ACCA

PAPER P4

ADVANCED FINANCIAL MANAGEMENT

In this May 2007 new edition

- We discuss the **best strategies** for revising and taking your ACCA exams

- We show you how to be well prepared for the **December 2007 exam**

- We give you **lots of great guidance** on tackling questions

- We show you how you can **build your own exams**

- We provide you with **three** mock exams including the **Pilot paper**

- We provide the **ACCA examiner's answers** as well as our own to the Pilot Paper as an additional revision aid ·

Our **i-Pass** product also supports this paper.

D1437731

FOR EXAMS IN DECEMBER 2007

BPP
LEARNING MEDIA

First edition May 2007

ISBN 9780 7517 3371 6

British Library Cataloguing-in-Publication Data
A catalogue record for this book
is available from the British Library

Published by

BPP Learning Media Ltd
BPP House, Aldine Place
London W12 8AA

www.bpp.com/learningmedia

Printed in Great Britain by
Cromwell Press
Trowbridge
BA14 0XB

Your learning materials, published by BPP Learning
Media Ltd, are printed on paper sourced from
sustainable, managed forests.

We are grateful to the Association of Chartered Certified
Accountants for permission to reproduce past
examination questions. The answers to past examination
questions have been prepared by BPP Learning Media
Ltd.

Contents

Question index

The headings in this checklist/index indicate the main topics of questions, but questions are expected to cover several different topics.

Mock exam 1

Questions to 61 to 65

Mock exam 2

Questions to 66 to 70

Mock exam 3 (Pilot paper)

Questions to 71 to 75

Planning your question practice

Our guidance from page 35 shows you how to organise your question practice, either by attempting questions from each syllabus area or **by building your own exams** – tackling questions as a series of practice exams.

Topic index

Listed below are the key Paper P4 syllabus topics and the numbers of the questions in this Kit covering those topics.

If you need to concentrate your practice and revision on certain topics or if you want to attempt all available questions that refer to a particular subject, you will find this index useful.

Syllabus topic	Question numbers
Adjusted present value	9, 14, Mock 1 Q1
Alpha values	6, 10
Arbitrage pricing theory	6
Barriers to trade	54, 58
Basis	43, 51, Mock 1 Q2
Black-Scholes model	12, 13, 15, Mock 2 Q3
Bonds	2
Capital asset pricing model	1, 5, 6, 10, 17, 19, 29, 30, 37, 44, 54
Capital structure	28-30
Caps	40
Collars	40, 41
Corporate failure	32, 33
Corporate governance	16, 20
Countertrade	46, 53
Covenants	2
Currency forward contracts	46, 50, 53, Mock 2 Q2, Mock 2 Q2
Currency futures	46, 51, Mock 1 Q2
Currency options	45, 46, 47, 50, 53, Mock 2 Q2
Currency swaps	45, 52
Debt problem of LDCs	31
Debt valuation	1
Delta hedge	59, 60
Demergers	37
Directors' remuneration	16
Divestment	37
Dividend policy	57, Mock 1 Q5, Mock 2 Q4
Economic exposure	43
Economic value added (EVA)™	3, 16
Efficient market hypothesis	21, 34
Ethics	55
Euromarkets	28, 46
Exchange rates	48, 49
Financial contagion	31
Financing	28, 29, 30, 32, 39, 52, Mock 1 Q1, Mock 2 Q1
Forecasts	4, 17, 39
Foreign investment	19, 23, 24, 54, Mock 2 Q1
Free cash flow	3, 4, 19, 22, 29, 33, 36
Greeks	59, 60
Hedging	13
Interest forward rate agreements	Mock 2 Q2
Interest rate futures	41, 42, Mock 2 Q2
Interest rate options	42, Mock 2 Q2
Interest rate swaps	44

Syllabus topic	Question numbers
Interest rate parity	49
Investment appraisal	7, 14, 17, 19, 23, 37, Mock 1 Q1, Mock 2 Q1
Management buy-out	38, 39
Modigliani and Miller	57, Mock 1 Q1
Money market hedge	53, Mock 1 Q2
Multilateral netting	50, 53
Multinationals	56, 68
Political risk	54, 55, Mock 1 Q1, Mock 2 Q1, Q5
Portfolio theory	6, 10, Mock 2 Q5
Profitability index	6
Purchasing power parity	17, 49, Mock 2 Q1
Ratio analysis	4, 32-35
Real options	9, 11, 14, 25, Mock 1 Q3
Reconstruction	36, 37
Share options	12, 16, 60
Share ownership	2
Share repurchase	57, Mock 1 Q4
Share valuation	20, 21, 29, Mock 1 Q1
Shareholder value analysis	3
Shareholders	2
Stock splits	Mock 1 Q4
Strategic planning	23, 32, 34, 37, Mock 1 Q1
Swaptions	45
Synergy	Mock 1 Q1
Takeovers and mergers	19-27, 35
Tax haven	48, Mock 1 Q5
Trade risks	56
Transaction exposure	43, 51
Transfer pricing	56
Translation exposure	34, 43, 51
Treasury management	53
Value at risk	1
Weighted average cost of capital	5, 6, 14, 22, 24, 27, 29, 30, 33, 36, 44, Mock 1 Q1, Mock 2 Q1
World Trade Organisation	58

Using your BPP Practice and Revision Kit

Tackling revision and the exam

You can significantly improve your chances of passing by tackling revision and the exam in the right ways. Our advice is based on feedback from ACCA examiners.

- We look at the dos and don'ts of revising for, and taking, ACCA exams
- We focus on Paper P4; we discuss revising the syllabus, what to do (and what not to do) in the exam, how to approach different types of question and ways of obtaining easy marks

Selecting questions

We provide signposts to help you plan your revision.

- A full **question index**
- A **topic index** listing all the questions that cover key topics, so that you can locate the questions that provide practice on these topics, and see the different ways in which they might be examined
- **BPP's question plan** highlighting the most important questions and explaining why you should attempt them
- **Build your own exams**, showing how you can practise questions in a series of exams

Making the most of question practice

At BPP we realise that you need more than just questions and model answers to get the most from your question practice.

- Our **Top tips** included for certain questions provide essential advice on tackling questions, presenting answers and the key points that answers need to include
- We show you how you can pick up **Easy marks** on some questions, as we know that picking up all readily available marks often can make the difference between passing and failing
- We include **marking guides** to show you what the examiner rewards
- We refer to the **2007 BPP Study Text** for detailed coverage of the topics covered in questions
- A number of questions include **Answer plans**, **Analysis** and **Helping hands** attached to show you how to approach them if you are struggling
- In a bank at the end of this Kit we include the **examiner's answers** to the Pilot paper. Used in conjunction with our answers they provide an indication of all possible points that could be made, issues that could be covered and approaches to adopt.

Attempting mock exams

There are three mock exams that provide practice at coping with the pressures of the exam day. We strongly recommend that you attempt them under exam conditions. **Mock exams 1 and 2** reflect the question styles and syllabus coverage of the exam; **Mock exam 3** is the Pilot paper.

Passing ACCA exams

BPP
LEARNING MEDIA

Revising and taking ACCA exams

To maximise your chances of passing your ACCA exams, you must make best use of your time, both before the exam during your revision, and when you are actually doing the exam.

- Making the most of your revision time can make a big, big difference to how well-prepared you are for the exam

- Time management is a core skill in the exam hall; all the work you've done can be wasted if you don't make the most of the three hours you have to attempt the exam

In this section we simply show you what to do and what not to do during your revision, and how to increase and decrease your prospects of passing your exams when you take them. Our advice is grounded in feedback we've had from ACCA examiners. You may be surprised to know that much examiner advice is the same whatever the exam, and the reasons why many students fail don't vary much between subjects and exam levels. So if you follow the advice we give you over the next few pages, you will **significantly** enhance your chances of passing **all** your ACCA exams.

How to revise

☑ Plan your revision

At the start of your revision period, you should draw up a **timetable** to plan how long you will spend on each subject and how you will revise each area. You need to consider the total time you have available and also the time that will be required to revise for other exams you're taking.

☑ Practise Practise Practise

The **more exam-standard questions** you do, the **more likely you are to pass** the exam. Practising full questions will mean that you'll get used to the time pressure of the exam. When the time is up, you should note where you've got to and then try to complete the question, giving yourself practice at everything the question tests.

☑ Revise enough

Make sure that your revision covers the breadth of the syllabus, as all topics could be examined in a compulsory question. However it is true that some topics are **key** – they are likely to appear often or are a particular interest of the examiner – and you need to spend sufficient time revising these. Make sure you also know the **basics** – the fundamental calculations, proformas and report layouts.

☑ Deal with your difficulties

Difficult areas are topics you find dull and pointless, or subjects that you found problematic when you were studying them. You mustn't become negative about these topics; instead you should build up your knowledge by reading the **Passcards** and using the **Quick Quiz** questions in the Study Text to test yourself. When practising questions in the Kit, go back to the Text if you're struggling.

☑ Learn from your mistakes

Having completed a question you must try to look at your answer critically. Always read any **Top tips guidance** in the answers; it's there to help you. Look at any **Easy marks** to see how you could have quickly gained credit on the questions that you've done. Aim to learn at least one new point from each question you attempt, a technical point perhaps or a point on style or approach.

☑ Read the examiners' guidance

ACCA's website contains articles by examiners which you **must** read, as they may form the basis of questions on any paper after they've been published.

Read through the examiner's answers to the Pilot paper included at the back of the Kit. In general these are far longer and more comprehensive than any answer you could hope to produce in the exam, but used in conjunction with our more realistic solutions, they provide a useful revision tool, covering all possible points and approaches.

☑ Complete all three mock exams

You should attempt the **Mock exams** at the end of the Kit under **strict exam conditions**, to gain experience of selecting questions, managing your time and producing answers.

How NOT to revise

☒ Revise selectively

Examiners are well aware that some students try to forecast the contents of exams, and only revise those areas that they think will be examined. Examiners try to prevent this by doing the unexpected, for example setting the same topic in successive sittings.

☒ Spend all the revision period reading

You cannot pass the exam just by learning the contents of Passcards, Course Notes or Study Texts. You have to develop your **application skills** by practising questions.

☒ Audit the answers

This means reading the answers and guidance without having attempted the questions. Auditing the answers gives you **false reassurance** that you would have tackled the questions in the best way and made the points that our answers do. The feedback we give in our answers will mean more to you if you've attempted the questions and thought through the issues.

☒ Practise some types of question, but not others

Although you may find the numerical parts of certain papers challenging, you shouldn't just practise calculations. These papers will also contain written elements, and you therefore need to spend time practising written question parts.

☒ Get bogged down

Don't spend a lot of time worrying about all the minute detail of certain topic areas, and leave yourself insufficient time to cover the rest of the syllabus. Remember that a key skill in the exam is the ability to **concentrate on what's important** and this applies to your revision as well.

☒ Overdo studying

Studying for too long without interruption will mean your studying becomes less effective. A five minute break each hour will help. You should also make sure that you are leading a **healthy lifestyle** (proper meals, good sleep and some times when you're not studying).

How to PASS your exams

☑ Prepare for the day

Make sure you set at least one alarm (or get an alarm call), and allow plenty of time to get to the exam hall. You should have your route planned in advance and should listen on the radio for potential travel problems. You should check the night before to see that you have pens, pencils, erasers, watch, calculator with spare batteries, also exam documentation and evidence of identity.

☑ Select the right questions

You should select the optional questions you feel you can answer **best**, basing your selection on the topics covered, the requirements of the question, how easy it will be to apply the requirements and the availability of easy marks.

☑ Plan your three hours

You need to make sure that you will be answering the correct number of questions, and that you spend the right length of time on each question – this will be determined by the number of marks available. Each mark carries with it a **time allocation** of **1.8 minutes**. A 20 mark question therefore should be selected, completed and checked in 36 minutes. With some papers, it's better to do certain types of question first or last.

☑ Read the questions carefully

To score well, you must follow the requirements of the question, understanding what aspects of the subject area are being covered, and the tasks you will have to carry out. The requirements will also determine what information and examples you should provide. Reading the question scenarios carefully will help you decide what **issues** to discuss, **techniques** to use, **information** and **examples** to include and how to **organise** your answer.

☑ Plan your answers

Six minutes of planning plus thirty minutes of writing is certain to earn you more marks than thirty six minutes of writing. Consider when you're planning how your answer should be **structured,** what the **format** should be and **how long** each part should take.

Confirm before you start writing that your plan makes **sense,** covers **all relevant points** and does not include **irrelevant material.**

☑ Show evidence of judgement

Remember that examiners aren't just looking for a display of knowledge; they want to see how well you can **apply** the knowledge you have. Evidence of application and judgement will include writing answers that only contain **relevant** material, using the material in scenarios to **support** what you say, **criticising** the **limitations** and **assumptions** of the techniques you use and making **reasonable recommendations** that follow from your discussion.

☑ Stay until the end of the exam

Use any spare time to **check and recheck** your script. This includes checking you have filled out the candidate details correctly, you have labelled question parts and workings clearly, you have used headers and underlining effectively and spelling, grammar and arithmetic are correct.

How to FAIL your exams

☒ Don't do enough questions

If you don't attempt sufficient questions on the paper, you are making it harder for yourself to pass the questions that you do attempt. If for example you don't do a 20 mark question, then you will have to score 50 marks out of 80 marks on the rest of the paper, and therefore have to obtain 63% of the marks on the questions you do attempt. Failing to attempt all of the paper is symptomatic of poor time management or poor question selection.

☒ Include irrelevant material

Markers are given detailed mark guides and will not give credit for irrelevant content. Therefore you should **NOT** braindump all you know about a broad subject area; the markers will only give credit for what is **relevant**, and you will also be showing that you lack the ability to **judge what's important.** Similarly forcing irrelevant theory into every answer won't gain you marks, nor will providing uncalled for features such as situation analyses, executive summaries and background information.

☒ Fail to use the details in the scenario

General answers or reproductions of Kit answers that don't refer to what is in the scenario in **this** question won't score enough marks to pass.

☒ Copy out the scenario details

Examiners see **selective** use of the right information as a key skill. If you copy out chunks of the scenario which aren't relevant to the question, or don't use the information to support your own judgements, you won't achieve good marks.

☒ Don't do what the question asks

Failing to provide all the examiner asks for will limit the marks you score. You will also decrease your chances by not providing an answer with enough **depth** – producing a single line bullet point list when the examiner asks for a discussion.

☒ Present your work poorly

Markers will only be able to give you credit if they can read your writing. There are also plenty of other things that will make it more difficult for markers to reward you. Examples include:

- Not using black or blue ink
- Not showing clearly which question you're attempting
- Scattering question parts from the same question throughout your answer booklet
- Not showing clearly workings or the results of your calculations

Paragraphs that are too long or which lack headers also won't help markers and hence won't help you.

Using your BPP products

This Kit gives you the question practice and guidance you need in the exam. Our other products can also help you pass:

- **Learning to Learn Accountancy** gives further valuable advice on revision

- **Passcards** provide you with clear topic summaries and exam tips

- **Success CDs** help you revise on the move

- **i-Pass CDs** offer tests of knowledge against the clock

- **Learn Online** is an e-learning resource delivered via the Internet, offering comprehensive tutor support and featuring areas such as study, practice, email service, revision and useful resources

You can purchase these products by visiting www.bpp.com/mybpp.

Visit our website www.bpp.com/acca/learnonline to sample aspects of Learn Online free of charge. Learn Online is hosted by BPP Professional Education.

Passing P4

BPP
LEARNING MEDIA

Revising P4

Topics to revise

Firstly we must emphasise that you will need a good knowledge of the **whole syllabus**. Any part of the syllabus could be tested within compulsory Section A. The two questions in this section are likely to be integrated, with ethics underpinning the whole paper.

That said, there are certain topics that are stressed in the syllabus and by the examiner, and therefore are core:

- Financial decision making in a corporation
- Ethical aspects of financial management
- Environmental considerations
- Corporate governance arrangements
- Investment appraisal methods
- Capital structure
- Mergers and acquisitions as corporate strategy
- Valuation issues in mergers and acquisitions
- Corporate restructuring
- International economic environment
- International operations
- Risk and treasury management functions
- Choosing the right risk management strategy
- Financial engineering

Your knowledge of other topic areas needs to demonstrate breadth. You need to have a good idea of:

- Different types of risk
- The measurement of risks
- Asset pricing models (CAPM etc)
- Valuations methods
- Capital and money market concepts
- The yield curve

It's also useful to keep reading the business pages during your revision period and not just narrowly focus on the syllabus. Remember that the examiner has stressed that this paper is about how organisations respond to real-world issues, so the more you read, the more practical examples you will have of how organisations have tackled real-life situations.

Question practice

You should use the Passcards and any brief notes you have to revise these topics, but you mustn't spend all your revision time passively reading. Question practice is vital; doing as many questions as you can in full will help develop your ability to analyse scenarios and produce relevant discussion and recommendations. The question plan on page 35 tells you what questions cover so that you can choose questions covering a variety of organisations and risk situations.

You should make sure you leave yourself enough time during your revision to practise 30 mark Section A questions as you cannot avoid them, as the scenarios and requirements of Section A questions are more complex and approach the syllabus in an integrated way. You should also leave yourself enough time to do the three mock exams.

Passing the P4 exam

Displaying the right qualities

The examiner will expect you to display the following qualities.

Qualities required	
Fulfilling the higher level question requirements	This means that when you are asked to show higher level skills such as **assessment or evaluation**, you will only score well if you demonstrate them. Merely describing something when you are asked to evaluate it will not earn you the marks you need.
Identifying the most important features of the organisation and its environment	You must use your **technical knowledge and business awareness** to identify the key features of the scenario.
Sorting the information in the scenario	You will get a lot of information, particularly in the Section A scenario, and will be expected to **evaluate how useful** it is and **use it** to support answers such as comparisons and discussions.
Selecting relevant real-life examples	You will gain credit for using **good examples.**
Arguing well	You may be expected to discuss both sides of a case, or present an argument in favour or against something. You will gain marks for the **quality** and **logical flow of your arguments**.
Making reasonable recommendations	The measures you recommend must be **appropriate** for the organisation; you may need to discuss their strengths and weaknesses, as there may be costs of adopting them. The recommendations should clearly state what has to be done.

Avoiding weaknesses

Our experience of, and examiner feedback from, other higher level exams enables us to predict a number of weaknesses that are likely to occur in many students' answers. You will enhance your chances significantly if you ensure you avoid these mistakes:

- **Failing to provide what the question verbs require** (discussion, evaluation, recommendation) or to write about the topics specified in the question requirements

- **Repeating the same material** in different parts of answers

- **Stating theories and concepts** rather than applying them

- **Quoting chunks of detail** from the question that don't add any value

- **Forcing irrelevancies into answers**, for example irrelevant definitions or theories, or examples that don't relate to the scenario

- **Giving long lists or writing down all that's known** about a broad subject area, and not caring whether it's relevant or not

- **Focusing too narrowly on one area** – for example only covering financial risks when other risks are also important

- **Letting your personal views prevent you from answering the question** – the question may require you to construct an argument with which you personally don't agree

- **Unrealistic or impractical recommendations**

- **Vague recommendations** - instead of just saying improve risk management procedures, you should discuss precisely **how** you would improve them

- **Failing to answer sufficient questions** because of poor time management

- **Not answering all parts of optional questions**

Using the reading time

We recommend that you spend the first part of the 15 minutes reading time choosing the Section B questions you will do, on the basis of your knowledge of the syllabus areas being tested and whether you can fulfil all the question requirements. Remember that Section B questions can cover different parts of the syllabus, and you should be happy with all the areas that the questions you choose cover. We suggest that you should note on the paper any ideas that come to you about these questions.

However don't spend all the reading time going through and analysing the Section B question requirements in detail; leave that until the three hours writing time. Instead you should be looking to spend as much of the reading time as possible looking at the Section A scenario, as this will be longer and more complex than the Section B scenarios and cover more of the syllabus. You should highlight and annotate the key points of the scenario on the question paper.

Choosing which questions to answer first

Spending most of your reading time on the compulsory Section A questions will mean that you can get underway with planning and writing your answer to the Section A questions as soon as the three hours start. It will give you more actual writing time during the one and a half hours you should allocate to it and it's writing time that you'll need. Comments from examiners of other syllabuses that have similar exam formats suggest that students appear less time-pressured if they do the big compulsory questions first.

During the second half of the exam, you can put Section A aside and concentrate on the two Section B questions you've chosen.

However our recommendations are not inflexible. If you really think the Section A questions looks a lot harder than the Section B questions you've chosen, then do those first, but **DON'T run over time on them.** You must leave yourself an hour and a half to tackle the Section A questions. When you come back to it, having had initial thoughts during the reading time, you should be able to generate more ideas and find the question is not as bad as it looks.

Tackling questions

Scenario questions

You'll improve your chances by following a step-by-step approach to Section A scenarios along the following lines.

Step 1   **Read the requirement**

You need to identify the knowledge areas being tested and what information will therefore be significant.

Step 2   **Identify the action verbs**

These convey the level of skill you need to exhibit and also the structure your answer should have. A lower level verb such as define will require a more descriptive answer; a higher level verb such as evaluate will require a more applied, critical answer.

The examiner has stressed that **higher level requirements and verbs** will be most significant in this paper, for example critically evaluating a statement and arguing for or against a given idea or position.

Action verbs that are likely to be frequently used in this exam are listed below, together with their intellectual levels and guidance on their meaning.

Intellectual level		
1	**Define**	Give the meaning of
1	**Explain**	Make clear
1	**Identify**	Recognise or select
1	**Describe**	Give the key features
2	**Contrast**	Make a comparison between things on the basis of the differences between them
2	**Analyse**	Give reasons for the current situation or what has happened
3	**Assess**	Determine the strengths/weaknesses/importance/ significance/ability to contribute
3	**Discuss**	Examine in detail by using arguments for and against
3	**Construct the case**	Present the arguments in favour, supported by evidence
3	**Evaluate**	Determine the value of
3	**Recommend**	Advise the appropriate actions to pursue in terms the recipient will understand

Step 3   Identify what each part of the question requires

When planning, you will need to make sure that you aren't reproducing the same material in more than one part of the question.

Also you're likely to come across part questions with two requirements that may be at different levels; a part question may for example ask you to explain X and discuss Y. You must ensure that you **fulfill both requirements** and that your discussion of Y shows greater depth than your explanation of X (for example by identifying problems with Y or putting the case for and against Y).

Step 4   Check the mark allocation to each part

This shows you the depth anticipated and helps allocate time.

Step 5   Read the scenario through quickly, highlighting key data

In the front pages of the text we discussed what the key data would be for questions covering different areas of the syllabus:

Investment appraisal
- Calculations of NPV and IRR
- Real options use

Mergers and acquisitions
- Advantages and disadvantages
- Overpricing
- Valuation of target company
- Restructuring methods

Risk management	• Instruments for managing interest rate risk
	• Instruments for managing exchange rate risks
	• Credit and political risks
International aspects	• International environment
	• Overseas investment appraisal
	• Dividend policy and exchange controls

Step 6   Read the scenario carefully

Put points under headings related to requirements (eg by noting in the margin to what part of the question the scenario detail relates).

Step 7   Consider the consequences of the points you've identified

Remember that in the answer you will often have to provide recommendations based on the information you've been given. Consider also that you may have to criticise the code, framework or model that you've been told to use. You may have to bring in wider issues or viewpoints, for example the views of different stakeholders.

Step 8   Write a plan

You may be able to do this on the question paper as often there will be at least one blank page in the question booklet. However any plan you make should be reproduced in the answer booklet when writing time begins.

Consider carefully when planning your answer to Section A the sorts of issues that will earn you professional marks. How should you present your answer? Do the arguments you use have a logical flow and are they supported by material from the scenario?

Step 9   Write the answer

Make every effort to present your answer clearly. The pilot paper and other questions suggest that the examiner will be looking for you to make a number of clear points. The best way to demonstrate what you're doing is to put points into separate paragraphs with clear headers.

Discussion questions

Remember that **depth of discussion** will be important. Discussions will often consist of paragraphs containing 2-3 sentences. Each paragraph should:

- **Make a point**
- **Explain the point** (you must demonstrate **why** the point is important)
- **Illustrate the point** (with material or analysis from the scenario, perhaps an example from real-life)

Gaining the easy marks

Knowledge of the core topics that we list under topics to revise should present you with some easy marks. The pilot paper suggests that there will be some marks available on certain part questions for definitions, explanations or descriptions that don't have to be related to the scenario. However don't assume that you can ignore all the scenarios and still pass!

As P1 is a Professional level paper, 4 or 5 **professional level marks** will be awarded. Some of these should be easy to obtain. The examiner has stated that some marks may be available for presenting your answer in the form of a letter, presentation, memo, report or briefing notes. You may also be able to obtain marks for the style and layout of your answer.

Formulae

Set out below are the formulae which you will be given in the exam, and formulae which you should learn. If you are not sure what the symbols mean, or how the formulae are used, you should go back to the Study Text.

Exam formulae

Modigliani and Miller Proposition 2 (with tax)

$$k_e = k_e^i + (1-T)(k_e^i - k_d)\frac{V_d}{V_e}$$

Two asset portfolio

$$s_p = \sqrt{w_a^2 s_a^2 + w_b^2 s_b^2 + 2w_a w_b r_{ab} s_a s_b}$$

The capital asset pricing model

$$E(r_i) = R_f + \beta_i(E(r_m) - R_f)$$ *The asset beta formula*

$$\beta_a = \left[\frac{V_e}{(V_e + V_d(1-T))}\beta_e\right] + \left[\frac{V_d(1-T)}{(V_e + V_d(1-T))}\beta_d\right]$$

The growth model

$$P_0 = \frac{D_0(1+g)}{(r_e - g)}$$

Gordon's growth approximation

$$g = br_e$$

The weighted average cost of capital

$$WACC = \left[\frac{V_e}{V_e + V_d}\right]k_e + \left[\frac{V_e}{V_e + V_d}\right]k_d(1-T)$$

The Fisher formula

$$(1 + i) = (1 + r)(1 + h)$$

Purchasing power parity and interest rate parity

$$s_1 = s_0 \times \frac{(1+h_c)}{(1+h_b)}$$

$$f_0 = s_0 \times \frac{(1+i_c)}{(1+i_b)}$$

The Black Scholes option pricing model	The FOREX modified Black and Scholes option pricing model
$c = P_a N(d_1) - P_e N(d_2)e^{-rt}$ Where $\quad d_1 = \dfrac{\ln\left(\dfrac{P_a}{P_e}\right) + (r + 0.5s^2)t}{s\sqrt{t}}$ $\quad\quad\quad d_2 = d_1 - s\sqrt{t}$	$c = e^{-rt}\, F_0 N(d_1) - XN(d_2)$ Or $p = e^{-rt}\, XN(-d_2) - F_0 N(-d_1)$ Where $\quad d_1 = \dfrac{\ln\left(\dfrac{F_0}{X}\right) + s^2\,\dfrac{T}{2}}{s\sqrt{T}}$ and $\quad d_2 = d_1 - s\sqrt{T}$

The put call parity relationship

$p = C - P_a + P_e e^{-rt}$

BPP
LEARNING MEDIA

Formulae to learn

Beta factor calculation

$$\beta_j = \frac{COV_{jm}}{\sigma_m^2} = \frac{P_{jm}}{\sigma_m} = \frac{\sigma_{syst}}{\sigma_m}$$

$$\beta = \frac{n\Sigma xy - \Sigma x \Sigma y}{n\Sigma x^2 - (\Sigma x)^2}$$

$$\beta = \frac{\sigma_s \rho_{sm}}{\sigma_m}$$

Interest rate parity

$$\frac{i_f - i_{uk}}{1 + i_{uk}} = \frac{\text{Forward rate}}{\text{Spot rate}} - 1$$

or

$$\frac{1 + i_f}{1 + i_{uk}} = \frac{\text{Forward rate}}{\text{Spot rate}} = \frac{\text{Expected future exchange rate}}{\text{Spot rate}}$$

International Fisher effect

$$\frac{1 + r_f}{1 + r_h} = \frac{1 + i_f}{1 + i_h}$$

Cost of debt capital

(1 – tax rate)(risk free rate + credit spread)

Yield on corporate bond

(Risk free rate + credit spread)

Delta

$$\frac{\Delta C}{\Delta S} = \frac{\text{change in call option price}}{\text{change in price of shares}}$$

Gamma

Change in delta value – change in price of underlying share

Vega

$$\frac{\Delta C}{\Delta \sigma} = \frac{\text{change in option price}}{\text{change in option's implied volatility}}$$

Exam information

The exam paper

The exam is a three-hour paper consisting of two sections.

Section A has two compulsory questions worth 60 marks in total. The questions will usually require the candidate to show a comprehensive understanding of issues from across the syllabus. The questions which will be in the form of a case study or scenario will address significant issues relevant to the senior financial manager or advisor. These will require students to demonstrate high-level capabilities to evaluate, relate and apply the information in the case study to the question requirements. Each question will contain a mix of computational and discursive elements with approximately 50 percent of the marks apportioned to each of the two elements. The maximum marks to be allocated to a single question in Section A will not exceed 40 marks.

Section B questions are more likely to assess a range of discrete subject areas from the main syllabus section headings; they may require evaluation and synthesis of information contained within short scenarios and application of this information to the question requirements.

		Number of marks
Section A:	2 compulsory case studies	60
Section B:	Choice of 2 from 3 questions (20 marks each)	40
		100

Pilot paper

Section A

1   Calculation of current cost of equity for unquoted company, the target of an acquisition, using CAPM; estimation of expected growth rate, required rate of return and value of target company using concept free cash flow. Advise board on proposed acquisition.

2   Discussion and evaluation of hedging policies for foreign currency exposure.

Section B

3   Advanced investment appraisal and project value at risk.

4   Estimation of the cost of debt and equity using the Modiagliani-Miller proposition; discussion of alternative sources of finance

5   Procedures for obtaining a listing; advantages and disadvantages of a listing for a medium sized company; ethical considerations of proposed course of action

The pilot paper is reproduced in full from page 359.

Useful websites

The websites below provide additional sources of information of relevance to your studies for *Strategic Financial Management*.

- www.accaglobal.com

  ACCA's website. Includes student section.

- www.bpp.com

  Our website provides information about BPP products and services, with a link to the ACCA website.

- www.ft.com

  This website provides information about current international business. You can search for information and articles on specific industry groups as well as individual companies.

- www.economist.com

  Here you can search for business information on a week-by-week basis, search articles by business subject and use the resources of the Economist Intelligence Unit to research sectors, companies or countries.

- www.invweek.co.uk

  This site carries business news and articles on markets from Investment Week and International Investment.

- www.pwcglobal.com/uk

  The PricewaterhouseCoopers website includes UK Economic Outlook.

- www.bbc.co.uk

  The website of the BBC carries general business information as well as programme-related content.

Planning your question practice

Planning your question practice

We have already stressed that question practice should be right at the centre of your revision. Whilst you will spend some time looking at your notes and Paper P4 Passcards, you should spend the majority of your revision time practising questions.

We recommend two ways in which you can practise questions.

- Use **BPP's question plan** to work systematically through the syllabus and attempt key and other questions on a section-by-section basis

- **Build your own exams** – attempt questions as a series of practice exams

These ways are suggestions and simply following them is no guarantee of success. You or your college may prefer an alternative but equally valid approach.

BPP's question plan

The BPP plan below requires you to devote a **minimum of 20 hours** to revision of Paper P4. Any time you can spend over and above this should only increase your chances of success.

Step 1   **Review your notes** and the chapter summaries in the Paper P1 **Passcards** for each section of the syllabus.

Step 2   **Answer the key questions** for that section. These questions have boxes round the question number in the table below and you should answer them in full. Even if you are short of time you must attempt these questions if you want to pass the exam. You should complete your answers without referring to our solutions.

Step 3   **Attempt the other questions** in that section.

Step 4   Attempt **Mock exams 1, 2 and 3** under strict exam conditions.

Syllabus section	2007 Passcards chapters	Questions in this Kit	Comments	Done ☑
Role and responsibility towards shareholders	1–5	2	Answer in full. This question tests your knowledge of corporate governance.	☐
Advanced investment appraisal	6–10	9	Answer in full. This is a wide ranging question, testing your knowledge of different methods of valuation for investment appraisal	☐
		11	Answer in full. This question focuses on the application of real options for investment appraisal	☐
Acquisitions and mergers	11–14	24	Answer in full. This question addresses the important issue of synergies in evaluating mergers	☐
		25	Answer in full. This question covers a number of important issues that arise in the valuation of companies for acquisitions.	
Corporate reconstruction and reorganisation	15–17	37	Answer in full. This question deals with the evaluation of restructuring strategies by means of a sell-off or a merger.	☐
		39	Answer in full. This question deals with the advantage and disadvantage of financing strategies for a management buyout.	☐
Treasury and advanced risk management techniques	18–22	40	Answer in full. This question discusses the management of currency risk using currency swaps.	
		42	Answer in full. This question addresses the various aspects of hedging interest rate risks using futures and options.	☐
Economic environment for multinationals	23–24	43	Answer in full. This question deals with the impact of exchange rate exposure on the cash flows of a multinational.	☐
		56	Answer in full. This question deals with transfer pricing policies of multinational companies.	☐
Emerging issues	26	59	Answer in full. This question deals with the management of risk of option positions using the Greeks.	☐

Build your own exams

Having revised your notes and the BPP Passcards, you can attempt the questions in the Kit as a series of practice exams.

	Practice exams		
	1	2	3
Section A			
1	Q3 Lion and Cub	Q7 Sleepon	Q25 Carpetshop
2	Q53 NTC	Q35 Stanzial	Q9 Trosoft
Section B			
3	Q18 Boxless	Q59 Uniglow	Q8 Cost of capital
4	Q26 Hotparts	Q55 Beela	Q38 Reflator
5	Q48 Exchange rates	Q31 Global financial markets	Q49 Gitlor

Whichever practice exams you use, you must attempt **Mock exams 1, 2 and 3** at the end of your revision.

Questions

ROLE AND RESPONSIBILITY TOWARDS STAKEHOLDERS

Questions 1 and 2 cover the role and responsibility towards stakeholders, the subject of Part A of the BPP Study Text for Paper P4.

---

1 Impex   54 mins

Impex, a major food and beverage retailer, is considering a takeover of a small unlisted competitor in order to build market share. The business is, however, concerned about volatility, and the Chairman, who has been talking to the company's stockbrokers, wishes to monitor the value at risk for the business and make appropriate assessments for any investment opportunities.

Impex has 268m shares in issue on which it recently paid a dividend of 156c per share. Dividends have been growing steadily at 2.5% pa and the brokers have informed the chairman that the shares of the company have a beta of 0.98.

The company is geared with $3.26bn of 5.8% perpetual debt in issue which has an AA credit rating.

The target company, Elfix, generated earnings per share excluding interest (and tax thereon) of 80c last year and has a policy of distributing 60% of its earnings. Elfix has $220m of 15 year 7% debt in issue that is rated A2. Elfix has 57 million shares in issue.

General market statistics are that the risk-free rate is 6% and the market is returning 10% at a risk of 8%. Yield spreads for the wholesale sector in basis points are

Rating	5 yr	10 yr	15 yr	30 yr
AA	15	20	30	50
A2	80	95	107	120

Assume a tax rate of 30%.

Required

(a) Calculate the equity, debt and total market values of both companies along with the equity, debt and overall betas for both companies and an estimate of the share price for Elfix. **(16 marks)**

(b) Calculate the 3 month value at risk at a 1% level for shareholders, debt holders and the company overall for each company assuming zero unsystematic risk in each company. **(8 marks)**

(c) Write a brief report to the Chairman of the uses and limitations of value at risk. **(6 marks)**

(Total = 30 marks)

2 Shareholders and bondholders   36 mins

(a) Discuss why conflicts of interest might exist between shareholders and bondholders. **(8 marks)**

(b) Provide examples of covenants that might be attached to bonds, and briefly discuss the advantages and disadvantages to companies of covenants. **(7 marks)**

(c) Details of the possible convertible loan stock issue for the purchase of a hotel are shown below. (100 centos = $1)

Raise $9 million by issuing 10% $100 convertible loan stock 20Z0, issued and redeemable at par. The loan stock is convertible into 60 ordinary shares at any date between 1 January 20Y0 and 31 December 20Y4. The loan stock is callable for conversion by the company subject to the company's ordinary share price exceeding 200 centos between 1 January 20Y2 and 31 December 20Y4, and puttable for redemption by the loan stock holders if the share price falls below 100 centos between the same dates. The current rate at which the company can borrow from the bank is 10%. The company's shares are currently trading at $0.46.

Discuss the implications for the company if the diversification is financed with convertible loan stock with these terms. **(5 marks)**

(Total = 20 marks)

ADVANCED INVESTMENT APPRAISAL

Questions 3 to 18 cover advanced investment appraisal, the subject of Part B of the BPP Study Text for Paper P4.

---

3 Lion and Cub   54 mins

(a)   Define free cash flow, discuss the possible conflicts that might exist between managers and shareholders over the use of free cash flows, and illustrate actions shareholders might take to reduce such conflicts.

(8 marks)

(b)   Discuss how effectively shareholder value analysis indicates the creation of economic value for shareholders.   **(5 marks)**

(c)   On 1 January 20X1 a rights issue will be made by Lion Inc of $15 million to fund a project which should increase the future earnings of Lion from 20X4.

The details of Lion's free cash flow forecasts for the next ten years are as follows:

Free cash flow forecast at 31 December 20X0 with no rights issue

	20X1	20X2	20X3–Y0
	$m	$m	$m
Sales	45	50	60
Operating costs excluding depreciation	(21)	(21)	(24)
Working capital	(2)	(3)	(3)
Replacement capital expenditure	(11)	(4)	(5)
Tax	(4)	(5)	(5)
Free cash flow	7	17	23

Lion discounts free cash flows at 10%.

Free cash flow forecast at 31 December 20X0 with rights issue

	20X3	20X4–Y0
	$m	$m
Sales	60	70
Operating costs excluding depreciation	(24)	(29)
Working capital	(3)	(3)
Replacement capital expenditure	(5)	(5)
Tax	(5)	(5)
Free cash flow	23	28

20X1 and 20X2 are as for the forecast with no rights issue.

Calculate the increase in market value added as a result of undertaking the new project.   **(2 marks)**

(d)   Discuss the benefits and drawbacks of Economic Value Added (EVA)™.   **(7 marks)**

(e)   The following data relates to Cub Inc

Income statement data

	20X1	20X2
	$m	$m
Revenue	995	1,180
Pre-tax accounting profit	210	265
Taxation	63	80
Profit after tax	147	185
Dividends	50	60
Retained earnings	97	125

Balance sheet data

	20X1 $m	20X2 $m
Non-current assets	370	480
Net current assets	400	500
	770	980
Financed by:		
Shareholders' funds	595	720
Medium and long-term bank loans	175	260
	770	980

Pre-tax accounting profit is taken after deducting the economic depreciation of the company's non-current assets (also the depreciation used for tax purposes).

Other relevant information

(i)   Economic depreciation was $95 million in 20X1 and $105 million in 20X2.
(ii)   Interest expenses were $13 million in 20X1 and $18 million in 20X2.
(iii)   Other non-cash expenses were $32 million in 20X1 and $36 million in 20X2.
(iv)   The tax rate in 20X1 and 20X2 was 30%.
(v)   Cub had non-capitalised leases valued at $35 million in each year 20X0-20X2.
(vi)   The company's pre-tax cost of debt was estimated as 7% in 20X1 and 8% in 20X2.
(vii)   The company's cost of equity was estimated as 14% in 20X1 and 16% in 20X2.
(viii) The target capital structure is 75% equity, 25% debt.
(ix)   Balance sheet capital employed at the end of 20X0 was $695 million. There were no loans at that date.

Required

Estimate the EVA™ for Cub Inc for 20X1 and 20X2, stating any assumptions that you make and discussing what the calculations demonstrate about the performance of the company.   **(8 marks)**

(Total = 30 marks)

4 Wurrall   54 mins

The board of directors of Wurrall Inc has requested the production of a four-year financial plan. The key assumptions behind the plan are:

(a)   Historically, sales growth has been 9% per year. Uncertainty about future economic prospects over the next four years from 20X5–20X8 however implies that this growth rate will reduce by 1% per year after the financial year 20X5 (eg to 8% in 20X6). After four years, growth is expected to remain constant at the 20X8 rate.

(b)   Cash operating costs are estimated to be approximately 68% of sales.

(c)   Tax allowable depreciation for the past few years has been approximately 15% of the net book value of plant and machinery at year end. This is expected to continue for the next few years.

(d)   Inventories, receivables, cash in hand and 'other payables' are assumed to increase in proportion to the increase in sales. Investments are expected to remain constant.

(e)   Investment in, and net book value of, plant and machinery is expected to increase in line with sales. No investment is planned in other non-current assets other than a refurbishment of buildings at an estimated cost of $40 million in late 20X7.

(f)   Any change in interest paid as a result of changes in borrowing may be assumed to be effective in the next year. Wurrall plans to meet any changes in financing needs, with the exception of the repayment of the fixed rate loan, by adjusting its overdraft.

(g)   Wurrall currently pays 7% per annum interest on its short-term borrowing.

(h)   Corporation tax is expected to continue at its present rate over the next four years.

(i)   For the last few years the company's dividend policy has been to pay a constant percentage of earnings after tax. No changes in this policy are planned.

(j)   Wurrall has borrowed extensively from the banking system, and covenants exist that prevent the company's gearing (book value of total loans to book value of total loans plus equity) exceeding forty percent for a period of more than one year.

(k)   The company's managing director has publicly stated that both profits before tax and Wurrall's share price should increase by at least 100% during the next four years.

Summarised financial accounts of Wurrall Inc
Income statement for the year ended March 20X4

	$m
Revenue	1,639
Operating costs before depreciation	(1,225)
EBITDA	414
Tax allowable depreciation	(152)
EBIT	262
Net interest payable	(57)
Profit on ordinary activities before tax	205
Tax on ordinary activities (30%)	(62)
Dividends	(80)
Amount transferred to reserves	63

Balance sheet as at 31 March 20X4

	$m	$m
Non-current assets		
Land and buildings	310	
Plant and machinery (net)	1,012	
Investments[1]	32	
		1,354
Current assets		
Inventories	448	
Receivables	564	
Cash in hand and short-term deposits	20	
		1,032
Payables: amounts falling due within one year:		
Short term loans and overdrafts	230	
Other payables	472	
		(702)
Payables: amounts falling due after one year:		
Borrowings (8% fixed rate)[2]		(580)
		1,104
Capital and reserves		
Called up share capital (10 pence par)		240
Reserves		864
		1,104

1   The investments yield negligible interest

2   Borrowings are scheduled to be repaid at the end of 20X6 and will be refinanced with a similar type of loan in 20X6.

The company's current share price is 210 cents, and its weighted average cost of capital is 11%.

Required

(a) Produce pro forma balance sheets and income statements for each of the next four years. Clearly state any assumptions that you make. **(12 marks)**

(b) Critically discuss any problems or implications of the assumptions that are made in each of points (i) to (iv) and point (ix) in the question. **(8 marks)**

(c) Using free cash flow analysis, evaluate and discuss whether or not the managing director's claims for the future share price are likely to be achievable. (The operating cash flow element of free cash flow may be estimated by: EBIT(1 − t) plus depreciation.) **(10 marks)**

(Total = 30 marks)

5 Your company   54 mins

Your company has produced a draft guidance manual to assist in estimating the cost of capital to be used in capital investment appraisal. Extracts from the manual, which includes worked examples, are reproduced below.

Guidance manual for estimating the cost of capital

(a) It is essential that the discount rate used reflects the weighted average cost of capital of the company.

(b) The cost of equity and cost of debt should always be estimated using market values.

(c) Inflation must always be included in the discount rate.

(d) The capital asset pricing model or the dividend valuation model may be used in estimating the cost of equity.

(e) The cost of debt is to be estimated using the redemption yield of existing debt.

(f) Always round the solution up to the nearest whole percentage. This is a safeguard if the cost of capital is underestimated.

Illustrative examples

The current date is assumed to be June 20X9, with four years until the redemption of the loan stock.

Relevant data

	Book values $m	Market values $m
Equity (50 million ordinary shares)	140	214
Debt 10% loan stock 20Y3 $80m	80	85

	Per share	Annual growth rates
Dividends	24 pence	6%
Earnings	67 pence	9%

The beta value of the company (asset beta) is 1.1

Other information

Market return	14%
Risk free rate	6%
Current inflation	4%
Corporate tax rate	30%

Illustration 1 – When the company is expanding existing activities

Cost of equity

Dividend valuation model: $\dfrac{D}{P} + g = \dfrac{24}{428} + 0.09 = 0.146 \text{ or } 14.6\%$

Capital asset pricing model:

$$ke = Rf + (Rm - Rf)\ beta$$
$$= 6\% + (14\% - 6\%)\ 1.1$$
$$= 14.8\%$$

Cost of debt

To find the redemption yield, with four years to maturity, the following equation must be solved.

Debt is assumed to be redeemed at par value and interest to be payable annually. Estimates are based upon total interest payments of $80m at 10% or $8m per year.

$$85 = \frac{8}{(1+kd)} + \frac{8}{(1+kd)^2} + \frac{8}{(1+kd)^3} + \frac{88}{(1+kd)^4}$$

By trial and error

At 9% interest

8 × 3.240	25.92
80 × 0.708	56.64
	82.56

9% discount rate is too high

At 7% interest

8 × 3.387	27.10
80 × 0.763	61.04
	88.14

Interpolating:

$$7\% + \frac{3.14}{3.14 + 2.44} \times 2\% = 8.13\%$$

The cost of debt is 8.13%

Market value of equity $214m
Market value of debt $85m

Weighted average cost of capital:

(CAPM has been used in this estimate. The dividend valuation model would result in a similar answer.)

$$14.8\% \times \frac{214}{299} + 8.13\% \times \frac{85}{299} = 12.90\%$$

Inflation of 4% must be added to the discount rate.

The discount rate to be used in the investment appraisal is 12.90% + 4% = 16.90% or 17% rounded up to the nearest whole percentage.

Illustration 2 – When the company is diversifying its activities

The asset beta of a similar sized company in the industry in which your company proposes to diversify is 0.90.

Gearing of the similar company

	Book values	Market values
	$m	$m
Equity	165	230
Debt	65	60

Cost of equity

The beta of the comparator company is used as a measure of the systematic risk of the new investment. As the gearing of the two companies differs, the beta must be adjusted for the difference in gearing.

Ungearing

$$\text{Beta equity} = \text{beta assets} \times \frac{E}{E + D(1 - t)}$$

$$\text{Beta equity} = 0.90 \times \frac{230}{230 + 60(1 - 0.3)} = 0.76$$

Using the capital asset pricing model:

$$
\begin{aligned}
ke &= R_f + (R_m - R_f)\,\text{beta} \\
&= 6\% + (14\% - 6\%)\,0.76 \\
&= 12.08\%
\end{aligned}
$$

Cost of debt

This remains at 8.13%

Market value of equity $214m
Market value of debt $85m

Weighted average cost of capital:

$$12.08\% \times \frac{214}{299} + 8.13\% \times \frac{85}{299} = 10.96\%$$

The discount rate to be used in the investment appraisal when diversifying into the new industry is 10.96% + 4% inflation, 14.96% or 15% rounded up to the nearest %.

Required

Produce a revised version of the draft manual for estimating the cost of capital. Revisions, including amended calculations, should be made, where appropriate to both written guidance notes and illustrative examples. Where revisions are made to any of the six guidance notes, or to the illustrations, brief discussion of the reason for revision should be included. State clearly any assumptions that you make.

(30 marks)

6 Jetter

54 mins

Summarised financial details of Jetter Inc are shown below.

Extract from the income statement

	$m
Revenue	582
Profit before tax	93
Taxation (30%)	(28)
Profit after tax	65
Dividends	(26)
Retained earnings	39

Extracts from the balance sheet

	$m
Non-current assets (net)	210
Current assets	186
Current liabilities	(153)
	243
Financed by:	
Ordinary shares (25 pence par)	50
Reserves	122
12% loan stock June 20X6	71
	243

The company's ordinary shares are currently trading at $2.20, and the loan stock at $105.50. The loan stock is redeemable at its par value of $100.

The company's equity beta is 1.25.

Jetter Inc is considering investing in one of three projects. The company has $50 million that is currently earning 5.8% in short-term money market deposits. Any surplus funds after the investment in one of the projects will continue to be invested in the money market.

The company has employed an external consultant to estimate risk/return data relevant to the three projects.

	Project 1	Project 2	Project 3
Investment cost ($ million)	35	40	28
Estimated correlation of returns with the market	0.76	0.63	0.58
Standard deviation of returns	8.4%	4.6%	14.3%
Expected return (IRR)	15%	11%	17%

Market return 15% per annum
Market standard deviation of returns 6.9%
Risk free rate 6% per annum

Required

(a) Evaluate which project should be selected. Do not use information provided later in the question requirements in your evaluation.

State clearly any assumptions that you make in all parts of the question. **(7 marks)**

(b) If it was later calculated that the profitability index for project 2 was 1.3, based upon equal cash inflows of $16 million per year from the project for four years, what does this imply about the accuracy of the beta estimated for the project? **(4 marks)**

(c) Estimate Jetter's cost of capital prior to undertaking the investment. Briefly discuss (do not calculate) what effect the project selected in (a) is likely to have on Jetter's cost of capital. **(7 marks)**

(d)   The consultant has suggested that beta estimates should be adjusted by using the formula: [(0.67 × unadjusted beta) + 0.33] in any estimate of required returns.

   (i)   Briefly discuss the reason for using an adjusted beta such as this.   **(2 marks)**
   (ii)   Calculate whether or not your choice of project in (a) above would have altered using adjusted betas.
                                                                                          (3 marks)

(e)   Discuss the advantages and disadvantages of using the Capital Asset Pricing Model and the Arbitrage Pricing Theory in investment appraisal.   **(7 marks)**

                                                                                          (Total = 30 marks)

7 Sleepon   54 mins

Sleepon Hotels Inc owns a successful chain of hotels. The company is considering diversifying its activities through the construction of a theme park. The theme park would have a mixture of family activities and adventure rides. Sleepon has just spent $230,000 on market research into the theme park, and is encouraged by the findings.

The theme park is expected to attract an average of 15,000 visitors per day for at least four years, after which major new investment would be required in order to maintain demand. The price of admission to the theme park is expected to be $18 per adult and $10 per child. 60% of visitors are forecast to be children. In addition to admission revenues, it is expected that the average visitor will spend $8 on food and drinks, (of which 30% is profit), and $5 on gifts and souvenirs, (of which 40% is profit). The park would open for 360 days per year.

All costs and receipts (excluding maintenance and construction costs and the realisable value) are shown at current prices; the company expects all costs and receipts to rise by 3% per year from current values.

The theme park would cost a total of $400 million and could be constructed and working in one year's time. Half of the $400 million would be payable immediately, and half in one year's time. In addition working capital of $50 million will be required from the end of year one. The after tax realisable value of non-current assets is expected to be between $250 million and $300 million after four years of operation.

Maintenance costs (excluding labour) are expected to be $15 million in the first year of operation, increasing by $4 million per year thereafter. Annual insurance costs are $2 million, and the company would apportion $2.5 million per year to the theme park from existing overheads. The theme park would require 1,500 staff costing a total of $40 million per annum (at current prices). Sleepon will use the existing advertising campaigns for its hotels to also advertise the theme park. This will save approximately $2 million per year in advertising expenses.

As Sleepon has no previous experience of theme park management, it has investigated the current risk and financial structure of its closest theme park competitor, Thrillall Inc. Details are summarised below.

Thrillall Inc, summarised balance sheet

	$m
Non-current assets (net)	1,440
Current assets	570
Less current liabilities	(620)
	1,390
Financed by:	
$1 ordinary shares	400
Reserves	530
	930
Medium and long term debt	460
	1,390

Other information

(a)   Sleepon has access to a $450 million loan at 7.5% fixed rate to provide the necessary finance for the theme park.

(b) $250 million of the investment will attract 25% per year capital allowances on a reducing balance basis, available with a one year lag.

49

(c) Corporate tax is at a rate of 30%.

(d) The average stock market return is 10% and the risk free rate 3.5%.

(e) Sleepon's current weighted average cost of capital is 9%.

(f) Sleepon's market weighted gearing if the theme park project is undertaken is estimated to be 61.4% equity, 38.6% debt.

(g) Sleepon's equity beta is 0.70.

(h) The current share price of Sleepon is 148 pence, and of Thrillall 386 pence.

(i) Thrillall's medium and long term debt comprises long term bonds with a par value of $100 and current market price of $93.

(j) Thrillall's equity beta is 1.45.

Required

Prepare a report analysing whether or not Sleepon should undertake the investment in the theme park. Your report should include a discussion of what other information would be useful to Sleepon in making the investment decision. All relevant calculations must be included in the report or as an appendix to it. State clearly any assumptions that you make. **(30 marks)**

8 Cost of capital

36 mins

(a) Discuss the merits and potential problems of using each of the weighted average cost of capital and adjusted present value to aid the evaluation of proposed capital investments. **(10 marks)**

(b) Your company is considering the possible effect on its cost of capital if conversion of a convertible loan stock occurs. Stock market prices have recently been very volatile, and could easily rise or fall by 10% or more during the next two months. The convertible is a $20 million 8% loan stock with four years to maturity, which was originally issued at its par value (face value) of $100. The loan stock may be converted into 20 ordinary shares during the next two months only. The loan stock's current market price is $110. Redemption in four years' time would be at the par value of $100. The company currently has other debts with a market value of $23 million.

Your company could currently issue straight debt at par of $100 with a redemption yield of 9%.

The company's current share price is 520 cents, the market value of ordinary shares is $180 million, and financial gearing 80% equity to 20% debt (by market values).

The systematic risk of the company's equity is similar to that of the market, and is thought to be unlikely to change in the near future.

The market return is 15%.

The corporate tax rate is 30%.

Required

Assuming that no major changes in interest rates occur during the next two months, estimate the impact on the company's cost of capital if:

(i) The company's share price in two months' time is 470 cents, and no conversion takes place.
(ii) The company's share price in two months' time is 570 cents, and conversion takes place.

State clearly any other assumptions that you make.

Comment on your findings. **(10 marks)**

(Total = 20 marks)

9 Trosoft

54 mins

Trosoft pte Ltd is a Singapore based company specialising in the development of business software. The company's managers believe that its future growth potential in the software sector is limited, and are considering diversifying into other activities. One suggestion is Internet auctions, and a member of the management team has produced the following draft financial proposal.

Internet auctions project

Year	0	1	2	3	4
	S$'000	S$'000	S$'000	S$'000	S$'000
Auction fees	–	4,300	6,620	8,100	8,200
Outflows:					
IT maintenance costs	–	1,210	1,850	1,920	2,125
Telephone	–	1,215	1,910	2,230	2,420
Wages	–	1,460	1,520	1,680	1,730
Salaries	–	400	550	600	650
Allocated head office overhead	–	85	90	95	100
Marketing	500	420	200	200	–
Royalty payments for use of technology	680	500	300	200	200
Market research	110	–	–	–	–
Rental of premises	–	280	290	300	310
Total outflows	1,290	5,570	6,710	7,225	7,535
Profit before tax	(1,290)	(1,270)	(90)	875	665
Tax	316	311	22	(214)	(163)
Other outflows:					
IT infrastructure	(2,700)	–	–	–	–
Working capital	(400)	(24)	(24)	(25)	(26)
Net flows	(4,074)	(983)	(92)	636	476

Additional information

(a) All data include the estimated effects of inflation on costs and prices wherever relevant. Inflation in Singapore is forecast to be 2% per year for the foreseeable future.

(b) The investment in IT infrastructure and the initial working capital will be financed by a 6 year 5.5% fixed rate term loan. Other year 0 outlays will be financed from existing cash flows.

(c) The Singapore government is expected to give a 1% per year subsidy to the cost of the loan to support the creation of jobs associated with this project.

(d) Highly skilled IT staff would need to be taken from other activities resulting in a loss of S$80,000 per year pre-tax contribution for three years.

(e) Head office cash flows for overheads will increase by S$50,000 as a result of the project in year one, rising by S$5,000 per year after year one.

(f) Corporate tax is at a rate of 24.5% per year, payable in the year that the tax liability arises. The company has other profitable projects.

(g) Tax allowable depreciation on IT infrastructure is 20% for the first year, and straight line thereafter. The IT infrastructure has an expected working life of six years after which major new investment would be required.

(h) The company's current weighted average cost of capital is 7.8%.

(i) The company's equity beta is 1.05.

(j) The average equity beta of companies in the Internet auctions sector is 1.42.

(k) The market return is 9.5% per year and the risk free rate 4% per year.

51

(l) Trosoft's capital gearing is:

Book value 55% equity, 45% debt
Market value 70% equity, 30% debt

(m) The average gearing of companies in the Internet auction sector is 67% equity, 33% debt by market values.

(n) The market research survey was undertaken three weeks ago.

(o) After tax operating net cash flows after year 4 are expected to stay approximately constant in real terms. The royalty payment will remain at S$200,000 in money terms.

(p) Issue costs on debt are 1.5%. These costs are not tax allowable.

Required

Acting as an external consultant you have been asked to prepare a report on the proposed diversification of the company into Internet auctions. The report must include a revised financial analysis. You should use the adjusted present value method for this purpose. Include in your report discussion of other financial and non financial factors, including real options, that Trosoft might consider prior to making the investment decision.

(30 marks)

10 Question with helping hand: Hasder   54 mins

Hasder plc currently operates only in the UK, but is considering diversifying its activities internationally into either Europe or East Asia, the latter including several developing economies. Estimates have been obtained of the likely risk and return of investments in these parts of the world, which are expected to vary during different economic states of the UK. After either diversification approximately 30% of the market value of the company would be represented by overseas investments.

| | | | Expected % IRR return | |
UK economic state	Probability	Invest in Europe	Invest in East Asia	Invest in UK
Low growth	0.3	7	2	6
Average growth	0.5	12	30	13
Rapid growth	0.2	21	15	17

Standard deviation of expected returns:

Europe	4.86
East Asia	12.26
UK	4.03

Covariances of expected returns:

UK/Europe	17.89
UK/East Asia	31.98

Members of Hasder's board of directors have different views about such diversification.

Director A believes that the company should focus exclusively upon the UK market as it always has, because 'overseas investments are too risky'.

Director B believes that overseas diversification will offer the company the opportunity to achieve a much better combination of risk and return than purely domestic investments, and 'will open up new opportunities'.

Director C considers that overseas investments are expensive, and overseas diversification will not be valued by shareholders who could easily achieve such diversification themselves.

Director D is in favour of the diversification, but considers East Asia to be a much better alternative than Europe.

Director E is also in favour of East Asia, but suggests that a much higher proportion of the company's activities should be located there, possibly between 50% and 70%.

Required

(a) Discuss the views of each of the five directors. Include in your discussion relevant calculations regarding portfolio risks and returns. What other factors might influence the investment decision?

State clearly any assumptions that you make. **(20 marks)**

(b) Estimate and explain the implications of the correlation coefficients between:

(i) UK/Europe; and
(ii) UK/East Asia. **(6 marks)**

(c) Hasder plc has also purchased CAPM based risk and return estimates from an investment bank.

	Relevant market return	*Relevant risk free rate*	*Relevant investment beta*
Europe	13%	5%	0.85
East Asia	18%	8%	1.32

Assuming this information is accurate, show how it might be used to assist the diversification decision.

(4 marks)

(Total = 30 marks)

Helping hand. Certain calculations are necessary in order to discuss the directors' views

Step 1 Calculate expected value of each area's investment

Step 2 Calculate weighted expected values of UK/Europe and UK/Asia combinations

Step 3 Use two asset portfolio equation $\sigma_p = \sqrt{\sigma_a^2 x^2 + \sigma_b^2(1-x)^2 + 2x(1-x)\rho_{ab}\sigma_a\sigma_b}$ to calculate standard deviation ie risk of each portfolio. $\rho_{ab}\sigma_a\sigma_b$ is the covariance

Step 4 Calculate coefficient of variation (Portfolio risk/Portfolio return) to show value for money of investment.

Directors' views

Director A — Is this always true?
Director B — Why might this view be true?
Director C — Are costs necessarily higher? When might individuals be able to do better and when might they not?
Director D — Results of calculations are relevant
Director E — Recalculate two-asset portfolio equation for revised weightings

Other considerations

As with many other questions, problems with the data, and further helpful information are worth discussing. In addition:

- Is it better to use systematic risk?
- How do the proposed policies fit in with overall strategy and financing?

(b) Correlation coefficient = $\dfrac{\text{Covariance}}{\text{Standard deviation investment 1} \times \text{Standard deviation investment 2}}$

(c) Compare expected return figures calculated in (a) with required returns figures calculated using CAPM formula $E(r_i) = r_f + [E(r_m) - r_f]\beta_i$. Expected return > Required return ∴ invest; Required return > Expected return ∴ don't invest?

11 Wit and Pratney

36 mins

Wit and Pratney have successfully tested a new scramjet engine that they believe could power the first generation of hypersonic planes cutting flight times from London to New York to 1½ hours. They are now considering whether to undertake the necessary development work in order to make it a viable commercial product. They believe the development phrase will take 3 years costing £247m pa following which the engine will have a market life of 12 years.

Demand is estimated to be 60 units pa production requires the use of a special steel alloy whose prices are quite volatile but would be £80m at today's prices and Wit and Pratney intends to sell at a 12.5% premium. Steel alloy prices are expected to rise at 4% pa subject to 22% volatility.

Wit and Pratney will need to take on a new production facility for this engine at the end of the 3 year development phase that will cost £3.14bn. Their cost at capital is 12% and risk-free rates are 5.5%.

Required

(a)   Estimate the current value at this opportunity and determine whether the company should proceed, assuming both production revenues and costs arise at the year-end.   **(12 mark)**

(b)   Your initial assessment shows that over 50% of all sales will be to the US market and all US Airline companies insist on being billed in US dollars. The board of directors are concerned about the level of exposure to the US dollar and have asked you to prepare a short paper identifying the risk resulting from such a level of exposure to the US dollar and how they should be managed.   **(8 marks)**

(Total = 20 marks)

12 AVT

54 mins

(a)   Discuss how a decrease in the value of each of the determinants of the option price in the Black-Scholes option-pricing model for European options is likely to change the price of a call option.   **(6 marks)**

(b)   AVT Inc is considering the introduction of an executive share option scheme.

The scheme would be offered to all middle managers of the company. It would replace the existing scheme of performance bonuses linked to the post-tax earnings per share of the company. Such bonuses in the last year ranged between $5,000 and $7,000. If the option scheme is introduced, new options are expected to be offered to the managers each year.

It is proposed for the first year that all middle managers are offered options to purchase 5,000 shares at a price of 500 cents per share after the options have been held for one year. Assume that the tax authorities allow the exercise of such options after they have been held for one year. If the options are not exercised at that time, they will lapse.

The company's shares have just become ex-div and have a current price of 610 cents. The dividend paid was 25 cents per share, a level that has remained constant for the last three years. Assume that dividends are only paid annually.

The company's share price has experienced a standard deviation of 38% during the last year.

The short-term risk free interest rate is 6% per annum.

Required

(i)   Discuss the relative merits for the company of the existing bonus scheme and the proposed share option scheme.   **(6 marks)**

(ii)   Evaluate whether or not the proposed share option scheme is likely to be attractive to middle managers of AVT Inc.   **(11 marks)**

(iii) When told of the scheme one manager stated that he would rather receive put options than call options, as they would be more valuable to him.

    (1) Discuss whether or not AVT should agree to offer him put options. **(3 marks)**

    (2) Calculate whether or not he is correct in his statement that put options would be more valuable to him. **(4 marks)**

(Total = 30 marks)

13 Daylon   36 mins

The managers of Daylon Inc are reviewing the company's investment portfolio. About 15% of the portfolio is represented by a holding of 5,550,000 ordinary shares of Mondglobe Inc. The managers are concerned about the effect on portfolio value if the price of Mondglobe's shares should fall, and are considering selling the shares. Daylon's investment bank has suggested that the risk of Mondglobe's shares falling by more than 5% from their current value could be protected against by buying an over the counter put option. The investment bank is prepared to sell an appropriate six month option to Daylon for $250,000.

Other information

(a) The current market price of Mondglobe's ordinary shares is 360 cents.
(b) The annual volatility (variance) of Mondglobe's shares for the last year was 169%.
(c) The risk free rate is 4% per year.
(d) No dividend is expected to be paid by Mondglobe during the next six months.

Required

(a) Evaluate whether or not the price at which the investment bank is willing to sell the option is a fair price.
(10 marks)

(b) Discuss what factors Daylon should consider before deciding whether or not to purchase the option.
(5 marks)

(c) Explain how the managers of Daylon could protect the entire portfolios from a more than a 5% fall in the market.
(5 marks)

(Total = 20 marks)

14 Fuelit   54 mins

Fuelit plc is an electricity supplier in the UK. The company has historically generated the majority of its electricity using a coal fuelled power station, but as a result of the closure of many coal mines and depleted coal resources, is now considering what type of new power station to invest in. The alternatives are a gas fuelled power station, or a new type of efficient nuclear power station.

Both types of power station are expected to generate annual revenues at current prices of £800 million. The expected operating life of both types of power station is 25 years.

Financial estimates:

	Gas	Nuclear
	£m	£m
Building costs	600	3,300
Annual running costs (at current prices)		
Labour costs	75	20
Gas purchases	500	–
Nuclear fuel purchases	–	10
Customer relations	5	20
Sales and marketing expenses	40	40
Interest expense	51	330
Other cash outlays	5	25
Accounting depreciation	24	132

Other information

(a) Whichever power station is selected, electricity generation is scheduled to commence in three years' time.

(b) If gas is used most of the workers at the existing coal fired station can be transferred to the new power station. After tax redundancy costs are expected to total £4 million in year four. If nuclear power is selected fewer workers will be required and after tax redundancy costs will total £36 million, also in year four.

(c) Both projects would be financed by Eurobond issues denominated in Euros. The gas powered station would require a bond issue at 8.5% per year. The bond for the nuclear project would be at 10%, reflecting the impact on financial gearing of a larger bond issue.

(d) Costs of building the new power stations would be payable in two equal instalments in one and two years' time.

(e) The existing coal fired power station would need to be demolished at a cost of £10 million after tax in three years time.

(f) The company's equity beta is expected to be 0.7 if the gas station is chosen and 1.4 if the nuclear station is chosen. Gearing (debt to equity plus debt) is expected to be 35% with gas and 60% with nuclear fuel.

(g) The risk free rate is 4.5% per year and the market return is 14% per year. Inflation is currently 3% per year in the UK and an average of 5% per year in the member countries of the Euro bloc in the European Union.

(h) Corporate tax is at the rate of 30% payable in the same year that the liability arises.

(i) Tax allowable depreciation is at the rate of 10% per year on a straight line basis.

(j) At the end of twenty-five years of operations the gas plant is expected to cost £25 million (after tax) to demolish and clean up the site. Costs of decommissioning the nuclear plant are much less certain, and could be anything between £500 million and £1,000 million (after tax) depending upon what form of disposal is available for nuclear waste.

Required

(a) Estimate the expected NPV of each of investment in a gas fuelled power station and investment in a nuclear fuelled power station.

State clearly any assumptions that you make.

(*Note.* It is recommended that annuity tables are used wherever possible) **(15 marks)**

(b) Discuss other information that might assist the decision process. **(6 marks)**

(c) An external advisor has suggested that the discount rate for the costs of decommissioning the nuclear power station should be adjusted because of their risk. Discuss whether or not this discount rate should be increased or decreased. **(3 marks)**

(d)   Explain the significance of the existence of real options to the capital investment decision, and briefly discuss examples of real options that might be significant in the power station decision process.   **(6 marks)**

(Total = 30 marks)

15 Bioplasm   36 mins

Bioplasm plc is a UK based company that has completed the preliminary development of a new drug to combat a major disease. Initial clinical trials of the drug have been favourable, and the drug is expected to receive approval from the regulatory authority in the near future. Bioplasm has taken out a patent on the drug that gives it the exclusive right to commercially develop and market the drug for a period of 15 years. Although it is difficult to produce precise estimates, the company believes that to commercially develop and market the drug for worldwide use will cost approximately £400 million at current prices. The expected present value from sales of the drug during the patent period could vary between £350 million and £500 million. The current long-term government bond yield is 5%. The annual variance of returns on similar biotech companies is estimated to be 0.185.

The finance director of Bioplasm can see from the possible NPVs that the company has a difficult decision as to whether or not to develop the drug, and wonders if option pricing could assist the decision.

Required

(a)   Using the Black-Scholes option pricing model for the life of the patent, estimate the call values of the option to commercially develop and market the drug. Provide a reasoned recommendation, based upon your calculations and any other relevant information, as to whether or not Bioplasm should develop the drug.

Note. Because the value of the returns from the patent will fall over the period before the drug is commercially developed, it is necessary to adjust the expected present value from sales of the drug. In all relevant parts of the Black-Scholes model, the present value from sales of the drug should be multiplied by $\exp^{(-0.067)(15)}$ to reflect this potential reduction in value according to when the drug is developed.   **(15 marks)**

(b)   Explain what is meant by real options and how they could be used by Bioplasm in this situation.   **(5 marks)**

(Total = 20 marks)

16 Remuneration package   36 mins

The remuneration committee of A Inc is discussing the remuneration package that might to be offered to the company's new managing director. Members of the committee have expressed different opinions. These include:

(a)   The managing director must be offered a salary at least 20% more than the average of similar sized companies in order to attract the best candidates.

(b)   It is essential to offer a salary linked to revenue.

(c)   The managing director should be offered share options, exercisable in one year's time, on at least 3,000,000 shares, at an exercise price of 25% below the current market price of 120 pence.

(d)   Remuneration should be a basic salary plus a proportion of the economic value added (EVA™) of the company. 1.5% per year was the suggested proportion.

In the ensuing debate one committee member stated that a friend had recently bought one year European style put options on the company's shares at a price of 35 cents. The options to be granted to the new managing director would therefore be worth several million pounds. Such generosity would not be well received given recent newspaper commentary about the excessive remuneration of senior managers in some companies.

Relevant company and market data is shown below:

	Year ended 31 March 20X4
	$ million
Revenue	546
Cost of sales	(369)
Depreciation	(52)
Advertising	(10)
Net interest	(26)
Profit before tax	89
Taxation	(27)
Available to shareholders	62

	$ million	
	31 March 20X3	31 March 20X4
Capital employed	420	458

Notes

(1) Accounting depreciation is approximately equal to economic deprecation.
(2) Advertising has been $10 million per year for the last four years.
(3) The company's cost of equity is 12%
(4) The company's weighted average cost of capital is 9.5%
(5) The risk free rate is 4%
(6) The corporate tax rate is 30%

Required

(a) Discuss the relative merits of each of the four suggestions.   **(6 marks)**

(b) Some committee members have expressed concern about how much some of the suggestions might cost the company.

For both the share option and EVA™ suggestions, estimate the potential cost to the company, and comment on your findings. For EVA™ the estimate should be based upon the most recent relevant published data.

(9 marks)

(c) Briefly describe the possible areas of conflict between the shareholders and the managers of the business. Outline possible strategies available to resolve any such conflicts.   **(5 marks)**

(Total = 20 marks)

17 Wickern   **54 mins**

Assume it is now the end of 20X5. Four years ago Wickern plc, a UK quoted company, invested in an ice-skating rink in Denmark. The capital cost was 60 million kroners, or £8 million at the exchange rate at the time. The rink is used most of the time for public skating sessions, but is also used by an ice hockey team and for concerts.

When the investment occurred the rink had an expected working life of eight years, after which significant new investment would be needed. If no new investment were to take place the building and site at the end of 20X9 would have an estimated value of 79 million kroners. Any new capital investment in 20X9 would cost an estimated 328 million kroners, and could lead to annual incremental after tax cash flows of between 50 million and 65 million kroners for the next ten years.

The value of the land and building if sold now is 100 million kroners.

The corporate tax rate between 20X2 and 20X5 was 30% in the UK, and 35% in Denmark. It was announced in December 20X5 that the Danish tax rate would be reduced to 28.5% in 20X6. The UK tax rate is expected to remain at 30% for the foreseeable future. A bilateral tax treaty exists between the UK and Denmark, where any tax suffered in Denmark will be fully available for credit in the UK.

Wickern plc has had other profitable capital investments in Denmark since before 20X2, and pays the full rate of taxation in Denmark.

Original forecast operating cash flows

| | | Kroners (million) | | | | | | | |
		20X2	20X3	20X4	20X5	20X6	20X7	20X8	20X9
Inflows	Public ice-skating	13.5	14.2	15.0	15.7	16.5	17.2	18.0	18.7
	Ice hockey matches	18.0	18.5	19.0	19.5	20.0	20.5	21.0	21.5
	Concerts	7.5	11.0	11.0	11.0	13.5	13.5	13.5	13.5
		39.0	43.7	45.0	46.2	50.0	51.2	52.5	53.7
Outflows	Public ice-skating	7.5	7.5	7.5	7.5	7.5	7.5	7.5	7.5
	Ice hockey matches	3.0	3.0	3.0	3.0	3.0	3.0	3.0	3.0
	Concerts	1.5	1.5	1.5	1.5	1.5	1.5	1.5	1.5
	General overheads	11.2	11.2	13.5	13.5	13.5	15.7	15.7	15.7
	Tax allowable depreciation	7.5	7.5	7.5	7.5	7.5	7.5	7.5	7.5
		30.7	30.7	33.0	33.0	33.0	35.2	35.2	35.2
Taxable net cash flows		8.3	13.0	12.0	13.2	17.0	16.0	17.3	18.5
Taxation (35%)		(2.9)	(4.6)	(4.2)	(4.6)	(6.0)	(5.6)	(6.1)	(6.5)
Remittable to the UK		12.9	15.9	15.3	16.1	18.5	17.9	18.7	19.5

| | £ (million) | | | | | | | |
	20X2	20X3	20X4	20X5	20X6	20X7	20X8	20X9
Remittable to the UK	1.72	2.12	2.04	2.15	2.47	2.39	2.49	2.60

The original cash flow forecasts proved to be inaccurate, and at the end of 20X5 the actual cash flows for the first years were produced for analysis, together with new cash flow forecasts for the next four years.

Actual (20X2 – 20X5) and revised projected future operating cash flows (post 20X5):

| | | Kroners (million) | | | |
		20X2	20X3	20X4	20X5
Inflows	Public ice-skating	11.2	12.0	12.0	12.0
	Ice hockey matches	11.2	11.2	12.0	13.5
	Concerts	6.0	7.5	6.0	11.2
		28.4	30.7	30.0	36.7
Outflows	Public ice-skating	7.5	7.5	7.5	7.5
	Ice hockey matches	3.0	3.0	3.0	3.0
	Concerts	3.0	3.0	3.0	4.5
	General overheads	13.5	13.5	14.2	14.2
	Tax allowable depreciation	7.5	7.5	7.5	7.5
		34.5	34.5	35.2	36.7
Taxable net cash flows		(6.1)	(3.8)	(5.2)	0
Taxation (35%)		2.1	1.3	1.8	0
Remittable to the UK		3.5	5.0	4.1	7.5

| | £ (million) | | | |
	20X2	20X3	20X4	20X5
Cash flows Remittable to the UK	0.44	0.56	0.41	0.68

		Kroners (million)			
		20X6	*20X7*	*20X8*	*20X9*
Inflows	Public ice-skating	13.8	13.8	13.8	13.8
	Ice hockey matches	15.1	15.1	15.1	15.1
	Concerts	13.1	13.1	13.1	13.1
		42.0	42.0	42.0	42.0
Outflows	Public ice-skating	7.2	7.2	7.2	7.2
	Ice hockey matches	3.3	3.3	3.3	3.3
	Concerts	4.6	4.6	4.6	4.6
	General	15.1	15.1	15.1	15.1
	Tax allowable depreciation	7.2	7.2	7.2	7.2
		37.4	37.4	37.4	37.4
Taxable amounts		4.6	4.6	4.6	4.6
Taxation (28.5%)		(1.3)	(1.3)	(1.3)	(1.3)

Inflation in Denmark is at the rate of 5% per year and in the UK 2% per year. These rates are expected to continue in the foreseeable future.

The spot rate at the end of 20X5 is 11.09 Kroners:£.

The beta of the investment in 20X2 was estimated to be 1.125. The risk free rate was 7% and the market return 15%. At the end of 20X5 the beta of the investment has been re-evaluated at 0.95, the risk free rate is 6% and the market return 13.5%.

Required

(a) Analyse the financial performance of the ice-skating rink between 20X2 and 20X5 inclusive. Include in your analysis discussion of reasons why the actual cash flows differed from those forecast and a calculation of the forecast NPV to 20X9. Recommend what corrective action might be taken. **(15 marks)**

(b) Prepare a report for the board of Wickern plc discussing whether or not the ice-skating rink should be sold now, retained for another four years or retained indefinitely. All relevant assumptions and calculations should be included in the report (or as an appendix to it). **(15 marks)**

(Total = 30 marks)

18 Boxless

36 mins

(a) Briefly discuss possible benefits and drawbacks to a multinational company from using a holding company based in a tax haven. **(5 marks)**

(b) Boxless plc has subsidiaries in three overseas countries, Annovia, Cardenda and Sporoon. Corporate taxes for the three countries are shown below:

	Corporate income tax rate	*Withholding tax on dividends*	*% of after tax income remitted to the UK*
Annovia	40%	10%	70
Cardenda	25%	–	40
Sporoon	20%	5%	80

The UK corporate tax rate is 30%, and bilateral tax treaties exist between the UK and each of the three countries. Under the treaties, any corporate tax paid overseas on income remitted to the UK may be credited against UK tax liability. Boxless currently remits income from its overseas subsidiaries direct to the UK parent company.

The UK government currently only taxes income from multinational companies' overseas subsidiaries when such income is remitted to the UK. UK tax liability is based upon the grossed up dividend distributions to the UK (grossed up at the local tax rate and before deduction of any withholding tax).

The UK government is now considering taxing the gross income earned by overseas subsidiaries. If such gross income were to be taxed, credit against UK tax liability would be available for all corporate tax paid overseas.

Required

(i) Estimate the impact on the cash flows of Boxless if the UK government alters the tax rules as detailed above.

Assume that the taxable income in each of the subsidiaries is the equivalent of £100,000.   **(7 marks)**

(ii) For each of the current and possible new tax rules, evaluate what benefit, if any, Boxless would experience if it were to transfer income from its overseas subsidiaries to the parent company via a tax haven holding company. Assume that the UK tax authorities would then treat all income from overseas subsidiaries as coming from a single source, the tax haven holding company. Comment upon your results.   **(4 marks)**

(c) Explain the possible risks that a multinational may face with respect to taxes.   **(4 marks)**

(Total = 20 marks)

ACQUISITIONS AND MERGERS

Questions 19 to 30 cover acquisitions and mergers, the subject of Part C of the BPP Study Text for Paper P4.

---

19 Intergrand   54 mins

The board of directors of Intergrand plc wishes to establish an operating subsidiary in Germany through the acquisition of an exiting German company. Intergrand has undertaken research into a number of German quoted companies, and has decided to attempt to purchase Oberberg AG. Initial discussions suggest that the directors of Oberberg AG may be willing to recommend the sale of 100% of the company's equity to Intergrand for a total cash price of 115 million Euro, payable in full on acquisition.

Oberberg has provided the managers of Intergrand with internal management information regarding accounting/cash flow projections for the next four years.

The projects are in money/nominal terms.

Oberberg AG, financial projections
Euro (million)

Year	20X3	20X4	20X5	20X6
Sales	38.2	41.2	44.0	49.0
Labour	11.0	12.1	13.0	14.1
Materials	8.3	8.7	9.0	9.4
Overheads	3.2	3.2	3.3	3.4
Interest	2.5	3.0	3.5	3.8
Tax allowable depreciation	6.3	5.8	5.6	5.2
	31.3	32.8	34.4	35.9
Taxable profit	6.9	8.4	9.6	13.1
Taxation (25%)	1.7	2.1	2.4	3.3
Incremental operating working capital	0.7	0.9	1.0	2.0
Replacement investment	4.2	4.2	4.2	4.2
Investment for expansion	–	–	9.0	–

Oberberg AG, pro forma summarised income statement
for the year ending 31 December 20X2

	Euro (million)
Revenue	35.8
Operating expenses	21.1
Interest expense	3.4
Depreciation	6.2
	30.7
Taxable profit	5.1
Taxation (25%)	1.3
Profit after tax	3.8

Oberberg AG, pro forma summarised balance sheet
as at 31 December 20X2

	Euro (million)
Non-current assets	73.2
Current assets	58.1
Current liabilities	(40.3)
	91.0
Financed by:	
Ordinary shares (100 Euro par value)	15.0
Reserves	28.0
Medium and long term bank loans	30.0
8% Bond 20X9 (par value 1,000 Euro)	18.0
	91.0

Notes

(a) The spot exchange rate between the Euro and pound is Euro 1.625/£.

(b) Inflation is at 4% per year in the UK and 2% per year in the Euro bloc. This differential is expected to continue unless the UK joins the Euro bloc.

(c) The market return is 11% and the risk free rate is 4%.

(d) Oberberg's equity beta is estimated to be 1.4.

(e) Oberberg's 8% bond is currently priced at 1,230 Euro and its ordinary share price is 300 Euro.

(f) Post-merger rationalisation will involve the sale of some non-current assets of Oberberg in 20X3 with an expected after tax market value of 8 million Euro.

(g) Synergies in production and distribution are expected to yield 2 million Euro per annum before tax from 20X4 onwards.

(h) £175,000 has already been spent researching into possible acquisition targets.

(i) The purchase of Oberberg will provide publicity and exposure in Germany for the Intergrand name and brand. This extra publicity is believed to be the equivalent of Intergrand spending 1 million Euro per year on advertising in Germany.

(j) The weighted average cost of capital of Intergrand is 10%.

(k) After tax cash flows of Oberberg after 20X6 are expected to grow at approximately 2% per year.

(l) Oberberg does not plan to issue or redeem any equity or medium and long-term debt prior to 20X6.

(m) After tax redundancy costs as a result of the acquisition are expected to be 5 million Euro, payable almost immediately.

(n) Operating working capital comprises receivables and inventory less payables. It excludes short-term loans.

(o) Current liabilities include negligible amounts of short-term loans.

(p) The corporate tax rate in Germany is 25% and in the UK 30%. A bilateral tax treaty exists between the two countries whereby tax paid in one country may be credited against any tax liability in the other country.

(q) If Intergrand acquires Oberberg existing exports to Germany yielding a pre-tax cash flow of £800,000 per annum will be lost. It is hoped that about half of these exports can be diverted to the French market.

Required

Intergrand has suggested that Oberberg should be valued based upon the expected present value (to infinity) of the operating free cash flows of Oberberg. These would be discounted at an all-equity rate and adjusted by the present value of all other relevant cash flows, discounted at an appropriate rate(s).

Acting as a consultant to Intergrand plc, prepare a report evaluating whether or not Intergrand should offer the 115 million Euro required to acquire Oberberg AG. Include in your report discussion of other commercial and business factors that Intergrand should consider prior to making a final decision.

Assume that it is now mid-December 20X2.

State clearly any other assumptions that you make.   **(30 marks)**

20 Demast

54 mins

Demast Ltd has grown during the last five years into one of the UK's most successful specialist games manufacturers. The company's success has been largely based on its Megaoid series of games and models, for which it holds patents in many developed countries. The company has attracted the interest of two plcs, Nadion, a traditional manufacturer of games and toys, and BZO International, a conglomerate group that has grown rapidly in recent years through the strategy of acquiring what it perceives to be undervalued companies.

Summarised financial details of the three companies are shown below.

Demast Ltd
Summarised balance sheet as at 31 December 20X3

	£'000	£'000
Fixed assets (net)		8,400
Current assets		
Stock	5,500	
Debtors	3,500	
Cash	100	
		9,100
Less *current liabilities*		
Trade creditors	4,700	
Tax payable	1,300	
Overdraft	1,200	
		7,200
		10,300
Medium and long-term loans		3,800
Net assets		6,500

	£'000
Financed by	
Ordinary shares (25 pence nominal)	1,000
Reserves	5,500
	6,500

Summarised profit and loss account for the year
ended 31 December 20X3

	£'000
Turnover	27,000
Profit before tax	4,600
Taxation	1,380
	3,220
Dividend	1,500
Retained earnings	1,720

Additional information

(a) The realisable value of stock is believed to be 90% of its book value.
(b) Land and buildings, with a book value of £4 million, were last revalued in 20W9.
(c) The directors of the company and their families own 25% of the company's shares.

	Demast	Nadion	BZO Int
Turnover (£m)	27	112	256
Profit before tax (£m)	4.6	11	24
Fixed assets (£m net)	8.4	26	123
Current assets (£m)	9.1	41	72
Current liabilities (£m)	7.2	33	91
Overdraft (£m)	1.2	6	30
Medium and long-term liabilities (£m)	3.8	18	35
Interest payable (£m)	0.5	3	10
Share price (pence)	-	320	780
EPS (pence)	80.5	58	51
Estimated required return on equity	16%	14%	12%
Growth trends per year:			
Earnings	12%	6%	13%
Dividends	9%	5%	8%
Turnover	15%	10%	23%

Assume that the following events occurred shortly after the above financial information was produced.

7 September. BZO makes a bid for Demast of two ordinary shares for every three shares of Demast. The price of BZO's ordinary shares after the announcement of the bid is 710 pence. The directors of Demast reject the offer.

2 October. Nadion makes a counter bid of 170 pence cash per share plus one £100 10% convertible debenture 20Y8, issued at par, for every £6.25 nominal value of Demast's shares. Each convertible debenture may be exchanged for 26 ordinary shares at any time between 1 January 20X7 and 31 December 20X9. Nadion's share price moves to 335 pence. This offer is rejected by the directors of Demast.

19 October. BZO offers cash of 600 pence per share. The cash will be raised by a term loan from the company's bank. The board of Demast are all offered seats on subsidiary boards within the BZO group. BZO's shares move to 680 pence.

20 October. The directors of Demast recommend acceptance of the revised offer from BZO.

24 October. BZO announces that 53% of shareholders have accepted its offer and make the offer unconditional.

Required

(a) Discuss the advantages and disadvantages of growth by acquisition. **(7 marks)**

(b) Discuss whether or not the bids by BZO and Nadion are financially prudent from the point of view of the companies' shareholders. Relevant supporting calculations must be shown. **(17 marks)**

(c) Discuss problems of corporate governance that might arise for the shareholders of Demast Ltd and BZO plc. **(6 marks)**

(Total = 30 marks)

21 Minprice

54 mins

The directors of Minprice plc, a food retailer with 20 superstores, are proposing to make a takeover bid for Savealot plc, a company with six superstores in the north of England. Minprice will offer four of its ordinary shares for every three ordinary shares of Savealot. The bid has not yet been made public.

Summarised accounts

Balance Sheets as at 31 March 20X0

	Minprice plc			Savealot plc		
	£m	£m	£m	£m	£m	£m
Land and buildings (net)			483			42.3
Fixed assets (net)			150			17.0
			633			59.3
Current assets						
Stock	328			51.4		
Debtors	12			6.3		
Cash	44			5.3		
		384			63.0	
Creditors: amounts falling due in less than one year						
Creditors	447			46.1		
Dividend	12			2.0		
Taxation	22			2.0		
		(481)			(50.1)	
			(97)			12.9
Creditors: amounts falling due after more than one year						
14% loan stock			(200)			
Floating rate bank term loans			(114)			(17.5)
			222			54.7
Shareholders' Funds						
Original shares 25 pence per			75	50 pence par		20.0
Reserves			147			34.7
			222			54.7

Profit and loss accounts for the year ending 31 March 20X0

	£m	£m
Turnover	1,130	181
Earnings before interest and tax	115	14
Net interest	(40)	(2)
Profit before tax	75	12
Taxation	(25)	(4)
Available to shareholders	50	8
Dividend	(24)	(5)
Retained earnings	26	3

The current share price of Minprice plc is 232 pence, and of Savealot plc 295 pence. The current loan stock price of Minprice plc is £125.

Recent annual growth trends:	Minprice plc	Savealot plc
Dividends	7%	8%
EPS	7%	10%

Rationalisation following the acquisition will involve the following transactions (all net of tax effects):

(a) Sale of surplus warehouse facilities for £6.8 million.

(b) Redundancy payments costing £9.0 million.

(c) Wage savings of £2.7 million per year for at least five years.

Minprice's cost of equity is estimated to be 14.5%, and weighted average cost of capital 12%. Savealot's cost of equity is estimated to be 13%.

Required

(a) Discuss and evaluate whether or not the bid is likely to be viewed favourably by the shareholders of both Minprice plc and Savealot plc. Include discussion of the factors that are likely to influence the views of the shareholders.

All relevant calculations must be shown. **(15 marks)**

(b) Discuss the possible effects on the likely success of the bid if the offer terms were to be amended to a choice of one new Minprice plc 10 year zero coupon debenture redeemable at £100 for every 10 Savealot plc shares, or 325 pence per share cash. Minprice plc could currently issue new 10 year loan stock at an interest rate of 10%.

All relevant calculations must be shown. **(7 marks)**

(c) The directors of Savealot plc have decided to fight the bid and have proposed the following measures:

(i) Announce that their company's profits are likely to be doubled next year.

(ii) Alter the Articles of Association to require that at least 75% of shareholders need to approve an acquisition.

(iii) Persuade, for a fee, a third party investor to buy large quantities of the company's shares.

(iv) Introduce an advertising campaign criticising the performance and management ability of Minprice plc.

(v) Revalue fixed assets to current values so that shareholders are aware of the company's true market values.

Acting as a consultant to the company, give reasoned advice on whether or not the company should adopt each of these measures. **(8 marks)**

(Total = 30 marks)

22 Paxis

54 mins

Paxis Inc will soon announce a takeover bid for Wragger Inc, a company in the same industry. The initial bid will be an all share bid of four Paxis shares for every five Wragger shares.

The most recent annual data relating to the two companies are shown below:

	$'000	
	Paxis	*Wragger*
Sales revenue	13,333	9,400
Operating costs	(8,683)	(5,450)
Tax allowable depreciation	(1,450)	(1,100)
Earnings before interest and tax	3,200	2,850
Net interest	(715)	(1,660)
Taxable income	2,485	1,190
Taxation (30%)	(746)	(357)
After tax income	1,739	833
Dividend	(870)	(458)
Retained earnings	869	375

Other information:

	Paxis	Wragger
Annual replacement capital expenditure ($'000)	1,600	1,240
Expected annual growth rate in sales, operating costs (including depreciation), replacement investment and dividends for the next four years	5%	6.5%
Expected annual growth rate in sales, operating costs (including depreciation), replacement investment and dividends after four years	4%	5%
Gearing (long term debt/long term debt plus equity by market value)	30%	55%
Market price per share (pence)	298	192
Number of issued shares (million)	7	8
Current market cost of fixed interest debt	6%	7.5%
Equity beta	1.18	1.38
Risk free rate	4%	
Market return	11%	

The takeover is expected to result in cost savings in advertising and distribution, reducing the operating costs (including depreciation) of Paxis from 76% of sales to 70% of sales. The growth rate of the combined company is expected to be 6% per year for four years, and 5% per year thereafter. Wragger's debt obligations will be taken over by Paxis. The corporate tax rate is expected to remain at 30%.

Sales and costs relevant to the decision may be assumed to be in cash terms.

Required

(a) Using free cash flow analysis for each individual company and the potential combined company, estimate how much synergy is expected to be created from the takeover. State clearly any assumptions that you make.

Note. The weighted average cost of capital of the combined company may be assumed to be the market weighted average of the current costs of capital of the individual companies, weighted by the current market value of debt and equity of the combined company, with the equity of Wragger adjusted for the effect of the bid price. **(15 marks)**

(b) Discuss the factors that might influence whether the initial bid is likely to be accepted by the shareholders of Wragger Inc. **(5 marks)**

(c) Estimate by how much the bid might be increased without the shareholders of Paxis suffering a fall in their expected wealth, and discuss whether or not the directors of Paxis should proceed with the bid. **(5 marks)**

(d) Once the bid is announced, discuss what defences Wragger Inc might use against the bid by Paxis Inc. **(5 marks)**

(Total = 30 marks)

23 Omnikit

54 mins

Omnikit plc is a manufacturer of kitchen furniture. The company's senior management have believed for several years that there is little opportunity to increase sales in the UK market and wish to set up a manufacturing subsidiary in Switzerland or the USA. Because of high transportation costs, exporting from the UK is not financially viable.

The Swiss subsidiary would involve the construction of a new factory on a 'green field' site. The projected costs are shown below.

Swiss subsidiary

	Now	Year 1
	SFr'000	SFr'000
Land	2,300	–
Building	1,600	6,200
Machinery	–	6,400
Working capital	–	11,500

Production and sales in year two are estimated to be 2,000 kitchens at an average price of SFr20,000 (at current prices). Production in each of years 3-6 is forecast at 2,500 units. Total local variable costs in Switzerland in year two are expected to be SFr11,000 per unit (at current prices). In addition a fixed royalty fee of £750,000 per year would be payable to the UK parent company. Tax allowable depreciation in Switzerland on machines is at 25% per year on a reducing balance basis. No tax allowable depreciation exists on other non-current assets.

The US investment would involve the purchase, via a takeover bid, of an existing kitchen furniture manufacturer based in Boston. The cost is not precisely known but Omnikit's managers are confident that a bid within the range $8m-10m will be successful. Additional investment of $2 million in new machines and $4 million in working capital would immediately be required, resulting in forecast pre-tax net cash flows (after tax savings from depreciation) in year one of $2 million (at current prices) rising to $3 million (at current prices) in year two and subsequent years.

All prices and costs in Switzerland and the USA are expected to increase annually by the current rate of inflation. The after-tax realisable value of the investments in six years' time is expected to be approximately SFr16.2 million and US$14.5 million at price levels then ruling, excluding working capital.

Inflation rates for each of the next six years are expected to be:

USA	6%
UK	3%
Switzerland	5%

Exchange rates

	SFr/£	$/£
Spot	2.3140 – 2.3210	1.5160 – 1.5210

Omnikit can borrow funds for the investment at 10% per year in the UK. The company's cost of equity capital is estimated to be 15%. After either proposed investment Omnikit's gearing will be approximately 50% debt, 50% equity by book value, and 30% debt, 70% equity by market value.

Corporate tax in Switzerland is at 40%, in the UK 33% and the USA 30%, Full bilateral tax treaties, exist between the UK and both Switzerland and the USA. Taxation is payable, and allowances are available, one year in arrears.

Required

(a)   Discuss the advantages and disadvantages of organic growth and growth by acquisition.   **(6 marks)**

(b)   Evaluate which, if either, of the two subsidiaries should be established by Omnikit. Include discussion of the limitations of your evaluation. State clearly any assumptions that you make.   **(24 marks)**

(Total = 30 marks)

24 X-Train   54 mins

You are the chief financial officer of X-Train a large listed company in the professional training business whose principal market activities are to offer professional training courses for the accountancy and legal qualifications. Its principal market base is London although it provides training courses throughout the UK. It has a small city based training business through its existing relationships. It has a good reputation within the professional training market earned through the quality of its service and exam success rate. Following the recent disinvestments of associated interest it has cash reserves of £2,064 million.

City-Train is a smaller unlisted company operating in London. It was founded in 1993 and has developed a strong position in the City and is the market leader in the provision of specialised City training courses to all the major financial institutions. In the year to 31 December 2006 its reported turnover was £4.08 billion and its profit after tax for the financial year was £120 million. It has recently expanded its training office premises to cope with the increased demand resulting from additional regulatory changes.

City-Train's cash flow statement for the current and preceding year is as follows:

City-Train Consolidated Cash Flow Statement (extract)

For the year ended 31 December 2006

	31 December 2006		31 December 2005	
	£m	£m	£m	£m
Net cash inflow from operating activities		504.00		228.00
Return on investment and servicing of finance				
Interest received	28.80		14.40	
Interest paid	(9.60)		(7.20)	
Interest element on finance leases	(15.60)		(9.60)	
		3.60		(2.40)
Taxation		(9.84)		(0.48)
Capital expenditure		(288.48)		(130.00)
Acquisition and disposals				
Proceeds from the sale of interest in joint ventures		24.00		86.00
Cash inflow before management of liquid resources and financing		233.28		81.12
Management of liquid resources				
Decrease/(increase) in short term deposits		85.20		(77.28)
Financing				
Increase/(decrease) in cash for the year		318.48		3.84

The statement below contains market data relating to X-Train:

Key Fundamentals

Forward P/E*	11.05	Dividend Yield	0.00
Price to Book value of equity	2.50	1 Yr Total Return (%)**	25.09
Price to cash flow	3.05	Equity Beta	2.05
1 Yr Sales Growth	−1.65	1 yr EPS Growth	80.55
Equity market cap	£3.5 bn		

You also note the following:

The current risk-free rate is 4.55% and the equity risk premium is estimated at 3.55%. The prevailing share price for X-Train is 295p per share and its P/E ratio is 10.5. The corporation tax for both companies is 30 per cent.

The balance sheet gearing ratio for X-Train, expressed as total debt to total capital (debt plus equity) is 50 per cent and as total debt to equity is 100 per cent.

You may assume that:

(1)   City-Train has undertaken a consistent programme of reinvestment.
(2)   The debt in both companies is all floating rate and is not expected to be sensitive to market risk.

There has been considerable consolidation in the training industry and you are advising your board of directors of X-Train on the value of City-Train as a potential target for acquisition. It is anticipated that over the longer term the training industry will settle to a rate of growth in line with GDP which stands at 4.5 per cent per annum (nominal). However, the current rates of growth for this company are likely to be sustained for the next five years before reverting to the GDP growth rate from the start of the sixth year forward.

Required

(a)   Estimate the current cost of equity capital for City-Train using the Capital Asset pricing Model, making notes on any assumptions that you have made.   **(9 marks)**

(b)   Estimate the expected growth rate of City-Train using the current rate of retention of free cash flows and your estimate of the required rate of return on equity for the future. Make notes on any assumptions you have made.   **(6 marks)**

(c)   Estimate the value of City-Train on the basis of its expected free cash flow to equity, explaining the limitations of the methods you have used.   **(7 marks)**

(d)   Write a brief report outlining the considerations your colleagues on the board of X-Train might bear in mind when contemplating this acquisition.   **(8 marks)**

(Total = 30 marks)

25 Carpetshop   54 mins

Carpetshop is a major nationwide carpet retailer that is considering the opportunity to acquire Copers Carpets, a smaller family owner unlisted competitor in this highly competitive sector. The companies are in discussion about the possibility of an immediate outright purchase but Copers have offered Carpetshop the choice of either a three month option or a six month option on the share capital of the company for $2.25bn.

Carpetshop have 1.136bn shares in issue on which a 46p dividend has just been paid. Carpetshop earnings are growing in line with the sector overall at an annual rate of 3% and its equity has a beta of 1.12. Carpetshop has $3.72bn of 5.25% irredeemable debt in issue with an A credit rating.

Copers Carpets has 98m shares in issue and were it ungeared it is estimated that it could have paid a 187p dividend last year and would slow growth in line with the sector. Copers do, however, have $960m at 6.5% irredeemable debt in issue with a B credit rating.

Neither Carpetshop nor Copers are considered to have any unsystematic risk.

General market statistics are that the risk-free rate is 5% and the market is returning 10% at a risk of 9%. Yield spreads for irredeemables are

Rating	bp
A	78
B	140

Carpetshop believes that the takeover offers potential cost saving synergies of $18m pa. If Carpetshop were to acquire Copers it would refinance the combined business such that, in market value terms, the debt to equity ratio would be 30%.

Assume a tax rate of 30%.

Required

(a)   Calculate the price of the 3 month and 6 month options on the shares of Copers.   **(16 marks)**

(b)   Calculate the value the combined businesses would have if there was an immediate takeover based on the estimated synergies and refinancing plans of Carpetshop. Assess the value and beta of the equity and debt.   **(8 marks)**

(c)   Prepare a brief report outlining the advantages and disadvantages of using options in this situation.   **(6 marks)**

(Total = 30 marks)

26 Hotparts

36 mins

You are the chief financial officer of Hotparts Co, and engineering company specializing in the manufacture of high performance car parts. The company has cash reserves of $975 million realised through the disposal of associated interests. Hotparts' stated objective is to become market leader and is now considering the following two options, both of which are on strategy:

Option 1

Expansion of operations through the acquisition of Spareparts Co. Spareparts is located approximately 100 miles from Hotparts' location. Spareparts, however has had quality control problems with the production of manufactured parts. Spareparts is know within the industry as the provider of cheap parts.

It is believed that Spareparts Co could be brought for $350 million and the operations director has estimated that it will be necessary to spend a further $50 million over two years to make the necessary adjustments to the plant to bring it in line with the operations at Hotparts. In addition, the operations director estimates a further $15 million to retrain the staff at Spareparts Co. The training costs are spread evenly over 3 years after the completion of the conversion of the factory, being paid at the start of each year. Spareparts currently generates net cash from its operations of $30 million though this will half over the factory refurbishment period and be at only 80% of this during staff retraining.

Option 2

There is a site ripe for development close to the existing Hotparts factory. The cost of development of the site can be summarised as follows:

- Acquisition of site $150 million

- Build and fit of factory $225 million spread out evenly over the next five years, payable at the start of each year

Once completed, both options would offer the same productive capacity and quality. The company's cost of capital is 8.5 per cent.

Required

(a) Prepare a memorandum, to be considered at the next board meeting , which summarises the arguments for and against growth through organic growth versus acquisition. **(12 marks)**

(b) You have been asked to produce a short report which evaluates both options and recommends the course of action most appropriate to fulfilling Hotparts stated corporate objective, making notes on any assumptions you have made. Your report should also detail how your proposal can be implemented, highlighting potential areas of concern requiring careful attention. **(8 marks)**

(Total = 20 marks)

27 Question with analysis: Laceto

(a)   Laceto Inc, a large retail group specialising in the sale of clothing and electrical goods is currently considering a takeover bid for a competitor, in the electrical goods sector, Omnigen Inc, whose share price has fallen by 205 cents during the last three months.

Summarised data for the financial year to 31 March 20X1

	$ million	
	Laceto	Omnigen
Revenue	420	180
Profit before tax (after interest payments)	41	20
Taxation	12	6
Non-current assets (net)	110	63
Current assets	122	94
Current liabilities	86	71
Medium and long-term liabilities	40	12
Shareholders' funds	106	74

The share price of Laceto is currently 380 cents, and of Omnigen 410 cents. Laceto has 80 million issued ordinary shares and Omnigen 30 million. Typical of Laceto's medium and long-term liabilities is 12% loan stock with three years to maturity, a par value of $100, and a current market price of $108.80.

The finance team of Laceto has produced the following forecasts of financial data for the activities of Omnigen if it is taken over.

	$ million			
Financial year	20X2	20X3	20X4	20X5
Net sales	230	261	281	298
Cost of goods sold (50%)	115	131	141	149
Selling and administrative expenses	32	34	36	38
Capital allowances (total)	40	42	42	42
Interest	18	16	14	12
Cash flow needed for asset replacement and forecast growth	50	52	55	58

Corporate taxation is at the rate of 30% per year, payable in the year that the taxable cash flow occurs.

The risk-free rate is 6% per year and market return 14% per year. Omnigen's current equity beta is 1.2. This is expected to increase by 0.1 if the company is taken over as Laceto would increase the current level of capital gearing associated with the activities of Omnigen. Laceto's gearing post acquisition is expected to be between 18% and 23% (debt to debt plus equity by market values), depending upon the final price paid for Omnigen.

Post-takeover cash flows of Omnigen (after replacement and growth expenditure) are expected to grow at between 3% and 5% per year after 20X5.

Additional notes

(i)   The realisable value of Omnigen's assets, net of all repayments, is estimated to be $82 million.

(ii)   The PE ratios of two of Omnigen's quoted competitors in the electrical industry are 13:1 and 15:1 respectively.

Required

Discuss and evaluate what price, or range of prices, Laceto should offer to purchase the shares of Omnigen. State clearly any assumptions that you make.

Approximately 17 marks are for calculations and 8 for discussion.

(b) Before making a bid for Omnigen the managing director of Laceto hears a rumour that a bid for Laceto might be made by Agressa.com Inc, an Internet retailer specialising in the sale of vehicles and electrical goods. Summarised financial data for Agressa.com are shown below.

Agressa.com	$m
Revenue	190
Operating profit	12
Interest	4
Taxation	2
Non-current assets (net)	30
Current assets	80
Current liabilities	30
Medium and long-term liabilities	40
Shareholders' funds	40

Agressa's current share price is $26.50, and the company has 15 million issued ordinary shares.

Required

Prepare a brief report for the managing director of Laceto which analyses how Laceto might defend itself from a takeover bid from Agressa.com.

27 Question with analysis: Laceto

54 mins

(a) Laceto Inc, a large retail group specialising in the sale of clothing and electrical goods is currently considering a takeover bid for a competitor, in the electrical goods sector, Omnigen Inc, whose share price has **fallen by 205 cents** during the last three months.

> Omnigen or sector problems

Summarised data for the financial year to 31 March 20X1

	$ million	
	Laceto	*Omnigen*
Revenue	420	180
Profit before tax (after interest payments)	41	20
Taxation	12	6
Non-current assets (net)	110	63
Current assets	122	94
Current liabilities	86	71
Medium and long-term liabilities	40	12
Shareholders' funds	106	74

> Minimum price

The share price of Laceto is currently 380 cents, and of Omnigen **410 cents**. Laceto has 80 million issued ordinary shares and Omnigen 30 million. Typical of Laceto's medium and long-term liabilities is **12%** loan stock with **three years to maturity**, a **par value of $100**, and a **current market price of $108.80**.

> Cost of debt details

The finance team of Laceto has produced the following **forecasts** of financial data for the activities of Omnigen if it is taken over.

> Accuracy?

	$ million			
Financial year	*20X2*	*20X3*	*20X4*	*20X5*
Net sales	230	261	281	298
Cost of goods sold (50%)	115	131	141	149
Selling and administrative expenses	32	34	36	38
Capital allowances (total)	40	42	42	42
Interest	18	16	14	12
Cash flow needed for asset replacement and forecast growth	50	52	55	58

> Cash flow valuation
>
> CF replacement
>
> Free cash flows

Corporate taxation is at the rate of 30% per year, payable in the year that the taxable cash flow occurs.

The **risk-free rate is 6%** per year and **market return 14% per year**. Omnigen's current equity beta is 1.2. This is expected to **increase by 0.1** if the company is taken over as Laceto would increase the current level of capital gearing associated with the activities of Omnigen. Laceto's gearing post acquisition is expected to be between **18% and 23%** (debt to debt plus equity by market values), depending upon the final price paid for Omnigen.

> CAPM
>
> New beta
>
> Gearing ratios for WACC calculations

Post-takeover cash flows of Omnigen (after replacement and growth expenditure) are expected to grow at **between 3% and 5%** per year **after 20X5**.

> Earnings growth model
>
> Time horizon

Additional notes

> NRV method

(i) The realisable value of Omnigen's assets, net of all repayments, is estimated to be **$82 million**.

(ii) The **PE ratios** of two of Omnigen's quoted competitors in the electrical industry are 13:1 and 15:1 respectively.

> PE method but are these comparable?

Required

Discuss and evaluate what price, or range of prices, Laceto should offer to purchase the shares of Omnigen. State clearly any assumptions that you make. **(25 marks)**

Approximately 17 marks are for calculations and 8 for discussion.

(b) Before making a bid for Omnigen the managing director of Laceto hears a rumour that a bid for Laceto might be made by Agressa.com Inc, an Internet retailer specialising in the sale of vehicles and electrical goods. Summarised financial data for Agressa.com are shown below.

Agressa.com	*$m*
Revenue	190
Operating profit	12
Interest	4
Taxation	2
Non-current assets (net)	30
Current assets	80
Current liabilities	30
Medium and long-term liabilities	40
Shareholders' funds	40

Agressa's current share price is $26.50, and the company has 15 million issued ordinary shares.

Required

Prepare a brief report for the managing director of Laceto which analyses how Laceto might defend itself from a takeover bid from Agressa.com. **(5 marks)**

(Total = 30 marks)

28 McTee

54 mins

McTee plc is a Scottish manufacturer of golf clubs. The company has decided to purchase an existing golf club manufacturer in the State of Florida, USA. The purchase will cost an agreed $72 million for fixed assets and equipment, and in addition $8 million of working capital will be needed. No additional external funding for the proposed US subsidiary is expected to be needed for at least five years, and sales from the subsidiary would be exclusively to the US market. McTee has no other foreign subsidiaries, and the company's managers are considering how to finance the US investment. McTee's bank has advised that, taking into account McTee's credit rating, the following alternatives might be possible, with finance available up to the amount shown:

(a) A one for four rights issue, at a price of 280 pence per share. Underwriting and other costs are expected to be 5% of the gross amount raised.

(b) Five year Sterling 7% fixed rate secured bank term loan of up to £50 million, initial arrangement fee 1%.

(c) $15 million one year commercial paper, issued at $US LIBOR plus 1.5%. This could be renewed on an annual basis. An additional 0.5% per year would be payable to a US bank for a back-up line of credit.

(d) 80 million Swiss Franc five year fixed rate secured bank loan at 2.5%. This may be swapped into fixed rate $ at an **additional** annual interest rate of 2.3%. An upfront fee of 3.0% is also payable.

(e) £42 million 10-year Sterling Eurobond issue at 6.85%. This may be swapped into $ at an annual interest rate of 4.95%. Eurobond issue costs of 2%, and upfront swap costs of 1.7% would also be payable.

(f) $40 million floating rate six year secured term loan from a US bank, at $US LIBOR plus 3%.

No currency swaps are available other than those shown. Currency swaps would involve swapping the principal at the current spot exchange rate, with the reversal of the swap at the same rate at the swap maturity date.

$US LIBOR is currently 3%.

Exchange rates:

	Spot	One year forward
$/£	1.7985 – 1.8008	1.7726 – 1.7746
SF/£	2.256 – 2.298	2.189 – 2.205

McTee's current balance sheet is summarised below.

	£m
Fixed assets	117.8
Investments	8.1
Current assets	98.1
Creditors: amounts falling due within one year	
Loans and other borrowings	(38.0)
Other creditors	(48.6)
	137.4
Creditors: amounts falling due after more than one year	
Medium and long-term bank loans	30.0
8% Bond 20X9 (par value £100)	18.0
	48.0
Capital and reserves	
Ordinary shares (25 pence par value)	20.0
Reserves	69.4
	137.4

A covenant exists that prevents the book value of McTee's debt finance from exceeding 50% of total assets. McTee's current dividend per share is 22.2 pence and dividend growth is approximately 4% per year. The company's current share price is 302 pence.

Interest payments on debt financing may be assumed to be made annually at the end of the year. Corporate tax in the UK, USA and Switzerland is at a rate of 30%. Issue costs and fees such as swap fees are not tax allowable.

Required

(a) Discuss the factors that McTee should consider before deciding how to finance the proposed US subsidiary.

(10 marks)

(b) Prepare a report discussing and evaluating each of the six possible sources of finance, and provide a reasoned recommendation of which source, or combination of sources, McTee should use. Supporting calculations, including costs, should be provided wherever relevant. **(20 marks)**

(Total = 30 marks)

29 Kulpar   54 mins

The finance director of Kulpar Inc is concerned about the impact of capital structure on the company's value, and wishes to investigate the effect of different capital structures.

He is aware that as gearing increases the required return on equity will also increase, and the company's interest cover is likely to decrease. A decrease in interest cover could lead to a change in the company's credit rating by the leading rating agencies.

He has been informed that the following changes are likely.

Interest cover	Credit rating	Cost of long term debt
More than 6.5	AA	8.0%
4.0 – 6.5	A	9.0%
1.5 – 4.0	BB	11.0%

The company is currently rated A.

Summarised financial data:

	$m
Net operating income	110.0
Depreciation	20.0
Earnings before interest and tax	90.0
Interest	22.0
Taxable income	68.0
Tax (30%)	20.4
Net income	47.6
Capital spending	20.0

Market value of equity is $458 million, and of debt $305 million.

Kuplar's equity beta is 1.4. The beta of debt may be assumed to be zero.

The risk free rate is 5.5% and the market return 14%.

The company's growth rate of cash flow may be assumed to be constant, and to be unaffected by any change in capital structure.

Required

(a)   Determine the likely effect on the company's cost of capital and corporate value if the company's capital structure was:

(i)   80% equity, 20% debt by market values

(ii)   40% equity, 60% debt by market values

Recommend which capital structure should be selected.

Any change in capital structure would be achieved by borrowing to repurchase existing equity, or by issuing additional equity to redeem existing debt, as appropriate.

The current total firm value (market value of equity plus market value of debt) is consistent with the growth model $(CF_1/(k-g))$ applied on a corporate basis. CF_1 is next year's free cash flow, k is the weighted average cost of capital (WACC), and g the expected growth rate. Company free cash flow may be estimated using EBIT $(l-t)$ + depreciation – capital spending.

State clearly any other assumptions that you make.   **(20 marks)**

(b)   Discuss possible reasons for errors in the estimates of corporate value in part (a) above.   **(10 marks)**

(Total = 30 marks)

30 Semer

54 mins

A proposal has been put to the board of directors of Semer Inc that the company should increase its capital gearing to at least 50%, in order to reduce the company's cost of capital and increase its market value.

The managing director of Semer is not convinced by the logic of the proposal, or the accuracy of the calculations, but is unable to explain the reasons for his reservations.

A summary of the proposal and its implications is shown below.

Proposal to increase the capital gearing of Semer Inc

The company's current weighted average cost of capital is estimated to be 10.6%. If the proportion of debt is increased to 50% of total capital, by the repurchase of ordinary shares at their current market value, the cost of capital may be reduced to 9.9%. A reduced cost of capital means that the value of the company will increase which will be welcomed by our shareholders. Calculations supporting the above proposal are shown below:

Existing cost of capital

Cost of equity using the capital asset pricing model:

$4\% + (10.5\% - 4\%)\,1.2 = 11.8\%$

Cost of debt: 8%

Weighted average cost of capital:

$11.8\% \times \dfrac{\$350m}{\$519m} + 8\% \times \dfrac{\$169m}{\$519m} = 10.56\%$

Estimated new cost of capital

$11.8\% \times \dfrac{\$259.5m}{\$519m} + 8\% \times \dfrac{\$259.5m}{\$519m} = 9.90\%$

Impact on the value of the company:

Current value $\dfrac{\$60m}{0.1056} = \$568$ million

Expected new value $\dfrac{\$60m}{0.099} = \$606$ million

Other information

(a) Most recent summarised balance sheet

	$ million
Semer Inc	
Non-current assets (net)	442
Current assets	345
Less current liabilities	(268)
	519
Issued ordinary shares (50 pence par)	80
Reserves	270
Liabilities falling due after one year:	
Bank loans	119
8% loan stock redeemable in 5 years ($100 par value)	50
	519

(b) The current price of Semer's ordinary shares is 410 pence.
(c) The market price of one 8% loan stock is $112.
(d) The market return is 10.5% and the risk free rate 4.0%.
(e) Semer's equity beta is 1.2.
(f) Semer currently pays $15 million in dividends.
(g) The corporate tax rate is 30%.
(h) The company currently generates a free cash flow of $60 million per year, which is expected to increase by approximately 3% per year.

Required

(a) What, if any, are the mistakes in the proposal? Correcting for any mistakes produce revised estimates of the company's *current* cost of capital and *current* value. Brief explanation of the reasons for any revisions should be included. **(15 marks)**

(b) Assuming that the cost of equity and cost of debt do not alter, estimate the effect of the share repurchase on the company's cost of capital and value. **(5 marks)**

(c) Acting as an external consultant to Semer, discuss the validity of the proposed strategy to increase gearing, and explain whether or not the estimates produced in (b) above are likely to be accurate. **(10 marks)**

(Total = 30 marks)

CORPORATE RECONSTRUCTION AND REORGANISATION

Questions 31 to 39 cover corporate reconstruction and reorganisation, the subject of Part D of the BPP Study Text for Paper P4.

---

31 Global financial markets   36 mins

The globalisation of financial markets has facilitated the transfer of funds to emerging markets but it has contributed to financial instability.

(a)   Discuss the reasons for the existence of the 'global debt problem'. Explain briefly what is meant by financial contagion and how financial contagion might affect the global debt problem.   **(7 marks)**

(b)   Explain the main attempts that have been made to resolve the global debt problem and how governments might try to limit financial contagion.   **(8 marks)**

(c)   During the period from April to October 2006 the credit rating of Italy has been downgraded from AA to A– by Standard & Poor and from AA to AA– by Fitch; over the same period the rating from Moody has remained stable at Aa2.

You are required to consider whether the Euro Government Bond market can be treated as homogenous so that there is no need to distinguish, from a credit perspective, between bonds issued by different members of the European Monetary Union.   **(5 marks)**

(Total = 20 marks)

32 Question with answer plan: Noifa Leisure   54 mins

(a)   Describe the main elements in corporate failure models and discuss the main limitations of these models.
                    (6 marks)

(b)   Extracts from the 20X9 annual report of Noifa Leisure plc are shown below.

Chairman's report

'The group's financial position has never been stronger. Turnover has risen 209% and the share price has almost doubled during the last four years. Since the end of the financial year the company has acquired Beddall Hotels for £100 million, financed at 9% per year by a euro floating rate loan which has little risk. Our objective is to become the largest hotel group in the United Kingdom within five years.'

Profit and loss account summaries
for the years ending 31 December

	20X6 £m	20X7 £m	20X8 £m	20X9 £m
Turnover	325	370	490	680
Operating profit	49	60	75	92
Investment income	18	10	3	1
	67	70	78	93
Interest payable	14	16	24	36
Profit before tax	53	54	54	57
Taxation	23	19	19	16
Profit attributable to shareholders	30	35	35	41
Dividends	12	12	12	12
Retained earnings	18	23	23	29

[1] Loss/gain on disposal of fixed assets

Balance sheet summaries as at 31 December

	20X6 £m	20X7 £m	20X8 £m	20X9 £m
Fixed assets				
Tangible assets	165	260	424	696
Investments	120	68	20	4
	285	328	444	700
Current assets				
Stock	40	45	70	110
Debtors	56	52	75	94
Cash	2	3	4	5
c/f	98	100	149	209
b/f	98	100	149	209
Less current liabilities				
Trade creditors	82	94	130	176
Taxation	18	19	19	20
Overdraft	–	–	42	68
Other	15	24	28	42
	115	137	219	306
Total assets less current liabilities	268	291	374	603
Financed by				
Ordinary shares (10 pence nominal value)	50	50	50	50
Share premium	22	22	22	22
Revaluation reserve	–	–	–	100
Revenue reserves	74	97	120	149
Shareholders' funds	146	169	192	321
Bank loans	42	42	102	102
13% debenture 20Y6-8	80	80	80	180
	268	291	374	603

Analysis by type of activity

	20X6 Turnover £m	20X6 Profit[1] £m	20X7 Turnover £m	20X7 Profit £m	20X8 Turnover £m	20X8 Profit £m	20X9 Turnover £m	20X9 Profit £m
Hotels	196	36	227	41	314	37	471	45
Theme park	15	(3)	18	(2)	24	3	34	5
Bus company	24	6	28	8	38	14	46	18
Car hire	43	7	45	8	52	12	62	15
Zoo[2]	5	(1)	6	(1)	9	0	10	(1)
Waxworks	10	1	11	3	13	4	14	5
Publications	32	3	35	3	40	5	43	5
	325	49	370	60	490	75	680	92

[1]Operating profit before taxation.   [2]The zoo was sold during 20X9.

	20X6	20X7	20X8	20X9
Noifa Leisure plc average share price (pence)	82	104	120	159
FT 100 Share Index	1,500	1,750	1,800	2,300
Leisure industry share index	178	246	344	394
Leisure industry P/E ratio	10:1	12:1	19:1	25:1

Required

In his report the chairman stated that 'the group's financial position has never been stronger'. From the viewpoint of an external consultant appraise whether you agree with the chairman. Discussion of the group's financing policies and strategic objective, with suggestions as to how these might be altered, should form part of your appraisal. Relevant calculations must be shown.   **(24 marks)**

(Total = 30 marks)

33 Snowwell   **54 mins**

The managing director of Snowwell Inc has received an unsolicited letter from a reputable organisation specialising in the prediction of corporate failure, which suggests that Snowwell has been identified as a probable failing company. The organisation has offered to supply details of the full report on Snowwell for $100,000.

Given the collapse of many companies' share prices during the last few years, the managing director of Snowwell is concerned that if the contents of the report become public knowledge, Snowwell's share price could also fall.

He has also read about various models which use combinations of financial ratios to attempt to predict corporate failure, including a leading business school's SO model (developed in 20X1) which produces a score based upon the following equation:

$$SO = 3.5S1 + 1.8S2 + 0.25S3 + 0.69S4$$

where S_1 = Earnings before interest and tax/market value of equity
 S_2 = Working capital/medium and long term capital employed
 S_3 = Market value of equity/market value of debt
 S_4 = The present value to infinity of current operating free cash flow/revenue

According to the SO system a company scoring less than 1 has a high probability of failure; a score of 1–2 suggests remedial action is necessary to improve corporate financial performance; and a score of over 2 means that a company has a high probability of survival for at least three years, which is the maximum claimed prediction period for the model.

Information about Snowwell:

(a)   The share price of Snowwell Inc is currently 232 pence.

(b)   The current redemption yield on loan stock of similar risk to that of Snowwell is 8%, which is also the current interest rate of the floating rate term loan.

(c)   Snowwell needs to invest approximately $35 million per year to maintain operations at current levels.

(d)   Tax allowable depreciation in 20X3 was $38 million.

(e)   Snowwell's cost of equity is estimated to be 12%.

(f)   Corporate tax is at the rate of 30% per year.

(g)   The average gearing of Snowwell's industry is 50% (measured by the market value of medium and long-term debt related to the market value of equity).

(h)   Snowwell's revenue is mostly retail sales of high quality jewellery and watches.

The latest summarised accounts of Snowwell Inc are shown below:

Balance sheets as at

	31 March 20X3 $ million	31 March 20X2 $ million
Non-current assets		
Land and buildings (net)	211	196
Other non-current assets (net)	247	235
	458	431

Current assets				
Inventory	156		127	
Receivables	32		34	
Cash	5		3	
		193		164
Payables: amounts falling due within 1 year				
Payables	196		166	
Dividend	12		12	
Taxation	7		10	
		(215)		(188)

	31 March 20X3	31 March 20X2
Payables: amounts falling due after more than 1 year		
14% loan stock redeemable at par December 20X6	(150)	(150)
Floating rate bank term loans	(94)	(64)
	192	193
Shareholders funds		
Ordinary shares (50 pence par)	75	75
Reserves	117	118
	192	193

Income statements for the years ending

	31 March 20X3 $ million	31 March 20X2 $ million
Revenue	620	580
Earnings before interest and tax	43	52
Interest	20	18
Profit before tax	23	34
Taxation	7	10
Available to shareholders	16	24
Dividend	17	17
Retained earnings	(1)	7

Required

You have been requested by the managing director of Snowwell Inc to prepare a briefing document that includes:

(a)   An estimate of the SO score for Snowwell Inc. **(11 marks)**

(b)   A discussion of the significance of this score for Snowwell Inc. **(4 marks)**

(c)   A brief discussion of alternative ways of assessing whether or not Snowwell Inc is likely to experience financial distress and/or corporate failure. **(4 marks)**

(d)   Recommendations as to whether or not Snowwell should take any action based upon your findings in (a) – (c) above and any other relevant information or analysis. **(7 marks)**

(e)   A discussion as to whether or not Snowwell should purchase the full report for $100,000. **(4 marks)**

(Total = 30 marks)

34 Vadener

54 mins

Vadener plc has instigated a review of the group's recent performance and potential future strategy. The Board of Directors has publicly stated that it is pleased with the group's performance and proposes to devote resources equally to its three operating divisions. Two of the divisions are in the UK, and focus on construction and leisure respectively, and one is in the USA and manufactures pharmaceuticals.

Recent summarised accounts for the group and data for the individual divisions are shown below:

Group data

Income statement

	20X3 £m	20X4 £m	20X5 £m
Turnover	1,210	1,410	1,490
Operating costs	800	870	930
Operating profit	410	540	560
Net interest	40	56	65
Profit before tax	370	484	495
Tax (30%)	111	145	149
Profit after tax	259	339	346
Equity dividends	146	170	185
Retained earnings	113	169	161

Balance sheet

	20X3 £m	20X4 £m	20X5 £m
Tangible fixed assets	1,223	1,280	1,410
Intangible fixed assets	100	250	250
Current assets			
Stock	340	410	490
Debtors	378	438	510
Cash	10	15	15
Total assets	2,051	2,393	2,675
Less current liabilities			
Creditors	302	401	430
Short term loans	135	170	201
Taxation	55	72	75
Dividends	73	85	93
	1,486	1,665	1,876
Financed by			
Long term liabilities	400	410	470
Shareholders' equity	1,086	1,255	1,406
	1,486	1,665	1,876

Note. The 20X5 amount for shareholders equity includes a £10 million loss on translation from the US division due to the recent weakness of the $US.

Other group data at year end

	20X3	20X4	20X5
Share price (pence)	1,220	1,417	1,542
Number of issued shares (million)	300	300	300
Equity beta			1.10

The company's share price has increased by an average of 12% per year over the last five years.

Other data at year end

	20X3	20X4	20X5
FT 100 index	3,700	4,600	4,960
PE ratio of similar companies	15:1	14:1	15:1
Risk free rate (%)			5
Market return (%)			12

Divisional data 20X5

	Construction	Leisure	Pharmaceuticals
Turnover (£m)	480	560	450
Operating profit	160	220	180
Estimated after tax return (%)	13	16	14

Data for the sector

Average asset beta 20X5	0.75	1.10	1.40

Required

(a) Evaluate and comment on the performance of Vadener plc and each of its divisions. Highlight performance that appears favourable, and any areas of potential concern for the managers of Vadener. Comment upon the likely validity of the company's strategy to devote resources equally to the operating divisions.

All relevant calculations must be shown. **(20 marks)**

(b) Discuss what additional information would be useful in order to more accurately assess the performance of Vadener plc and its divisions. **(5 marks)**

(c) Discuss the possible implications for Vadener plc of the £10 million loss on translation, and recommend what action, if any, the company should take as a result of this loss. **(5 marks)**

(Total = 30 marks)

35 Stanzial
54 mins

Stanzial plc is a UK based telecommunications company listed on the FTSE 250 index. The company is considering the purchase of Besserlot Co, an unlisted company that has developed, patented and marketed a secure, medium range, wireless link to broadband. The wireless link is expected to increase Besserlot's turnover by 25% per year for three years, and by 10% per year thereafter. Besserlot is currently owned 35% by its senior managers, 30% by a venture capital company, 25% by a single shareholder on the board of directors, and 10% by about 100 other private investors.

Summarised accounts for Besserlot for the last two years are shown below:

Profit and loss accounts for the years ended 31 March (£'000)

	20X6	20X5
Turnover	22,480	20,218
Operating profit before exceptional items	1,302	820
Exceptional items	(2,005)	–
Interest paid (net)	(280)	(228)
Profit before taxation	(983)	592
Taxation	(210)	(178)
Dividend	(200)	(100)
Retained earnings	(1,393)	314

Balance sheets as at 31 March (£'000)

	20X6	20X5
Fixed assets (net)		
Tangible assets	5,430	5,048
Goodwill	170	200
Current assets		
Stocks	3,400	2,780
Debtors falling due within one year	2,658	2,462
Debtors falling due after more than one year	100	50
Cash at bank and in hand	48	48
Creditors		
Amounts falling due within one year	5,520	4,823
Net current assets	686	517
Net assets	6,286	5,765
Capital and reserves:		
Called up share capital (25 pence par)	2,000	1,000
Profit and loss account	3,037	4,430
Other reserves	1,249	335
Total equity shareholders funds	6,286	5,765

Other information relating to Besserlot:

(a)   Non-cash expenses, including depreciation, were £820,000 in 20X5–6.

(b)   Corporate taxation is at the rate of 30% per year.

(c)   Capital investment was £1 million in 20X5–6, and is expected to grow at approximately the same rate as turnover.

(d)   Working capital, interest payments and non-cash expenses are expected to increase at the same rate as turnover.

(e)   The estimated value of the patent if sold now is £10 million. This has not been included in fixed assets.

(f)   Operating profit is expected to be approximately 8% of turnover in 20X6–7, and to remain at the same percentage in future years.

(g)   Dividends are expected to grow at the same rate as turnover.

(h)   The realisable value of existing stocks is expected to be 70% of its book value.

(i)   The estimated cost of equity of Besserlot is 14%.

Information regarding the industry sector of Besserlot:

(a)   The average PE ratio of listed companies of similar size to Besserlot is 30:1.
(b)   Average earnings growth in the industry is 6% per year.

Required

(a)   Estimate the value of Besserlot Ltd using:

   (i)   Asset-based valuation
   (ii)   P/E ratios
   (iii)   Dividend valuation
   (iv)   The present value of expected future cash flows

   Discuss the potential accuracy of each of the methods used and recommend, with reasons, a value, or range of values that Stanzial might bid for Besserlot.

   State clearly any assumptions that you make.   **(25 marks)**

(b)   Discuss how the shareholder mix of Besserlot and type of payment used might influence the success or failure of the bid.   **(5 marks)**

(Total = 30 marks)

36 Evertalk

54 mins

Evertalk Inc manufactures mobile phones and operates a mobile phone network. In order to offer the latest hand-held videophone technology the company has borrowed extensively on the international bond market. Unfortunately the new technology has proved to be unpopular with consumers, and sales of new handsets and network subscriptions have been less than forecast. As a result the company's share price has fallen to only 10 pence, from a high two years ago of 180 pence. Capital investment of approximately $100 million per year is required for the company to continue operating at current levels – $20 million for the manufacturing division and $80 million for the network division. Approximately 25% of the sales of the manufacturing division are to the network division.

Income statements for the years ending 31 March 20X2 and 20X3

	20X2 $m	20X3 $m
Inflows		
Manufacturing division	280	320
Network division	410	470
	690	790
Outflows		
Manufacturing division	190	230
Network division	490	560
Tax allowable depreciation	50	60
	730	850
Pre-tax losses	(40)	(60)

Balance sheet as at 31 March 20X3

	$m	$m
Land and buildings (net)		120
Other non-current assets (net)		175
		295
Current assets		
Inventory	260	
Receivables	85	
Cash	5	
		350
Payables: amounts falling due within 1 year		
Floating rate bank loans[1]	40	
Payables	209	
		(249)
Payables: amounts falling due after more than 1 year		
12% unsecured bonds due in 7 years' time		(300)
		96
Shareholders' funds		
Ordinary shares (10 pence par)		50
Reserves		46
		96

1   Currently 8% interest

Evertalk's board of directors has arranged a crisis meeting and is considering three proposals:

(a)   Cease trading and close the company.

(b)   A corporate restructuring, in which bonds are converted to equity, and which gives control of the company to the current bond holders.

(c)   Sale of the company's shares to Globtalk Inc, which operates a successful rival mobile phone network, for the sum of $50 million. This deal would be conditional upon Globtalk not taking over the liability for any of Evertalk's loans.

The restructuring has the following proposed conditions:

(a) Existing ordinary shares will be cancelled and replaced by 100 million new ordinary shares with a par value of 50 pence each. 95 million of these will be given to the existing bondholders in exchange for the cancellation of all existing bonds. The bondholders will also make available $100 million of new 10% fixed rate loans.

(b) Existing shareholders will be offered one 5% convertible loan stock ($100 nominal value) free of charge in exchange for every 1,000 shares they now own. Conversion into new ordinary shares is available at any time during the next five years at a conversion rate of 50 shares for every $100 convertible loan stock held.

(c) 5 million new shares will be given to existing participants in the company's share option scheme in exchange for cancellation of their existing options to purchase 10 million old shares.

Other information

(a) All existing payables have equal claims for repayment against the company's assets.

(b) No dividends have been paid on ordinary shares for the last three years.

(c) Losses may not be carried forward for tax purposes.

(d) Surplus land and buildings could be disposed of for $40 million in order to repay the bank loan.

(e) The value of receivables, cash, non-current assets and payables represented by the two divisions is approximately equal. 90% of the inventory is represented by the manufacturing division.

(f) The $300 million bond has been borrowed by the network division, and the $40 million bank loan by the manufacturing division.

(g) If the restructuring and new investment does not take place, earnings before tax (after interest payments) are expected to stay at approximately the 20X3 level. If new investment takes place, forecast earnings before interest and tax are expected to increase by $30 million as a result of some rationalisation of the network division.

(h) The current market price of ordinary shares is 10 cents, and of loan stock $121. The par value and redemption value of each loan stock is $100.

(i) Corporate tax is at the rate of 30%. The risk free rate is 5% and the market return 14%. The equity beta of the company is 1.15, with the manufacturing division equity beta approximately 0.9, and the network division equity beta approximately 1.35. The company's analysts believe that market weighted gearing of about 60% equity, 40% debt is appropriate for the entire sector, but currently this cannot be achieved due to the low share price.

(j) Realisable values of assets if not sold as part of a going concern are estimated to be:

	$m
Land and buildings	140 (including the surplus $40 million)
Other non-current assets	50
Inventory	100
Receivables	70

(k) Redundancy and closure costs of approximately $100 million would be payable if the company was closed, all payable before any other payables. These costs relate equally to the two divisions. All realisable values and closure values are after tax.

Required

Acting as an independent consultant prepare a report for the board of directors of Evertalk. Your report should consider the advantages and disadvantages of each of the three proposals, from the viewpoint of each group of existing stakeholders in the company. It should also identify any other strategy(ies) which might be possible for Evertalk Inc.

State clearly any assumptions that you make.

(30 marks)

37 Romage

54 mins

Romage Inc has two major operating divisions, manufacturing and property sales, with revenues of $260 million and $620 million respectively

Balance sheet for Romage Inc

	$m
Land and buildings	80
Plant and machinery	140
Current assets	250
Current liabilities	180
	290
Financed by:	
Ordinary shares (25 cents par)	50
Reserves	130
Secured term loan	60
13% loan stock 2015 ($100 par)	50
	290

Summarised cash flow data for Romage Inc:

	$m
Cash revenue	880
Divisional operating expenses	803
Central costs	8
Interest	11
Taxation	14
Dividends	15

The company's current share price is 296 cents, and the market value of a loan stock is $131.

Projected real (ie excluding inflation) per tax financial data ($ million) of the two divisions are:

Year	1	2	3	4	5	6 onwards
Manufacturing:						
Operating net cash flows	45	48	50	52	57	60
Allocated central costs	4	4	4	4	4	4
Tax allowable depreciation	10	8	7	8	8	8
Property sales:						
Operating net cash flows	32	40	42	44	46	50
Allocated central costs	4	3	3	3	3	3
Tax allowable depreciation	5	5	5	5	5	5

Corporate taxation is at the rate of 31% per year, payable in the year that the relevant cash flow arises.

Inflation is expected to remain at approximately 3% per year.

The risk free rate is 5.5%, and the market return 14%.

Romage's equity beta is 1.15.

The company is considering a demerger whereby the two divisions are floated separately on the stock market. The loan stock would be serviced by the property division and the term loan by the manufacturing division. The existing equity would be split evenly between the divisions, although new ordinary shares would be issued to replace existing shares.

The average equity betas in the manufacturing and property sectors are 1.3 and 0.9 respectively, and the gearing levels in manufacturing and property sales by market values are 70% equity 30% debt, and 80% equity 20% debt respectively.

Notes

(1)   Allocated central costs reflect actual cash flows. If a demerger occurs these costs would rise to $6 million per year for each company.

(2)   A demerger would involve a one-off after tax cost of $16 million in year one which would be split evenly between the two companies. There would be no other significant impact on expected cash flows.

(3)   The current cost of the loan stock and term loan are almost identical.

(4)   The loan stock is redeemable at par.

Required

(a)   Discuss the potential advantages for Romage Inc of undertaking the divestment of one of its divisions by means of:

   (i)   A sell-off and
   (ii)   A demerger   **(6 marks)**

(b)   Using real cash flows, evaluate whether or not it is expected to be financially advantageous to the original shareholders Romage Inc for the company to separately float the two divisions on the stock market. Your evaluation should use both a 15 year time horizon and an infinite time horizon.

   In any gearing estimates the manufacturing division may be assumed to comprise 55% of the market value of equity of Romage Inc, and the property sale division 45%.

   State clearly any additional assumptions that you make.   **(24 marks)**

                                                                          (Total = 30 marks)

38 Reflator   36 mins

A division of Reflator Inc has recently experienced severe financial difficulties. The management of the division is keen to undertake a buyout, but in order for the buyout to succeed it needs to attract substantial finance from a venture capital organisation. Reflator Inc is willing to sell the division for $2.1 million, and the managers believe that an additional $1 million of capital would need to be invested in the division to create a viable going concern.

Possible financing sources

Equity from management $500,000, in 50 cents ordinary shares.

Funds from the venture capital organisation

Equity $300,000, in 50 cents ordinary shares
Debt: 8.5% fixed rate loan $2,000,000
9% subordinated loan with warrants attached $300,000.

The warrants are exercisable any time after four years from now at the rate of 100 ordinary shares at the price of 150 cents per share for every $100 of subordinated loan.

The principal on the 8.5% fixed rate loan is repayable as a bullet payment at the end of eight years. The subordinated loan is repayable by equal annual payments, comprising both interest and principal, over a period of six years.

The division's managers propose to keep dividends to no more than 15% of profits for the first four years. Independently produced forecasts of earnings before tax and interest after the buyout are shown below:

	$'000			
Year	*1*	*2*	*3*	*4*
EBIT	320	410	500	540

Corporate tax is at the rate of 30% per year.

The managers involved in the buyout have stated that the book value of equity is likely to increase by about 20% per year during the first four years, making the investment very attractive to the venture capital organisation. The venture capital organisation has stated that it is interested in investing, but has doubts about the forecast growth rate of equity value, and would require warrants for 150 shares per $100 of subordinated loan stock rather than 100 shares.

Required

(a) Briefly discuss the potential advantages of management buyouts. **(5 marks)**

(b) On the basis of the above data, estimate whether or not the book value of equity is likely to grow by 20% per year. **(7 marks)**

(c) Evaluate the possible implication of the managers agreeing to offer warrants for 150 ordinary shares per $100 of loan stock. **(3 marks)**

(d) You have been asked to produce a short memorandum explaining the role of a venture capitalist in this management buyout. You should also mention the typical requirements the venture capital organisation will demand from the buyout team. **(5 marks)**

(Total = 20 marks)

39 Airgo
54 mins

The directors of ASTER Inc have decided to concentrate the company's activities on three core areas, bus services, road freight and taxis. As a result the company has offered for sale a regional airport that it owns. The airport handles a mixture of short-haul scheduled services, holiday charter flights and air freight, but does not have a runway long enough for long-haul international operations.

The existing managers of the airport, along with some employees, are attempting to purchase the airport through a leveraged management buy-out, and would form a new unquoted company, Airgo Inc. The total value of the airport (free of any debt) has been independently assessed at $35 million.

The managers and employees can raise a maximum of $4 million towards this cost. This would be invested in new ordinary shares issued at the par value of 50p per share. ASTER Inc, as a condition of the sale, proposes to subscribe to an initial 20% equity holding in the company, and would repay all debt of the airport prior to the sale.

EPP Bank is prepared to offer a floating rate loan of $20 million to the management team, at an initial interest rate of LIBOR plus 3%. LIBOR is currently at 10%. This loan would be for a period of seven years, repayable upon maturity, and would be secured against the airport's land and buildings. A condition of the loan is that gearing, measured by the book value of total loans to equity, is no more than 100% at the end of four years. If this condition is not met the bank has the right to call in its loan at one month's notice. Airgo would be able to purchase a four year interest rate cap at 15% for its loan from EPP Bank for an up-front premium of $800,000.

A venture capital company, Allvent Inc, is willing to provide up to $15 million in the form of unsecured mezzanine debt with attached warrants. This loan would be for a five year period, with principal repayable in equal annual instalments, and have a fixed interest rate of 18% per year.

The warrants would allow Allvent to purchase 10 Airgo shares at a price of 100 pence each for every $100 of initial debt provided, at any time after two years from the date the loan is agreed. The warrants would expire after five years.

91

Most recent annual income statement of the airport

	$'000
Landing fees	14,000
Other revenue	8,600
	22,600
Labour	5,200
Consumables	3,800
Central overhead payable to ASTER	4,000
Other expenses	3,500
Interest paid	2,500
	19,000
Taxable profit	3,600
Taxation (33%)	1,188
Retained earnings	2,412

ASTER has offered to continue to provide central accounting, personnel and marketing services to Airgo for a fee of $3 million per year, with the first fee payable in year one. All revenues and cost (excluding interest) are expected to increase by approximately 5% per year.

Required

(a)   Prepare a report for the managers of the proposed Airgo Inc discussing the advantages and disadvantages for the management buy-out of the proposed financing mix. Include in your report an evaluation of whether or not the EPP Bank's gearing restriction in four years' time is likely to be a problem. All relevant calculations must be shown. State clearly any assumptions that you make.   **(22 marks)**

(b)   As a possible alternative to obtaining finance from Allvent, assume that a venture capital company that you are employed by has been approached by the management buy-out team for a $10 million loan. Discuss what information, other than that provided above, would be required from the MBO team in order to decide whether or not to agree to the loan.   **(8 marks)**

(Total = 30 marks)

> **ADVANCED RISK MANAGEMENT TECHNIQUES AND MULTINATIONAL ISSUES**
>
> Questions 40 to 58 cover advanced risk management techniques and the economic environment for multinationals, the subjects of Parts E and F of the BPP Study Text for Paper P4.

40 Troder
36 mins

(a) Discuss the advantages of hedging with interest rate caps and collars. **(5 marks)**

(b) Current futures prices suggest that interest rates are expected to fall during the next few months. Troder Inc expects to have $400 million available for short-term investment for a period of 5 months commencing late October. The company wishes to protect this short-term investment from a fall in interest rates, but is concerned about the premium levels of interest rate options. It would also like to benefit if interest rates were to increase rather than fall. The company's advisers have suggested the use of a collar option.

LIFFE short sterling options ($500,000), points of 100%

Strike price	Calls		Puts	
	Sept	Dec	Sept	Dec
95250	0.040	0.445	0.040	0.085
95500	0.000	0.280	0.250	0.170
95750	0.000	0.165	0.500	0.305

LIBOR is currently 5% and the company can invest short-term at LIBOR minus 25 basis points.

Required

(i) Assume that it is now early September. The company wishes to receive more than $6,750,000 in interest from its investment after paying any option premium. Illustrate how a collar hedge may be used to achieve this. (N.B. It is not necessary to estimate the number of contracts for this illustration). **(6 marks)**

(ii) Estimate the maximum interest that could be received with your selected hedge. **(2 marks)**

(c) Solter Co has recently obtained a contract to build a number of electricity generating stations (EGSs) in an Eastern European country (EE). The EGSs will be paid for by the EE government at a fixed price of 2,000 million EE marks 12 months after the start of the contract. Solter Co will need to spend 750 million EE marks immediately and an additional 750 million EE marks in 6 months' time. The company has not worked in Eastern Europe before and has no other business in this region.

The treasurer of Solter Co is discussing the possibility of a fixed-rate currency swap with an EE-based company that trades in the US. The swap would be taken out immediately for the full expected expenditure of 1,500 million EE marks at a swap rate of 15 EE marks to the $.

Interest of 20% each year would be payable on the full 1,500 million EE mark swap by Solter Co to the EE-based company. Payment would be in EE marks. The EE-based company will pay interest to Solter Co on the dollar value of the swap at 12%. Payment would be in USD. Assume interest payments are made annually at the end of the year.

There are no formal capital markets in the EE country and therefore no forward rates are available for the EE mark against the $. Forecasts of inflation rates for next year are 3% in the US and 25% in the EE country.

Assume the value of the EE mark is allowed to float freely by the EE government. The current spot rate is 18 EE marks to the $.

Required

Explain the procedure for a currency swap, and recommend, with appropriate supporting calculations, whether Solter Inc should enter into the currency swap with the EE-based company. **(7 marks)**

(Total = 20 marks)

41 FNDC

54 mins

Several months ago FNDC plc, a television manufacturer, agreed to offer financial support to a major sporting event. The event will take place in seven months' time, but an expenditure of £45 million for temporary facilities will be necessary in five months' time. FNDC has agreed to lend the £45 million, and expects the loan to be repaid at the time of the event. At the time the support was offered, FNDC expected to have sufficient cash to lend the £45 million from its own resources, but new commitments mean that the cash will have to be borrowed. Interest rates have been showing a rising trend, and FNDC wishes to protect itself against further interest rate rises when it takes out the loan. The company is considering using either interest rate futures or options on interest rate futures.

Assume that it is now 1 December and that futures and options contracts mature at the relevant month end.

LIBOR is currently 4%. FNDC can borrow at LIBOR plus 1·25%.

Euronext.LIFFE STIR £500,000 three month sterling futures. Tick size 0·01%, tick value £12·50
December 96·04
March 95·77
June 95·55

Euronext.LIFFE options on three month £500,000 sterling futures. Tick size 0·005%, tick value £6·25. Option premiums are in annual %.

		CALLS			PUTS	
	December	March	June	December	March	June
9400	1.505	1.630	1.670	–	–	–
9450	1.002	1.130	1.170	–	–	–
9500	0.502	0.630	0.685	–	–	0.015
9550	0.252	0.205	0.285	0.060	0.115	0.165
9600	0.002	0.025	0.070	0.200	0.450	0.710

Required

(a) Discuss the relative merits of using short-term interest rate futures and market traded options on short-term interest rates futures to hedge short-term interest rate risk. **(6 marks)**

(b) If LIBOR interest rates were to increase by 0·5% or to decrease by 0·5% estimate the expected outcomes from hedging using:

(i) An interest rate futures hedge; and
(ii) Options on interest rate futures.

Briefly discuss your findings.

Note: In the futures hedge the expected basis at the close-out date should be estimated, but basis risk may be ignored. **(16 marks)**

(c) Calculate and discuss the outcome of a collar hedge which would limit the maximum interest rate paid by the company to 5·75%, and the minimum to 5·25%. (These interest rates do not include any option premium.) **(5 marks)**

(d) The company has been advised that it can increase income by writing (selling) options. Discuss whether or not this is correct, and provide a reasoned recommendation as to whether or not FNDC plc should adopt this strategy. **(3 marks)**

(Total = 30 marks)

42 HYK

36 mins

The monthly cash budget of HYK Communications plc shows that the company is likely to need £18 million in two months' time for a period of four months. Financial markets have recently been volatile, due to uncertainties about the impact of a major computer bug. If computer problems occur in January 20X0, the finance director of HYK plc fears that short term interest rates could rise by as much as 150 basis points. If few problems occur then short term rates could fall by 50 basis points. LIBOR is currently 6.5% and HYK plc can borrow at LIBOR + 0.75%.

The finance director does not wish to pay more than 7.50%, including option premium costs, but excluding the effect of margin requirements and commissions.

LIFFE £500,000 3 month futures prices. The value of one tick is £12.50

December	93.40
March	93.10
June	92.75

LIFFE £500,000 3 months options prices (premiums in annual %)

Exercise Price	Calls December	Calls March	Calls June	Puts December	Puts March	Puts June
92.50	0.33	0.88	1.04	–	–	0.08
93.00	0.16	0.52	0.76	–	0.20	0.34
93.50	0.10	0.24	0.42	0.18	0.60	1.93
94.00	–	0.05	0.18	0.36	1.35	1.92

Assume that it is now 1 December and that exchange traded futures and options contracts expire at the end of the month. Margin requirements and default risk may be ignored.

Required

(a) Estimate the results of undertaking *each of* an interest rate futures hedge and an interest rate options hedge on the LIFFE exchange, if LIBOR

    (i)   Increases by 150 basis points, and

    (ii)   Decreases by 50 basis points.

    Discuss how successful the hedge would have been.

    State clearly any assumptions that you make.   **(15 marks)**

(b) Discuss the relative advantages of using exchange traded interest rate options and over-the-counter (OTC) interest rate options.   **(5 marks)**

(Total = 20 marks)

43 Pondhills

54 mins

(a) Discuss the significance to a multinational company of translation exposure and economic exposure.

(8 marks)

(b) Pondhills Inc is a US multinational company with subsidiaries in the UK and Africa. The currency of the African country is pegged against the dollar, with a current exchange rate of 246.3 dinars/$US. In recent months political unrest and an increasing inflation rate has led the finance director of Pondhills to become concerned about a possible devaluation of the dinar. He believes that the dinar could devalue by up to 15% relative to the dollar during the next few months.

Summarised financial data for the African subsidiary, Ponda SA, are shown below:

	Million dinars
Revenue	2,300
Non-current assets	510
Current assets	
Cash	86
Receivables	410
inventory	380
	876
Short-term payables	(296)
Long-term loans	(500)
	590

Shareholders' equity = 590

Current exchange rates are:

$US/£	1.5780
Dinar/$US	246.3

Notes

(i)   All sales from the African subsidiary are denominated in US dollars, and all receivables are therefore payable in dollars.

(ii)   50% of payables are debts owed in sterling to the UK subsidiary by Ponda SA.

(iii)   The cost of goods sold and other operating expenses (excluding interest) for Ponda SA are 70% of revenue. 40% of this is payable in dollars or sterling and 60% in dinars.

(iv)   The interest rate on loans is 12%.

(v)   No significant changes in exchange rates are expected between the dollar and other major currencies.

Required

Calculate:

(i)   The balance sheet transaction exposure of Pondhills Inc, AND the potential profit or loss on translation of the balance sheet using the current or closing rate method where all exposed assets and liabilities are translated at the current exchange rate. **(9 marks)**

(ii)   The expected impact on the dollar value of Ponda SA's annual cash flow in the first full year after devaluation. The time value of money may be ignored. **(6 marks)**

(c)   Comment upon whether or not Pondhills Inc should hedge against the exposures estimated in (b) (i) and (b) (ii). **(3 marks)**

(d)   Provide examples of possible longer term economic/cash flow implications of the possible devaluation for Pondhills Inc. **(4 marks)**

(Total = 30 marks)

44 Somax   54 mins

(a)   Somax plc wishes to raise 260 million Swiss Francs in floating rate finance for a period of five years.

The funds are to be used to establish a new production plant in the eastern region of Switzerland. Somax evaluates its investments using NPV, but is not sure what cost of capital to use in the discounting process. The company is also proposing to increase its equity finance in the near future for UK expansion, resulting overall in little change in the company's market weighted capital gearing. The summarised financial data for the company before the expansion are shown below.

Profit and loss account for the year ending 31 March 20X6

	£m
Turnover	1,984
Gross profit	432
Profit after tax	81
Dividends	37
Retained earnings	44

BALANCE SHEET AS AT 31 MARCH 20X6

	£m
Non-current assets (net)	846
Working capital	350
	1,196
Medium and long-term loans[1]	(210)
	986
Shareholders' funds	
Issued ordinary shares (50 pence par)	225
Reserves	761
	986

[1]Including £75m 14% fixed rate bonds due to mature in five years time and redeemable at £100. The current market price of these bonds is £119.50. Other medium and long-term loans are floating rate UK bank loans at base rate plus 1%.

Corporate rate tax may be assumed to be at the rate of 33% in both the UK and Switzerland. The company's ordinary shares are currently trading at 376 pence.

Somax's equity beta is estimated to be 1.18. The systematic risk of debt may be assumed to be zero. The risk free rate is 7.75% and market return 14.5%. Bank base rate is currently 8.25%.

The estimated equity beta of the main Swiss competitor in the same industry as the new proposed plant in the eastern region of Switzerland is 1.5, and the competitor's capital gearing is 35% equity, 65% debt by book values, and 60% equity, 40% debt by market values.

Exchange rates

Spot	SFr2.3245 – 2.3300/£
6 months forward	SFr2.2955 – 2.3009/£

Required

Estimate the sterling cost of capital that Somax should use as the discount rate for its proposed investment in eastern Switzerland. State clearly any assumptions that you make. **(12 marks)**

(b) Somax's bank has suggested a five year interest rate swap. Somax would issue a five year sterling fixed rate bond, and make the following swap with a Swiss company that is also a client of the bank.

Somax would pay the Swiss company SFr LIBOR + 1% per year. The Swiss company would pay Somax 9.5% per year.

A 0.2% per year fee would also be payable by each company to the bank. There will be an exchange of principal now, and in five years time, at today's middle spot foreign exchange rate. The Swiss company can borrow fixed rate sterling at 10.5% per annum, and floating rate SFr finance at SFr LIBOR + 1.5%.

Somax can borrow in SFr at a floating rate of between 5.75% and 6% depending upon which form of borrowing is selected (ie in the Euromarkets or the Swiss domestic markets).

SFr LIBOR is currently 5%.

Required

(i) Estimate the annual interest cost to Somax of issuing a five year sterling fixed rate bond, and calculate whether the suggested swap would be of benefit to both Somax plc and the Swiss company. **(10 marks)**

(ii) Excluding cheaper finance, discuss the possible benefits and the possible risks of such a swap for the two companies and the intermediary bank. **(8 marks)**

(Total = 30 marks)

45 Galeplus

54 mins

(a) From the perspective of a corporate financial manager, discuss the advantages and potential problems of using currency swaps. **(8 marks)**

(b) Galeplus plc has been invited to purchase and operate a new telecommunications centre in the republic of Perdia. The purchase price is 2,000 million rubbits. The Perdian government has built the centre in order to improve the country's infrastructure, but has currently not got enough funds to pay money owed to the local constructors. Galeplus would purchase the centre for a period of three years, after which it would be sold back to the Perdian government for an agreed price of 4,000 million rubbits. Galeplus would supply three years of technical expertise and training for local staff, for an annual fee of 40 million rubbits, after Perdian taxation. Other after tax net cash flows from the investment in Perdia are expected to be negligible during the three year period.

Perdia has only recently become a democracy, and in the last five years has experienced inflation rates of between 25% and 500%. The managers of Galeplus are concerned about the foreign exchange risk of the investment. Perdia has recently adopted economic stability measures suggested by the IMF, and inflation during the next three years is expected to be between 15% per year and 50% per year. Galeplus's bankers have suggested using a currency swap for the purchase price of the factory, with a swap of principal immediately and in three years' time, both swaps at today's spot rate. The bank would charge a fee of 0.75% per year (in sterling) for arranging the swap. Galeplus would take 75% of any net arbitrage benefit from the swap, after deducting bank fees. Relevant borrowing rates are:

	UK	Perdia
Galeplus	6.25%	PIBOR + 2.0%
Perdian counterparty	8.3%	PIBOR + 1.5%

Note. PIBOR is the Perdian interbank offered rate, which has tended to be set at approximately the current inflation level. Inflation in the UK is expected to be negligible.

	Exchange rates
Spot	85.4 rubbits/£
3 year forward rate	Not available

Required

(i) Estimate the potential annual percentage interest saving that Galeplus might make from using a currency swap relative to borrowing directly in Perdia. **(6 marks)**

(ii) Assuming the swap takes place as described, provide a reasoned analysis, including relevant calculations, as to whether or not Galeplus should purchase the communications centre. The relevant risk adjusted discount rate may be assumed to be 15% per year. **(8 marks)**

(c) As alternatives to the currency swap the bank has suggested:

(i) A swaption with the same terms as the currency swap, and an upfront premium of £300,000.

(ii)   A European style three year currency put option on the total expected net cash flow in year 3 at an exercise price of 160 rubbits/£, and an upfront premium of £1.7 million.

Required

Discuss and evaluate the relative merits of these suggestions for Galeplus.   **(8 marks)**

(Total = 30 marks)

46 Polytot   **54 mins**

Assume that it is now 1 July. Polytot plc has received an export order valued at 675 million pesos from a company in Grobbia, a country that has recently been accepted into the World Trade Organisation, but which does not yet have a freely convertible currency.

The Grobbian company only has access to sufficient $US to pay for 60% of the goods, at the official $US exchange rate. The balance would be payable in the local currency, the Grobbian peso, for which there is no official foreign exchange market. Polytot is due to receive payment in four months' time and has been informed that an unofficial market in Grobbian pesos exists in which the peso can be converted into pounds. The exchange rate in this market is 15% worse for Polytot than the 'official' rate of exchange between the peso and the pound.

Exchange rates

	$/£
Spot	1.5475 – 1.5510
3 months forward	1.5362 – 1.5398
1 year forward	1.5140 – 1.5178

	Grobbian peso/£
Official spot rate	156.30

	Grobbian peso/$
Official spot rate	98.20

Philadelphia SE £/$ options £31,250 (cents per pound)

	CALLS			PUTS		
	Sept	Dec	March	Sept	Dec	March
1.5250	2.95	3.35	3.65	2.00	3.25	4.35
1.5500	1.80	2.25	2.65	3.30	4.60	5.75
1.5750	0.90	1.40	1.80	4.90	6.25	7.35
1.6000	0.25	0.75	1.10	6.75	8.05	9.15

£/$ Currency futures (CME, £62,500)

September	1.5350
December	1.5275

Assume that options and futures contracts mature at the relevant month end.

Required

(a)   Discuss the alternative forms of currency hedge that are available to Polytot plc and calculate the expected revenues, in £ sterling, from the sale to the company in Grobbia as a result of each of these hedges. Provide a reasoned recommendation as to which hedge should be selected.   **(17 marks)**

(b)   The Grobbian company is willing to undertake a countertrade deal whereby 40% of the cost of the goods is paid for by an exchange of three million kilos of Grobbian strawberries. A major UK supermarket chain has indicated that it would be willing to pay between 50 and 60 pence per kilo for the strawberries.

Discuss the issues that Polytot should consider before deciding whether or not to agree to the countertrade.   **(6 marks)**

(c)   The Grobbian company has asked for advice in using the Euromarkets to raise international finance.

Required

Provide a briefing memo for the company discussing the advantages of the Euromarkets, and any potential problems for the Grobbian company in using them. **(7 marks)**

(Total = 30 marks)

47 Microchip Engineering   54 mins

You are the finance director of Microchip Engineering. This has substantial operations in the UK, US and Europe. The company has an opportunity to expand its European operations and expect that a bit to build a further new plant in Europe may be accepted in three months time. If the contract is accepted, an immediate capital spend of ☐250 million will be required in three months and the company will receive a ☐125 million grant from the European Development Fund in nine months time. The current Euro/sterling rate is EUR 0.6700 to the pound.

Three month and nine month Euro LIBOR is 2.6765 per cent and 3.0195 per cent respectively. The three and nine month sterling LIBOR is 4.2613 per cent and 4.3701 per cent respectively. You have decided to hedge the exchange rate risk by the purchase of EUR/STERLING at the money options which have a contract size of 100,000 Euros. The monthly volatility of the Euro against sterling is 6.25 per cent. At the current exchange rate, the project has a net present value of £60 million and the company's cost of capital is 8 per cent.

The board of directors are concerned about the use of derivatives in managing the firms treasury operations. They argue that the diversity of the firms interests in Europe, the UK and the United States means that such hedging transactions are unnecessary.

Required

(a)   Prepare a memorandum, to be considered at the next board meeting, which summarises the arguments for and against foreign currency risk hedging and recommends a general policy concerning the hedging of foreign exchange risk. **(10 marks)**

(b)   Prepare a short report justifying your use of derivatives to minimise the firm's exposure to foreign exchange risk. Your report should contain:

(i)   The likely option price for an at-the-money option, stating the circumstances in which the option would be exercised. You should use the Grabbe variant of the Black-Scholes model for both transactions, adjusted on the basis that deposits generate a rate of return of LIBOR. **(10 marks)**

(ii)   A calculation of the number of contracts that would be required to eliminate the exchange rate risk and the cost of establishing a hedge to cover the likely foreign currency exposure. **(4 marks)**

(iii)   A summary of the issues the board should bear in mind when reviewing a hedging proposal such as the, taking into account the limitations of the modelling methods employed and the balance of risk to which the firm will be exposed to when the position is hedged. **(6 marks)**

(Total = 30 marks)

48 Exchange rates   36 mins

Discuss the possible foreign exchange risk and economic implications of each of the following types of exchange rate system for multinational companies with subsidiaries located in countries with these systems:

(a)   A managed floating exchange rate;
(b)   A fixed exchange rate linked to a basket of currencies; and
(c)   A fixed exchange rate backed by a currency board system.
(d)   An adjustable peg system

(20 marks)

49 Gitlor

36 mins

At a luncheon meeting the managing director of Gitlor plc has told two of his colleagues, who hold senior executive positions in different companies, that he has recently obtained from his bank forecasts of exchange rates in one year's time. His two colleagues also work for companies that are heavily engaged in international trade, and both agree to obtain their own forecasts. The following week the three again meet for lunch and compare the forecasts made by their banks. These forecasts are shown below.

	$/Euro	£/Euro	Yen/$	$/£
Bank 1	0.76	0.56	120	1.36
Bank 2	0.84	0.64	140	1.31
Bank 3	1.00	0.65	140	1.54
Current spot rates	0.88	0.62	125	1.42

	USA	UK	Euro block	Japan
Annual inflation rates	3%	2%	3%	(1%)
Annual short-term interest rates	3.25%	4.75%	4.18%	0.01%

The three senior executives are puzzled by this information.

Required

Prepare a report discussing and analysing the above information, and explaining why the banks' forecast might differ. Your analysis should include calculations based upon inflation rates and interest rates.

Discuss in the report the mechanisms influencing future exchange rates and whether or not it is possible to accurately forecast such future exchange rates, and if so under what circumstances.

Your report should identify the link between factors affecting exchange rates in the long and short term and how risk can be controlled. **(20 marks)**

50 MJY

36 mins

Assume that it is now 31 December. MJY plc is a UK based multinational company that has subsidiaries in two foreign countries. Both subsidiaries trade with other group members and with four third party companies (company 1 – company 4).

Projected trade transactions for three months' time are shown below. All currency amounts are in thousands.

Receipts (read across) '000'	Payments (read down) '000'						
	Co 1	Co 2	Co 3	Co 4	MJY	Subsidiary 1	Subsidiary 2
MJY	$90	£60	€75	–	–	£40	$50
Subsidiary 1	£50	€85	$40	$20	€72	–	€20
Subsidiary 2	£15	–	€52	$30	£55	€35	–
Company 1	–	–	–	–	–	–	–
Company 2	–	–	–	–	$170	–	–
Company 3	–	–	–	–	$120	€50	–
Company 4	–	–	–	–	–	–	€65

Foreign exchange rates	$/£	€/£
Spot 1	1.7982 – 1.8010	1.4492 – 1.4523
3 months forward	1.7835 – 1.7861	1.4365 – 1.4390

Currency options. £62,500 contract size. Premium in cents per £

	Calls		Puts	
Strike price	February	May	February	May
1.80	1.96	3.00	3.17	5.34
1.78	2.91	3.84	2.12	4.20

Required

(a)   Working from the perspective of a group treasurer, devise a hedging strategy for the MJY group, and calculate the expected outcomes of the hedges using forward markets, and, for the dollar exposure only, currency options. **(15 marks)**

(b)   You have been asked to produce a paper, to be presented at the next board meeting which justifies your proposed hedging strategy for the group. You should also briefly outline the procedural/policy considerations that need to be addressed in order to finalise the strategy. **(5 marks)**

(Total = 20 marks)

51 KYT
36 mins

(a)   KYT Inc is a company located in the USA that has a contract to purchase goods from Japan in two months' time on 1 September. The payment is to be made in yen and will total 140 million yen.

The managing director of KYT Inc wishes to protect the contract against adverse movements in foreign exchange rates and is considering the use of currency futures. The following data are available.

Spot foreign exchange rate

Yen/$ 128.15

Yen currency futures contracts on SIMEX (Singapore Monetary Exchange)

Contract size 12,500,000 yen, contract prices are $US per yen.

Contract prices:

September   0.007985
December   0.008250

Assume that futures contracts mature at the end of the month.

Required

(i)   Illustrate how KYT might hedge its foreign exchange risk using currency futures. **(3 marks)**

(ii)   Explain the meaning of basis risk and show what basis risk is involved in the proposed hedge.

(4 marks)

(iii) Assuming the spot exchange rate is 120 yen/$ on 1 September and that basis risk decreases steadily in a linear manner, calculate what the result of the hedge is expected to be. Briefly discuss why this result might not occur. Margin requirements and taxation may be ignored. **(5 marks)**

(b)   The KYT business plan for the next 5 years shows a significant increase in business with Japan. The general manager tells you that the operations director is presenting the business case for setting up a wholly owned subsidiary in Japan. To that end, he was asked you to prepare a paper, to be presented at the board meeting, explaining the foreign exchange exposure risks which would result from such an investment.

In particular, he tells you he would like to explain transaction and translation exposure as he has heard that translation exposure risk is only a book entry and not a 'real cost' and so can be ignored. **(8 marks)**

(Total = 20 marks)

52 Ethnic Designs

36 mins

You are the chief financial officer of Ethnic Designs, a multi-national company based in the United States. Ethnic Designs imports textiles from India which are the sold on to couture houses. Ethnic Designs trades extensively with the UK and Europe as well as the US. Given the increased demand for the textiles, your company is considering expanding and opening an operation in the South East of England (which would be responsible for servicing the European customers). This would leave the US branch to focus on the US market. Your market research indicates that the demand both in the US and Europe is considerably greater than your company's current ability to supply and, moreover, establishing a UK base would reduce much of the currency risk associated with the non US business. Your assessment is that the company will need to raise the equivalent of $450 million of the new finance over 10 years, of which $150 million could come from the company's existing liquid reserves. You have completed a review of the financial merits of the case and the project offers a rate of return in excess of 80%. The company's current credit standing is assessed at AA+, its total market capitalisation is $4.5 bn which includes a 10 year syndicated loan of $0.5bn due for retirement in five years. The balance of the firm's capital is in the form of ordinary shares trading on the New York and London Stock Exchanges. You believe that the company can borrow the money but that the increase in gearing will drop the firm's credit rating to AA – (60% chance) or AA – (40% chance). The company's existing weight average cost of capital (tax adjusted at the company's average corporation tax rate of 30%) is 7.0%.

The current yield spreads for the industry are shown below:

RATING	1YR	2YR	3YR	5YR	7YR	10YR	30YR
AAA	4	8	12	18	20	30	50
AA+	8	12	20	30	32	35	60
AA	15	24	30	34	40	50	65
AA –	24	35	40	45	54	56	78
A +	28	37	44	55	60	70	82
A	55	65	75	85	95	107	120

Required

(a) Estimate the expected cost of capital for this project on the assumption that the additional finance is raised through a bond issue in the US market. **(10 marks)**

(b) Given the US $ debt raised through the bond issues is, in its entirety, to finance a project in the UK where the base currency is £, the Board has asked you to produce a short briefing note discussing how the US organisation can mange the currency risk exposure. You have also been asked to outline the alternative sources of finance available to finance this project, including a brief discussion of the advantages and disadvantages and the likely impact of each alternative source upon the firm's cost of capital. **(10 marks)**

(Total = 20 marks)

53 NTC

54 mins

(a) Discuss the advantages and disadvantages of centralised treasury management for multinational companies. **(5 marks)**

(b) NTC plc is a UK multinational with subsidiaries in Spain, Hong Kong and the USA. Transactions between companies within the group have historically been in all of the currencies of the countries where the companies are located and have not been centrally co-ordinated, with the currency of the transaction varying in each deal. Transactions due in approximately three months' time are shown below. All receipts and payments are in thousand units of the specified currencies.

Assume that it is now mid-June.

Receipts (read across)	UK	Payments (read down) Spain	Hong Kong	USA
UK	–	E210	$HK720	$US110
Spain	£100	–	E80	–
Hong Kong	$HK400	–	–	–
USA	$US430	E120	$HK300	–

Exchange rates

	$US/£	Euro/£	$HK/£
Spot	1.4358 – 1.4366	1.6275 – 1.6292	11.1987 – 11.2050
3 months forward	1.4285 – 1.4300	1.6146 – 1.6166	11.1567 – 11.1602

Note. The Hong Kong dollar is pegged against the US dollar.

Interest rates available to NTC and its subsidiaries (annual %)

	Borrowing	Investing
UK	6.9	6.0
Spain	5.3	4.5
Hong Kong	n/a	6.1
USA	6.2	5.4

Currency options

Philadelphia Stock exchange $/£ options, £31,250 contracts. Premium is in cents per £.

		Calls			Puts	
Exercise price	July	August	Sept	July	August	Sept
1.42	1.42	2.12	2.67	0.68	1.42	2.15
1.43	0.88	1.60	1.79	1.14	1.92	3.12
1.44	0.51	1.19	1.42	1.77	2.51	4.35

Option premiums are payable upfront. Contracts may be assumed to expire at the end of the relevant month.

Required

(i) The parent company is proposing that inter-company payments would be settled in sterling via multilateral netting. Demonstrate how this policy would reduce the number of transactions.

(Foreign exchange spot mid-rates may be used for this purpose.) **(5 marks)**

(ii) If payments were to continue to be made in various currencies, illustrate three methods by which the UK parent company might hedge its transaction exposures for the next three months. Discuss, showing relevant calculations, which method should be selected. Include in your discussion an evaluation of the circumstances in which currency options would be the preferred choice.

(*Note.* NTC plc wishes to minimise the transaction costs of hedging.) **(15 marks)**

(iii) NTC plc has been approached by a Russian company that wishes to purchase goods from NTC plc in exchange for wheat. The Russian currency is not freely convertible.

Discuss the potential advantages and disadvantages of such countertrade to NTC plc. **(5 marks)**

(Total = 30 marks)

54 Question with analysis: Avto

Avto plc is considering an investment in Terrania, a country with a population of 60 million that has experienced twelve changes of government in the last ten years. The investment would cost 580 million Terranian francs for machinery and other equipment, and an additional 170 million francs would be necessary for working capital.

Terrania has a well-trained, skilled labour force and good communications infrastructure, but has suffered from a major disease in its main crop, the banana, and the effect of cheaper labour in neighbouring countries.

Terrania is heavily indebted to the IMF and the international banking system, and it is rumoured that the IMF is unwilling to offer further assistance to the Terranian government. The Terranian government has imposed temporary restrictions on the remittance of funds from Terrania on three occasions during the last ten years.

The proposed investment would be in the production of recordable DVD players, which are currently manufactured in the UK, mainly for the European Union market. If the Terranian investment project was undertaken the existing UK factory would either be closed down or downsized. Avto plc hopes to become more competitive by shifting production from the UK.

Additional information:

(i)   UK corporate tax is at the rate of 30% per year, and Terranian corporate tax at the rate of 20% per year, both payable in the year that the tax charge arises. Tax allowable depreciation in Terrania is 25% per year on a reducing balance basis. A bilateral tax treaty exists between Terrania and the UK.

(ii)   The after tax realisable value of the machinery and other equipment after four years is estimated to be 150 million Terranian francs.

(iii)   £140,000 has recently been spent on a feasibility study into the logistics of the proposed Terranian investment. The study reported favourably on this issue.

(iv)   The Terranian government has offered to allow Avto plc to use an existing factory rent free for a period of four years on condition that Avto employs at least 300 local workers. Avto has estimated that the investment would need 250 local workers. Rental of the factory would normally cost 75 million Terranian francs per year before tax.

(v)   Almost all sales from Terranian production will be to the European Union priced in Euros.

(vi)   Production and sales are expected to be 50,000 units per year. The expected year 1 selling price is 480 Euros per unit.

(vii) Unit costs throughout year 1 are expected to be:

Labour: 3,800 Terranian (T) francs based upon using 250 workers
Local components: 1,800 T francs
Component from Germany: 30 Euros
Sales and distribution: 400 T francs

(viii) Fixed costs in year 1 are 50 million T francs

(ix)   Local costs and the cost of the German component are expected to increase each year in line with Terranian and EU inflation respectively. Due to competition, the selling price (in Euros) is expected to remain constant for at least four years.

(x)   All net cash flows arising from the proposed investment in Terrania would be remitted at the end of each year back to the UK.

(xi)   If the UK factory is closed Avto will face tax allowable redundancy and other closure costs of £35 million. Approximately £20 million after tax is expected to be raised from the disposal of land and buildings.

(xii) If Avto decides to downsize rather than close its UK operations then tax allowable closure costs will amount to £20 million, and after tax asset sales to £10 million. Pre tax net cash flows from the downsized operation are expected to be £4 million per year, at current values. Manufacturing capacity in Terrania would not be large enough to supply the market previously supplied from the UK if downsizing does not occur.

(xiii)   The estimated beta of the Terranian investment is 1.5 and of the existing UK investment 1.1.

(xiv)   The relevant risk free rate is 4.5% and market return 11.5%.

(xv)   Money market investment in Terrania is available to Avto paying a rate of interest equivalent to the Terranian inflation rate.

(xvi)   Forecast % inflation levels:

	UK and the EU	Terrania
Year 1	2%	20%
Year 2	3%	15%
Year 3	3%	10%
Year 4	3%	10%
Year 5	3%	10%

(xvii)   Spot exchange rates:

Terranian francs/£ 36.85
Terranian francs/Euros 23.32

Required

(a)   Prepare a financial appraisal of whether or not Avto plc should invest in Terrania and close or downsize its UK factory. State clearly all assumptions that you make.

(b)   Discuss the wider commercial issues that the company should consider, in addition to the financial appraisal, before making its decision on whether to invest.

(c)   Estimate the possible impact of blocked remittances in Terrania for the planning horizon of four years, and discuss how Avto might react to blocked remittances.

(28 marks in total are available for calculations, and 12 for discussion)

BPP
LEARNING MEDIA

54 Question with analysis: Avto

54 mins

Avto plc is considering an investment in Terrania, a country with a population of 60 million that has experienced **twelve changes of government** in the last ten years. The investment would cost **580 million Terranian** francs for machinery and other equipment, and an additional 170 million francs would be necessary for **working capital**.

Terrania has a well-trained, skilled labour force and good communications infrastructure, but has suffered from a major disease in its main crop, the banana, and the effect of cheaper labour in neighbouring countries.

[box: +/– investment]

[box: Happen again?]

Terrania is heavily indebted to the IMF and the international banking system, and it is rumoured that the IMF is unwilling to offer further assistance to the Terranian government. The Terranian government has imposed **temporary restrictions** on the remittance of funds from Terrania on three occasions during the last ten years.

The proposed investment would be in the production of recordable DVD players, which are currently manufactured in the UK, mainly for the European Union market. If the Terranian investment project was undertaken the existing UK factory would either be **closed down or downsized**. Avto plc hopes to become more competitive by shifting production from the UK.

[box: Appraise alternatives]

Additional information:

[box: Extra tax calculation]

(i)   UK corporate tax is at the rate **of 30%** per year, and Terranian corporate tax at the rate of **20%** per year, both payable in the year that the tax charge arises. Tax allowable depreciation in Terrania is **25%** per year on a reducing balance basis. A bilateral tax treaty exists between Terrania and the UK.

[box: Calculate]

(ii) The after tax **realisable value** of the machinery and other equipment after four years is estimated to be 150 million Terranian francs.

[box: Year 4]

(iii) £140,000 has recently been spent on a **feasibility study** into the logistics of the proposed Terranian investment. The study reported favourably on this issue.

[box: Relevant cost?]

(iv) The Terranian government has offered to allow Avto plc to use an existing factory rent free for a period of four years on condition that Avto employs at least **300 local workers**. Avto has estimated that the investment would need **250 local workers**. Rental of the factory would normally cost **75 million Terranian francs** per year before tax.

[box: Calculate which cheaper]

[box: Translate into Francs]

(v)   Almost all sales from Terranian production will be to the European Union priced in **Euros**.

(vi) Production and sales are expected to be 50,000 units per year. The expected year 1 selling price is 480 Euros per unit.

(vii) Unit costs throughout year 1 are expected to be:

Labour: 3,800 Terranian (T) francs based upon using **250 workers**

[box: See (iv)]

Local components: 1,800 T francs
Component from Germany: **30 Euros**
Sales and distribution: 400 T francs

[box: Translate]

(viii) Fixed costs in year 1 are 50 million T francs

[box: Adjust for inflation]

(ix) Local costs and the cost of the German component are expected to **increase each year in line with Terranian and EU inflation respectively**. Due to competition, the selling price (in Euros) is expected to remain constant for at least four years.

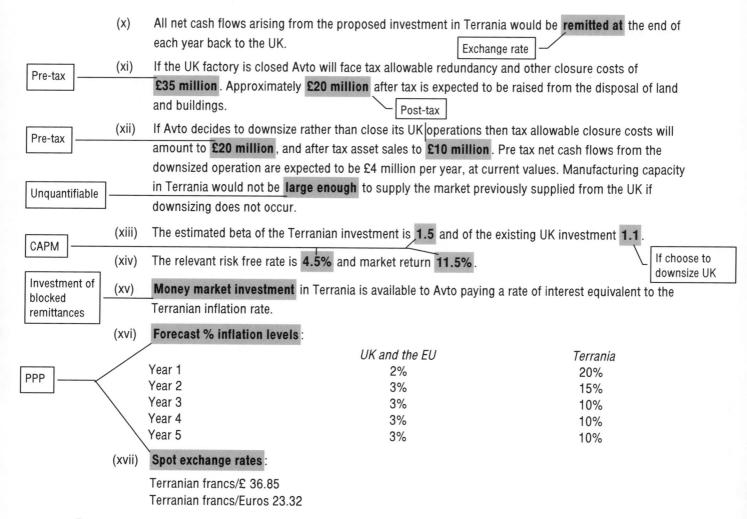

(x) All net cash flows arising from the proposed investment in Terrania would be **remitted at** the end of each year back to the UK.

Exchange rate

Pre-tax

(xi) If the UK factory is closed Avto will face tax allowable redundancy and other closure costs of **£35 million**. Approximately **£20 million** after tax is expected to be raised from the disposal of land and buildings.

Post-tax

Pre-tax

(xii) If Avto decides to downsize rather than close its UK operations then tax allowable closure costs will amount to **£20 million**, and after tax asset sales to **£10 million**. Pre tax net cash flows from the downsized operation are expected to be £4 million per year, at current values. Manufacturing capacity in Terrania would not be **large enough** to supply the market previously supplied from the UK if downsizing does not occur.

Unquantifiable

CAPM

(xiii) The estimated beta of the Terranian investment is **1.5** and of the existing UK investment **1.1**.

(xiv) The relevant risk free rate is **4.5%** and market return **11.5%**.

If choose to downsize UK

Investment of blocked remittances

(xv) **Money market investment** in Terrania is available to Avto paying a rate of interest equivalent to the Terranian inflation rate.

(xvi) **Forecast % inflation levels**:

PPP

	UK and the EU	Terrania
Year 1	2%	20%
Year 2	3%	15%
Year 3	3%	10%
Year 4	3%	10%
Year 5	3%	10%

(xvii) **Spot exchange rates**:

Terranian francs/£ 36.85
Terranian francs/Euros 23.32

Required

(a) Prepare a financial appraisal of whether or not Avto plc should invest in Terrania and close or downsize its UK factory. State clearly all assumptions that you make.

(b) Discuss the wider commercial issues that the company should consider, in addition to the financial appraisal, before making its decision on whether to invest.

(c) Estimate the possible impact of blocked remittances in Terrania for the planning horizon of four years, and discuss how Avto might react to blocked remittances.

(30 marks)

55 Beela

36 mins

The finance department of Beela Electronics has been criticised by the company's board of directors for not undertaking an assessment of the political risk of the company's potential direct investments in Africa. The board has received an interim report from a consultant that provides an assessment of the factors affecting political risk in three African countries. The report assesses key variables on a scale of −10 to +10, with −10 the worst possible score and +10 the best.

	Country 1	Country 2	Country 3
Economic growth	5	8	4
Political stability	3	−4	5
Risk of nationalisation	3	0	4
Cultural compatibility	6	2	4
Inflation	7	−6	6
Currency convertibility	−2	5	−4
Investment incentives	−3	7	3
Labour supply	2	8	−3

The consultant suggests that economic growth and political stability are twice as important as the other factors.

The consultant states in the report that previous clients have not invested in countries with a total weighted score of less than 30 out of a maximum possible 100 (with economic growth and political stability double weighted). The consultant therefore recommends that no investment in Africa should be undertaken.

Required

(a) Discuss whether or not Beela Electronics should use the technique suggested by the consultant in order to decide whether or not to invest in Africa. **(8 marks)**

(b) Discuss briefly how Beela might manage political risk if it decides to invest in Africa. **(7 marks)**

(c) Briefly discuss ethical issues that might need to be considered as part of a multinational company's investment decision process. **(5 marks)**

(Total = 20 marks)

56 Shegdor

36 mins

(a) Briefly discuss the possible objectives of transfer pricing strategies used by multinational companies.
(4 marks)

(b) Shegdor plc, a UK based multinational company, has subsidiaries in three countries – Umgaba, Mazila and Bettuna.

   (i) The subsidiary in Umgaba manufactures specialist components, which may then be assembled and sold in either Mazila or Bettuna.

   (ii) Production and sales volume may each be assumed to be 400,000 units per year no matter where the assembly and sales take place.

   (iii) Manufacturing costs in Umgaba are $16 per unit and fixed costs (for the normal range of production) $1.8 million.

   (iv) Assembly costs in Mazila are $9 per unit and in Bettuna $7.5 per unit. Fixed costs are $700,000 and $900,000 respectively.

   (v) The unit sales price in Mazila is $40 and in Bettuna $37.

   (vi) Corporate taxes on profits are at the rate of 40% in Umgaba, 25% in Mazila, 32% in Bettuna and 30% in the UK. No tax credits are available in these three countries for any losses made. Full credit is given by the UK tax authorities for tax paid overseas.

109

(vii)   Tax allowable import duties of 10% are payable on all goods imported into Mazila.

(viii)   A withholding tax of 15% is deducted from all dividends remitted from Umgaba.

(ix)   Shegdor expects about 60% of profits from each subsidiary to be remitted direct to the UK each year.

(x)   Cost and price data in all countries is shown in US dollars.

Required

Evaluate and explain:

(i)   If the transfer price from Umgaba should be based upon fixed cost plus variable cost, or fixed cost plus variable cost plus a mark up of 30%.

(ii)   Whether assembly should take place in Mazila or Bettuna.   **(8 marks)**

(c)   Comment upon the likely attitude of the governments of each of the four countries towards the transfer price and assembly location selected in (b)(i) and (b)(ii) above.   **(3 marks)**

(d)   Outline the mechanisms which prevent transfer price manipulation by multinationals.   **(5 marks)**

    (Total = 20 marks)

57 Serty   36 mins

(a)   Discuss whether or not an increase in dividends is likely to benefit the shareholders of a listed company.

    (8 marks)

(b)   The board of directors of Serty Inc is discussing the level and nature of the company's next dividend payment. Three options are under consideration:

(i)   A cash dividend of 15 pence per share, or

(ii)   A 5% scrip dividend, or

(iii)   The company repurchases 10% of the ordinary share capital at the current market price and then pays a cash dividend as in (i) above.

Summarised financial accounts for Serty are shown below:

Income statement ($ million)

Revenue	150.0
Operating profit	15.0
Net interest earned	4.0
	19.0
Taxation	6.3
Available to shareholders	12.7

Balance Sheet ($ million)

Non-current assets (net)		60
Current assets Inventory	20	
Receivables	20	
Cash and bank	40	80
Less current liabilities		(30)
		110
Shareholders funds		
Issued ordinary shares (50p par)		20
Reserves		90
		110

Serty's current share price is 400 pence cum div.

Required

Calculate the expected effect of each suggestion on a shareholder in Serty owning 1,000 shares. Explain briefly how accurate your estimates are likely to be. **(7 marks)**

(c) Discuss whether or not a company should pay dividends that are equal to free cash flow to equity. **(5 marks)**

(Total = 20 marks)

58 World Trade Organisation   36 mins

(a) Provide examples of how countries might impose protectionist measures to control the volume of imports. **(5 marks)**

(b) Briefly state the arguments in favour and against protection. **(5 marks)**

(c) Discuss the role and main objectives of the World Trade Organisation (WTO), and its potential effect on protectionist measures. **(6 marks)**

(d) Briefly discuss the possible effects of the activities of the WTO for a multinational company with foreign direct investment in a developing country that has recently joined the WTO. **(4 marks)**

(Total = 20 marks)

59 Uniglow
36 mins

(a) Briefly discuss the meaning and importance of the terms 'delta', 'theta' and 'vega' (also known as kappa or lambda) in option pricing. **(5 marks)**

(b) Assume that your company has invested in 100,000 shares of Uniglow Inc, a manufacturer of light bulbs. You are concerned about the recent volatility in Uniglow's share price due to the unpredictable weather in its home country. You wish to protect your company's investment from a possible fall in Uniglow's share price until winter in three months' time, but do not wish to sell the shares at present. No dividends are due to be paid by Uniglow during the next three months.

Market data

Uniglow's current share price	200 pence
Call option exercise price	220 pence
Time to expiry	3 months
Interest rates (annual)	6%
Volatility of Uniglow's shares	50% (standard deviation per year)

Assume that option contracts are for the purchase or sale of units of 1,000 shares.

Required

(i) Devise a delta hedge that is expected to protect the investment against changes in the share price until winter. Delta may be estimated using $N(d_1)$. **(8 marks)**

(ii) Comment upon whether or not such a hedge is likely to be totally successful. **(2 marks)**

(c) Given investors can diversity away all risks by including the shares of the company in a portfolio explain why companies would choose to hedge against risk. **(5 marks)**

(Total = 20 marks)

60 Folter
36 mins

Folter Inc has short-term equity holdings in a number of companies that it considers might be future take-over targets.

The equity market has recently been very volatile, and the finance director is considering how to protect the equity portfolio from adverse market movements, in case some of the holdings need to be sold, at short notice, by the end of October.

The finance director is particularly concerned about 2 million shares that are currently held in Magterdoor Inc. The shares are trading at 535 cents.

Assume that it is now 1 June and that option contracts mature at the month end.

LIFFE Traded options (1,000 shares)

	CALLS			PUTS		
	July	October	January	July	October	January
500	37.5	52.5	60.5	2.0	24.5	35.0
550	6.5	24.0	34.0	21.0	51.0	60.0

Required

(a) Illustrate how Folter Inc might use traded options to protect against a fall in the share price of Magterdoor Inc. Assuming that Folter has to sell the shares at the end of October at a price of 485 cents, evaluate the outcome of the hedge(s). **(4 marks)**

(b) Assume that the option delta of Magterdoor is 0.47. Illustrate how a delta neutral hedge might be used to protect against price movements of the shares of Magterdoor. Comment upon any practical problems of using a delta hedge for this purpose. **(4 marks)**

(c) Discuss the reasons why the January 550 call option premium is not the same as the intrinsic value of the option. **(4 marks)**

(d) The managing director of Folter suggests increasing its holding in Magterdoor from 2% to 6% of that company's issued shares. Discuss briefly the advantages and disadvantages of this strategy. **(3 marks)**

(e) Outline any measures that management of the target companies may take to resist any hostile bids. **(5 marks)**

(Total = 20 marks)

Answers

1 Impex

(a) **Impex**

$\beta_g = 0.98$, hence the **required return of shareholders** is

$r_e = r_f + \beta(r_m - r_f) = 6 + 0.98(10 - 6) = 9.92\%$

From this we can calculate the **share price** as

$E_{XD} = \dfrac{d_1}{r_e - g} = \dfrac{156 \times 1.025}{0.098 - 0.025} = 2155c$ or 21.55

Given that there are 268m shares in issue, the **equity market value** is

$E = \$21.55 \times 268m = \$5,775.4m$

The debt of Impex is perpetual with a coupon of 5.8% and a credit rating of AA. Taking the 30 year bond as representative, this suggests a yield spread of 50bp or 0.5% giving a **required return to debt holders** of

$r_d = r_f + \text{spread} = 6\% + 0.5\% = 6.5\%$

And from this, the **value of the perpetual debt** can be calculated as

$D_{XT} = \dfrac{c}{r_d} = \dfrac{5.8}{0.065} = \$89.23$

Giving a **market value for the \$3.26bn of debt** as

$D = 89.23 \times \left(\dfrac{3.26bn}{100}\right) = \$2,908.9m$

Now, the required return to debt holders of 6.5% is above the risk-free rate of 6%. Since we are told there is no unsystematic risk, the 0.5% premium must be to compensate for systematic risk, ie the debt has a beta. The **beta of the debt** can be calculated by rearranging CAPM as follows.

$r = r_f + \beta(r_m - r_f)$

so

$(r - r_f) = \beta(r_m - r)$

hence

$\beta = \dfrac{r - r_f}{r_m - r_f} = \dfrac{6.5 - 6.0}{10 - 6} = 0.125$

we can use this to calculate the following

(i) **Asset beta of Impex**

$$\beta_a = \left[\dfrac{E}{E + D(1-T)}\beta_e\right] + \left[\dfrac{D(1-T)}{E + D(1-T)}\beta_d\right]$$

$$= \left[\dfrac{5,775.4}{5,775.4 + 2,908.9 \times 0.7} \times 0.98\right] + \left[\dfrac{2,908 \times 0.7}{5,775.4 + 2,908.9 \times 0.7} \times 0.125\right] = 0.757$$

(ii) **The overall beta of Impex (beta of the WACC)**

The overall beta can be calculated as the weighted average of the equity debt betas as follows

$$\beta_{WACC} = \dfrac{5,775.4}{8,684.3} \times 0.98 + \dfrac{2,908.9}{8,684.3} \times 0.125 = 0.6936$$

So for Impex we have

	Market value $m	Beta	$\sigma_s = \beta\sigma_m$ (needed below)
Equity (E)	5,775.4	0.98	7.84%
Debt (D)	2,908.9	0.125	1.00%
Total (V)	8,684.3	0.6936	5.5488%

Elfix

Since Impex and Elfix are competitors in the same sector it is reasonable to presume that their asset betas are identical at the 0.757 calculated above

If Elfix were ungeared it would, therefore, have a **required return to shareholders** of

$r_e = r_f + \beta (r_m - r_f) = 6 + 0.757 (10 - 6) = 9.18\%$ which, in this situation, would be both its cost of equity and WACC.

Given that the policy of Elfix is to distribute 60% of earnings and retain 40% its **growth rate** would be

$g = rb = 9.18\% \times 0.4 = 3.672\%$

Here we are assuming that Elfix is also growing steadily in a highly competitive market so that the return achieved on reinvested earnings is simply the WACC.

We are given an EPS figure (excluding interest and tax thereon) of 80p. Given the distribution policy, the last dividend were the company ungeared would be 48p. From this we can determine the **ungeared share price** as

$$E = \frac{d_1}{r_e - g} = \frac{4.8 \times 1.03672}{0.0918 - 0.03672} = 903.46\text{p or }\$9.0346$$

And with 57m shares in issue this gives an **ungeared equity value** of

$U = \$9.0346 \times 57\text{m} = \$514.972\text{m}$

Now Eflix has \$220m of 15 year 7% debt in issue with an A2 rating corresponding to a yield spread of 107bp or 1.07%.

As a result, the **required return for Elfix's debt holders** is 7.07% (6 + 1.07) and its **market value** is

Time	Cash flow	Discount factor	PV $
1-15	7.00	$\frac{1}{0.0707}\left(1 - \frac{1}{1.0707^{15}}\right)$	63.474
15	100.00	$\frac{1}{1.0707^{15}}$	35.891
			99.365

And hence the **market value of Elfix's debt** is

$$V_d = \$99.365 \times \frac{220\text{m}}{100} = \$218.603$$

of which \$139.643m represents the present value of the coupon.

In addition, as for Impex, the **beta of Elfix's debt** can be calculated as

$$\beta_d = \frac{7.07 - 6.00}{10 - 6} = 0.2675$$

Applying Modigliani and Miller we have

V = U + PV (tax shield) = 514.972 + 139.643 × 0.3 = 556.865

Giving

	$m
Total value of geared business	556.865
Debt value	218.603
Equity value of geared business	338.262

Which, when spread over 57m shares, gives a **share price** of $5.93 per share.

The **beta of the equity** in this geared company can now be found using

$$\beta_g = \beta_u + (\beta_u - \beta_d) \frac{V_d}{V_e} (I - T)$$

$$= 0.795 + (0.795 - 0.2675) \times \frac{218.603}{338.262} \times 0.7 = 1.034$$

And the **overall beta** established as

$$\beta_{WACC} = \frac{338.262}{556.865} \times 1.034 + \frac{218.603}{556.863} \times 0.2675 = 0.7331$$

So for Elfix we have

	Market value $m	Beta	$\sigma_s = \beta\sigma_m$ (needed below)
Equity	338.262	1.034	8.272%
Debt	218.603	0.2675	2.14%
Total	556.865	0.7331	5.8648%

(b) The value at risk can be established as

$$VAR = S\phi\sigma \sqrt{t}$$

Where

S = current value
ϕ = normal distribution value corresponding to the described confidence level
σ = standard deviation
t = time

Since we are told that there is no unsystematic risk, then the total risk is the systematic risk calculated above. At the 1% level ϕ = N (0.95) = 2.325, hence the three month value at risk for each component is

Impex

$$\text{Equity VAR} = \$5,775.4m \times 2.325 \times 0.0784 \times \sqrt{\frac{3}{12}} = \$526.4m$$

$$\text{Debt VAR} = \$2,908.9m \times 2.325 \times 0.01 \times \sqrt{\frac{3}{12}} = \$33.8m$$

$$\text{Total VAR} = \$8,684.3m \times 2.325 \times 0.055488 \times \sqrt{\frac{3}{12}} = \$560.2m$$

Eflix

Equity VAR $= \$338.262 \times 3.325 \times 0.08272 \times \sqrt{\dfrac{3}{12}} = \$32.528m$

Debt VAR $= \$218.603m \times 2.325 \times 0.0214 \times \sqrt{\dfrac{3}{12}} = \$5.438m$

Total VAR $= \$556.865m \times 2.325 \times 0.058648 \times \sqrt{\dfrac{3}{12}} = \$37.966$

Note. In this question the total VAR is the sum of the equity VAR and debt VAR. This will only be the case in situations like this where there is no unsystematic risk or where debt and equity risks are perfectly positively correlated.

(c)   To: Chairman
       From: A N Other
       Date: 20 June 200X
       Subject: **Uses and limitations of VAR**

The **purpose** of VAR is to indicate the **potential scale of any loss of value** that may arise in extreme circumstances. What VAR gives is the **amount by which a value may fall over a given period of time at a given level of probability**, though perhaps this should say minimum amount. For example if VAR is $1m at 5% over one week then there is a 5% chance that over a one week period we could lose $1m **or more**. As such, VAR does not place a limit on the scale of any potential losses, its aim is to quantify potential extremes.

To evaluate VAR we need to have:

• A unit of measure, eg $s
• A specified time period
• A specified probability level (usually between 1% and 5%)
• A distribution for asset returns/values

The latter of those points is the most problematic and a number of different methods have been developed to deal with this, including

(i)   **Parametric VAR** – where it is assumed that returns, are normally distributed, making it relatively easy to assess. However share returns have not been observed to be normal and the returns from option type assets are far from normally distributed

(ii) **Historical simulation VAR** – where the distribution of returns is assessed using various financial models (eg Black-Scholes for options). This is again easy to understand and assess but requests extensive market data.

(iii) **Monte Carlo Simulation** – where returns from various assets are assumed to follow historical partners and a series of simulations is run combining various possibilities across all assets to get an overall distribution

None of these methods are foolproof and VAR appears to be **most effective** for **frequently traded assets** (for example it is used to determine the initial margin on futures contracts).

VAR should not be viewed in isolation, rather it should be considered as just **one of many evaluation techniques**. As we noted above VAR tells little about how large the risk may be under extreme circumstance. The **application** of VAR ideas over different assets, classes and currencies, especially when overlaid with derivatives such as options and swaps proves very **problematic**.

2 Shareholders and bondholders

Text references. Chapters 1 and 4.

Top tips. The key to (a) is realising the different attitudes to risk and return of bondholders and shareholders. Bondholders will be willing to take the company into liquidation if they believe it is the only certain way of realising their loan, but will be less willing if bankruptcy costs mean there is insufficient money left to repay loans. Hence it is fine to say that in some circumstances bondholders will prefer liquidation, but not others.

In (b) covenants can be broadly grouped as positive (company must do something), negative (company is prevented from doing something) and quantitative (essentially the accounting covenants, fulfilling financial limits).

Easy marks. (a) is probably more mainstream and you certainly need to realise why stakeholder conflicts occur, but if you know about covenants, there's nothing very difficult in (b) either.

(a)   (i)   **Different attitudes to risk and return**

Shareholders may want the company to undertake **risky projects** with correspondingly **high expected levels of returns**. Bondholders will want the company to undertake projects that guarantee sufficient returns to pay their interest each year, and ultimately to repay their loans.

(ii)   **Dividends**

Large (albeit) legal dividends may be preferred by shareholders, but may concern bondholders, because the payments leave low cash balances in the company and hence **put at risk** the **company's ability** to meet its commitments to the bondholders.

(iii)   **Priority in insolvency**

Bondholders may wish to take the company into **liquidation** if there are problems paying their interest, to guarantee their investment. Shareholders however may wish the company to **continue trading** if they expect to receive nothing if the company does go into liquidation.

(iv)   **Attitudes to further finance**

Shareholders may prefer the company to **raise additional finance** by means of loans, in order to **avoid having to contribute themselves** in a rights issue, or the risk of dilution of their shareholding and hence power if an open stock market issue is made. Bondholders may **not wish the company** to take on the burden of additional debt finance, because it may increase the risk that the **interest** that they are **due** will not be paid, or the company will have problems repaying their loans, particularly if the new loans rank above theirs.

(v)   **Restrictions imposed by bondholders**

Restrictions imposed by bondholders to protect their loans, such as charges preventing the company from selling assets or covenants, may limit the company's ability to maximise returns for shareholders.

(vi)   **Bankruptcy costs**

If the **costs of bankruptcy**, such as receivers and lawyers' fees, are likely to be **significant**, bondholders may be much less willing than shareholders for the company to bear any risk. Significant bankruptcy costs may mean that there is insufficient money left to repay their loans.

(b) A covenant in a loan agreement is an obligation placed on the borrower over and above repaying the loan according to terms.

The types of covenant are:

(i) **Positive covenants**

These require a borrower to do something, for example to **provide the bank** with its regular management accounts. This would allow the bank to **check** on the **financial performance** of the company, and to ensure that it is likely to be able to repay the loan as planned.

(ii) **Loan covenants**

The borrower may pledge **not to take out further loans** until the current loan has been repaid, or not to take further loans ranking above existing loans. The purpose of this is to protect the position of the lender, and to ensure that the risk of default is not increased, or the level of security diluted.

(iii) **Asset covenants**

There may be restrictions on the company's ability to **acquire, or dispose of, assets**.

(iv) **Accounting covenants**

These set **limitations on the borrower's financial position**. For example, the company might agree that its total borrowings should not exceed 100% of shareholder's funds. The purpose of this is to keep the gearing, and hence the level of risk to the lender, within certain limits.

(v) **Dividend covenants**

Covenants may **restrict the levels of dividends** borrowers can pay, or restrict the company's ability to purchase its own shares.

(vi) **Investment covenants**

Covenants may **limit the investments** the borrower can undertake, or prevent the borrower merging or making an acquisition.

(vii) **Repayment covenants**

The lender may be required to **build up a fund over time** to be drawn on to redeem bonds at the end of their life.

Advantages of covenants include:

(i) The main advantage of covenants is that lenders may be prepared to lend **more money** to the company if it provides the security of a covenant.

(ii) Covenants may mean that the costs at which the company can **borrow money** are **lower**.

(c) A number of factors must be taken into account when evaluating the financing of the diversification by means of the convertible loan stock issue, as follows.

(i) **Gearing**

The current gearing (debt:equity) based on book values is 31.8% ($7m/22m). The immediate effect of an issue of $9m debt would increase this to 72.7% (16/22), although on conversion there would be a substantial fall in the ratio. However, it would still be high for a significant period, especially for a company in a declining industry. The **level of financial risk** is therefore high with the company having to meet annual interest costs of nearly $1m during the period prior to conversion.

(ii) **Cost**

The **coupon rate of the loan stock** is 10%. This is the same as the current rate at which the company can borrow from the bank. Since one of the benefits of convertibles is that they can usually carry a lower coupon rate due to the attractiveness of conversion, this rate seems to be **high**. Presumably this is due to the effect on the gearing described above.

(iii)   **Conversion price**

The **effective conversion price** is $100/60 = $1.67 per share. This is a premium of $1.21 over the current market price of $0.46, a percentage increase of 263.0% over five years or $\sqrt[5]{3.63} - 1 = 29.4\%$ annually. While this may be possible if the market as a whole goes up, it is certainly not guaranteed.

(iv)   **Call option**

This allows the company to **restrict the potential gains** made by the loan stock holders. If the share price rises to $2 between 1 January 20Y2 and 31 December 20Y4, then the company can force the loan stock holders to convert, thus restricting their capital gain on conversion to $0.33 per share. Such an option may be unpopular with potential investors since it both restricts their possible gains and could force them to convert at a time that is inappropriate from the point of view of their personal tax position.

(v)   **Put option**

If the share price only rises to $1, the company can be forced to **redeem the loan stock at par**. This is a risky position for the company to be in, since if the share price is performing that badly in five years' time, it is likely that it will not be generating the level of revenues anticipated in the forecasts. The implication of this is that it could be very difficult for the company to raise the funds required to repay the loan stock holders, either from reserves or through its restricted ability to raise and to service additional debt.

3 Lion and Cub

Text references. Chapter 6 on the different valuation methods; Chapter 2 covers manager – shareholder conflicts.

Top tips. (a) is a good summary of manager – shareholder conflicts which the examiner often tests. (a) asks for actions shareholders can take to reduce conflicts, and our answer indicates what they can actually do in practice. Whilst they are trying to make management pay them the surplus cash, it is not legally correct to say that they can insist on increased dividends or share repurchase.

Note how free cash flow is calculated in the question details given in part (c). This reflects the approach taken by the examiner. In other questions you could be expected to carry out the calculation yourself. Remember to deduct capital subscribed when calculating market value added.

In (d) the adjustments to profits made when economic value added is used are ultimately meant to produce a figure for cashflows, but may not accurately do this.

In (e) the question makes clear that economic depreciation has been taken into account so you don't need to deduct it again. The interest payment should be added back **net** of tax. Leases should be included when calculating capital employed even if they are not on the balance sheet. Remember that the economic value added for a period is calculated on the capital employed at the **start** of that period. The target gearing, not the actual gearing, is used to calculate the WACC.

Easy marks. (d) is a straightforward discussion, but (b) should be reasonable as well, and you should revise these areas if you struggled with either part.

(a)   **Free cash flow**

The key element of the free cash flow model is the strategic need of companies to reinvest in new plant to maintain or increase current operating cash flows.

The free cash flow model is a present value model. It thus suggests that companies can maximise their value by undertaking projects with a positive net present value as well as replacing assets. If, when all available projects have been undertaken, there is still surplus cash, management should return the cash to shareholders by **paying large dividends** or by **buying back shares**.

Priorities

However management-shareholder priorities may differ.

(i)   **Profitability**

Whilst management may wish to invest in projects with a **large net present value**, shareholders may wish for a more **immediate or steadier return** than these maybe long-term projects offer.

(ii)   **Control**

Management may dislike the **loss of control** implicit in returning possibly large cash balances to shareholders. The **status** of having large amounts of money to exercise control over may be a significant motivation. Status is also linked into company size, and there may also be more tangible rewards arising from increasing company size, such as **remuneration increases.** These may motivate management to grow the company to a size greater than that required to maximise shareholder wealth.

Hence rather than returning monies to investors, managers may undertake investments with **questionable risk-return trade-offs**. If these produce negative returns, then dividends may suffer and the market value of shares decrease.

(iii)   **Survival**

On the other hand in times of recession management may be more concerned about ensuring the company's (and their own) survival rather than maximising shareholder wealth. Again this may lead to increased investment, but investment designed to reduce risk, for example by **diversification**.

Shareholder actions

Shareholders ultimately have the **right to remove directors** at the annual general meeting, and can indicate their disapproval in other ways at the meeting, for example **voting down the annual report and accounts**, or voting to reject the **report of the remuneration committee**. Legally they cannot however force management to pay more than the dividend they recommend. Nor can they force managers to buy back shares or increase the level of gearing, which will increase interest payments and reduce the cash flows available for management investment. There is a general legal rule that shareholders cannot usurp the power of the directors to manage the company.

(b)   **Shareholder value analysis**

Shareholder value analysis focuses on the creation of economic value for shareholders, as measured by the share price performance and the flow of dividends. Under shareholder value analysis key decisions with implications for cash flow and risk are specified. These will be decisions that impact upon **value drivers,** factors that have the greatest impact on shareholder value, such as sales growth rate, profit margin, working capital investment and the required rate of return.

Under the model:

| **Corporate value** | = | **PV of free cash flows** | + | **Current value of marketable securities and other non-operating investments** |

and Shareholder value = Corporate value − Debt

Limitations of shareholder value analysis model

(i) The model makes the questionable assumptions that **sales growth rates** are **constant,** that **operating profit rates** are **also constant** and that **tax** is a **constant percentage** of operating profit.

(ii) Some of the **necessary data** may not be readily available.

(iii) The present values of all the business's activities have theoretically to be taken to **infinity**. This difficulty can be overcome by taking a **terminal value** at some point in the future. However this introduces a further problem; not only do future cash flows have to be estimated, but a decision is needed on when those estimates cease to be realistic, and the terminal value has to be taken. Also the **terminal value** may prove difficult to **estimate.**

(iv) The **value drivers** that the business is focusing on may not always give the **same message**.

(c) **Present value of free cash flow at 31 December 20X0 without rights issue**

Time	Cash flow $m	Discount factor 10%	Net present value $m
1 (20X1)	7	0.909	6.363
2 (20X2)	17	0.826	14.042
3–10 (20X3 – 20Y0)	23	(6.145 – 1.736) = 4.409	101.407

Net present value = $121.812 million

Present value of free cash flow at 31 December 20X0 with rights issue

Time	Cash flow $m	Discount factor 10%	Net present value $m
1 (20X1)	7	0.909	6.363
2 (20X2)	17	0.826	14.042
3 (20X3)	23	0.751	17.273
4–10 (20X4 – 20Y0)	28	(6.145 – 2.487) = 3.658	102.424

Net present value = $140.102 million

	$m
Net present value with rights issue	140.102
Net present value without rights issue	121.812
Increase in net present value	18.290
Capital subscribed	15.000
Market value added	3.290

(d) **Benefits of economic value added**

(i) **Net present value**

Economic value added focuses on the **long-term net present value of a company.** Managerial performance will be improved by investing in positive NPV projects.

(ii) **Financing**

By including a financing element, the **cost of capital** is emphasised, and hence managers must have regard to **careful investment** and **control of working capital.** If managers choose negative NPV projects, the imputed capital charge will ultimately be greater than earnings.

(iii) **Cash flows**

The adjustments within the model mean that economic value added should be based on **cash flows** rather than accounting data and hence it may be **less distorted** by the **accounting policies** chosen.

(iv) **Clarity of measure**

Economic value added is a **monetary figure** rather than a ratio, and one that can be easily **linked to financial objectives.**

Drawbacks of economic value added

(i) **Failure to measure short-term position**

Economic value added does **not measure NPV** in the short-term. Projects with good long-term NPV, but large initial cash investments or poor initial returns, may be rejected by managers who are being judged on their **short-term performance.**

(ii) **Use of historical accounts**

Economic value added is based on historical accounts which may be of **limited use** as a guide to the future. In practice also the influences of accounting policies on the starting profit figure may not be completely negated by the adjustments made to it in the economic value added model.

(iii) **Other value drivers**

Other value drivers such as non-capitalised goodwill may be important despite being **excluded from the accounts**.

(iv) **Adjustments**

Making the necessary adjustments can be **problematic** as sometimes a large number of adjustments are required.

(v) **Cost of capital**

The cost of capital used is calculated by the **capital asset pricing model,** and is therefore based upon the **assumptions** of that model such as **no change in risk.**

(vi) **Inter-company comparisons**

Companies which are **larger in size** may have larger economic value added figures for this reason. **Allowance for relative size** must be made when inter-company comparisons are performed.

(e) **Economic value added**

Economic value added = Net operating profit after tax (NOPAT) − (Capital employed × Cost of capital)

Cub Inc

Net operating profit after tax

Net operating profit after tax is arrived at after making a number of adjustments.

	20X1 $m	20X2 $m
Profit after tax	147.0	185.0
Add: Non-cash expenses	32.0	36.0
Add: Interest after tax		
Charge (1 − 0.3))	9.1	12.6
NOPAT	188.1	233.6

Capital employed

Capital employed is on start of year figures

20X1 Capital employed	= Capital employed at end of 20X0 + Leases
	= 695 + 35
	= $730 million

20X2 Capital employed	= Book value of shareholders' funds + Bank loans + Leases
	= 595 + 175 + 35
	= $805 million

Weighted average cost of capital

20X1 cost of capital = $(0.75 \times 14\%) + (0.25 \times (7\%(1 - 0.3)))$
= 11.7%

20X2 cost of capital = $(0.75 \times 16\%) + (0.25 \times (8\%(1 - 0.3)))$
= 13.4%

Economic value added

20X1 EVA™ = $188.1 - (0.117 \times 730)$
= \$102.7 million

20X2 EVA™ = $233.6 - (0.134 \times 805)$
= \$125.7 million

On this measure, the company has created significant value in both 20X1 and 20X2 and appears to be on a rising trend.

4 Wurrall

Text references. Chapter 15 covers forecasts and ratio analysis, though you'll also need to look at Chapter 6 if you're unsure about free cash flow.

Top tips. The question requires you to calculate proforma income statements and balance sheets so you should use the same level of detail in your answer as you're given in the question. The way to approach this question is:

1   Copy out the proformas as per the question

2   Fill in all the figures that change by the percentages specified in the question for all of the four years (you need to show some figures for all of the four years; note the examiner's comment about giving limited credit for 1-2 years)

3   Work out the remaining figures for the income statement in 20X5 (interest, tax, dividends and retentions)

4   Calculate the reserves for year 1 and add up that half of the balance sheet

5   Calculate the short-term loan figures as the balancing figures

6   Repeat stages 3-5 for years 20X6 – 20X8

The key for the discussion of assumptions (ii) – (iv) is commenting on what relation these figures will or should have to sales. Assumption (ix) is a standard comment on dividend policy.

In (c) the change in assets represents the reinvestment figure you need to calculate free cash flow. Working capital = Total current assets – Total current liabilities.

(d) is a fairly typical ratio analysis part with calculations **and** comments required on profitability, liquidity and particularly gearing, discussion including problems **and** solutions.

Easy marks. The discussion in (b). The question requirement prompts you to discuss these points; however you would also have mentioned them if the discussion requirement had been more vaguer.

(a) **Pro forma accounts**

Pro forma income statement for the years ended March 20X5–20X8

	20X5	20X6	20X7	20X8
	$m	$m	$m	$m
Revenue	1,787	1,929	2,064	2,188
Operating costs before deprecation	(1,215)	(1,312)	(1,404)	(1,488)
	572	617	660	700
Tax allowable depreciation	(165)	(179)	(191)	(203)
Earnings before interest and tax	407	438	469	497
Net interest payable (Note)	(63)	(65)	(66)	(70)
Profit on ordinary activities before tax	344	373	403	427
Tax on ordinary activities	(103)	(112)	(121)	(128)
Profit after tax	241	261	282	299
Dividends	(135)	(146)	(158)	(167)
Amount transferred to reserves	106	115	124	132

Note. Interest = (8% × 580,000) + (7% × previous year's balance on short-term loans and overdrafts)

Pro forma balance sheets as at 31 March 20X5–20X8

	20X5	20X6	20X7	20X8
	$m	$m	$m	$m
Non-current assets				
Land and buildings	310	310	350	350
Plant and machinery (net)	1,103	1,191	1,275	1,351
Investments	32	32	32	32
	1,445	1,533	1,657	1,733
Current assets				
Inventories	488	527	564	598
Receivables	615	664	710	753
Cash in hand and short term deposits	22	24	25	27
	1,125	1,215	1,299	1,378
Payables: amounts falling due within one year:				
Short term loans and overdrafts (balance figure)	266	287	332	320
Other payables	514	556	595	630
	(780)	(843)	(927)	(950)
Payables: amounts falling due after one year:				
Borrowings (Note)	(580)	(580)	(580)	(580)
	1,210	1,325	1,449	1,581
Capital and reserves				
Called up share capital (10 cents par)	240	240	240	240
Reserves	970	1,085	1,209	1,341
	1,210	1,325	1,449	1,581

Note. Repaid at end of 20X6 and refinanced with a similar type of loan in 20X6.

(b) **Implications of the assumptions**

General assumptions

The pro forma accounts model treats **sales as the major variable** and makes forecasts of changes in several other factors dependent on sales. While this is basically a sensible approach where sales is the **limiting factor**, the relationships used are probably too simplistic and **not enough scenarios** of sales performance are considered.

Assumption (i)

The sales forecasts represent one possible scenario of the company's future performance. **Simulation analysis** could be used to generate other scenarios including best and worse cases, which may result in **different financing decisions** being made. The assumption that sales will continue to grow at 6% to perpetuity after 20X8 is over-optimistic.

Assumption (ii)

Presumably analysis of past data has shown that **cash operating costs** have been on average 68% of sales. This is too simplistic a formula, because costs will contain some **fixed elements** and some **variable costs** that **depend on a number of drivers**, not just sales. For example some variable costs are driven by number of employees and others by purchase quantities. Some costs are subject to price increases from inflation whereas others can be reduced as efficiency improvements take effect. A more detailed cost model, based on different categories of costs, would be more helpful in the forecasting process.

Assumption (iii)

The assumption that **plant and machinery** will **increase in line with sales** is unlikely to be **true even in the long term** and certainly not for the purposes of annual forecasts. Tax depreciation will not be a simple percentage of equipment value. Depreciation on new purchases of equipment will be higher than depreciation lost on old equipment. Any changes in tax depreciation rates and rules need to be reflected.

Assumption (iv)

Working capital does not need to increase in direct proportion to sales. For example according to inventory models, **optimum inventories** are likely to **vary with the square root of sales**. Receivables can be **controlled** so that they **grow less quickly than sales** whereas optimum use of payables implies obtaining as much finance as possible without harming trading relationships.

Assumption (ix)

A policy of paying dividends as a constant proportion of earnings each year could result in **volatile dividends**, and is less common than one of attempting to **maintain a steady growth of dividends** in line with the long run growth of profits. However, in the forecasts produced for the next four years there is no real difference between these policies because profit rises steadily.

(c)   Operating cash flow is estimated by EBIT(1-t) plus depreciation. To find free cash flow, this needs to be adjusted for changes in working capital and expenditure on non-current assets.

Changes in working capital and non-current assets

	20X5 $m	20X6 $m	20X7 $m	20X8 $m
Change in land and buildings	–	–	40	–
Change in plant and machinery	91	88	84	76
Change in working capital	15	27	–	56
Change in assets	106	115	124	132

Free cash flow

	20X5 $m	20X6 $m	20X7 $m	20X8 $m
EBIT (1-t)	285	307	328	348
Depreciation	165	179	191	203
Change in assets	(106)	(115)	(124)	(132)
Free cash flow	344	371	395	419

Assuming growth to perpetuity of 6% per year after 20X8, the present value of free cash flow as at 31 March 20X8 is estimated as:

Free cash flow $(1 + g)/(\text{WACC} - g) = 419 \times 1.06/(0.11 - 0.06) = \$8{,}883$ million.

Loans at 31 March 20X8, as estimated in the pro forma accounts, will be 580 + 320 = $900 million. Subtracting this from the PV of free cash flow leaves $7,983 million as the value of equity. There are 2,400 million shares, so share price at 31 March 20X8 is estimated as $7,983/2,400 = 333 cents per share.

This represents an **increase of 59%** over the current share price of 210 cents. On the basis of these figures, and the fact that the projected growth rate of 6% is probably over-optimistic, the managing director's claim that the share price will double in four years appears to be unfounded. However a lot will depend on the performance of the stock market over the next few years.

5 Your company

Revised guidance manual

(a) **Discount rate**

The discount rate for a project should reflect the **cost of finance** for that project, taking into account its risk. There are two main ways of doing this.

(i) The discount rate for a project should reflect the weighted average cost of capital for the company **only** if both the **business risk** and **financial risk** of the project are the same as the company's.

(ii) If the project finance will change the company's gearing, the **adjusted present value method** should be used.

(b) **Cost of debt and equity**

The cost of equity and cost of debt should always be estimated using **market values (no change from the original)**.

(c) **Inflation**

If project cash flows include estimates for expected inflation, the **discount rate** should also **allow for inflation**. Discount rates calculated by the normal methods described in this manual will automatically contain this inflation allowance. If project cash flows are estimated in real terms (at today's prices), the discount rate will also need to be **adjusted** to real terms, by removing the expected inflation rate.

(d) **Estimating cost of equity**

To estimate the cost of equity capital for a project we recommend the **Capital Asset Pricing Model** (CAPM), which relates the cost of capital to the project's systematic risk. The cost of equity capital for the whole company can also be estimated from the CAPM or from the **dividend valuation model** which relates the cost of capital to the company's share price and expected future dividend payments. Both models contain theoretical simplifications and require estimates which are subject to inaccuracies.

(e) **Estimating cost of debt**

The company's cost of debt should be estimated from the **current market rate** it is paying. For some types of loan the market rate is quoted transparently. For others it is necessary to **compute** the **redemption yield**, taking into account **interest** and **capital payments** compared with current market value. In each case, the cost to the company is after allowing for **corporate tax relief** on interest. Where there are several forms of company debt, the weighted average can be taken.

(f) **Rounding**

There is **no need** to **round** the cost of capital to the nearest whole percentage, although it must be appreciated that the estimate is usually subject to a high margin of error. The practice of rounding *up* to be more prudent is wrong, as this may cause **potentially profitable projects** to be **incorrectly rejected**. It is good practice, however, to use sensitivity analysis to gauge the risk of accepting the project.

Revised illustrative examples

Illustration 1 – when the company is expanding existing activities

Cost of equity

Dividend valuation model

The model should be based on next year's dividend D_1. g should be estimated dividend growth, not earnings growth.

$D_1 = D_0 (1 + g)$
$= 24 \times 1.06$
$= 25.44$ cents

Market price per share $= \$214m/50m$
$= 428$ cents

Cost of equity $= \dfrac{D_1}{P} + g$
$= 25.44/428 + 0.06$
$= 0.119$
$= 11.9\%$

Capital Asset Pricing Model

The company's equity beta, not asset beta, should be used to estimate the cost of equity shares. Assuming that debt is risk free (and beta of debt is therefore zero):

$\beta_a = \beta_e \dfrac{E}{E+D(1-t)}$

$\therefore 1.1 = \beta_e \times 214/[214 + 85(1 - 0.3)]$
$= \beta_e \times 214/273.5$

and $\beta_e = 1.1 \times 273.5/214$
$= 1.41$

The cost of equity, Ke $= 6\% + (14\% - 6\%)\ 1.41 = 17.3\%$.

The two estimates of cost of equity are now very different. The CAPM estimate is used in the computation of WACC.

Cost of debt

The loan stock has a book value of \$80m and a market value of \$85m. Annual interest payments are 10% of \$80m = \$8m and result in tax savings of 30%, for which the timing difference is ignored, giving a net interest cost of \$8m $\times$ 0.7 = \$5.6m.

Assuming the debt is redeemed at par of \$80 million:

Rough cost $= 5.6/85 + \left[\dfrac{(80 - 85)}{85 \times 4}\right] = 5.1\%$

For a more accurate answer, find the cost by estimating the IRR of the cash flows at 5% and 6% and interpolate:

Year	$m	Discount factor 5%	PV $m	Discount factor 6%	PV $m
0	(85.0)	1.000	(85.0)	1.000	(85.0)
1–4	5.6	3.546	19.9	3.465	19.4
4	80.0	0.823	65.8	0.792	63.3
			0.7		(2.3)

By interpolation, cost of debt $= 5\% + 0.7/(0.7 + 2.3)$
$= 5.23$, say 5.2%

Weighted Average Cost of Capital (WACC)

$$WACC = Ke_g \left(\frac{E}{E+D}\right) + Kd(1-t)\left(\frac{D}{E+D}\right)$$

$$= 17.3\left(\frac{214}{214+85}\right) + 5.2\left(\frac{85}{214+85}\right)$$

$$= 13.9\%$$

The discount rate for the project is 13.9%. No further adjustment is needed because the market costs of equity and debt already allow for expected inflation.

Illustration 2 – when the company is diversifying its activities

Cost of equity

The asset beta of a similar sized company in the industry in which the company proposes to diversify is 0.90. This can be used as the asset beta of the new project. (**This does not need to be 'ungeared' as in the original example, as it is an asset beta not an equity beta**).

To estimate the equity beta for our company for the new project, we use the formula:

$$\beta_a = \beta_e \frac{E}{E+D(1-t)}$$

$$\therefore \beta_e = 0.90 \times 273.5/214$$
$$= 1.15 \text{ (same computation as in illustration 1 with a different asset beta)}$$

Using the CAPM, $Ke = 6\% + 8\% \times 1.15$
$$= 15.2\%$$

Cost of debt

This is unchanged at 5.2%.

$WACC = 15.2\% \times 214/299 + 5.2\% \times 85/299$
$$= 12.4\%$$

6 Jetter

Text references. Chapter 7 on WACC basics, Chapter 4 Appendix on CAPM and arbitrage pricing theory.

Top tips. (a) requires you to understand the determinants of beta, and relate the correlation of returns from the investment and returns from the market to the market standard deviation.

Remember that the formula for calculating beta is not given in the exam, so you need to learn it. The beta you calculate is used in CAPM to find the expected return and then the expected return is compared with the actual return, the alpha value calculated and whether the investment is worthwhile is assessed.

Work through the answer to (b) carefully, seeing how it's built up, first calculating the net present value, then using that in the IRR calculation to find the discount rate, and substituting the discount rate into CAPM to find the beta.

(c) should be a fairly straightforward WACC calculation provided you use IRR to find the cost of redeemable debt and weighted by market values. For (d) you just need to follow the instructions.

Many of the criticisms of CAPM in (e) can be applied to other techniques, that is unrealistic assumptions, dependence on historical data which may not reflect the future and limited time frame.

Easy marks. The assumptions of CAPM in (e) are core knowledge.

(a) Using the formula:

$$\beta_j = \frac{P_{jm}\sigma_j}{\sigma_m}$$

where P_{jm} = Project correlation coefficient (correlation with market returns)
  β_j = Project standard deviation
  β_m = Market standard deviation

we can then calculate the required return using the CAPM formula:

$E(r_j) = r_f + [E(r_m) - r_f]\,\beta_j$

and the abnormal return as:

Abnormal return = Expected return − Required return

Project 1

$$\beta_j = \frac{0.76 \times 8.4}{6.9}$$

  = 0.925

$E(r_j)$ = 6 + (15 − 6) 0.925
  = 14.33%

Abnormal return = 15 − 14.33
  = 0.67%

Project 2

$$\beta_j = \frac{0.63 \times 4.6}{6.9}$$

  = 0.42

$E(r_j)$ = 6 + (15 − 6) 0.42
  = 9.78%

Abnormal return = 11 − 9.78
  = 1.22%

Project 3

$$\beta_j = \frac{0.58 \times 14.3}{6.9}$$

  = 1.202

$E(r_j)$ = 6 + (15 − 6) 1.202
  = 16.82%

Abnormal return = 17 − 16.82
  = 0.18%

Selection of project

All three projects could be selected as they all generate positive **abnormal returns**. If only one project is to be chosen, Project 2 may be the project selected as:

(i) It has the largest **abnormal return**
(ii) It requires the largest **investment**

However the best way to select projects would be to calculate the **net present value**, and we cannot do that on the available data.

Money market returns are not relevant as assuming **market efficiency**, investment in the money market will have a zero NPV.

(b)   Present value of cash flows = Profitability index × Initial investment

$$= 1.3 \times 40$$

$$= \$52.0 \text{ million}$$

We can estimate the discount rate by selecting two discount rates.

Year	Cash flow $m	Discount factor 10%	PV $m	Discount factor 5%	PV $m
1–4	16	3.170	50.72	3.546	56.74

Discount rate $= 5 + (10 - 5) \times \dfrac{56.74 - 52.0}{56.74 - 50.72}$

$$= 8.93\%$$

Alternative solution

Annuity factor $= \dfrac{52}{16}$

$$= 3.250$$

This lies between 8% and 9%

Discount rate $= 8 + \dfrac{3.312 - 3.250}{3.312 - 3.240}$

$$= 8.86\,\%$$

$8.93 = 6 + (15 - 6)\,\beta_j$

$\beta_j = 0.326$

This implies the estimated Beta of 0.42 for Project 2 was too high.

(c)   Using CAPM

Cost of equity, $Ke = r_f + [E(r_m) - r_f]\beta_j$

$$= 6 + [15 - 6]\,1.25$$

$$= 17.25\%$$

Calculate after tax cost of debt Kd $(1 - t)$ using IRR. Starting rate 2/3 of coupon rate 12% ie 8%.

Year		Cash flow $	Disc factor 8%	DCF $	Disc factor 5%	DCF $
20X2	Investment	(105.50)	1.000	(105.50)	1.000	(105.50)
20X3–6	Interest net of tax	8.40	3.312	27.82	3.546	29.79
20X6	Redemption	100.00	0.735	73.50	0.823	82.30
				(4.18)		6.59

Cost of debt $= 5 + (8 - 5) \dfrac{6.59}{(6.59 - (-4.18))}$

$$= 6.8\%$$

Market value of equity, E = 200 million × 2.20

= 440 million

Market value of debt, D = 71 million × 1.0550

= 74.905 million

$$\text{WACC} = \text{Ke}\,\frac{E}{E+D} + \text{Kd}(1-t)\frac{D}{E+D}$$

$$= 17.25\,\frac{440}{440+74.905} + 6.8\frac{74.905}{440+74.905}$$

$$= 15.73\%$$

Impact of business risk

The **business risk** of the new investment appears to be low, with an asset beta of 0.33, and an equity beta only a little higher due to the company's mix of finance. This will result in some **decrease in the cost of equity** and hence the **weighted average cost of capital**, but this decrease is unlikely to be significant.

Impact of financial risk

The **financial risk** of Jetter is unlikely to change significantly because the investment is being financed by internal funds which will result in a change in the distribution of assets but no immediate change in the financial risk. If the investment does make the profits forecast, these will ultimately accrue to the shareholders, resulting in a decrease in gearing.

(d) (i) The main reason for using this formula is a belief that CAPM **overestimates betas** that are high or **underestimates betas** that are low.

(ii) **Revised betas**

Project 1 (0.67) 0.925 + 0.33 = 0.950
Project 2 (0.67) 0.42 + 0.33 = 0.611
Project 3 (0.67) 1.202 + 0.33 = 1.135

Project 1

$E(r_j)$ = 6 + (15 − 6) 0.950
= 14.55%

Abnormal return = 15 − 14.55
= 0.45%

Project 2

$E(r_j)$ = 6 + (15 − 6) 0.611
= 11.50%

Abnormal return = 11 − 11.50
= (0.5%)

Project 3

$E(r_j)$ = 6 + (15 − 6) 1.135
= 16.22

Abnormal return = 17 − 16.22
= 0.78%

Project 2 now would fail to achieve the return expected, and thus would not be selected.

(e)   **Advantages of CAPM**

Risk and return

CAPM links risk and return by attempting to **describe the difference in returns** in terms of a single variable, **systematic risk**, measured by the beta factor. The beta factor represents the **sensitivity** of the company's shares to the risk of 'the economy'.

Uses

CAPM can be used to estimate **expected return** from an investment.

Limitations of CAPM

Assumptions of CAPM

Many of the assumptions behind the CAPM are not very realistic. For instance it is assumed that:

(i)   All investors hold **well-diversified portfolios** and all make the same unbiased forecasts of future performance of shares.

(ii)   **Return, risk and correlation** can be **evaluated** over a **single time period**.

(iii)   Investors are only interested in **mean returns and risk**, measured entirely by **variability of returns**.

(iv)   Investors can **invest or borrow** at the **risk-free rate**.

(v)   The **capital market** has **perfect efficiency**, with no one individual dominating it, and **no tax** or **transaction costs**.

(vi)   The economy can be described in terms of a **single variable**.

(vii)   **Costs of insolvency** are **zero**.

There is a body of evidence concerning inaccurate predictions made by the CAPM, for example when it is applied to certain days of the week or months of the year.

Use of historical data

Furthermore, the only feasible way of estimating a company's beta factor or the market risk premium ($R_m - R_f$) is by **examining historical data** and making the assumption that the future will be the same as the past.

Different circumstances

It is hard to use CAPM to estimate returns on projects under **different economic environments**, market returns under different economic environments and the probabilities of the various environments.

Different times

The CAPM is really just a **single period model**. Few investment projects last for one year only and to extend the use of the return estimated from the model to more than one time period would require both project performance relative to the market and the economic environment to be reasonably stable.

In theory, it should be possible to apply the CAPM for each time period, thus arriving at successive discount rates, one for each year of the project's life. In practice, this would exacerbate the estimation problems mentioned above and also make the discounting process much more cumbersome.

Focus on shareholders

When applied to capital investment appraisal, the CAPM makes the additional assumption that companies **make decisions** on **behalf of shareholders only**. This ignores the position of other stakeholders who have different attitudes to risk because they find it more difficult to diversify their position than shareholders do.

Advantages of APT

Arbitrage pricing theory (APT) explains return in terms of several independent economic factors, such as the rate of inflation, the level of interest rates, and the index of industrial production. Different shares will have different sensitivities to each of these factors and, if these sensitivities can be estimated, the return of the share can be predicted. APT can be used to **compare the pricing of shares** with **each other**, rather than with the **market**.

Problems with APT

APT is difficult to implement in practice because:

(i)   It is not clear **how many factors** should be **used** in the model and what they should be.

(ii)   It is difficult to **measure the sensitivity of a company's shares** to these factors (APT is certainly not the only financial theory to fall foul of the problems of multiple regression analysis).

(iii)   APT uses the **assumptions of portfolio theory** and hence many of the assumptions of CAPM including an efficient market.

7 Sleepon

> **Text references.** Chapter 6 for the investment appraisal methods and complications.
>
> **Top tips.** A very similar question to many that this examiner has set before, both in terms of the calculation requirements and the points that should be brought out in the discussion.
>
> You should do the calculation first as an appendix for the report, aiming to spend about 50 minutes on it. The reference to costs being at current prices, and the fact that some costs were increasing at different rates, meant that you had to adjust most of the figures for inflation each year. The details given about the competitor should also have given you a big enough clue to identify the need to ungear and regear beta. Sleepon's current WACC and equity beta are not relevant.
>
> The most complicated requirements are towards the end of the calculation, so you should be able to pick up enough marks on the earlier part and in the discussion to have a good chance of passing the question. It would have been acceptable to assume working capital was recovered in year 6 rather than year 5.
>
> The strategic considerations are fairly basic – is diversification necessary (remember its disadvantages)? How will the competition respond? The bulk of the discussion consists of going through the major figures in the appraisal and considering how they might change or why they might not be accurate, also considering anything the appraisal may have missed out (real options).
>
> **Easy marks.** The discussion should be fine if you questioned the figures given in the scenario. Most of the calculations though just consist of calculating the effect of inflation increases.

Report on the investment theme park

This report discusses the financial appraisal of the potential investment in the theme park, shown in an appendix, and other factors that the board of Sleepon should consider when making their assessment, including the further information required.

Financial appraisal

The appraisal shows a negative net present value, indicating that on financial grounds, the investment is not worthwhile.

Other factors

However there are a number of factors that Sleepon's board should consider.

ANSWERS

Need for diversification

The board should asses whether the **strategic decision** to diversify is the correct one; it may be better to look for further investments in the hotel sector, in which Sleepon has experience. Sleepon is likely to have to **recruit managers and staff** with experience of running theme parks; this will be **costly** and successful recruitment is not completely certain.

Extent of diversification

Even if diversification is the best policy, there may be better investments in the theme park or leisure facility sector. The directors also need to investigate how much the theme park income is **correlated** with the hotel income. Will the factors causing a fall in demand for hotel accommodation (customers holidaying abroad for example) also affect the demand for theme parks.

Competition

Sleepon should not only investigate the current position of likely competitors, but also how the competition is likely to **respond** if the new theme park is opened.

Further information and calculations

The expected values given represent only one possible scenario. Appraisal is needed of other possible scenarios and information obtained about, or estimations made of:

- The effect on revenue of **different scales of admission charges**

- The effect on revenue of **different spending** within the theme park, if for example more attractions were offered

- The impact of **tighter control on working capital** as this is a major item of expenditure in the early years

- **Cost patterns** – is the assumption that all costs will increase in line with inflation too pessimistic

- The **accuracy of the realisable value estimate** in year 5 and what the effect would be on realisable value of extending the analysis beyond five years

- Whether disposal value would differ if the park was sold after 5 years as a **going concern** rather than its assets sold separately

- The **accuracy of the discount rate estimate** – Thrillall's activities may not be of the same risk, and maybe the future figures have been over-discounted

- The effect of extending the analysis beyond five years, calculating at what stage the park is likely to break even, and whether this **payback** period could be tolerated

- The impact of **scaling down** the **initial investment** on operating income and costs – would this decrease the payback period significantly

- The possibility of **real options** – further investment at a later date if the theme park proved more successful than expected

Simulations should be carried out under a number of different assumptions and **sensitivity analysis applied** to key figures in the scenario.

Appendix

	Working	0 $m	1 $m	2 $m	3 $m	4 $m	5 $m
Receipts							
Adult admission	1			41.2	42.5	43.8	45.1
Child admission	1			34.4	35.4	36.5	37.6
Food	1			13.7	14.2	14.6	15.0
Gifts	1			11.5	11.8	12.2	12.5
Total receipts				100.8	103.9	107.1	110.2
Expenses							
Labour	2			42.4	43.7	45.0	46.4
Insurance	2			2.1	2.2	2.3	2.3
Maintenance				15.0	19.0	23.0	27.0
Capital allowances	3			62.5	46.9	35.2	26.4
Total expenses				122.0	111.8	105.5	102.1
Taxable profits				(21.2)	(7.9)	1.6	8.1
Taxation 30%				6.4	2.4	(0.5)	(2.4)
Capital allowances				62.5	46.9	35.2	26.4
Initial cost		(200.0)	(200.0)				
Realisable value							250.0
Working capital	4		(51.5)	(1.5)	(1.6)	(1.6)	56.2
Net cash flow		(200.0)	(251.5)	46.2	39.8	34.7	338.3
Discount factors 11%	5	1.000	0.901	0.812	0.731	0.659	0.593
Present value		(200.0)	(226.6)	37.5	29.1	22.9	200.6

Net present value = $(136.5) million.

Note. The market research, advertising and the apportioned overheads are not relevant cash flows.

Workings

1 Income

Estimated income × $(1.03)^2$ year 2 etc

Estimated income is:
Adult admission 6,000 × 360 × 18
Child admission 9,000 × 360 × 10
Food 15,000 × 360 × 8 × 0.3
Gifts 15,000 × 360 × 5 × 0.4

2 Labour and insurance

Current costs × $(1.03)^2$ year 2 etc

3 Capital allowances

Assume first allowance available for yr 1 for all expenditure $125,000 + $125,000 and benefit received in yr 2. Allowances available up to and including yr 4, no allowance claimable for yr 5 in yr 6 as after-tax realisable value given.

Assume allowances can be claimed against liabilities elsewhere in the group.

Year of claim	Written down value $m	Capital allowance $m	Year payable
1	250.0	62.5	2
2	187.5	46.9	3
3	140.6	35.2	4
4	105.4	26.4	5

ANSWERS

4 **Working capital**

50.00 × 1.03 = 51.50 yr 1, 3% increase yrs 2-4, assume repaid end of yr 5.

5 **Discount factor**

E = 400 × 3.86 = $1,544m
D = 460 × 0.93 = $428m

Ungearing Thrillall's equity beta

$$\beta_a = \beta_e \frac{E}{E+D(1-t)}$$

$$\beta_a = 1.45 \frac{1,544}{1,544+428(1-0.3)}$$

= 1.21

Regearing asset beta to reflect Sleepon's gearing

$$\beta_e = 1.21 \frac{61.4+38.6(1-0.3)}{61.4}$$

= 1.74

Using CAPM

$$Ke = r_f + [E(r_m) - r_f]\beta_j$$

= 3.5 + (10 − 3.5)1.74 = 14.8%

Kd = 7.5%

WACC = (14.8 × 0.614) + (7.5 (1 − 0.3) 0.386)

= 11.1%, say 11%

8 Cost of capital

(a) **WACC**

A company's weighted average cost of capital (WACC) is the **average of the after-tax costs** of the **different sources of finance** that it uses, **weighted in proportion to the market values** of those funds. WACC can be used as a **discount rate** to evaluate the company's potential projects provided that:

(i) There is **no significant change in the capital structure** of the company as a result of the investment

(ii) The **operating (systematic) risk of the new project** is the **same** as the **company's existing systematic risk**

If these conditions are true then a project whose return exceeds the WACC will be worthwhile and its NPV will indicate the expected increase in shareholder value if it is accepted.

Problems of WACC

(i) One practical problem is whether to **include short-term debt** (eg overdraft) in the computation. This depends on whether the **short-term debt** is effectively used as a **long term source of finance**.

(ii) If the new project has **different systematic risk** to the company's existing business (ie condition (ii) above is untrue) then a risk-adjusted version of the WACC must be computed if the method is to give reasonable results.

140 BPP LEARNING MEDIA

(iii)   WACC cannot be used if the finance for the new project would cause a **significant change to the company's capital structure** (ie condition (i) above is untrue).

(iv)   It is also difficult to use WACC if there are **specific financing opportunities**, for example subsidised loan finance, or complex tax allowances.

Adjusted present value

Adjusted present value (APV) is a more advanced method that can be used for any project appraisal exercise, but it is in the more complex cases (involving a **change in capital structure** and/or **other complex finance problems**) that it is the most useful.

(i)   The first stage is to **evaluate the base case NPV** of operating cash flows by discounting at the ungeared cost of equity.

(ii)   The **present value of each individual financing side effect** is then evaluated separately. The sum of the base case NPV and the PV of financing side effects is the APV.

The method has the advantage over basic net present value using WACC that it allows **each different type of cash flow** to be **discounted at a rate specific to the risk** of that cash flow. It also allows the effects of more complex financing situations to be considered.

Problems with APV

The main practical problem is to **identify correctly the financing side effects** and their appropriate discount rates. Theoretical weaknesses of the method stem from simplifications introduced by the Modigliani and Miller model of capital structure. For example:

- It is assumed that the only effect of debt issued at market rates is the **tax relief on debt** interest
- The computation of an asset beta assumes that **cash flows** are perpetuities

(b)   (i)   **No conversion: share price is 470 cents**

If no conversion takes place, the value of the convertible will be as debt with 4 years to maturity. Its value is found by **discounting interest** and **redemption** value at 9%, which is the company's pre-tax cost of debt.

Year		$	9% factors	PV $
1–4	Interest	8	3.240	25.92
4	Redemption	100	0.708	70.80
				96.72

(Note that the value per share for conversion to take place would need to be at least $96.72/20 = 484 cents).

Total market value of the loan stock   = 96.72/100 × $20 million
                                                              = $19.34 million

Other debt has a market value of $23m, giving total debt value of $42.34m and a cost of 9%(1 − 0.3) = 6.3% after tax.

If the share price falls to 470 cents

Total market value of shares = 470/520 × $180m
                                                 = $162.69 million

The cost of equity is 15% because its systematic risk is the same as that of the market.

Total value of debt plus equity   = $42.34m + $162.69m
                                                     = $205.03 million

Weighted average cost of capital   = 15% × 162.69/205.03 + 6.3% × 42.34/205.03
                                                        = 13.2%

(ii) **Conversion: share price is 570 cents**

Number of new shares issued = 20 × $20m/$100

= 4 million

Value of new shares issued = 4m × 570p

= $22.8 million

Value of existing shares = 570/520 × $180m

= $197.31 million

Value of all shares = $220.11 million

Debt remaining = $23 million

Total value of equity and debt = £243.11 million

Assuming the cost of equity and debt are unchanged

Weighted average cost of capital = 15% × 220.11/243.11 + 6.3% × 23/243.11

= 14.2%

The cost of capital is higher if conversion takes place because **cheaper debt** has been **replaced** with **more expensive equity shares.**

Conclusion

This calculation is unlikely to be correct because the **assumption** that the costs of equity and debt are unchanged by the conversion is probably **wrong**. When debt is reduced, the **financial risk** to shareholders **decreases**, causing a reduction in the cost of equity. However, it is unlikely that the cheaper equity will compensate for the loss of cheap debt in the capital structure because **debt interest** is **tax allowable** whereas dividends to shareholders are not.

9 Trosoft

Text references. Chapter 7 on WACC basics and adjusted present value.

Top tips. Do the NPV calculation first before looking at any of the APV adjustments as there would be ten or 11 marks for this.

Complications included being given non-relevant costs (it's worth noting these in your answer, saying that you've ignored them) and the fact that you were given enough data to enable you to calculate six years worth of cash flows. You are expected to calculate flows for as many years as you are given data; though you will gain some marks for correct technique if you calculate for a limited number of years, you will limit the credit you are given.

With the APV, the risk-free rate is chosen, as tax relief from a stable government is virtually risk-free provided the company has other profitable projects. The tax relief is only given for a limited number of years so you have to use the cumulative discount factor rather than the tax relief/risk-free rate perpetuity formula.

Easy marks. The discussion in (b) brings in a number of points that are relevant in many other questions– data limitations, real options, whether in practice the company can cope with diversification and compatibility with strategy.

To: Directors of Trosoft pte ltd
From: Financial Management Consultant

Report on the proposed diversification into internet auctions

Introduction

Our assessment of the proposed investment takes into account **financial and non-financial factors** and considers the **effect of the diversification** on the **overall business strategy** of the company.

Time period of analysis

Four years of financial estimates were provided in your original brief. However, because the **IT infrastructure** underlying the project is expected to last six years before renewal is required, **the estimates have been extended to six years**, assuming that costs (apart from royalty payments and depreciation) and working capital rise at the current rate of inflation, 2% per year after year 4.

Method of analysis

The **adjusted present value** method has been used for the financial evaluation, first computing the base case NPV and then the PV of financial side effects.

Base case NPV

Year	Working	0	1	2	3	4	5	6
		S$'000	S$'000	S$'000	S$'000	S$'000	S$'000	S$'000
Auction fees			4,300	6,620	8,100	8,200	8,364	8,531
Costs								
IT maintenance costs			1,210	1,850	1,920	2,125	2,168	2,211
Telephone costs			1,215	1,910	2,230	2,420	2,468	2,518
Wages			1,460	1,520	1,680	1,730	1,765	1,800
Salaries			400	550	600	650	663	676
Incremental head Office overhead	2		50	55	60	65	66	68
Marketing		500	420	200	200	–	–	
Royalty payments for use of technology		680	500	300	200	200	200	200
Lost contribution From other activities			80	80	80	–	–	–
Rental of premises			280	290	300	310	316	323
Tax allowable depreciation	3		540	432	432	432	432	432
		1,180	6,155	7,187	7,702	7,932	8,078	8,228
Profit before tax		(1,180)	(1,855)	(567)	398	268	286	303
Tax (24·5%)		289	454	139	(98)	(66)	(70)	(74)
		(891)	(1,401)	(428)	300	202	216	229
Add back depreciation:			540	432	432	432	432	432
Other outflows:								
IT infrastructure		(2,700)						
Working capital	4	(400)	(24)	(24)	(25)	(26)	(10)	509
Net flows		(3,991)	(885)	(20)	707	608	638	1,170
10% discount factors	5	1	0.909	0.826	0.751	0.683	0.621	0.564
Present values		(3,991)	(804)	(17)	531	415	396	660

The expected base case NPV is (S$2,810,000)

Workings

1 The market research cost has been left out of the computation, as it is a sunk cost.

2 Only incremental head office overheads have been included. Other allocated overheads are irrelevant.

3 Depreciation = $\dfrac{2,700}{5}$ = 540 year 1 and $\dfrac{(2,700-540)}{5}$ = 432 in years 2–6.

4 Working capital in year 5 is assumed to increase by the 2% inflation rate. Accumulated working capital at year 4 = 400 + 24 + 24 + 25 + 26 = 499. 2% × 499 = 10. Total working capital at year 5 (509) is assumed to be released at the end of year 6.

5   Cost of equity

For the base case NPV the **ungeared cost of equity** has been used for the new project as the discount rate. To find this we ungeared the average equity beta of companies in the internet auction sector to find the asset beta:

Assuming corporate debt to be virtually risk free:

$\beta_a = \beta_e E/[E + D](1 - t)]$
$\beta_a = 1.42 \times 67/[67 + 33 (1 - 0.245)] = 1.035$

Using CAPM

$Ke_u = r_f + (r_m - r_f) \beta_a$
$Ke_u = 4\% + (9.5\% - 4\%) 1.035 = 9.69\%$

We have approximated this result to 10% as the discount rate for the base case NPV computation.

Financing side effects

Tax shield (tax relief on interest payments)

The 6 year term loan covers IT infrastructure S$2.7 million plus working capital S$0.4 million = S$3.1 million.

The subsidised interest rate is 5.5% – 1% = 4.5%.
Annual interest = S$3.1m × 4.5% = S$139,500.
Annual tax relief = 24.5% × S$139,500 = S$34,177.
Discount this at the risk free rate 4%
The present value of tax relief for 6 years is: S$34,177 × 5.242 = S$179,156.

Alternatively the tax shield could be based upon the percentage debt capacity of the company.

Government interest rate subsidy

Annual interest saving net of tax is S$3,100,000 × 1% × (1 – 0.245) = S$23,405.
Present value for six years, discounted at the risk free rate, is S$23,405 × 5.242 = **S$122,689**.

Issue costs

Issue costs are S$3,100,000 × 1.5% = **S$46,500**.

Adjusted present value

The estimated APV of the investment is –S$2,810,000 + S$179,156 + S$122,689 – S$46,500 = **(S$2,554,655)**

Results of evaluation

On the basis of the financial estimates made, the **investment is not worthwhile**, having a large negative adjusted present value. Alternative investment opportunities are likely to produce much better results, and should be investigated. However, the negative APV of this project is subject to a **large margin of error**, as there are major potential benefits and uncertainties that have not been valued in the computation, such as **realisable value**, or **benefits after six years.**

The discount rate used is based on the **capital asset pricing model**, which has a number of theoretical weaknesses. However, any errors in the discount rate are probably immaterial compared with **uncertainties in the cash flows** themselves. Some of the **cash flow estimates** may be **wrong** because of **lack of underlying information**. More information should be obtained to substantiate the forecast sales figures, and **sensitivity** and/or **simulation analysis** should be used to investigate the impact of different assumptions on net cash flows.

Other factors

Real options

There are several possible alternatives that have not been brought into the evaluation. These will add value as real options. They include the **option to sell the project as a going concern** at various points in its life (a **put option**), the **option to increase investment and market share**, and the **option to cross-sell other company products** to the project's clientele (**call options**). Although valuing these options is difficult, it is better to attempt an estimate rather than ignore their value altogether.

Lack of experience

The company has **no experience in this field of business** and may make **management mistakes** as it goes through the learning curve. For example, there may be **technological problems or legal regulations** that have not been fully explored. Also, **marketing and pricing** may prove **difficult** if existing suppliers decide to react to the **increased competition**.

Strategic considerations

Before engaging in a different market sector it is always wise to **revisit the company's overall business strategy**. A major risk is that this investment may divert management resources from the core business and cause long term problems.

10 Question with helping hand: Hasder

Text references. Chapter 4.

Top tips. The key to (a) is realising that you have to calculate:

- Expected returns using probability and return details
- Risk using the two investment portfolio model
- Coefficient of variation: Risk/return

The discussion is mainly about various aspects of portfolio theory, focusing on the advantages of diversification the view that shareholder diversification is better than company diversification, and the practical limitations to these arguments (is the company able to take advantage of opportunities to diversify, are shareholders able and willing to diversify themselves.)

For (b) you need to know what the correlation coefficient is; remember it's not given on your formula sheet. The correlation coefficient can vary between -1 and $+1$, so both portfolios show reasonably strong positive correlation.

The key to (c) is realising the purpose of the CAPM data – to enable you to calculate the required return and compare it with the expected return calculated in (a).

Easy marks. The discussion of other factors to consider offers half a dozen reasonable marks, as it contains a number of issues that will normally be important (limitations of existing data, further information required, compatibility with overall strategy).

(a) **Europe**

Growth	Probability	Return %	Expected value %
Low	0.3	7	2.1
Average	0.5	12	6.0
Rapid	0.2	21	4.2
			12.3

East Asia

Growth	Probability	Return %	Expected value %
Low	0.3	2	0.6
Average	0.5	30	15.0
Rapid	0.2	15	3.0
			18.6

UK

Growth	Probability	Return %	Expected value %
Low	0.3	6	1.8
Average	0.5	13	6.5
Rapid	0.2	17	3.4
			11.7

Expected return UK/Europe = (0.7 × 11.7) (0.3 × 12.3) = 11.88%
Expected return UK/Asia = (0.7 × 11.7) (0.3 × 18.6) = 13.77%

Use two asset portfolio equation to measure the total risk of the portfolio, where $\rho_{ab}\sigma_a\sigma_b$ = Covariance as per question

UK/Europe

$$\sigma = \sqrt{\sigma_a^2 x^2 + \sigma_b^2(1-x)^2 + 2x(1-x)\rho_{ab}\sigma_a\sigma_b}$$

$$= \sqrt{4.03^2 0.7^2 + 4.86^2 0.3^2 + 2(0.7)(0.3)17.89}$$

$$= 4.19$$

UK/East Asia

$$\sigma = \sqrt{\sigma_a^2 x^2 + \sigma_b^2(1-x)^2 + 2x(1-x)\rho_{ab}\sigma_a\sigma_b}$$

$$= \sqrt{4.03^2 0.7^2 + 12.26^2 0.3^2 + 2(0.7)(0.3)31.98}$$

$$= 5.91$$

Risk and return

	Portfolio return	Portfolio risk	Coefficient of variation
UK alone	11.70	4.03	0.34
UK/Europe	11.88	4.19	0.35
UK/East Asia	13.77	5.91	0.43

As risk increases, so does return. The coefficient of variation is lowest for the UK investment, indicating that that offers the best value, although other factors need to be considered, as below.

Director A

In one sense Director A may be right, and Hasder's **lack of experience in serving overseas markets** may handicap it. Nevertheless there still may be overseas investments, the risk of which would be lower than further investment in the UK.

Director B

Director B assumes that Hasder will be in a position to exploit overseas investments. If it is, some overseas investments may offer **higher returns** as well as **lower risk**. Investing in a portfolio may also offer lower risk (or risk levels within acceptable limits) for higher returns, so B is correct in assuming that there could be new opportunities from investing internationally. Risk and correlation levels may vary as different countries are at different stages of the trade cycle, and natural resources and economic policies may vary considerably.

Director C

Director C's statement that overseas investments are expensive (presumably compared by the UK) is a generalisation that often won't be true, since **costs of production** will be lower in many overseas countries than in the UK. Also if overseas investments are negatively correlated with UK investments, Hasder can reduce its systematic risk and **reduce the variability of its cash flows**. Lower risk levels may result in **lower costs of finance from finance providers**. There may however be **higher transaction** and **information costs**.

The view that shareholders can achieve **diversification** may be true in that investors can purchase investments in multinational companies, or investment trusts which include proportions of overseas investments, and can do so at **lower costs** than Hasder will incur investing overseas. However this assumes that available investments such as unit trusts are allowed to purchase in overseas markets; not all countries allow portfolio investment. Hasder may be able to invest in these countries and thus offer its shareholder 'clientele' the combination of risk and return that it requires.

Director D

Judged by potential returns, having some investments in East Asia would be a better alternative than investing in Europe. However the risk is also higher and the coefficient of variation is lower, suggesting that it offers **less value for risk**.

Director E

If 50% is invested:

Expected return UK/Asia = $(0.5 \times 11.7) (0.5 \times 18.6) = 15.15\%$

$$\text{Risk} = \sqrt{4.03^2 0.5^2 + 12.26^2 0.5^2 + 2(0.5)(0.5)31.98}$$

$$= 7.59$$

If 70% is invested:

Expected return UK/Asia = $(0.3 \times 11.7) (0.7 \times 18.6) = 16.53\%$

$$\text{Risk} = \sqrt{4.03^2 0.3^2 + 12.26^2 0.7^2 + 2(0.3)(0.7)31.98}$$

$$= 9.41$$

This underlines the discussion of Director D's views, that East Asia offers much higher potential returns, but at a much higher risk. It is only recommended if Hasder is seeking **very high returns**, as it may cause disruption to the UK operations if these are to be operated on a reduced scale.

Other factors

Data limitations

These include:

(i)   We do not know the basis on which **estimates of returns** have been **made**, or the basis on which **probabilities** have been **assigned**.

(ii)   The data looks to have been oversimplified; possibly for example the **lowest returns** if low **growth** takes place might be materially lower than expected.

(iii)   We haven't been told of **any other investments** that the company might have, or any **real options** attached to these investments.

Further information

The following would be helpful:

(i)   Market analysis, also an idea of potential competition.
(ii)   Assessment of various risks, including political and exchange risks.

Systematic risk

It may be better to assess the portfolios using systematic risk and the **capital asset pricing model**: if it is assumed that unsystematic risk can be diversified away.

Strategic factors

The **investment strategy** must be **consistent** with Hasder's overall business strategy; major investment overseas will amount to a significant change in focus. Investment overseas may only produce **significant returns in the longer-term**, which may not fit in with the demands of shareholders for dividend levels to be maintained. Also a strategy of **vertical integration** (for example buying up suppliers) may be better than the horizontal integration that is being proposed.

Finance

We are also not told how Hasder intends to finance overseas investment; availability of finance and the chance for Hasder to reduce exchange risk by taking out loans in the local overseas currency may impact on the decision.

(b)   Correlation coefficient $= \dfrac{\text{Covariance}}{\sigma_{UK}\sigma_{Europe}}$

(i)   UK/Europe $= \dfrac{17.89}{4.03 \times 4.86} = 0.91$

This indicates a high degree of positive correlation; the portfolio standard deviation is not very different from the individual standard deviations. Little risk reduction will take place if the company invests in Europe as well.

(ii)   UK/East Asia $= \dfrac{31.98}{4.03 \times 12.26} = 0.65$

Again positive correlation exists, but not as highly as between the UK and Europe. In particular the risk of investing in East Asia decreases substantially if it is part of a portfolio as indicated.

(c)   Using CAPM

$E(r_j) = r_f + [E(r_m) - rf]\beta_j$

Europe

Expected return = 12.3%

Required return = 5 + (13 − 5)0.85 = 11.8%

Europe is showing a higher return than would be required by the investment's systematic risk.

Asia

Expected return = 18.6%

Required return = 8 + (18 − 8)1.32 = 21.2%

Asia's expected return is less than would be suggested by the systematic risk.

On this basis the European investment would be recommended, the Asian investment would not be. However other strategic factors might also be important.

11 Wit and Pratney

(a) Wit and Pratney must pay today (development cost) in order to have the opportunity/option to enter into production in 3 years time. They will only choose to do this if the production option value exceeds the present value of the development cost.

Development cost

Time	Cash flow £m	DF	AV £m
0	247	1	247.0
1	247	$\dfrac{1}{1.12^1}$	220.5
2	247	$\dfrac{1}{1.12^2}$	196.9
PV of development cost			664.4

Production option

To evaluate this real call option we need to establish

S = PV of all volatile future cash flows if the project is undertaken

X = PV **at the option expiry date** of any non-volatile cash flows arising if the project is undertaken.

σ = Volatility of the returns from S

r_f = Risk – free rate

t = Time of expiry

Considering the future volatile cash flows, at todays prices the unit production cost will be £80m with a selling price at 90m (12½% margin) giving a net cash inflow at £10m per unit or £600m pa (60 units pa). These figures are exposed to an average annual inflation at 4% subject to 22% volatility.

With a cost of capital of 12% and inflation at 4% there is a real required return that can be calculated as

$1.12 = (1 + r) \times 1.04$

$(1 + r) = \dfrac{1.12}{1.04} = 1.07692$

r = 0.07692 or 7.692% pa

From the date the production commences we can view the return as a 12 year annuity at £600m to be discounted at a rate at 7.692%, ie

Time	Cash flow £m	DF	AV £m
1-12	600	$\dfrac{1}{0.07692}(1-\dfrac{1}{1.07692^{12}})$	4,595
PV of volatile production cash flows at time = 3			4,595
Discount factor to bring to time = 0			$\dfrac{1}{1.07692^3}$
PV at volatile production cash flows at time = 0 (S)			3,679

So we have

S = £3,679m

X = £3,3140m

$\sigma = 22\%$ pa

$r_f = 5.5\%$ pa

$t = 3$ years

$$d_1 = \frac{\ln\left[\dfrac{3{,}679}{3{,}140}\right] + (0.055 + 0.5 \times 0.22^2) \times 3}{0.22 \times \sqrt{3}} = 1.039$$

$d_2 = d_1 - \sigma\sqrt{t} = 1.039 - 0.22 \times \sqrt{3} = 0.658$

$N(d_1) = N(1.04) = 0.5 + 0.3508 = 0.8508$

$N(d_2) = (0.66) = 0.5 + 0.2454 = 0.7454$

$C = SN(d_1) - Xe^{-rt}N(d_2)$

$C = 3{,}679 \times 0.8508 - 3140 \times e^{-0.0555 \times 3} \times 0.7454 = £1{,}145.6m$

Conclusion

	£m
Value of developments call option	1,145.6
PV of development costs	664.4
NPV of development opportunity	481.2

Hence Wit and Pratney should proceed with the development.

(b) **Paper on managing risk arising from US $ fluctuations**

Given the significant proportion (over 50%) of anticipated sales are expected to be settled in US dollars then clearly Wit and Pratney have a **considerable exposure to fluctuations in the US $ exchange** rate. There are number of **differing options** available in order to manage the exposure to an acceptable level. The exposure to the risk presented by currency fluctuations is **usually** managed through a means of hedging.

(i) A **forward exchange contract** can be used to hedge against transaction exposure by allowing the company (Wit & Pratney) to arrange for a bank to buy or sell an agreed quantity of foreign currency at a future date, at an agreed rate.

(ii) Alternatively, the company can take out a **currency futures contract** to hedge against the risk. Once again, the currency futures contract would be for the purchase or sale of an agreed quantity of foreign currency at a future date at an agreed rate.

Thus, both forward exchange contracts and currency future contracts have the **advantage** of specifying with **certainty**, the amount and timing of all cash flows which would **allow the company to plan** accordingly. The difference between these two instruments is that the forward exchange contacts are over the counter between the buyer and seller and thus not tradeable. Therefore, in the event that the contract between the US airline and Wit and Pratney was cancelled, the **currency futures contract** would provide a greater degree of **flexibility** to Wit and Pratney.

An **alternative instrument** available for the purpose of hedging against currency risk is a **currency option**. This is an agreement involving a right, but not an obligation, to buy or sell a certain amount of currency at a stated exchange at some time in the future. The currency option involves paying a premium which is the most buyer of the option can lose. This is likely to be the most appropriate instrument to use the hedging against currency in this instance as there is a degree of uncertainty whether the production of engines will proceed given the volatility of the price of steel.

Lastly, the **final option** would be **not to hedge** against the currency risk. This is only appropriate if it was felt that the US $ was appreciating against the UK £.

12 AVT

> **Text references.** Chapter 8 for Black-Scholes; Chapter 1 for share option schemes.
>
> **Top tips.** This question illustrates how the data that you need to use in the Black-Scholes formula may be given in an exam question. Remember in (a) that decreases in time and volatility are to the detriment of the option holder as they decrease the chances of the option holder benefiting from an increase in the security price.
>
> The key issues in (b)(i) are how well remuneration is linked to controllable results and problems with the figures used for controllable results.
>
> The data given in the question indicates you can use simple discounting to adjust the value of future dividends in (b)(ii). In a more complex scenario, you may have to adjust future dividends by e-rT.
>
> You need a scientific calculator for the Black-Scholes formula. In is also known as log e and should be on your calculator.
>
> $e^{-0.06} = 1/e^{0.06}$. Again you need your calculator for this.
>
> As d_1 and d_2 are both positive, we need to add 0.5 to the value obtained from the normal distribution tables.
>
> The main Black-Scholes calculation would probably be worth 6-7 marks; you should achieve most of these marks by demonstrating clearly that you were putting the correct figures into the correct place in the formula, even if your figure slipped on your calculator when you carried out the calculation. A good conclusion would have earned you a couple more marks. The put-call parity formula is given in the exam.
>
> **Easy marks.** If you struggled with (a) learn the answer.

(a)   The value of the option depends on the following variables.

    (i)   **The price of the security**

        A decrease in the price of the security will mean that a call option becomes **less valuable.** Exercising the option will mean purchasing a security that has a lower value.

    (ii)   **The exercise price of the option**

        A decrease in the exercise price will mean that a call option becomes **more valuable**; the profit that can be made from exercising the option will have increased.

    (iii)   **Risk free rate of return**

        A decrease in the risk free rate will mean that a call option becomes **less valuable.** The purchase of an option rather than the underlying security will mean that the option holder has spare cash available which can be invested at the risk free rate of return. A decrease in that rate will mean that it becomes less worthwhile to have spare cash available, and hence to have an option rather than having to buy the underlying security.

    (iv)   **Time to expiry of the option**

        A decrease in the time of expiry will mean that a call option becomes **less valuable,** as the time premium element of the option price has been decreased.

    (v)   **Volatility of the security price**

        A decrease in volatility will mean that a call option becomes **less valuable.** A decrease in volatility will decrease the chance that the security price will be above the exercise price when the option expires.

(b)   (i)   **Advantages for the company**

        To the company's shareholders the main advantage of any employee incentive scheme should be that employees are highly **motivated** to improve their own wealth and that in doing so they also increase shareholder returns.

Basic salary plus bonus related to the pre-tax profit of the employee's department

Advantages for the company

The main advantage is that **salary costs** will automatically be **lower** in **years of poor performance**. In other words, the conversion of a fixed salary cost to a variable one lowers the company's operating risk.

Disadvantages for the company

(1) The measure is based upon **accounting profits** rather than **cash flows** and may be distorted by the **accounting policies chosen** or **manipulation** by the senior managers.

(2) Middle managers can be encouraged to take a **short-term view of profits** (eg a cost-cutting approach, minimising new investment). This may cause the share price to drop.

A basic salary plus a share option scheme

Advantages for the company

(1) Middle managers will be **motivated** to work towards the **same goal** as **shareholders**, ie maximising share values.

(2) The scheme will **not motivate a short-term outlook** unless the time to maturity is too short. From a shareholder's point of view the longer the time horizon the better, but there must be a trade-off with the manager's reduction in motivation if the time horizon is too long. A typical compromise period would be two to three years.

Disadvantages for the company

(1) Earnings will be **diluted** when the options are exercised.

(2) Middle managers may believe that their decisions will have **little effect** on the share price. This will depend on the extent of the responsibility they are given, and how much the share price is influenced by **factors other than the company's actions**.

(ii) The Black Scholes formula is:

Call price = $P_s N(d_1) - Xe^{-rT} N(d_2)$

The **share price** must be adjusted by the dividends expected to be paid during the option period discounted at the risk-free rate.

$$P_s = 610 - \frac{25}{1.06}$$
$$= 586.42$$

$$d_1 = \frac{\ln(Ps/X) + rT}{\sigma\sqrt{T}} + 0.5\,\sigma\,\sqrt{T}$$

$$= \frac{\ln(586.42/500) + 0.06(1)}{0.38 \times \sqrt{1}} + (0.5 \times 0.38 \times \sqrt{1})$$

$$= \frac{0.1594 + 0.06}{0.38} + 0.19$$
$$= 0.7674$$

$$d_2 = 0.7674 - (0.38 \times \sqrt{1})$$
$$= 0.3874$$

$$N(d_1) = 0.5 + 0.2786$$
$$= 0.7786, \text{ using interpolation}$$

$N(d_2)$ = 0.5 + 0.1507

= 0.6507, using interpolation

Call price = $(586.42 (0.7786)) - (500 \, e^{-0.06 \times 1} (0.6507))$

= 456.59 - 306.40

= 150.19

The expected option call price is 150.19p per share, giving a current option value of 5,000 × 150.19 = $7,510

This is some way above the bonuses that would have been paid over the last few years. The options are in the money and would appear to be more attractive to employees. However their attitude to **risk** will also influence their decisions, as the two schemes have different risks. The value of the Black-Scholes model is very dependent on the assumption that the **previous volatility** of the share price will **continue,** and this may not be the case.

(iii) (1) **Put options**

AVT should not grant the manager put options, allowing shares to be sold at a fixed price. A holder of a put option will benefit from the company's **share price value falling** below the exercise price of the option, and therefore has an incentive to take actions that will **decrease the company's value.**

(2) $Pp = Pc - Ps + Xe^{-rT}$

= 150.19 - 586.42 + 470.88

= 34.65c

Call options are thus **more valuable** in this situation.

13 Daylon

Text references. Chapter 8.

Top tips. An attempt was made to disguise the fact that this is a Black-Scholes question, but the giveaways are mentioning risk-free rate and variance in the context of options. Remember though that you must use the standard deviation, not the variance in the calculation. The exercise price is 5% lower than the market price as that is the protection provided, and six months is clearly the time period. Hopefully you remembered that Black-Scholes is used to value call (buy) options, and that you need to carry out the extra stage of using the put-call parity calculation which is on your formulae sheet.

Note that the square root of 169% is taken as 13%.

Key points in (b) are limitations of Black-Scholes, the limitation in terms of time period and amount of portfolio and possible alternatives.

Easy marks. (b) is reasonable, though if you found (a) a real struggle, you probably shouldn't have chosen this question.

(a) Put option on shares being offered

(i) Use Black-Scholes to calculate value of call option

(ii) Use Put-Call parity theorem to calculate value of equivalent put option

Price of call option, $P_c = P_s \, N(d_1) - Xe^{-rT} \, N(d_2)$

$$d_1 = \frac{\ln(P_s / X) + rT}{\sigma\sqrt{T}} + 0.5\sigma\sqrt{T}$$

$$d_2 = d_1 - \sigma\sqrt{T}$$

Where P_s = 360 cents

X = 360 (1 − 0.05) = 342 cents

r = 0.04

$\sigma = \sqrt{169\%}$ = 13% or 0.13

T = 0.5 (6 months)

$d_1 = \dfrac{\ln(360/342) + (0.04 \times 0.5)}{0.13\sqrt{0.5}} + 0.5 \times 0.13 \times \sqrt{0.5}$

  = 0.7756 + 0.0460

  = 0.8216

$d_2 = 0.8216 - (0.13 \times \sqrt{0.5})$

  = 0.7297

$N(d_1) = 0.5 + 0.2939 + 0.16(0.2967 - 0.2939)$

  = 0.7943

$N(d_2) = 0.5 + 0.2642 + 0.97(0.2673 - 0.2642)$

  = 0.7672

$P_0 = (360)(0.7943) - (342)(e^{-0.04 \times 0.5})(0.7672)$

  = 28.76c

Using put-call parity

$P_p = 28.76 - 360 + (342)(e^{-0.04 \times 0.5})$

  = 3.99c

Total value of shares = 5.55 million × $0.0399 = $221,445

Overcharge by bank = 250,000 − 221,445 = $28,555

The price at which the bank is willing to sell the option appears overvalued by $28,555.

(b) **Factors to be considered**

Limitations of Black-Scholes

There are a number of problems with relying on the Black-Scholes model.

(i) The assumptions may not be realistic. Examples include the assumptions that there are **no transaction costs, borrowing** is possible at the **risk-free rate** and **volatility is consistent and the same as it has been historically** over the life of the option.

(ii) The model fails to take into account tax; if gains are made, Daylon may be liable to tax.

Time period

The option is limited to six months. The managers may wish to hedge for a longer period than that, but will incur further costs of using additional hedging instruments.

Rest of portfolio

The managers may also wish to consider **hedging the rest of the investment portfolio**.

Other derivatives

Cheaper alternatives may include **stock index futures** and **collars**.

(c)   The managers would either need to hedge each individual share within the portfolio or hedge the portfolio overall.

In order to **hedge each individual share** appropriate derivatives would need to be available in the market or available on the OTC market. Though hedging each individual security separately would achieve the best hedge, the **cost** of this strategy and **availability** of hedging products would probably render it **impractical**.

The alternative would be to **use a readily available index product to hedge the portfolio overall**. Managers would need to consider the beta of the portfolio and its unsystematic risk (which cannot be hedged with index derivatives). This hedge would be much **quicker** and **cheaper** to establish, requiring just one derivatives trade, however it would leave Daylon **open to unsystematic risk**.

A third hybrid version may be worth considering. Daylon could **individually hedge securities making up more than, say, 10% of the investment portfolio, and hedge the remainder as one unit with index derivatives**. This may reduce the residual unsystematic risk exposure, though it does depend on the build-up of the portfolio.

14 Fuelit

Text references. Chapter 6 on investment basics, Chapter 7 on WACC and Chapter 8 on real options.

Top tips. In (a) ensure that you answer the question and present two separate computations of NPV. Split computations into operational cash flows, which can be handled by annuities, and specific one-off cash flows, which cannot. The discount rate should be a risk adjusted WACC for each project, in each case inflation-adjusted to real terms.

Don't be too depressed about getting aspects of the calculations wrong; instead carefully work through the answer to see why you went wrong and make sure you don't make the same mistake next time! Do also give yourself credit for the parts of the answer you got right; the marking scheme basically set down 1 mark for each correct figure.

We suggest that the easiest marks on the question are:

- Netting off the 800m revenues and costs
- The after tax demolition and redundancy costs which are given
- The t1 and t2 building costs
- The tax allowable depreciation
- The cost of debt for each option

The harder marks are for:

- The timings of cash flows
- The t4 – t28 operating cash in current terms
- The discount factor for the t28 demolition costs
- The cost of equity for each option

The best answers will have correctly calculated:

- WACC
- The real cost of capital
- The discounted cash flows

The discussion parts of the question are probably worth half the marks and you should make sure you spend enough time on these, as it should be easier to gain marks on (b) and (d) in particular than on the more difficult calculations. The assumptions discussed in (b) range from those that only affect certain figures to those that change the whole picture (political changes or a disaster). Alternative scenarios, using different assumptions, may be helpful.

> (c) indicates how uncertainty can be incorporated; the key points were understanding that risk might be different and that the discount rate should be reduced. Make sure that you have a knowledge of real options, as there may well be a discussion part at the end of a compulsory question similar to (d). As well as the options described, the option to delay investments may also be significant.
>
> **Easy marks.** The calculations listed above in (a) and particularly (b) of the written parts. (b) requires you to look closely at your assumptions, and also think about wider issues that might affect strategy (stakeholder interests for example).

(a) **NPV of the two investments**

We need to calculate a WACC and convert it to a real cost of capital to discount the real cash flows of the investments.

Gas

$$Ke = r_f + [E(r_m) - r_f] B_j$$
$$= 4.5 + [14 - 4.5]\, 0.7$$
$$= 11.15\%$$

$$Kd = 8.5\,(1 - 0.3)$$
$$= 5.95\%$$

$$WACC = (\text{Equity weighting} \times Ke) + (\text{Debt weighting} \times Kd)$$
$$= (0.65 \times 11.15) + (0.35 \times 5.95)$$
$$= 9.33\%$$

As WACC is a nominal rate, convert to real rate.

$$\text{Real rate} = \frac{(1 + \text{nominal rate})}{(1 + \text{inflation rate})} - 1$$

$$= \frac{1.0933}{1.03} - 1$$

$$= 6.15\%,\ \text{say } 6\%$$

Nuclear

$$Ke = 4.5 + (14 - 4.5)\, 1.4$$
$$= 17.8\%$$

$$Kd = 10\,(1 - 0.3)$$
$$= 7\%$$

$$WACC = (0.4 \times 17.8) + (0.6 \times 7)$$
$$= 11.32\%$$

$$\text{Real rate} = \frac{1.1132}{1.03} - 1$$

$$= 8.08\%,\ \text{say } 8\%$$

Discounted cash flow estimates: Gas

Annual operating cash flows Years	First 10 years 4–13	Last 15 years 14–28
	£m	
Annual revenues	800.000	
Annual costs		
Labour	75.000	
Gas purchases	500.000	As for years 4–13
Sales and marketing expenses	40.000	
Customer relations	5.000	
Other cash outlays	5.000	
	625.000	
Incremental taxable	175.000	
Tax at 30%	52.500	
After tax cash flows	122.500	
Tax credit on depreciation	18.000	
Incremental cash flow	140.500	122.500
Annuity factors at 6%		
Years 4-13		
(8.853 – 2.673)	6.180	
Years 14-28		
(13.406** – 8.853)		4.553
Present value	868.300	557.700

* Tax credit on building costs depreciation $600 \times 10\% \times 30\% = \$18m$.

** Using formula $\dfrac{1-(1+r)^{-n}}{r}$ for annuity 1-28.

Other cash flows

Year	1	2	3	4	28
After tax redundancy costs (£m)				4	
Building costs (2 instalments) (£m)	300	300			
After tax demolition of coal fired station (£m)			10		
After tax demolition of gas plant (£m)					25
6% factors	0.943	0.890	0.840	0.792	0.196
Present value of costs (£m)	282.9	267.0	8.4	3.2	4.9

Total net present value = 868.3 + 557.7 − (282.9 + 267.0 + 8.4 + 3.2 + 4.9)

= £ 859.6 million

Note: Interest is ignored from annual cost estimates because it (and the tax relief it attracts) is included in the after tax discount rate.

Discounted cash flow estimates: Nuclear power

Annual operating cash flows	First 10 years	Last 15 years
Years	4–13	14–28
	£m	£m
Annual revenues	800.000	
Annual costs		
Labour	20.000	
Nuclear fuel purchases	10.000	as for years 4–13
Sales and marketing expenses	40.000	
Customer relations	20.000	
Other cash outlays	25.000	
	115.000	
Incremental taxable cash flows	685.000	
Tax at 30%	205.500	
After tax cash flows	479.500	479.500
Tax credit on depreciation	99.000	
Incremental cash flow	578.500	479.500
Annuity factors at 8%		
Years 4-13		
(7.904 – 2.577)	5.327	
Years 14-28		
(11.051** – 7.904)		3.147
Present value	3,081.700	1,509.000

* Tax credit on building costs depreciation
   3,300 × 10% × 30% = £99m
** Using annuity formula

Other cash flows

Year	1	2	3	4	28
After tax redundancy costs (£m)				36	
Building costs (2 installments) (£m)	1,650	1,650			
After tax demolition of coal fired station(£m)			10		
After tax decommissioning of nuclear plant(£m)					1,000
8% factors	0.926	0.857	0.794	0.735	0.116
Present value of costs (£m)	1,527.9	1,414.1	7.9	26.5	116.0

Total net present value = 3,081.7 + 1,509.0 – (1,527.9 + 1,414.1 + 7.9 + 26.5 + 116.0)
                  = **£1,498.3 million**

Note: If the lowest estimate of nuclear plant decommissioning cost was used, the net present value would be £1,558 million.

Conclusion

On the basis of net present values applied to the estimates given, the nuclear plant should be chosen.

(b)   The most significant factors to affect the decision which have not been taken into account above are:

(i)   **Social and political acceptability of more nuclear powered station**

If **public opinion** is heavily **against** nuclear power, the government is unlikely to risk its political majority by deciding in favour of it. Even if a vocal minority is the only opposition, construction could be severely delayed by demonstrations and sabotaging actions. **Social and political intelligence** is therefore vital information.

(ii)   **Risk of a rapid change in political acceptability of nuclear plants**

Future political acceptability may be influenced by a number of events. For example a number of **small leakages** could cause a nuclear plant to abandoned at any time during its life because of a fall in public acceptability. Threat of **terrorist action** may also cause political opinion to change. **Risk scenarios** need to be constructed and **contingency plans** devised.

(iii)   **Risk of a large-scale nuclear accident or gas explosion**

Such risks are not easily analysed by expected values and NPV computations, but both events have actually happened in the past. Information needs to be collected to **model** these events as **scenarios**.

(iv)   **Technical information**

It would be useful to evaluate the **technical information** underlying the projected construction and operation of the plants to ensure that best practice, particularly in **safety testing,** is envisaged and that costs are realistic to achieve the necessary quality. This may indicate how likely delays are during construction. **Industry information** on current developments would aid an evaluation of **how long** the stations would be **in operation**, and the consequences if technology changes. It might also enable a narrower estimate of the rage of **decommissioning costs** to be made.

(v)   **Economic information**

More details and accurate estimates could be obtained on, for example, expected future **demand** for power, annual **inflation** rate estimates (both in general and for individual cost items), and **interest rate movements.** The likelihood of the United Kingdom **joining the euro currency zone** is also significant. If the UK does not join the euro zone in the near future, there may be **uncertainties** attached to the **cost of debt**, which is denominated in euros for both projects. Based on existing predictions of inflation levels, the **euro** is likely to **depreciate** against the pound, making the cost of debt cheaper.

(vi)   **Fiscal changes**

Expected **future tax rates** and **capital allowances** may have a significant impact, including the possibility of 'green' taxes or constraints on polluting industries and likely treatment of gas and nuclear power under these taxes.

(vii)   **CAPM implications**

It would be useful to get more information about the **systematic risk** of the power industry, and how **different gearing levels** would affect the assessment of other projects and the company's overall valuation.

(viii) **The value of real options associated with each project**

As discussed in part (d) below, these are likely to be **higher** for the gas fuelled power station.

On the basis however of the estimates made, the NPV of the nuclear power alternative is so much higher than the gas alternative that further information on the accuracy of other general cash flow estimates is unlikely to change the decision.

(c) **Highest cost estimate**

Perhaps the simplest way of dealing with the range of options available is to use the **highest cost estimate.**

Discount rate

A further way of dealing with the high uncertainty attached to the cost of decommissioning is to **decrease the discount rate** for the cost figure used.

Risk free rates

An alternative method of handling risk is to **discount at the risk free rate** and to **convert all cash forecasts to certainty-equivalents**. The certainty-equivalent for this cost would be **higher** than the expected value.

(d)   **Real options**

An option is a choice which need only be exercised if it is to the investor's advantage. A '**real option**' is such a **choice or opportunity** which exists because of a capital investment. The choice may involve being able to change plans once the project is underway. The opportunity also may not have been envisaged when the original plans were made, but may arise later on.

Options associated with the project

Options associated with the projects are in the main more valuable for the gas fuelled than for the nuclear power project. They include the following:

(i)   **The option to abandon the project early**

This may be needed for a variety of reasons, for example because of falling demand or because of the emergence of a new technology. High decommissioning costs make this a problem for the nuclear powered project.

(ii)   **The option to expand if demand increases**

This is easier for gas because of the lower investment costs.

(iii)   **The option to switch power source in the future**

This is more valuable for gas, because the technology could be adapted for other fossil fuels, such as oil. Nuclear power technology has no easy power source alternatives.

The significance of these options is that they **add value** to the project and should be taken into account in the **investment appraisal**. Although the valuation is difficult, even a rough estimate is better than no estimate at all. On this basis, the gas fuelled project is likely to be relatively more valuable than shown in the original calculations.

15 Bioplasm

> **Text references.** Chapter 8.
>
> **Top tips.** It is fairly clear how most of the data given in the question relates to the Black-Scholes model. The 350 – 500 prices must be the share values as these are the expected present values of future returns. The 400 is the exercise price as the company is deciding whether or not to spend the money. Remember also that you need to use the standard deviation, not the variance, and thus you have to calculate the square root of the variance.
>
> The calculations in this question are time-pressured, partly because of the complications of having to calculate two call prices and having to adjust the expected present value.
>
> **Easy marks.** The discussion on possible problems includes many important features including variations in forecasts, dependence of results on time period, rate of interest and variance assumed.

(a) $P_s = 350\, e^{(-0.067)(15)} = £128$

or $= 500\, e^{(-0.067)(15)} = £183$

$X = 400$
$r = 5\%$
$T = 15$ years
$\sigma = \sqrt{0.185} = 0.430$

(i)   Ps = 128

Calculate d_1

$$d_1 = \frac{\ln(P_s/X) + rT}{\sigma\sqrt{T}} + 0.5\sigma\sqrt{T}$$

$$d_1 = \frac{\ln(128/400) + 0.05(15)}{0.43\sqrt{15}} + 0.5(0.43)\sqrt{15}$$

$$= -0.234 + 0.833$$
$$= 0.599$$

Calculate $N(d_1)$

$$N(d_1) = 0.5 + 0.2224 + 0.9(0.2257 - 0.2224)$$
$$= 0.7254$$

Calculate d_2

$$d_2 = d_1 - \sigma\sqrt{T}$$

$$d_2 = 0.599 - 0.43\sqrt{15}$$
$$= -1.066$$

Calculate $N(d_2)$

$$N(d_2) = 0.5 - 0.3554 - 0.6(0.3577 - 0.3554)$$
$$= 0.1432$$

$$P_c = P_s N(d_1) - Xe^{-rT} N(d_2)$$
$$= 128(0.7254) - 400\, e^{(-0.05)(15)}\, 0.1432$$
$$= £66 \text{ million}$$

(ii)   Ps = 183

Calculate d_1

$$d_1 = \frac{\ln(P_s/X) + rT}{\sigma\sqrt{T}} + 0.5\sigma\sqrt{T}$$

$$d_1 = \frac{\ln(183/400) + 0.05(15)}{0.43\sqrt{15}} + 0.5(0.43)\sqrt{15}$$

$$= -0.019 + 0.833$$
$$= 0.814$$

Calculate $N(d_1)$

$$N(d_1) = 0.5 + 0.2910 + 0.4(0.2939 - 0.2910)$$
$$= 0.7922$$

Calculate d_2

$$d_2 = d_1 - \sigma\sqrt{T}$$

$$d_2 = 0.814 - 0.43\sqrt{15}$$
$$= -0.851$$

Calculate $N(d_2)$

$$N(d_2) = 0.5 - 0.3023 - 0.1[0.3051 - 0.3023]$$
$$= 0.1974$$

$$P_c = P_s N(d_1) - Xe^{-rT} N(d_2)$$
$$= 183\ (0.7922) - 400\ e^{(-0.05)\ (15)}\ 0.1974$$
$$= £108\ \text{million}$$

In both cases the value of the option exceeds the value of the net present value estimates.

For net present value of £350 million, the extra expenditure of £400 million will give a revised negative net present value of £50 million, compared with a call option value of £66 million.

For net present value of £500 million, the extra expenditure will give a revised net present value of £100 million compared with the call option value of £108 million.

On the figures therefore the company **should develop the patent, whatever the expected present value**

Further factors to consider

The main drawback with the financial analysis is that it depends on potentially unreliable estimates.

(1)   The **net present value forecasts** are subject to **wide variation**. They may also depend upon factors unknown at present, but which may impact significantly over time, for example **competitors** developing rival products.

(2)   The net present value forecasts depend upon the **discount rate chosen**.

(3)   The net present value forecasts **only cover a 15 year period**, and there may be significant returns after that period.

(4)   The estimated development costs of £400 million may be subject to a **considerable margin of error**, particularly if new techniques or new technology are needed to develop the drug.

(5)   The Black-Scholes model is dependent upon the **variance**, and this again may be difficult to estimate as this is a new product and may not be comparable with those developed by other companies. In addition the variance may not remain constant over time.

(6)   Arguably as the drug could be developed at any time, the option is an **American option** whereas the Black-Scholes model is designed to value **European options**.

Because of these uncertainties, Bioplasm should consider other factors including the **strategic importance** of developing the drug, before coming to a final decision.

(b)   In many project evaluation situations, the firm has one or more options to make strategic changes to the project during its life. These **strategic options** which are known as **real options** are typically ignored in standard discounted cash flow analysis where a single expected present value is computed. These real options, however, can **significantly increase the value of a project by eliminating unfavourable outcomes**.

Real options in capital projects requires a further decision being made sometime in the future, whether to **continue in the same direction** (and make a follow-on investment) or to **change direction** (make a start on a project the company has previously been waiting to start) or to **abandon** a project that has been previously started.

Bioplasm has a number of strategic decisions which it needs to consider. From the calculations in part (a) it is clear that the **option to abandon is not viable** since the value of the call option exceeds the value of the net present value. Thus, Bioplasm must decide whether it is to delay the development of the drug to a future date or whether it intends to develop the drug now.

The **Black Scholes** model can be used to estimate the value of real option. However, there are certain differences between the application of the Black Scholes model to real options. The **main practical problem** is the **estimation of volatility**. As the underlying asset is not traded, it is very difficult to establish the volatility of the value. The main method to overcome this problem is to use simulation methods to estimate the volatility.

The **value of a real option can be determined by reference** to:

- The present value of the future benefit streams of the follow-on project
- The initial cost of the follow-on project
- The time within which the option must be exercised
- The variability of expected project returns
- The risk rate of interest.

16 Remuneration package

Text references. Chapter 1 discusses aligning directors' and company interests: the call option calculation is covered in Chapter 8.

Top tips. The key to (a) is discussing how well the different proposals link salary with controllable company success, and what the consequences of management manipulation will be.

(b) is a good illustration of the information you'll be given when you're expected to use the put-call parity formula. Remember as the manager will have the option to **buy** shares, he'll be given **call** options; you aren't given the call price, but are given the put price and other information (exercise and share prices, time and risk-free rate) to help you calculate the call price. Remember that advertising counts as investment expenditure and is added back to profit, but taken into account when calculating capital employed. The adjustment you make for advertising needn't necessarily be three years' worth.

Easy marks. Hopefully you spotted that some of the measures in (a) were not really linked with cash flow and profitability at all.

(a) **Relative merits of the four suggestions**

(i) **Above average salary**

The purpose of offering a salary 20% above the competition is to **attract ambitious applicants** for the job who have **good track records** with existing companies in the sector. It may also **attract applicants from other higher earning sectors** who may bring expertise, ability and fresh ideas. However if the new managing director is likely to be chosen from within the company's ranks there is **little point** in paying an **above average salary** before he or she has proven ability at the job. There is **no conclusive evidence** that a high salary by itself will **motivate the managing director**. At its worst, it might actually motivate him or her to fail, thus achieving a high severance pay-off. There might also be a general escalation of management salaries within the firm, causing increased management costs and dissatisfaction among employees, shareholders and customers.

(ii) **Salary linked to revenue**

This is not recommended because it would be easy for the managing director to **earn a higher salary** while **reducing company profitability**. A salary linked to revenue can motivate the managing director to introduce strategies which are **expansionary** but **not profitable**, for example reducing product prices to increase sales at the expense of profit margins, or acquiring new businesses at prices which are too high to recover the investment cost. If salary is to be linked to accounting results, some version of profitability must be included in the formula.

(iii) **Share options**

Share options are a popular way of **motivating key management staff**. Their advantage is that they motivate managers to think of the shareholders' viewpoint when making decisions and should thus **reward wealth creation** rather than management empire building. They should also discourage strategies that increase short term profitability only, or achieve profitability at the expense of taking undue risks.

Problems with share options

The problem with rewards based on share options prices is that **share prices** are only **partially dependent on company performance**. The **changes to the general state** of the **economy** and **stock market** may in any given year **outweigh the company's specific successes or failures**, resulting in either unjustified rewards being given to the managing director, or a lack of rewards when credit is due. Rewards which are based on share price performance compared with the sector average are probably a fairer method.

It is also **difficult** to **evaluate how many share options** should be given to the managing director and over **what period** the **exercise right** should be allowed. Quite often large companies have been over-generous in the packages they have offered, prompting discussion that remuneration committees do not understand option values.

(iv) **Bonus based on EVA™**

Economic Value Added (EVA™) is a version of the measure that is called **residual income** in **management accounting** textbooks. The expected operating profit (capital employed × cost of capital) is subtracted from actual operating profit to determine the **excess operating profit**, or EVA™. This type of measure rewards an **absolute increase in profitability** rather than achieving a high *rate* of return, which can be achieved by shrinking the company down to its most profitable components. The EVA™ method also identifies cash flows which are **in reality investment** but which are usually treated as expenses (eg advertising).

Problems with EVA™

However like all methods of this type it is still subject to common problems, for example:

(i) If capital employed is low, as for example in a service company, the **EVA™** is high and may be **overstated**.

(ii) It is **vulnerable to short term manipulation** by management at the expense of longer-term wealth creation (eg not replacing written down non-current assets).

If the remuneration scheme is to be based on EVA™, it would probably be better to consider the increase in EVA™ that the new managing director achieves, rather than the absolute EVA™.

(b) **Cost of the share option scheme**

The suggestion is to offer the managing director call options at an exercise price 25% below current market price, ie 75% × 120p = 90p.

A one year put option on the company's shares costs 35 pence. We must assume in the absence of information that the exercise price for the put option is also 90p.

The value of the managing director's options can be estimated using the put-call parity formula, $P^P = P^C - P^S + Xe^{-rT}$

Thus $P^C = P^P + P^S - Xe^{-rT}$
$= 35 + 120 - [90 \times 2.718^{-(0.04)(1)}]$
$= 35 + 120 - [90 \times 0.9607]$
$= 68.5$ pence

The value of 3 million call options would therefore be $2.055 million.

This is a very generous price and is in fact misguided. The **exercise price of the options** should be set at a **price above current market price**, not below it, so that when the options are issued they have only a **small value** and encourage the managing director to **work to improve the share price** to above the exercise price.

The **one year period** for the option is also too short to encourage long term strategies. A three to five year period would be better.

Cost of the EVA™ scheme

To estimate EVA™ it is first necessary to compute net operating profit after tax (NOPAT) by adding back interest and advertising costs and recalculating the tax charge, as follows:

	$m
Profit before tax	89.0
Add back:	
Advertising	10.0
Interest	26.0
	125.0
Taxation (30%)	37.5
NOPAT	87.5

Capital employed at the **start of the year** is $420 million. This is adjusted by adding three years worth (say) of advertising investment: $420m + ($10m × 3) = $450 million.

The **expected NOPAT** for the company would be capital employed × WACC = $450m × 9.5% = $42.75m

Thus the EVA™ is the excess NOPAT: $87.5m – $42.75m = $44.75 m.

If the managing director receives 1.5% of this, it amounts to approximately $670,000 per annum. As discussed above, the scheme would be better linked to the increase in EVA™ after the new managing director has been appointed.

(c)   The fact that managers of a company are not necessarily the owners of the company leaves open the possibility that managers may not act in the interests of the owners of the company.

Possible **areas of conflict** are:

(i)   The short term drive to cut costs and increase profits thereby **increasing share price and hence managerial reward at the expense of the long-term investment** which would jeopardise the long-term prospects of the company.

(ii)   Managers may pursue policies which **seek to maximise benefits to themselves** rather than to shareholders. An example of one such policy is to focus on the sales of a company but not on its profits.

(iii)   Managers may not be acting in the interests of the shareholders when evaluating takeovers or mergers. Thus, their decision may be to **protect their own interests** rather than to maximise shareholder wealth.

(iv)   The pursuit of short-term cost reduction may lead to the company taking **decisions which adversely affect its relationship with stakeholders**. Possible examples are making employees redundant or reducing the product lines available to customers etc. In the long term the affected stakeholders will move to other companies and thereby impact the long term performance of the company.

There are a number of **strategies** which are available for **resolution of conflict** between shareholders and managers. All such strategies seek to promote **goal congruence**. Goal congruence is accordance between the objectives of agents acting within an organisation and the objectives of the organisation as a whole.

Goal congruence may be better achieved by devising **remuneration strategies** which are related to the overall profitability of the company or its share price. Examples of such incentives are profit related bonuses, employee share schemes or executive share option plans.

An alternative approach is attempt to monitor managers' behaviour through the adoption of a **corporate framework of decision making that restricts the powers of managers** and increases the role of independent external parties in the monitoring of their duties. This could be achieved by establishing management audit procedures or by introducing additional reporting requirements.

17 Wickern

> **Text references.** Chapter 6.
>
> **Top tips.** In questions like (a) don't be afraid to speculate why changes have occurred; provided your suggestions are intelligent, you can gain considerable credit and give yourself an advantage over most candidates, as the examiner's report emphasises.
>
> Remember in (b) it is the future cash flows we are interested in; the cash flows from 20X2 – 20X5 are not relevant. In (a) no extra tax was forecast to be payable in the UK, as Danish tax rates were above UK tax rates, but in (b) extra tax will be payable as Danish tax rates have fallen.

(a)   **Expected values**

	20X1 £m	20X2 £m	20X3 £m	20X4 £m	20X5 £m	20X6 £m	20X7 £m	20X8 £m	20X9 £m
Remitted to the UK		1.72	2.12	2.04	2.15	2.47	2.39	2.49	2.60
Initial investment	(8.00)								
Realisable value (W1)									10.53
Net cash flows	(8.00)	1.72	2.12	2.04	2.15	2.47	2.39	2.49	13.13
Discount factors (W2)	1.000	0.862	0.743	0.641	0.552	0.476	0.410	0.354	0.305
Present values	(8.00)	1.48	1.58	1.31	1.19	1.18	0.98	0.88	4.00

Expected net present value = £4.6 million

Workings

1   **Realisable value**

$$\text{Realisable value} = \frac{79}{7.5}$$

$$= 10.53$$

2   **Discount factors**

Using $Ke = r_f + [r_m - r_f] J_j$

$Ke = 7 + (15 - 7)\ 1.125$

$= 16\%$

Actual values

	20X2 £m	20X3 £m	20X4 £m	20X5 £m
Remitted to the UK	0.44	0.56	0.41	0.68
Net cash flows	0.44	0.56	0.41	0.68
Discount factors	0.862	0.743	0.641	0.552
Present values	0.38	0.42	0.26	0.38

Actual net present value = £1.44 million

Comparison of actual and expected performance

Difference = 1.48 + 1.58 + 1.31 + 1.19 – 1.44

= £4.12 million

Actual performance was £4.12 million worse than predicted at the opening of the rink. This also compares with a total net present value for the eight years of the project of £4.6 million.

Reasons for adverse performance

(i)   **Income from ice-skating**

Income from ice-skating was below expectations in all four years, total actual income for the four years being Kr47.2 million compared with projected income of Kr58.4 million. As income figures appear to have stabilised over the last three years at Kr12.0 million, projected income for the next four years of Kr13.8 million (a 15% increase) appears to be **optimistic**. A **major marketing and sales promotion** will be needed if income is to reach projections over the next four years.

(ii) **Income from ice-hockey matches**

Income from ice-hockey matches was also below expectations for each of the four years, Kr47.9 million in total compared with expectations of Kr75 million. Again an **advertising** campaign might help. If the shortfall is due to a lack of success by the team using the rink, and Wickern has any influence over the running of the team, perhaps Wickern might to be able to engineer a **change in the team management.** However the shortfall could also be due to factors largely beyond Wickern's control, for example attendance figures for the sport as a whole being less than expected over the period.

(iii) **Income from concerts**

Except in the last year, income from concerts was lower than expectations, Kr 30.7 million compared with expected income for the period of Kr40.5 million. In addition actual costs at Kr13.5 million are more than double projected costs of Kr6 million. As well as looking at the **promotion** of concerts, Wickern must analyse the reasons for **variances**, and take action to **control costs**.

(iv) **General overheads**

These were higher than expected, actual costs for the four years of Kr55.4 million exceeding expected costs of Kr49.4 million. Again action must be taken to **control costs**, particularly as they exceed budget despite activity being lower than budget.

(v) **Exchange rates**

Remittances to the UK were affected by the **depreciation of the kroner** against the £. Had income and costs been as forecast, remittances to the UK over the four years would have been £6.39 million compared with expected remittances of £8.03 million. Wickern should assess its methods for **forecasting exchange rate differences** to see if the original forecasts were over-optimistic.

(b)   To: Board
        From: Accountant
        Date: 23 January 20X6
        Subject: **Possible sale of ice-rink**

This report evaluates the financial consequences of various options for the future of the ice-rink.

Exchange rates

In order to evaluate these options, we need to use the purchasing power parity equation, $\dfrac{i_f - i_{uk}}{1 + i_{uk}}$ or

$\dfrac{1 + i_f}{1 + i_{uk}} - 1$) to predict future exchange rates.

$$\text{Change in rates} = \frac{0.05 - 0.02}{1.02} \text{ or } \left(\frac{1.05}{1.02} - 1\right)$$

$$= 2.94\%$$

This represents an annual depreciation of the kroner against the £.

(i) **Continuing operations and disposal in 20X9**

	20X6	20X7	20X8	20X9
Kr cash flows				
Remittable cash flows (Krm)	10.5	10.5	10.5	10.5
(42.0 – 37.4 – 1.3 + 7.2)				
Exchange rate (× 1.0294 each year) (Krm)	11.41	11.75	12.10	12.45
£ cash flows				
Remittable cash flows	0.92	0.89	0.87	0.84
Tax (1.5%) (£m)	(0.01)	(0.01)	(0.01)	(0.01)
Net cash flows (£m)	0.91	0.88	0.86	0.83
Discount factors 13% (W)	0.885	0.783	0.693	0.613
Present values (£m)	0.81	0.69	0.60	0.51

Net present value of operations = £2.61 million

Working

$$K_e = 6 + (13.5 - 6)\,0.95$$
$$= 13.13\%, \text{ say } 13\%$$

Realisable value in 20X9 = 79/12.45 × 0.613
$$= £3.89 \text{ million}$$

NPV if operations continued to 20X9 = 2.61 + 3.89
$$= £6.5 \text{ million}$$

(ii) **Continuing operations beyond 20X9**

	20X9	20Y0–Y9	20Y0–Y9
Investment (Krm)	(328.000)		
Cash flows (Krm)		50.000	65.000
Discount factor Yr 4, 13%	0.613		
Annuity factor, Yrs 5–4, 13% *		3.328	3.328
Present value (Krm)	(201.060)	166.400	216.320
20X9 forecast exchange rate	12.450	12.450	12.450
Present value £m	(16.150)	13.370	17.380

* Annuity factor yrs 5 – 14 = Annuity factor yrs 1 – 14 – Annuity factor yrs 1 – 4
$$= 6.302 - 2.974$$
$$= 3.328$$

Cash flows Kr50 million, net present value = 2.61 – 16.15 + 13.37
$$= £(0.17 \text{ million})$$

Cash flows Kr65 million, net present value = 2.61 – 16.15 + 17.38
$$= £3.84 \text{ million}$$

(iii) **Immediate disposal**

Proceeds = 100/11.09
$$= £9.02 \text{ million}$$

Conclusion

On the basis of the calculations above, immediate disposal offers the highest net present value. However this conclusion is dependent on the assumptions:

(i) That the business could not be sold as a **going concern** for a higher value than site value in 20X9.

(ii) Cash flows will be **constant** for the ten years after 20X9, and will not continue beyond then, and that **realisable value** at the end of that period will be 0.

18 Boxless

Text references. Chapters 9, 24.

Top tips. Detail can help you score well in (a), not just commenting that a tax haven reduces tax, but how it can be used (to avoid certain taxes eg capital gains and reduce other taxes such as withholding taxes).

Planning a proforma such as (b) is helpful as the best format will depend on how the tax is charged. The key stages are

- Calculating the income on which the three taxes (local corporate, withholding and UK income) are charged
- Calculating what these tax liabilities are
- As the last stage of the proforma calculating how much foreign tax can be set off against the UK tax
- Finally, adding the three tax liabilities

The comment at the end should earn you 1-2 marks.

Easy marks. You need good understanding of how transfer pricing works to answer both parts of this question well.

(a)   **Inability to offset tax burden**

Taxable income coming from several overseas subsidiaries is treated separately for UK tax purposes. It is likely that for subsidiaries in high tax countries the **local tax suffered** is too high to be **fully relieved** against the UK corporate tax liability, and also cannot be offset against UK tax liabilities of other foreign subsidiaries.

Benefits of tax haven

If a **tax haven holding company is used**, and all remittances to UK are made from this company, the **income is pooled and treated** as if it all comes from this single source. This can allow the total of foreign tax paid to be offset against the total UK tax liability of the tax haven holding company. This result is often that foreign tax credits are more **effectively used**.

In addition the use of tax haven may **enable capital gains to escape tax free** and a **reduction in withholding** tax on dividends if they are paid by the tax haven holding company. It is also often more **tax efficient** to channel cash from cash-rich subsidiaries to those requiring finance via a tax haven, rather than via the parent company. The use of tax havens may mean that the company's affairs may be less transparent as most tax havens have tough privacy laws and often bank secrecy arrangements.

Drawbacks of tax haven

There may be risks to post tax earnings levels as governments seek to close tax loopholes affecting tax havens. In addition, there are some annual incorporation costs involved in registering a tax haven. Finally, a political climate that is becoming more unfavourable to tax avoidance, and scandals involving companies registered in tax havens, may mean that there is a degree of risk to reputation involved in using them.

(b) (i) **Existing tax position**

	Annovia £'000	Carden £'000	Sporoon £'000	Total £'000
Taxable income (as given)	100.0	100	100.0	300.0
Local corporate income tax (40%/25%/20%) (1)	40.0	25	20.0	85.0
After-tax income	60.0	75	80.0	215.0
Dividend remitted to UK (70%/40%/80%)	42.0	30	64.0	136.0
Withholding tax on dividend (10%/–/5%) (2)	4·2	–	3·2	7.4
Dividend remitted to UK	42.0	30	64.0	136.0
Grossed up for UK tax purposes:				
× 100/(100 – local corporate tax rate):	70.0	40	80.0	190.0
UK tax liability (30%)	21.0	12	24.0	57.0
Foreign tax offset:				
70%/40%/80% of local corporate tax charge	28.0	10	16.0	54.0
Withholding tax	4.2	0	3.2	7.4
Total	32.2	10	19.2	61.4
Offset against UK tax liability	21.0 (max)	10	19.2	50.2
UK tax payable (3)	–	2	4.8	6.8
Total tax payable (1) + (2) + (3)	44.2	27	28.0	99.2

Total taxation is £99,200.

UK government taxes total income

	Annovia £'000	Cardenda £'000	Sporoon £'000	Total £'000
Income	100.0	100	100.0	300.0
Local corporate income tax (1)	40.0	25	20.0	85.0
Available for distribution	60.0	75	80.0	215.0
Dividend remitted to UK	42.0	30	64.0	136.0
Withholding tax on dividend (2)	4·2	–	3·2	7.4
Income for UK tax purposes	100.0	100	100.0	300.0
UK tax liability (30%)	30.0	30	30.0	90.0
Foreign tax offset: corporate tax	40.0	25	20.0	85.0
withholding tax	4.2	–	3.2	7.4
Total	44.2	25	23.2	92.4
Offset against UK tax liability	30.0 (max)	25	23.2	78.2
UK tax payable (3)	–	5	6.8	11.8
Total tax payable (1) + (2) + (3)	44.2	30	30.0	104.2

Total taxation is £104,200, an increase of £5,000.

(ii) **Using a tax haven holding company**

Figures are extracted from the total columns above.

	Existing tax position £'000	Total income taxed £'000
Taxable income	300.0	300.0
Local corporate income tax (1)	85.0	85.0
Total dividend to UK from holding company	136.0	136.0
Withholding tax (2)	7.4	7.4
Grossed up income for UK tax purposes	190.0	300.0
UK tax liability (30%)	57.0	90.0
Foreign tax offset:		
[92.4 but max 57; 92.4 but max 90]	57.0 (max)	90.0 (max)
UK tax payable (3)	–	–
Total taxation	92.4	92·4

Total tax payable in both cases is £92,400.

The tax haven holding company enables Boxless plc to **offset all the foreign tax** against UK tax payable. Without the tax haven, tax credits available from Annovia are too high to be fully usable against UK tax.

(c) **Multinational companies investing or trading aboard** may **risk** a **high tax burden** through suffering local taxes that are particularly heavy on foreign investors or through tariffs and customs charges.

In many instances a multinational will establish a **branch** and utilise its initial losses against other profits and then turn the branch into a subsidiary when it starts making profits.

In some cases, there may be a risk that the company's profits may be **taxed twice**, once in the country in which they are earned, the other in the company's country of residence. However, most countries give **double taxation relief**, a tax credit for taxes on income paid to the host country to prevent this. In addition, in many countries the remitted profits of a subsidiary will be taxed at a higher rate than those of a branch, as profits paid in the form of dividends are likely to be subject to withholding tax. However the double tax treaty existing between most countries means that foreign tax credits are available for withholding taxes on sums paid to other countries as dividends, interest and royalties.

19 Intergrand

Top tips. The main calculation is the adjusted present value – debt calculation. Although the free cash flows is the most significant working, and the additional tax is dependent on the calculations of the free cash flows, it is better exam technique to work out the easier figures first before attempting the free cash flow calculations to make sure you get the marks for these.

The publicity costs are discounted at Intergrand's WACC because they are quoted at an equivalent figure for Intergrand.

You have to assume that the exchange rate in 20X6 applies in perpetuity.

The research is a sunk cost and should thus be excluded from the calculation.

There are several possible ways of calculating the tax shield on debt acquired. You can simply calculate the market value x tax relief, and assume that the loans similar to the current bonds will be available to infinity. More prudently, you can take the question at face value and assume that the tax relief on the bonds will be available until 20X9 when the bonds are redeemed, and that further bonds won't be issued. We have discounted the tax relief at the risk-free rate, but it would also be acceptable (though involve more calculations) to discount it at the cost of debt, calculating the cost of debt by an IRR calculation or using the interest yield.

It is definitely easier to round the base case cost of capital to the nearest whole number and thus be able to make use of discount tables.

The sale of assets and the extra investment both relate to Oberberg, so they should be discounted at its cost of capital, but they do not form part of the free cash flows. The interest should also be excluded from the free cash flows but the synergies should be included. The free cash flows and additional tax post 20X6 can be found using the dividend valuation model formula, but don't forget to discount these because they start from 20X7 (year 5).

Easy marks. Despite all the complications in the calculations, you can easily score marks on the discussion. Most of the discussion points will be raised in other investment appraisals.

Adjusted present value of investment

	Working	Euro m
Redundancy		(5.0)
Publicity	1	7.0
Lost exports	2	(4.3)
Tax shield	3	9.7
Sale of assets	5	7.3
Investment for expansion	6	(6.9)
Free cash flows	7	171.2
Additional tax	8	(10.5)
Adjusted present value		168.5
Value of outstanding loans (30 + ((1230/1000) × 18)		(52.1)
Value of Oberberg		116.4

Using free cash flows and adjusted present value, the value of Oberberg is €116.3 million which suggests an offer of €115 million is reasonable, although the estimate is subject to a large margin of approximation.

Workings

1   **Publicity**

$$\text{Benefit} = \frac{\text{Annual cash flows } (1 - t)}{\text{Intergrand's WACC}}$$

$$= \frac{1(1 - 0.3)}{0.1}$$

$$= €7\text{million}$$

2   **Lost exports**

Cost of lost exports = £800,000 × 0.5 × (1 − 0.3) = £280,000

However the exchange rate is not constant.

Under purchasing power parity, next year's euro/£ exchange rate is $\dfrac{1 + 0.02}{1 + 0.04}$ of this year's exchange

	20X3	*20X4*	*20X5*	*20X6*
Exchange rate	1.594	1.563	1.533	1.504
Cost of lost exports € million	0.45	0.44	0.43	0.42
Discount at Intergrand's WACC, 10%	0.909	0.826	0.751	0.683
Present value	0.41	0.36	0.32	0.29

	€ million
Present value 20X3 – 6	1.38
Present value 20X7 – infinity ($\frac{0.42}{0.1}$) – (0.42 × 3.170)	2.87
	4.25

3 Tax shield

	€ million
Bank loans (Dt) (30 × 0.25)	7.5
Bonds: Annual interest charge × Tax relief × 4% Cumulative discount factor (18 × 0.08 × 0.25 × 6.002)	2.2
	9.7

The tax shield on the bonds has been discounted at the risk-free rate, on the assumption that tax relief is virtually certain to be received.

4 Discount rate

Discount at appropriate rate for Oberberg.

Use $\beta_a = \beta_e \dfrac{E}{E+D(1-t)} + \beta_d \dfrac{D(1-t)}{E+D(1-t)}$

Assuming debt is risk-free,

$\beta_a = \beta_e \dfrac{E}{E+D(1-t)}$

E $= 15 \times (300/100) = 45$

D $= 30 + (18 \times 1.23) = 52.14$

$\beta_a = 1.4 \dfrac{45}{45 + 52.14(1-0.25)}$

$= 0.749$

Using CAPM

$Ke_u = r_f + [E(r_m) - r_f]\beta_j$
$= 4 + (11 - 4)\, 0.749$
$= 9.24\%$, say 9%.

This is used for the base case free cash flow calculation, before calculation of financing side effects.

5 Sale of assets

Present value $= 8.0 \times$ 9% Discount factor year 1
$= 8.0 \times 0.917$
$= €7.3$ million

6 Investment for expansion

Present value $= 9.0 \times$ 9% Discount factor year 3
$= 9.0 \times 0.772$
$= €6.9$ million

7 **Free cash flows**

	20X3 €m	20X4 €m	20X5 €m	20X6 €m
Sales	38.2	41.2	44.0	49.0
Synergies		2.0	2.0	2.0
Labour	(11.0)	(12.1)	(13.0)	(14.1)
Materials	(8.3)	(8.7)	(9.0)	(9.4)
Overheads	(3.2)	(3.2)	(3.3)	(3.4)
Tax allowable depreciation	(6.3)	(5.8)	(5.6)	(5.2)
Taxable profit	9.4	13.4	15.1	18.9
Taxation	(2.4)	(3.4)	(3.8)	(4.7)
Add back tax allowable depreciation	6.3	5.8	5.6	5.2
Working capital	(0.7)	(0.9)	(1.0)	(2.0)
Replacement investment	(4.2)	(4.2)	(4.2)	(4.2)
Free cash flows	8.4	10.7	11.7	13.2
Discount factor 9%	0.917	0.842	0.772	0.708
Present value	7.7	9.0	9.0	9.3

Free cash flows 20X3 – 20X6 = €35 million

Free cash flows post 20X6 $= 13.2 \dfrac{(1+g)}{Ke - g} \times 9\%$ Discount factor year 4

$$= 13.2 \frac{(1 + 0.02)}{0.09 - 0.02} \times 0.708$$

$$= €136.2 \text{ million}$$

Free cash flows = 136.2 + 35

$$= €171.2 \text{ million}$$

8 **Additional tax**

Discount at Intergrand's cost of capital as relates to UK liability.

Taxable profit	9.4	13.4	15.1	18.9
Extra tax at 5%	0.47	0.67	0.76	0.95
Discount factor 10%	0.909	0.826	0.751	0.683
Present value	0.43	0.55	0.57	0.65

Additional tax 20X3 – 20X6 = €2.2 million

Additional tax post 20X6 $= 0.95 \dfrac{(1+g)}{Ke - g} \times 10\%$ Discount factor year 4

$$= 0.95 \frac{(1 + 0.02)}{0.1 - 0.02} \times 0.683$$

$$= €8.3 \text{ million}$$

Extra tax = 2.2 + 8.3 = €10.5 million

Other factors to be considered

(a) **Assumptions**

The **assumptions** used in the forecasts need to be **examined carefully** and alternative forecasts prepared under different assumptions, for example the need for additional investment at a later date, tax changes or assuming that all the exports will be lost.

(b)   **Risk**

Further work needs to be done on **assessing risks**, as the risk assessments upon which the beta factor calculation is **based** may **not be accurate** and risks may change over time, particularly as we are looking at cash flows to infinity. Sensitivity analysis needs to be **undertaken** to see how much key figures may change before the decision is affected.

(c)   **Timescale**

The majority of the benefits from Oberberg will be **obtained after 20X6**, and the directors of Intergrand must **consider** whether this is **too long a timescale** for its investors.

(d)   **Real options**

The existence of real options, the **chance to take decisions** in the future that could **further enhance** the value of Oberberg should be considered.

(e)   **Economic exposure**

If inflation rates stay the same, the value of the euros and hence the value of the investment will **continue to appreciate**. However the investment's value will be affected by a UK decision to join the Euro.

(f)   Implications of acquisition

The board needs to consider the implications of diversification. Although the acquisition can **reduce risk by diversification**, it can also create **difficulties of integration**, particularly if Oberberg is significant in size relative to Intergrand. Intergrand's board needs to consider carefully any synergies involved and how reliable forecasts of these are, measured against the costs of changing the structure and culture of Oberberg. Intergrand's board should also consider carefully the attitudes of Oberberg's staff in the light of the planned redundancies, and what will be required to retain staff who are important for Oberberg's continued success.

(g)   **Other strategies**

Intergrand's board should try to **ascertain** whether there are other investments in Germany or elsewhere that offer **higher present values** or are **better strategic fits**.

20 Demast

Text references. Chapter 12 on valuation methods, Chapter 11 on acquisition issues.

Top tips. Many of the advantages (and disadvantages) in (a) are to do with size. Other questions on mergers and acquisitions have also started with a discussion about the general advantages and disadvantages of acquisition, possibly in comparison with internal growth.

In (b) it is helpful to make an evaluation of the likely purpose of the two bidders in making their offers for Demast. On the basis of this, it is possible to suggest appropriate valuation techniques to estimate a fair price for the company. The full value of the various offers can then be calculated and compared with the valuations to determine whether the bids are appropriate under the circumstances.

For most questions of this type, you will be comparing bid terms with net assets, price/earnings and dividend growth valuation methods.

In (c) the answer is in terms of the principles the directors must follow.

Easy marks. (a) is a straightforward discussion; you should learn the list of factors if you struggled with it.

(a)   A company planning to grow must decide on whether it will try to achieve this through organic growth alone or through some combination of **organic growth** and **acquisition**.

Advantages of growth by acquisition

(i)   **Faster growth**

The company may be able to **grow much faster** than would be possible through purely organic development. This is particularly true if the company is seeking to **expand into a new product or market** area when acquisition will allow the company to gain technical skills, goodwill and customer contracts which would take it a long time to develop by itself.

(ii)   **Use of share exchange**

If the acquisition is financed through a share exchange, then the company will **not face the pressures on cash** that often result during a time of organic growth. However, it must take account of the likely affect of such an acquisition on the share price, earnings per share and gearing. If the target company is financially more stable it may be able to improve its liquidity and ability to raise further finance.

(iii)   **Critical mass**

In some markets it is argued that a company **requires 'critical mass'** in order to operate effectively. This is particularly true in industries where a high level of capital investment is required. Acquisition may allow a company to reach an efficient size much more quickly than if it were to try to get there through organic growth.

(iv)   **Risk levels**

A larger company with a better spread of products, customers and markets faces a **lower level of operating risk** than a small company which may be more dependent on a small number of customers and suppliers. Acquisition will therefore allow the company to reduce its operating risk more quickly. This effect is enhanced if the company is using acquisition as a means of diversification into new product/market areas.

(v)   **Operating economies**

Acquisition may permit the company to make **operating economies** through the rationalisation and elimination of duplication in areas such as research and development, debt collection and corporate relations.

(vi)   **Asset backing**

Acquisition may allow the company to achieve a **better level of asset backing** if it has a high ratio of sales to assets.

(vii)   **Opportunities**

The acquisition may be to some **extent opportunistic** if the bidding company identifies a firm where the assets are undervalued.

Problems of growth by acquisition

(i)   **Failure to integrate the management and operations effectively**

The merged firm does not achieve the planned economies of scale. A recent report highlighted frequent failure to achieve an amalgamation of corporate cultures post-merger. It was the realisation of the inherent difficulties of this process that caused the proposed merger of the Leeds and the National Provincial building societies to be called off fairly recently.

(ii) **Overpriced acquisition**

If an acquisition is being made for strong strategic reasons there may be **competition between bidding companies** which forces the price up to a level beyond that which can be justified on financial grounds. If too high a price is paid then the post-merger financial performance is likely to be disappointing. The costs of mounting the bid and of the subsequent reorganisations may also mean that earnings are depressed, at least in the short term.

(iii) **Returns**

The acquisition may lead to **inequalities in returns** between the shareholders of the bidding and the target companies. It is often the case that the shareholders in the target company do disproportionately well when compared with the shareholders in the bidding company. This is likely to be the case when the price paid for the acquisition is towards the top of the projected range.

(b) **Appropriate valuation technique**

The appropriate valuation technique will depend on the plans which the bidding company has for Demast post-merger. Demast is an unlisted company and therefore there is no market price available. It is assumed that Nadion would intend to continue the operations as a going concern and therefore an earnings based valuation is appropriate in this case. BZO might also plan to continue to operate the business in its present form, or alternatively it might be planning to asset strip if it believes the assets are significantly undervalued. If this is the case, then the company should be valued on a net assets basis.

(i) **Asset basis valuation**

Demast's net assets currently amount to £6.5m at book values. However, the stock must be written down by 10% to its realisable value, giving a revised net assets figure of £5.95m or £1.49 per share. This valuation does not take into account a number of factors including:

(1) The **land and buildings** have **not been revalued** since 20W9. Property prices have fallen since then during the recession and therefore they may be overvalued.

(2) The **patents are excluded** from the balance sheet and may have a significant value if there are a number of years left to run.

(3) There is no information to suggest whether the **other components** of the asset base are realistically valued, in particular any plant and equipment.

(ii) **Earnings basis valuations**

(1) **P/E ratio**

If it is reasonable to assume that Demast should operate on a similar P/E ratio to Nadion since they are both in the same sector, then Nadion's P/E ratio can be used in calculations. This should be approximately correct since although Nadion is much bigger and is a listed company, Demast is showing a much higher rate of growth.

Nadion's P/E ratio is 320/58 = 5.517

If applied to Demast's earnings, this would suggest a valuation of £4.44 per share (80.5 × 5.517).

(2) **Dividend valuation model**

This approach allows the calculation of the theoretical share price based on the projected dividend stream and the cost of capital:

$$P_0 = \frac{D_0(1+g)}{(r-g)}$$

Where P_0 = theoretical share price

D_0 = dividend in year 0 (37.5p per share)

g = expected rate of growth in dividends

r = cost of equity capital

$$P_0 = \frac{37.5\,(1+0.09)}{(0.16-0.09)} = £5.84 \text{ per share}$$

The **value of the various bids** can now be calculated.

(i) **7 September**

BZO bids 2 for 3 at a price of 710p = £4.73/share

(ii) **2 October**

Nadion bids:

	£
Cash per share	1.70
Debentures: £100 for (6.25/0.25 =) 25 shares equates to cash per share	4.00
Total value at date of merger	5.70

In addition the shareholders gain the opportunity to purchase new shares in 5 years' time at £3.85 (£100/26). This is 15% above Nadion's current share price and therefore if the current rates of growth continue should provide the opportunity to acquire new shares at a significant discount to the prevailing market price.

(iii) **19 October**

BZO bids in cash £6.00 per share.

Nadion's bid

Considering firstly the bid by Nadion, it is assumed that the company intends to continue to operate Demast as a **going concern**. The bid of £5.70 per share is 14 pence below the most optimistic theoretical share price calculated on the basis of the dividend growth model. This would appear to be a **realistic but prudent bid** from the point of view of Nadion's shareholders. The 5% rise in the price of Nadion's shares following the announcement of the bid suggests that the market also believes that the acquisition would be financially beneficial.

BZO's initial bid

BZO's initial bid of £4.73 per share is **well above** the **net assets valuation** of £1.49 per share. However it is in line with the **P/E ratio valuation** of £4.44 per share. Thus if BZO were intending to continue to operate Demast as a going concern, the bid appears to be prudent. However, if BZO's purpose in acquiring Demast is to dispose of all or part of the assets and to change fundamentally the structure of the company, then the bid does not appear sensible. This view is confirmed by the markets which down-valued BZO's shares 9% on the announcement of the offer.

BZO's final bid

BZO's final cash offer of £6.00 per share is above the **most optimistic valuation based** on the dividend growth model. In view of BZO's previous deals, it must be assumed that the management perceive Demast to be in possession of significantly undervalued and under-used assets. Additionally, the use of the term loan to finance the offer will increase BZO's level of debt from £65m to £89m. The current level of gearing is:

$$\frac{£30m + £35m}{£123m + £72m - £91m - £35m} = 94\%$$

Therefore, a further significant increase in this level would not appear to be a prudent move from the point of view of the shareholders in BZO. This view is confirmed by the further slide in the share price to 680 pence.

(c) **Responsibilities of directors**

Corporate governance was defined in the Cadbury Report as 'the **system** by which **companies are directed** and **controlled**'. The directors are responsible for the corporate governance of the company and should act in the best interests of shareholders, taking account of the needs of other groups such as employees, creditors and customers.

City Code

During the conduct of a takeover bid the directors are additionally bound by the rules of the **City Code** concerning the way in which the bid is conducted. The directors of both companies are required to disregard their own interests when advising their shareholders.

Shareholders' interests

As has been outlined above, it is doubtful whether the directors of BZO are acting in the best interests of their shareholders by bidding such a high price and by taking on a further £24m of debt. They appear to be following a strategy of **growth at any price** which may not be in the best long-term interests of the group.

Directors' interests

When the final bids of Nadion and BZO are compared, they appear to be very close, particularly when the likely capital gain on conversion in the Nadion offer is taken into account. It therefore seems surprising that the directors of Demast should advise acceptance of the BZO offer in preference to the Nadion offer, particularly since **continuity of the current operations** is more likely if Nadion gained ownership. It appears that they may have been swayed by the offer of directorships by BZO and the prospect of continued well paid employment in advising acceptance of the offer. If this is the case then they were acting in their own best interests and not fully taking into account the needs of the owners of the remaining 75% of the shares.

Other parties' interests

The bid by BZO is also less likely to be to the benefit of other interested parties such as employees and customers since the prospects of at least a partial breakup and asset disposal are more likely if BZO gains ownership.

21 Minprice

Text references. Chapters 12 to 14.

Top tips. Roughly one third of the marks for (a) would be for estimating the effect on EPS and share price of the takeover. Also important are existing share price valuation using the dividend valuation model and a discussion of gearing.

Don't be too disheartened if you did not cope very well with the discussion about market efficiency. Although this topic is important, the other calculations plus reasonable discussion would have gained you more than half marks.

Important points in the discussion in (a) which will often need to be brought into discussions on takeovers and mergers include:

- Views of shareholders
- State of market efficiency
- Valuation of shares using one or more methods and problems of methods used. Consider whether market is under or overvaluing shares
- Combined company issues – gearing, dividend policies, post-acquisition strategies

In (b) the yield on the zero coupon bond and its estimated value need to be computed. The bulk of the marks were available for these. The cash offer comments are standard. Remember of course that companies have to find the cash for a cash offer!

Easy marks. Scoring a very feasible 6–7 marks in (c) would only have left you needing 8–9 out of 22 on the other parts to pass this question.

(a) **Views of shareholders**

Since the terms of the bid involve a share-for-share swap, shareholders will be highly interested in the fundamentals underlying the current market value of shares in both companies, in the **potential economic gains** that can be made by combining the companies and the likely effect of the takeover on share prices, including the proportion in which the gains are likely to be split between the two sets of shareholders.

Shareholders of Savealot are unlikely to accept unless they receive a **premium** over their existing share price, whereas Minprice shareholders will not wish to offer **too high a premium** because this will cause them to lose out. Other factors are also at play in this proposed takeover, one of which is that Minprice may be seeking to reduce its high gearing by taking over the comparatively ungeared Savealot.

Existing share prices

The reasonableness of each company's existing share price can be tested against the dividend valuation model:

Latest dividend per share: Minprice: £24m/300m = 8 pence. Savealot:
£5m/40m = 12.5 pence.

Share values from the dividend valuation model: $D_0(1 + g)/(Ke - g)$:

Minprice: $8 \times 1.07/(14.5\% - 7\%) = 114$ pence
Savealot: $12.5 \times 1.08/(13\% - 8\%) = 270$ pence

If the stock market is efficient, the companies' current market share prices provide the best indicator of the 'true' value of their shares. However, on the basis of the **dividend valuation model** (using past growth rates as an indicator of expected future growth) Minprice's actual share price of 232 pence is more than twice as high as it 'should' be. Although the DVM is a simplistic model, this might signal caution to Savealot's shareholders, whose actual price of 295 pence seems comparatively reasonable. It is clear that future growth for both companies is expected to be better than the past. This may reflect expectations of a general upturn in the sector, or may be the effect of general market feelings that takeovers will be taking place.

Earnings per share are: Minprice: £50m/300m = 16.67p. Savealot: £8m/40m = 20p.

The **P/E ratios are:** Minprice: 232/16.67 = 13.9. Savealot: 295/20 = 14.75.

Unfortunately, no P/E ratios or other statistics for the food retail industry are available for comparison. However, the P/E of Minprice, which is nearly as high as that of Savealot, seems over-rated on the basis of its poorer growth record and higher cost of equity capital.

Potential economic gains from the takeover

The present value of the proposed rationalisation transactions following the takeover is £7.5 million:

	£m
Warehouse sale	6.8
Redundancy	(9.0)
Wage savings for 5 years: £2.7m × 3.605*	9.7
	7.5

* The annuity factor for 5 years at 12%, the WACC of Minprice. Wage savings may last for more than 5 years, giving a higher present value.

Assuming this gain in value from combining the companies is achievable, it indicates that the takeover is economically worthwhile.

The bid has not yet been made public. The effect of the potential gains from the takeover terms is **unlikely** to have been **reflected** in the share prices of either company. However, it is just as probable that shareholders already have some expectations of takeovers in the industry, in which case synergetic gains would already have been anticipated in share prices, even under the semi-strong view of market efficiency.

Effect of the takeover announcement on share prices

There are a number of different ways of examining the effect of the takeover information being made public.

(i)   **Poor market efficiency**

Assume first that shareholders had **no previous expectations** that the takeover would take place and are taken totally by surprise when the synergetic gains of £7.5 million are announced.

They will estimate the value of the combined business as:

	£m
Value of firms before takeover:	
Minprice: 300m × 232p	696.0
Savealot: 40m × 295p	118.0
	814.0
Post takeover synergy	7.5
Estimated value after takeover	821.5

Minprice will issue 4/3 × 40m new shares = 53.333m new shares to the shareholders of Savealot. The total number of shares in Minprice will rise to 353.333m.

The **expected share price** for Minprice after the takeover is announced will be £821.5m/353.333m = 232.5 pence. This is only a 0.5p gain to Minprice shareholders, who will have allowed all the advantage of synergy to accrue to Savealot.

Savealot shares will be expected to reflect the announcement by rising to 4/3 × 232.5p = 310p, giving them a 15p gain, an increase of 5%.

The **reconciliation** of the gains is: Minprice 300m shares × 0.5p = £1.5m and Savealot 40m shares × 15p = £6m, giving a total of £7.5m.

On this assumption, shareholders of Savealot would be fairly happy with the terms of the offer and Minprice shareholders would not lose from their existing position.

Total equity earnings from the combination will be £50m + £8m = £58m, assuming that wage savings are offset against redundancy cost write-offs and before any expected earnings growth.

This will give an **expected earnings per share** of £58/353.333 = 16.4 pence. This represents a drop from Minprice's existing 16.67p, but Savealot shareholders would receive the equivalent of 4/3 × 16.4p = 21.9p compared with their existing 20p.

(ii)   **Stronger market efficiency**

Suppose however that shareholders had **already guessed** that the takeover would take place and share prices had **already increased** to reflect expected gains (a stronger view of market efficiency).

The **value of the combined business** would then be £814m and the expected value of Minprice's shares after the terms of the offer were announced would be £814/353.333 = 230.3 pence, a drop of nearly two pence.

Minprice shareholders would be disappointed with the terms of the offer. Savealot shareholders would still be better off, with an expected increase in share price to 4/3 × 230.3p = 307 pence (a premium of 4%).

(iii)   **Over-valuation of Minprice shares**

As a third possibility, Minprice's shares may be **temporarily over-valued** by the market, as indicated by the high share price compared with that predicted from the DVM.

Such an over-valuation might occur, for example, if investors had false hopes of Minprice's opportunities in the takeover market. A fair price for Minprice's shares based on its existing business might be 114p, giving a total value of 300m × 114p = £342m.

Then the value of the combined company would be £342m + £118m + £7.5m = £467.5m, giving an expected share price after the takeover announcement of £467.5/353.333 = 132.3 pence.

This would represent very favourable takeover terms to Minprice, but would be unacceptable to Savealot, whose equivalent share value would fall from 195p to 4/3 × 132.3p = 176.4p.

Conclusion

In summary, the takeover terms appear to be fair and acceptable, provided that Minprice's shares are not temporarily over-valued by false expectations. Savealot shareholders need to evaluate the stability of Minprice's share price before accepting the offer.

Other factors

(i)   **Gearing**

Minprice is very highly geared. Even if only long term debt is considered, gearing (D/E) in terms of book value is 314/222 = 141% and in terms of market value is 364/696 = 52%.

By comparison, Savealot's gearing is only 17.5/54.7 = 32% in book terms and 17.5/118 = 15% in market value terms.

In addition, Minprice has high current creditors resulting in net current liabilities. While this is not unusual for a supermarket chain, it indicates that gearing in real terms is even higher. The shareholders of Minprice will favour the share issue terms for the takeover of Savealot which should reduce their gearing substantially, whereas Savealot's shareholders are unlikely to see this as an advantage.

(ii)   **Dividend policy**

The companies have different dividend yields and covers, which may influence the views of some shareholders.

	Minprice	Savealot
Dividend yield	3.4%	4.2%
Dividend cover	2.1	1.6

(iii)   **Management plans**

The composition of the board of directors and senior managers will be fundamental to the success of the business after the takeover. Savealot seems to have been performing better than Minprice recently and may be able to argue for more than proportional representation on the board. Shareholders of both companies will be interested in these plans.

(b)   **325 pence per share cash offer**

For the shareholders of Savealot this represents a **premium of 10%** over the current market price of 295p and is significantly better than the most optimistic estimate of the share offer's value, which was 310 pence.

The **cash offer** gives a **risk free return** compared with the risk of shares. For this reason cash offers are usually less in value than the equivalent share offers. Since this offer is *more* than the share offer it represents good value to Savealot shareholders. However, they will suffer immediate capital gains tax on the disposal.

From Minprice's point of view, the cash offer is **unlikely** to be **feasible**, given its high gearing and weak liquidity position.

Zero coupon debenture

If Savealot shareholders accept the zero coupon debenture they could either sell it or hold it. Holding it would imply a **reduction in the risk** of their investment portfolio.

Each debenture would effectively have a cost of $10 \times 295p = £29.50$ and could be redeemed in 10 years for £100. The rate of return can be estimated from $£29.50(1+r)^{10} = £100$. Thus $1/(1+r)^{10} = 0.295$. Looking at the 10 year row in the PV tables, 0.295 implies a return of 13%. Since this is high compared with the 10% expected return on equivalent-risk corporate debt, the debenture represents good value.

To estimate its value, discount the £100 redemption value for 10 years at 10%. This gives a value of £38.60, or 386 pence per Savealot share, representing a premium of 31%. The debenture is clearly the most attractive of the three forms of offer to Savealot shareholders.

To Minprice it is less attractive than cash in the longer term but more attractive in the short term because **no cash payments** are **required** for 10 years. However, earnings per share will suffer if the cost of the debt is amortised over 10 years.

(c) To: Board of Directors of Savealot plc
From: Consultant

In the UK, defences made by a publicly quoted company against a takeover bid must be legal and be allowed by the City Code on Takeovers and Mergers and Stock Exchange regulations. Our advice on your proposals is as follows.

(i) **Doubling profits**

If your profits are likely to double, then **now** is a good time to **announce** the fact. You will need to substantiate your claims with clear evidence that can be verified by shareholders. This is very likely to halt the bid, or at least secure better terms.

(ii) **Alteration of articles**

Stock Exchange regulations **prohibit** the alteration of articles of association to require more than a 51% majority to accept an offer for acquisition.

(iii) **Third party investor**

This defence, which was used for example in the Guinness case, is illegal under the Companies Act, as it is tantamount to the company **purchasing its own shares**.

(iv) **Advertising campaign**

As with defence (i) this can be a very effective form of defence provided that the **information** is **true** and can be substantiated, otherwise a libel action might result.

(v) **Revaluation of fixed assets**

Revaluation of fixed assets is a good idea, provided that it is carried out by an independent valuer and the values can be **substantiated**. However, the effect on share values may be less significant than might be thought as, in an efficient market, these true asset values will already have been estimated by institutional shareholders.

22 Paxis

Text references. For the calculations Chapter 6 on free cash flows and Chapter 7 on cost of capital are helpful; Chapters 12 and 13 cover the discussion issues relating to mergers.

Top tips. Arguably as all the free cash flows increase by the same % each year in each of the three appraisals, you only need to do a full analysis in year 1, and then increase the free cash flows before discount by x% each year. However, if you do this, a slip in the calculation will cost you marks as there are no workings, so it's better to do the full analysis unless you are short of time.

Depreciation can be combined with other operating costs in the calculation in (a), but remember it needs to be added back. Replacement capital expenditure needs to be subtracted, and interest and dividends not included at all. (If you'd been given profit before tax, you would have to have had to add back interest to get earnings before interest and tax, but that's not necessary here). All WACCs can be rounded to the nearest whole number, so that you can use annuity tables, but this does make quite a difference to the answer of free cash flows for the combined company.

Note that the combined market values of equity and debt are not the same as the value of combined free cash flows, but you have to calculate the combined figure for equity and debt, to be able to weight the WACC calculation.

(b) is a standard discussion on an appraisal – the technique is to question all the key figures you use, and also consider what's not there. (c) is concerned with what the Wragger shareholders get out of the process, (d) the benefits for Praxis (and might the directors be better off looking elsewhere?)

Easy marks. The easiest discussion marks are in (e) although you need to be careful only to discuss defences that are legitimate once the bid has been announced. Most of the calculations in (a) are simply increasing figures by x%.

(a)   **Paxis**

	1	2	3	4
	$'000	$'000	$'000	$'000
Sales	14,000	14,700	15,435	16,207
Operating costs inc depn	(10,640)	(11,172)	(11,730)	(12,317)
EBIT	3,360	3,528	3,705	3,890
Tax 30%	(1,008)	(1,058)	(1,112)	(1,167)
Add back depreciation	1,523	1,599	1,679	1,762
Replacement investment	(1,680)	(1,764)	(1,852)	(1,945)
Free cash flow	2,195	2,305	2,420	2,540
Discount factor 10% (W)	0.909	0.826	0.751	0.683
Present value	1,995	1,904	1,817	1,735

Free cash flows years 1-4 = 7,451,000

Working

Ke

$$E(r_j) = r_f + [E(r_m) - r_f]\beta_j$$

$$= 4 + (11 - 4)1.18$$

$$= 12.3\%$$

$$WACC = Ke_g \frac{E}{E+D} + Kd(1-t)\frac{D}{E+D}$$

$$= (12.3 \times 0.7) + (6 \times (1 - 0.3) \times 0.3)$$

$$= 9.9\%, \text{ say } 10\%$$

Free cash flows beyond year 4 $= \dfrac{\text{Cashflow Yr } 4 \times (1+g)}{WACC - g} \times \text{Yr 4 Discount Factor}$

$$= \frac{2,540(1.04)}{0.1 - 0.04} \times 0.683$$

$$= 30,070,000$$

Total free cash flows = 7,451,000 + 30,070,000 = 37,521,000

Wragger

	1	2	3	4
	$'000	$'000	$'000	$'000
Sales	10,011	10,662	11,355	12,093
Operating costs inc depn	(6,976)	(7,429)	(7,912)	(8,426)
EBIT	3,035	3,233	3,443	3,667
Tax 30%	(911)	(970)	(1,033)	(1,100)
Add back depreciation	1,172	1,248	1,329	1,415
Replacement investment	(1,321)	(1,406)	(1,498)	(1,595)
Free cash flow	1,975	2,105	2,241	2,387
Discount factor 9% (W)	0.917	0.842	0.772	0.708
Present value	1,811	1,772	1,730	1,690

Free cash flows years 1–4 = 7,003,000

Working

Ke

$$E(r_j) = r_f + [E(r_m) - r_f]\beta_j$$

$$= 4 + (11 - 4)1.38$$
$$= 13.7\%$$

$$\text{WACC } Ke_g \frac{E}{E+D} + Kd(1-t)\frac{D}{E+D} = (13.7 \times 0.45) + (7.5 \times (1 - 0.3) \times 0.55)$$

$$= 9.1\%, \text{ say } 9\%$$

$$\text{Free cash flows beyond year 4} = \frac{2,387(1.05)}{0.09 - 0.05} \times 0.708$$

$$= 44,362,000$$

Total free cash flows = 7,003,000 + 44,362,000 = 51,365,000

Combined value

		$'000
Paxis	Equity 7,000 × 2.98	20,860
	Debt 20,860 × 0.3/0.7	8,940
Wragger	Equity 8,000 × 2.98 × 4/5	19,072
	Debt 8,000 × 1.92 × 0.55/0.45	18,773
		67,645

Free cash flows

	1	2	3	4
	$'000	$'000	$'000	$'000
Sales combined + 6%	24,097	25,543	27,075	28,700
Operating costs inc depn 70% of sales	(16,868)	(17,880)	(18,953)	(20,090)
EBIT	7,229	7,663	8,122	8,610
Tax 30%	(2,169)	(2,299)	(2,437)	(2,583)
Add back depreciation combined + 6% per year	2,703	2,865	3,037	3,219
Replacement investment combined + 6% per year	(3,010)	(3,191)	(3,382)	(3,585)
Free cash flow	4,753	5,038	5,340	5,661
Discount factor 10% (W)	0.909	0.826	0.751	0.683
Present value	4,320	4,161	4,010	3,866

Present value years 1-4 = $16,357,000

Working

$$\text{WACC} = \frac{(20,860 \times 12.3) + (8,940 \times 6(1 - 0.3)) + (19,072 \times 13.7) + (18,773 \times 7.5(1 - 0.3))}{67,645}$$

= 9.7%, say 10%

$$\text{Free cash flows beyond year 4} = \frac{5,661(1.05)}{0.1 - 0.05} \times 0.683$$

$$= 81,196$$

Total free cash flows = 16,357,000 + 81,196,000 = $97,553,000

Total free cash flows of individual companies = 37,521,000 + 51,365,000 = 88,886,000

Synergy = $8,667,000

(b)   (i)   **Level of consideration**

This is the key factor. On current market prices, Paxis is offering $11.92 (four sharesworth) for $9.60 (five sharesworth) in Wragger. This is a premium of 24% which appears generous.

(ii)   **Expectations of future profits**

If the shareholders of Wragger plan to retain shares in the combined group, they want to know that expectations of **future profits** and **synergies** are reasonable.

(iii)   **Future dividend policy**

Shareholders may be sensitive to the dividend policy possibly being **less generous** than they have been used to with Wragger. In the most recent year Wragger's dividend payout ratio was 55% compared with Paxis's ratio of 50%.

(iv)   **Their tax position**

The shareholders may prefer a **future capital gain** on sale of shares in Praxis to cash consideration, or instant sale of any shares they are given.

(v)   **Changes in share prices**

Shareholders will also **take account** of **any changes in share prices** that occur during the bid process.

(c)   (i)   **Potential for increase**

Paxis could increase its bid by the amount of the synergy, $8.667m, less the amount of the existing premium (2.32 × 8m/5) = $3.712 m, ie $4.955m.

(ii)   **Options**

Acquiring Wragger may give rise to **strategic options** that have not been valued in the appraisal process.

(iii)   **Strategic process**

There may be other good strategic grounds for bidding for Wragger, although Paxis's board may also consider buying an **alternative (cheaper?) company**. Given that Wragger is in the same industry, expectations of synergies through economies of scale may be reasonable, although the acquisition may not represent much of a diversification of risk.

(iv)   **Costs of resistance**

Paxis's directors should consider whether the bid is likely to be **resisted**, and how **difficult** and **costly** it will be to overcome the resistance.

Conclusion

As the merger appears to create wealth for shareholders of both companies through synergies, the directors should proceed with the bid.

(d) **Possible defences**

(i) **Propaganda against Paxis and for Wragger**

Directors could try to persuade shareholders that Paxis shares are poor value compared with Wragger shares, **concentrating on Paxis's lower growth rates and its lower predicted value for free cash flows.** The directors could also revalue Wragger's assets.

(ii) **Regulatory authorities**

The directors could lobby to have the bid referred to the **regulatory authorities**.

(iii) **Counterbid**

As the companies are of fairly **similar size**, Wragger could make a counter-bid for Paxis's shares.

(iv) **Poison pills**

The directors should make use of any **anti-takeover devices** in the company's constitution relating to bidding, although it may be rather difficult to introduce others at this stage.

(v) **White knight**

The directors could try to find another company that is willing to offer Wragger's shareholders a **better deal**.

23 Omnikit

Text references. Chapter 9 on the investment appraisal: Chapter 11 includes points that you could have discussed.

Top tips. Two foreign investment appraisals in one question! For this sort of question, which is relatively common and contains many computational techniques, you need to develop a standard approach and practice it hard, because a look at the marking scheme shows that not many marks are awarded for each computational element. Never miss out the discussion parts of a question like this: they are far better value for time than the computational parts. Our answer shows you the best sequence in which to tackle the problem, and provides further hints at the various key stages.

Easy marks. The figures and workings at the start of each appraisal before you get onto the more complicated workings. The discussion part in (a) should be fairly straightforward, and the limitations of the assumptions are common to most questions of this type.

(a) **Advantages of organic growth**

(i) It can be carefully planned to fulfil strategic objectives.

(ii) It is more likely to involve existing front-line managers than growth by acquisition and hence can be more motivating.

Disadvantages of organic growth

However, the costs of **entering new lines of business** can be high and the lead times involved might be too long to enable the business to gain competitive advantage. The new business has to researched, developed and planned, production facilities have to be acquired and suitable staff hired. The organisation then goes through a learning curve, often repeating the mistakes made by competitors.

Advantages of growth by acquisition

(i) It provides a **quicker method of entering new markets** or acquiring new technology or patents, sometimes enabling very rapid growth

(ii) **It enables increased market power** by eliminating competitors

(iii) **It provides economies of scale** by elimination of duplicated resources, combining complementary resources, etc

Disadvantages of growth by acquisition

By its nature, however, growth by acquisition cannot be **planned** in as much detail as organic growth. Quick decisions sometimes have to be made in response to acquisition opportunities, often without as much information as the acquiring company would like. Major acquisitions may change the company's strategic direction. Staff problems are more likely to arise as attempts are made to integrate or change the cultures of merged organisations.

(b) **Contribution to organisational objectives**

The evaluation of each of the two alternatives is made in terms of how well each one contributes to the **achievement of organisational objectives** and strategies. The information given enables a financial appraisal of each alternative to be made. This will only be part of the input to the final decision, albeit an important part. Many non-financial factors will also have to be taken into account.

Approach used

The financial appraisal is shown below. The basic approach is to estimate cash flows in the foreign currency, convert them to the home currency and discount them at a rate based on home country cost of capital.

Financial appraisal of the two alternative investments

The time horizon for appraisal of both investments is 7 years: six years of operation plus one further year to allow for the tax delay.

Appraisal of Swiss investment

Year	0	1	2	3	4	5	6	7
Production/sales units			2,000	2,500	2,500	2,500	2,500	
Cont. per unit, SFr (W1)			9,923	10,419	10,940	11,487	12,061	
	SFr '000	SFr '000	SFr '000	SFr '000	SFr '000	SFr '000	SFr '000	SFr '000
Total contribution			19,846	26,048	27,350	28,718	30,153	
Royalty(£750,000 ÷ exch.rate)			(1,806)	(1,841)	(1,877)	(1,914)	(1,951)	
Operating cash flow			18,040	24,207	25,473	26,804	28,202	
Tax at 40%				(7,216)	(9,683)	(10,189)	(10,722)	(11,281)
Tax saved by dep'n all. (W2)				1,120	360	270	202	152
Land	(2,300)							
Building	(1,600)	(6,200)						
Machinery		(6,400)						
After tax realisable value							16,200	
Working capital (W3)		(11,500)	(575)	(604)	(634)	(666)	(699)	14,678
Cash remitted to UK	(3,900)	(24,100)	17,465	17,507	15,516	16,219	33,183	3,549
Exchange rate SFr/£ (W4)	2.3175	2.3625	2.4084	2.4551	2.5028	2.5514	2.6010	2.6515
	£'000	£'000	£'000	£'000	£'000	£'000	£'000	£'000
Cash remitted from Switzerland	(1,683)	(10,201)	7,252	7,131	6,199	6,357	12,758	1,338
Royalty received			750	750	750	750	750	
Tax at 33% on royalty				(248)	(248)	(248)	(248)	(248)
Net cash	(1,683)	(10,201)	8,002	7,633	6,701	6,859	13,260	1,090
12.51% d.f. (W5)	1.000	0.889	0.790	0.702	0.624	0.555	0.493	0.438
Present value	(1,683)	(9,069)	6,322	5,358	4,181	3,807	6,537	477

The Swiss investment has a positive net present value of **£15.93 million.**

> **Top tips.** Appraisal of the US investment follows the same lines but is easier.

Appraisal of US investment

Year	0	1	2	3	4	5	6	7
	$'000	$'000	$'000	$'000	$'000	$'000	$'000	$'000
Pre-tax cash flow		2,120	3,371	3,573	3,787	4,014	4,255	
Tax at 30%			(636)	(1,011)	(1,072)	(1,136)	(1,204)	(1,277)
Cost of acquisition (assume maximum)	(10,000)							
Machinery	(2,000)							
After tax realisable value							14,500	
Working capital (W6)	(4,000)	(240)	(254)	(270)	(286)	(303)	(321)	5,674
Cash remitted to/from USA	(16,000)	1,880	2,481	2,292	2,429	2,575	17,230	4,397
Exchange rate (W4)	1.5185	1.5627	1.6082	1.6551	1.7033	1.7529	1.8040	1.8565
Cash remitted to/from USA	(10,537)	1,203	1,543	1,385	1,426	1,469	9,551	2,368
Additional UK tax (3%) (W7) (See Note below)			(41)	(63)	(65)	(67)	(69)	(71)
Net cash	(10,537)	1,203	1,502	1,322	1,361	1,402	9,482	2,297
12.51% d.f. (W5)	1.000	0.889	0.790	0.702	0.624	0.555	0.493	0.438
Present value	(10,537)	1,069	1,187	928	849	778	4,675	1,006

Net present value = (£45,000)

Workings

1   **Contribution per unit – Switzerland**

	SFr
At current prices (year 0):	
Sales price	20,000
Variable costs	11,000
Contribution	9,000

This will increase by 5% per year. Contribution per unit in year 2 will be $9,000 \times 1.05^2 = $ SFr 9,923.

2   **Tax saved by tax-allowable depreciation (machinery only) in Switzerland**

(Figures in SFr'000)

Year	1	2	3	4	5	6	7
Asset value at start of year	6,400	4,800	3,600	2,700	2,025	1,519	
25% depreciation	1,600	1,200	900	675	506	380	
Tax saved at 40%			1,120	360	270	202	152

It is assumed that, because the Swiss subsidiary earns no profits in year 1, the tax depreciation in year 1 cannot be claimed until year 2. The allowance in year 2 will therefore be 2,800, giving rise to a tax saving of 1,120 in year 3.

No **balancing allowance** has been shown, as the asset will still be in use after year 6 and its value is included in the after-tax realisable value of the investment, SFr16.2m.

3   **Investment in working capital – Switzerland**

It is assumed that total working capital requirement increases with inflation at 5% per year and is returned at the end of year 7. It is assumed that the amount of working capital at year 6 is *not* included in the value of the investment at that stage.

> **Top tips.** In the absence of clear instructions, reasonable assumptions have to be made, but clearly alternatives are possible.

(Figures in SFr'000)

Year	1	2	3	4	5	6	7
Total working capital	11,500	12,075	12,679	13,313	13,979	14,678	
Investment in WC	(11,500)	(575)	(604)	(634)	(666)	(699)	14,678

4 Computation of exchange rates for the next 7 years

For ease of computation, the spot rate will be taken as the mid-market exchange rate.

Spot rate for SFr = (2.3140 + 2.3210)/2 = 2.3175
Spot rate for $ = (1.5160 + 1.5210)/2 = 1.5185

Using purchasing power parity theory, each year the SFr/£ exchange rate is multiplied by 1.05/1.03 and the $/£ rate is multiplied by 1.06/1.03.

> **Top tips.** Alternatively multiply by $\dfrac{0.05-0.03}{1+0.03}+1$ and $\dfrac{0.06-0.03}{1+0.03}+1$

Year	SFr/£	$/£
0	2.3175	1.5185
1	2.3625	1.5627
2	2.4084	1.6082
3	2.4551	1.6551
4	2.5028	1.7033
5	2.5514	1.7529
6	2.6010	1.8040
7	2.6515	1.8565

5 Discount rate for the investments

Because both investment alternatives represent an expansion of the existing business, the company's existing weighted average cost of capital can be used as a discount rate.

The debt is borrowed in the UK where interest will save tax at the rate of 33%. Its after tax cost is 10%(1 − 0.33) = 6.7%

Market values should be used as weights.

WACC = 0.7 × 15% + 0.3 × 6.7% = 12.51%

6 Working capital – US investment

Year	0	1	2	3	4	5	6	7
	$'000	$'000	$'000	$'000	$'000	$'000	$'000	$'000
Total working capital	4,000	4,240	4,494	4,764	5,050	5,353	5,674	
Investment in WC	(4,000)	(240)	(254)	(270)	(286)	(303)	(321)	5,674

7 Additional tax – US investment

Additional tax of 3% (33% − 30%) is suffered in the UK on US taxable profits. This is computed by converting the pre-tax cash flow at the exchange rate for the year and then multiplying by 3%. eg Year 1: 2,120 ÷ 1.5627 × 3% = 40.69, rounded to 41.

The net present value of the US investment is **negative £45,000** if the investment cost is the maximum $10 million.

If the cost is only $8m, the NPV is increased by $2m/1.5185 = £1.317m, giving a **positive NPV of £1.272m.**

Conclusion

From the financial appraisal, the Swiss investment is the better alternative. If the US investment is thought to have a positive NPV, then both investments could be undertaken (they are not mutually exclusive) provided adequate funds and management resources were available.

Assumptions

The financial appraisals are based on several assumptions, which are stated during the course of the computation.

Uncertainties

Most of the estimates are subject to considerable uncertainty, for example:

(i)   Estimates of future exchange rates are based upon forecast inflation levels and purchasing power parity theory.

(ii)   Inflation is unlikely to remain at the levels given and may affect different types of costs and revenues in different ways.

(iii)   Tax rates may change.

(iv)   As in most financial appraisals, the most difficult figure to estimate is the residual value at the end of the time horizon of six years.

(v)   Estimates for the Swiss sales figures are more difficult to make than for the US investment, because it is a start-up business.

(vi)   The systematic risk of both investments is assumed to be the same as Omnikit's existing business. If this is not the case then project specific discount rates should be used.

(vii)   Sensitivity analysis could be used to provide more information on which of the above uncertainties cause the most problems.

24 X-Train

(a)   The cost of equity capital can be derived from the Capital Asset Pricing Model.

For X-Train we have:

Market value of equity V_e = £3,500m
Price to book value of equity   = 2.5
Book value of equity   = £1,400m
Debt to equity ratio   = 100%
Book value of debt   = £1,400m

Now the debt is noted as being floating rate with the result that it will be priced at par, hence

Market value of debt V_d =   £1,400m

Since the debt is noted as free of market risk we can calculate the asset beta of X-Train as

$$\beta_a = \frac{3,500}{3,500 + 1,400\,(1-0.3)} \times 2.05 = 1.602$$

From the cash flow statement it is clear that the net debt of City-Train is negligible, hence it may be considered an ungeared company. Since both companies operate in the same sector it is reasonable to presume that their asset betas are the same. As a result, for City-Train we have

$\beta_e = \beta_a = 1.602$

And so through CAPM we can determine the cost of equity of City-Train as

Re $= r_f + \beta_e\,(r_m - r_f)$
    $= 4.55\% + 1.602\,(3.55\%) = 10.2371\%$

The assumptions inherent in the above calculations are those made in the development of CAPM and the theories of Mobdhani and Miller, specifically:

- There is a single risk free rate at which investors can freely invest or borrow.
- Investors are rational and risk-averse.
- Investor expectations are homogeneous.
- Capital markets are perfect.

Other assumptions made in the above calculations are:

- The market risks of the two calculations are identical, hence they have the same asset beta.
- There are no other risk factors (such as size of default risk) that need to be incorporated.

(b)   We can determine the reinvestment rate (b) from the cash flow statement figures as follows

	2006 £m	2005 £m
Net cash from operating activities	504.00	228.00
Net interest	(3.60)	(2.40)
Taxation	(9.84)	(0.48)
Free cash flow to equity (pre-reinvestment)	490.56	225.12
Capital expenditure	288.48	130.00
Free cash flow to equity (post reinvestment)	202.08	95.12
Reinvestment rate $\left(\dfrac{\text{Capital expenditure}}{\text{Freecash flow (pre)}}\right)$	0.588	0.577

Average reinvestment rate = $\dfrac{0.588 + 0.577}{2} = 0.5825$

The return on reinvestment income (r) is more difficult to ascertain. The current figure could be determined as the IRR of the current business portfolio and, since the business is ungeared, this should correspond to the cost of equity of 10.2371%, giving

G = rb = 10.2371 × 0.5825 = 5.963%

Estimate growth rates of the future years are

Year	1	2	3	4	5	6 onwards
Growth	5.963%	5.963%	5.963%	5.963%	5.963%	4.5%

(c)

Time	Cash flow £m	DF	PV £m
1	$202.08 \times 1.05963 = 214.13$	$\dfrac{1}{1.102371}$	194.24
2	$202.08 \times 1.05963^2 = 226.90$	$\dfrac{1}{1.102371^2}$	186.71
3	$202.08 \times 1.05963^3 = 240.43$	$\dfrac{1}{1.102371^3}$	179.48
4	$202.08 \times 1.05963^4 = 254.77$	$\dfrac{1}{1.102371^4}$	172.52
5	$202.08 \times 1.05963^5 = 269.96$	$\dfrac{1}{1.102371^5}$	165.83
5	Future perpetuity* 6,600.41	$\dfrac{1}{1.102371^5}$	4,054.45
			4,953.23

* At time 5, we have constant future growth of 4.5% pa hence at that time we can use

$$E_5 = \frac{FCFE_5\ (1+g)}{r_e - g} = \frac{269.96 \times 1.045}{0.102371 - 0.05963} = £6,600.41m$$

to value all future free cash flows

The assumptions underlying this calculation are:

- The current operating cash flows are sustainable in the long term.
- The estimated growth rates will be achieved.
- The investors required rate of return will remain constant.
- The business is a going concern and can be expected to have an infinite future life.

One important thing to note here which is typical in these types of valuation is that the vast majority (here over 80%) comes from the valuation of the future perpetuity.

As a result, the value is highly susceptible to any variability in the figures used to determine this, particularly

- Future growth rates
- Future cost of capital

(d)   To whomsoever it may concern

The proposed acquisition of City-Train represents a substantial capital investment for your training company X-Train. There are a number of issues which need to be considered before making the acquisition. These are detailed out below:

(i)   **Business synergies**

Given the respective markets of X-Train and City-Train there would be considerable advantages in integration. These can be summarised as follows.

(ii)   **Revenue synergies**

There are likely to be a considerable enhancement in your ability to capture market share that would add shareholder value. Given that City-Train is an unquoted company the shareholders will not be able to achieve this increased value at a lower cost or even by attempting to diversify. The markets in which both companies operate are complementary and there is likely to be substantial opportunities for cross-over business. It would, especially in the short to medium term, be advisable to maintain both companies as independent business where each is able to advise their respective clients about the course provided by the other company. Given the markets; ie accountancy, legal and city training it is more than likely that clients will wish to use more than one set of training courses.

(iii)   **Cost synergies**

There are likely to be cost saving opportunities in the combination of these operations. For example, the administration and client billing system for both companies could be consolidated into a single system thereby provided better management information. The additional printing/publishing requirements may also present opportunities to discuss unit cost reductions from your publishers. In addition, there may be opportunities to save on accommodation costs if the training facilities could be shared to some extent.

(iv)   **Financial synergies**

The larger company would have greater opportunities to acquire finance at more favourable rates and under better conditions.

25 Carpetshop

(a)   **Carpetshop**

Equity

$\beta = 1.12$

Hence the required return to shareholders is

$r = r_f + \beta\,(r_m - r_f) = 5 + 1.12\,(10 - 5) = 10.6\%$

Based on this, the current share price is

$E_{xd} = \dfrac{46 \times 1.03}{0.106 - 0.03} = 623.42c$ or $\$6.2342$

Giving a total equity value on the 1,136m shares of

$E = \$7,082.1m$ ($\$6.2342 \times 1,136m$)

Debt

The required return on its debt based on the 78bp spread is 5.78% giving a debt value of

$D_{xi} = \dfrac{5.25}{0.0578} = \$90.83$

Hence the total value of the $3.72bn debt is

$D = \$3,378.9m$ ($90.83 \times \dfrac{3.72bn}{100}$)

Since the company has no unsystematic risk, the 78bp premium is to cover market risk, ie the debt has a beta of

$\beta_d = \dfrac{5.78 - 5.00}{10 - 5} = 0.156$

Ungeared

If Carpetshop was, therefore, ungeared we would have

$\beta_u = \left[\dfrac{7,082.1}{7,082.1 + 3,378.9 \times 0.7} \times 1.12\right] + \left[\dfrac{3,378.9 \times 0.7}{7,082.1 + 3,378.9 \times 0.7} \times 0.156\right] = 0.87865$

And using the ideas of Modiglian and Miller we could have

$V = U + DT$

Now $V = E + D = 7,082.1 + 3,378.9 = \$10,461.0m$, hence

$10,4610.0 = U + 3,378.9 \times 0.3$

giving

$U = 10,461.0 - 3,378.9 \times 0.3 = \$9,447.33m$

Copers Carpets

Ungeared

Since Copers operated in the same sector and is, therefore, subject to the same market risks we assume that as an ungeared company it would have the same beta, ie $\beta = 0.87865$

As a result, the required return on its equity would be

$r_e = 5 + 0.87865 (10 - 5) = 9.39325\%$

Giving, since it is growing at the same 3% rate as the sector, a share price of

$$E_{xd} = \frac{187 \times 1.03}{0.0939325 - 0.03} = 3{,}012.71p \text{ or } \$30.1271$$

And an capitalisation value on its 98m shares of

$U = \$2{,}952.5m \ (\$30.1271 \times 98m)$

Debt

Having B rated debt requires a 140bp premium over the risk-free rate, hence the debt holders required return will be

$r_d = 5 + 1.40 = 6.40\%$

Giving a debt value of

$$D_{XD} = \frac{6.5}{0.064} = 101.5625$$

And a market value for the $960m debt of

$$D = \$975m \ (\$101.5625 \times \frac{960m}{100})$$

The beta of this debt, since all risk is market risk, will be

$$\beta_d = \frac{6.4 - 5.0}{10 - 5} = 0.28$$

Geared

Using M&M we can calculate the total value of Copers as

$V = U + DT = 2{,}952.5 + 975 \times 0.3 = \$3{,}245m$

Which can be broken down as

	$m
Total value	3,245
Debt value	975
Equity value	2,270

The beta of these shares can be calculated using

$$\beta_g = \beta_u + (\beta_u - \beta_d) \frac{D}{E} (I - T)$$

$$= 0.87865 + (0.87865 - 0.18) \times \frac{975}{2{,}270} \times 0.7 = 1.05864$$

Hence the systematic risk inherent in the shares is

$\sigma_s = \beta\sigma_m = 1.05864 \times 9\% = 9.52776\%$

Options

We need to use the Black-Scholes model to evaluate a call option where

S = $2,270m – current share value
X = $2,250m – exercise price
σ = 9.52776% pa
t = $\frac{3}{12}$ (3 months) or $\frac{6}{12}$ (6 months)

3 month option

$$d_1 = \frac{\ln\left(\dfrac{2,270}{2,250}\right) + (0.05 + 0.5 \times 0.0952776^2) \times \dfrac{3}{12}}{0.0952776 \times \sqrt{\dfrac{3}{12}}} = 0.472$$

$$d_2 = d_1 - \sigma\sqrt{t} = 0.4720 - 0.0952726 \times \sqrt{\frac{3}{12}} = 0.424$$

$N(d_1) = N(0.47) = 0.6808$
$N(d_2) = N(0.42) = 0.6628$

Hence the value at a three month call is

$C = SN(d1) - Xe^{-rt}N(d_2)$

$= 2,270 \times 0.6808 - 2,250 \times e^{-0.05 \times 3/12} \times 0.6628 = \$72.64m$

6 month option

$$d_1 = \frac{\ln\left(\dfrac{2,270}{2,250}\right) + (0.05 + 0.5 \times 0.0952776^2) \times \dfrac{6}{12}}{0.0952776 \times \sqrt{\dfrac{6}{12}}} = 0.536$$

$$d_2 = d_1 - \sigma\sqrt{t} = 0.536 - 0.0952726 \times \sqrt{\frac{6}{12}} = 0.469$$

$N(d_1) = N(0.54) = 0.7054$
$N(d_2) = N(0.47) = 0.6808$

Hence the value of a six month call is

$C = 2,270 \times 0.7054 - 2,250 \times e^{-0.05 \times 6/12} \times 0.6808 = \$107.3m$

(b) For the ungeared business we have ß = 0.87865, giving a cost of capital of

r_e = 5 + 0.87865 (10 − 5) = 9.39325% as we saw earlier

The synergistic gain from the merger will, therefore, be

$$\text{Synergy gain} = \frac{\$18m}{0.093925} = \$191.6m$$

assuming the cost savings into perpetuity.

So for the ungeared combination we have

	$m
Carpetshop	9,447.3
Copers Carpets	2,952.5
Synergy gain	191.6
	12,591.4

And the beta of the combined entity would be 0.87865

If the combined business is re-financed with a debt to equity ratio at 30%, then in proportionate terms we could have

Equity (E)	100
Debt (D)	30
Total (V)	130

And hence $D = \dfrac{30}{130} V$

Now, assuming the debt remains irredeemable we can apply the following

$V = U + DT$

$V = U + \dfrac{30}{130} V \times 0.3$

$V = U + \dfrac{9}{130} V$

$\dfrac{121}{130} V = U$

$V = \dfrac{130}{121} U = \dfrac{130}{121} \times 12{,}591.4 = \$13{,}528m$

Which will be

	$m
Equity $\dfrac{100}{130} \times 12{,}591.4$	10,406
Debt $\dfrac{30}{130} \times 12{,}591.4$	3,122
Total	13,528

Assuming the credit rating of the new enlarged Carpetshop remains unaltered we would have $\beta_d = 0.156$, hence the beta of the equity would be

$\beta_g = \beta_u + (\beta_u + \beta_d) \dfrac{D}{E} (I - T)$
$= 0.87865 + (0.87865 - 0.156) \times 30\% \times 0.7 = 1.03$

(c) To: Whoever
From: A N Other
Date: 20 June 200X
Subject: **Pros and cons of using call options**

A call option gives the right, but not the obligation, to buy an asset at a given price either on (European style), or on or before (America style) a given date. This **right does not come free**, however, and a price or premium must be paid to acquire it. Our analysis above gave the costs of 3 and 6 month options at a strike price of $2.25bn

	$m
3 month option	72.6
6 month option	107.3

against out estimate of the current value of $2.27bn. These options are both clearly $20m in-the-money ($2,270m – $2,250m) and so we can **analyse these premiums** as

	Total premium $m	Intrinsic value $m	Time value $m
3 month	72.6	20.0	52.6
6 month	107.3	20.0	87.3

If we buy either of these options we are paying a significant sum in the form of time value which will never be recovered. Then again, if we buy Copers outright now for $2.72bn and the market takes a downturn then losses could be massive. These time value figures just 1.9% and 3.2% of the current value of Copers.

The **usefulness** of options hinges on our business **view on the likely near-term volatility** of markets. If we believe that markets are liable to be fairly stable then there is little to be gained by paying either of these premiums. If, however, we believe that markets may be more volatile over the next six month then the flexibility afforded by the option will prove advantageous.

26 Hotparts

(a)   To: Board of Directors
From: Chief Financial Officer
Re: **Organic Growth versus Acquisition**

There are a number of factors which need to be considered in evaluating the two options available. These are summarised below

Option 1: Acquisition of Spareparts Co

The operations of Spareparts are **well established** and will only require small modifications to bring them into line with our processes. Thus, the acquisition of Spareparts will offer us a **more rapid entry route** to the market.

Although Spareparts is not a direct competitor, it does operate in the same broad market. Thus the acquisition of Spareparts would be a means of **removing a potential competitor** and could also lead to **increased market share**.

There are considerable **synergies** between Spareparts and our business Hotparts, such as business knowledge, management skills and business processes. This will make the **assimilation** of Spareparts into Hotparts relatively **straightforward and easy**.

The acquisition of Spareparts will incur **lower initial cost** as there will be no set-up cost. Our costs, after acquisition, would be limited to modifications of plant and staff training.

Spareparts would also provide **access to additional distribution channels** and could also lead to an increase in market share.

In addition, the acquisition of an established company with existing assets would provide **additional debt capability** for the new larger organisation.

However, there are **strategic problems** associated with acquisition which need to be considered. Spareparts is an independent organisation and the problems associated with its assimilation into Hotparts Co should not be underestimated. For example, Spareparts has its own customers, suppliers, markets, employees, business systems and processes. The **integration** of all of the above will require careful planning and implementation. Consideration will need to be given to whether there is sufficient capacity at Hotparts to enable successful integration or whether it is likely to lead to management overload.

Like all organisations, Spareparts will have its own individual culture and proposed takeover and integrations of Spareparts into Hotparts may cause **resentment amongst the staff** at all levels as well as amongst Spareparts existing customers and suppliers.

In addition, give the respective locations of Hotparts and Spareparts the **distance between the two** sites will increase the problem of integration.

Finally, is the **purchase price** for Spareparts **too expensive**? Have we had to offer more to buy agreement from reluctant directors who were unwilling to sell?

Option 2: Development of site near Hotparts' site

Growing organically by developing the site **may be cheaper in the long run** as it is more likely to be financed entirely by retained earnings and will not involve paying a premium for a desirable subsidiary.

Hotparts will be developing a new vehicle which has our group's existing culture rather than acquiring a subsidiary with a different culture (which is always hard to change).

Hotparts Co will be able to **use its existing staff and systems** to create the growth projects. This will provide career opportunities for staff and hence lead to **increased staff morale**. Any new staff required would be trained in the ways of Hotpart's current culture and processes and so would easily fit into the new larger organisation.

The overall **expansion and growth can be planned more efficiently**. The proximity of the proposed site to the existing factory will help the organisational efficiency as there will be reduced transport costs. It should also mean that there is no duplication of resources with existing operations.

Economics of scale can be achieved from more efficient use of central head office functions such as finance, purchasing, personnel and management service. With the acquisition of Spareparts we would have had to buy its head office function, leading to either fewer economics of scale or more redundancies.

Growth via the development of the nearby site would allow us to develop in our existing market where we have expertise and thus limit the risk of failure. The different profiles and expectations of our customers and suppliers compared to those of Spareparts could lead to misunderstandings which in turn could affect the success or otherwise of the new larger organisation.

Although the advantages associated with pursuing a policy of organic internal growth are considerable there are also a number of **disadvantages**.

Growth via the development of the site will be **slower** and thus it will be longer before we see positive cash flows from our capital outlaw.

Internal growth will **not provide us access to a new market** which we may be able to develop for our larger organisation.

Growth through acquisition would be immediate, leading to a larger organisation with increased purchasing power from the outset. In the instance of internal growth the benefits of the new larger organisation would not be realised until a considerably later date.

(b)
To: Board of Directors
From: Chief Financial Officer
Date: 20 June 2006
Subject: **Spareparts takeover**

We are considering two alternative expansion options. Both will take five years to complete and, once completed, will offer identical productive capacity and quality. **Assuming the end result will be identical** either way, then from a financial perspective it would be **best to adopt the minimum net cost alternative**.

As we can see from the analysis below, the **minimum cost alternative is to acquire Spareparts** assuming it is available at the estimated $350m. Indeed this option would be preferable up to a price at $361m beyond which option 2 is preferable.

Option 1 – Spareparts

Time	Net revenue $m	Costs $m	Cash flow $m	Discount factor	PV $m
0	–	(350)	(350)	1	(350.0)
0	–	(25)	(25)	1	(25.0)
1	15	(25)	(10)	$1/1.085$	(9.2)
2	15	(5)	10	$1/1.085^2$	8.5
3	24	(5)	19	$1/1.085^3$	14.9
4	24	(5)	19	$1/1.085^4$	13.7
5	24		24	$1/1.085^5$	16.0
NPV					(331.1)

Option 2 – Development site

Time	Cash flow $m	Discount factor	PV $m
0	(150)	1	(150.0)
0	(45)	1	(45.0)
1	(45)	$\dfrac{1}{1.085}$	(41.5)
2	(45)	$\dfrac{1}{1.085^2}$	(38.2)
3	(45)	$\dfrac{1}{1.085^3}$	(35.2)
4	(45)	$\dfrac{1}{1.085^4}$	(32.5)
NPV			(342.4)

Clearly option 1 has an $11.3m lower cost NPV and is therefore, the preferred option.

27 Question with analysis: Laceto

Text references. Chapters 12 and 14 on the calculations, whilst Chapter 13 covers the merger discussion issues.

Top tips. The most important element of (a) is the calculation of the free cash flows and the weight of the marks reflects this. The complications in this calculation are:

- The weighted average cost of capital calculation; we use Omnigen's equity beta (which reflects the systematic risk of Omnigen's activities) to calculate the cost of equity and the loan stock example to calculate the cost of debt.

- The post 20X5 position: the dividend valuation equation can be used to estimate the cash flows given the growth in earnings

Note that the marking guide highlights the need for adjustment of debt values for the equity bid, a suggested minimum price and a reasonable range of prices.

In (b) we give more of the possible suggestions than you would need to gain full marks. We have excluded lobbying for a Competition Commission referral on the grounds that this is unlikely to succeed given the size of the company. We have also excluded the 'white knight', friendly bidder solution, as we have assumed that Laceto does not wish to be taken over. To gain high marks, you needed to mention the financial data in the report.

Easy marks. Although you are well rewarded for the calculations in (a), there are a number of marks available for discussion including predictably limitations of the methods you use. (b) offers a good chances to score well.

(a)   **Minimum price**

The minimum price that Laceto could possibly pay is the **current market price** of the shares, 410p. This would value Omnigen at $123 million. However unless Omnigen's shareholders were expecting the company's share price to fall in the near future, they are likely to be looking for an offer in excess of market price so Laceto will have to pay a **premium**. To decide what the company should pay, it is necessary to look at a range of valuation methods.

Realisable values

The realisable value of Omnigen's assets is **$82 million**. This is below the current market value of Omnigen's shares, reflecting market expectations of Omnigen's future profitability. The shareholders of Omnigen would clearly not accept an offer as low as this, but realisable value has some use of a measure of **comparison**, indicating the possible loss if Omnigen fails to make the necessary dividend payments.

P/E ratios

If the P/E ratios of Omnigen's two competitors were used to provide either end of a range within which the offer price would be located, then the offer price would be somewhere between earnings after tax, $14 million, multiplied by 13 and 15, to give a range of between **$182 million and $210 million**.

Problems with using P/E ratios

(i)   Omnigen's **prospects** may differ substantially from both the companies used as comparisons, thus justifying its lower P/E ratio of $8.78/1 \left(\dfrac{123}{14} \right)$. The fall in the market price over the past few years may be an indication that a strong or semi-strong efficient market is taking a realistic view of Omnigen's future earnings.

(ii)   We are not told anything of the **other factors** that may influence P/E ratios such as Omnigen's **asset backing**, **gearing** or **status** within the industry as compared with its competitors.

Cash flows

Basing the offer on the **present value of the future cash flows** of Omnigen is likely to be a more reliable method than realisable values or P/E ratios, since Laceto is offering to buy the company with a view to develop its operations and hence generate future cash flows. In particular use of **free cash flows,** which take into account plans for **asset replacement** and **future investment**, focus on the strategic aspects of acquisition.

	20X2	20X3	20X4	20X5
	$m	$m	$m	$m
Net sales	230	261	281	298
Cost of goods sold	(115)	(131)	(141)	(149)
Selling/admin expenses	(32)	(34)	(36)	(38)
Capital allowances	(40)	(42)	(42)	(42)
Taxable profits	43	54	62	69
Taxation	(13)	(16)	(19)	(21)
Profits after tax	30	38	43	48
Add: Capital allowances	40	42	42	42
Less: Cash flow needed for asset replacement/growth	(50)	(52)	(55)	(58)
Net cash flow	20	28	30	32
Discount factors 14% (W)	0.877	0.769	0.675	0.592
Present values	18	22	20	19

Working

Cost of equity

Having Omnigen's predicted equity beta and assuming that any variation in gearing between 18% and 23% will not change equity beta,

$$K_e = r_f + [E(r_m) - r_f]\beta_j$$
$$= 6 + 1.3(14 - 6)$$
$$= 16.4\%$$

Cost of debt

Assume Laceto's cost of debt will remain unchanged on acquisition of Omnigen, as Omnigen currently has a lower gearing than Laceto.

Year		Cash flow $	Disc factor 5%	Present value $	Disc factor 6%	Present value
0	MV	(108.80)	1.000	(108.80)	1.000	(108.80)
1–3	Interest (1 – 0.3)	8.4	2.723	22.87	2.673	22.45
3	Redemption	100	0.864	86.40	0.840	84.00
				0.47		(2.35)

$$\text{Cost of debt} = 5 + \frac{(0.47)}{(0.47 + 2.35)}$$

$$= 5.2\%$$

Weighted average cost of capital

At 18% gearing

WACC = (16.4 × 0.82) + (5.2 × 0.18)
     = 14.4%

At 23% gearing

WACC = (16.4 × 0.77) + (5.2 × 0.23)
     = 13.8%

14% is near midway point, therefore use 14%.

Present values if growth is 3% after 20X5

$$\text{Present values} = \text{Present values (20X2-5)} + \frac{\text{20X5 earnings}\,(1+g)}{(r-g)}$$

$$= (18 + 22 + 20 + 19) + \frac{19(1+0.03)}{(0.14 - 0.03)}$$

$$= \$257 \text{ million}$$

Present values if growth is 5% after 20X5

$$\text{Present values} = (18 + 22 + 20 + 19) + \frac{32(1+0.05)}{(0.14 - 0.05)} \times 0.592$$

$$= \$300 \text{ million}$$

Value of shares

Present values are total values of equity. Assuming 3% growth, the value of shares will be between 77% and 82% of $257 million, between $198 million and $211 million. Assuming 5% growth, value will be between 77% and 82% of $301 million, between $232 million and $247 million.

Problems with value calculation

(i)   **Predictions of operating cash flows** may not be accurate.

(ii) **Capital allowances** would not be less than **asset replacement flows indefinitely**.

(iii) Cash flow calculations have been based on an assumed investor time horizon of **infinity**, but in practice the time horizon may not exceed ten years.

Conclusion

Laceto must offer a premium, but must keep this premium as low as possible to **maximise the value to its own shareholders**. An initial offer of $160 million would be halfway between current market value and value of equity under the free cash flows assuming lower (3%) growth and maximum gearing. This would be a premium of about 30% on the current price, but does give Laceto reasonable scope to increase the offer should it initially be refused by shareholders.

(b) **Methods of defence**

Pre-acquisition

Improve asset utilisation

This may be achieved by **taking cash off low-interest deposit accounts**; by **selling redundant non-current assets** such as under-utilised property; **by rationalising operations** to make full use of business assets; or by **improving efficiency of working capital management** (eg reducing inventories and speeding up receivables' collections). In each case the cash released can be returned to shareholders. The effect may be to **boost share price** and persuade shareholders to vote against the bid.

Communicate information about Laceto

Release of information concerning **improved future cash flows** may persuade shareholders that the offer price is too low, and that they should not sell but retain their shares to benefit from future profits. Laceto should concentrate particularly on communicating with key shareholders such as institutional shareholders. A P/E ratio of 10.5:1, lower than other companies in its sector, suggests that Laceto may have scope to do this.

Poison pills

Laceto can grant **rights** to shareholders, to purchase shares at a discount or to exchange shares for **cash or debt securities** at a price in excess of what is likely to be offered by Agressa. It can also provide **golden parachutes,** expensive severance contracts, for directors and senior staff that Agressa would have to honour if they took Laceto over and made the directors or staff redundant.

Articles

The directors of Laceto can attempt to have the company's **articles altered** to require a large yes vote from shareholders to approve an acquisition.

Repurchase

Laceto could use any surplus cash to **re-purchase its own shares** and hence push the price up to a level that Agressa could not afford.

Strategic shareholdings

The directors of Laceto might arrange for a **friendly party to take a significant share** in the company.

Post-acquisition

Present a rational argument against plans

Documents justifying the **company's existing management and strategy** and criticising the bidding company's strategic plans are an important part of the defence procedures when a hostile bid is received. This could include a general analysis of Agressa's future prospects. Laceto's defence could **highlight the volatility of earnings** in the dot-com sector.

Counter-bid

Laceto could make a **counter-bid** for Agressa's shares; Agressa is a much smaller company than Laceto and is smaller than Omnigen. However its P/E ratio is a lot higher, and its activities may not fit well with Laceto's.

Acquisition of Omnigen

Successful acquisition of Omnigen by Laceto may make a successful takeover bid by Agressa less likely as the **combined market capitalisation** may be in excess of what Agressa can afford.

28 McTee

Text references. Chapter 4 covers financing strategy in general. Chapter 14 relates the discussion to different sources of finance. Chapter 7 gives guidance on the cost of capital calculations and Chapter 9 covers the issues involved in international investment.

Top tips. (a) should have been about the financing decision, not the investing (see the examiner's comments).

In his report on (b), the examiner highlighted that he was looking for a logical approach, discussing the strengths and weaknesses of each method, and in particular:

- Cost (requiring calculations)

- Risk (foreign exchange risk is most important)

- Maturity (the need to match a long-term investment in the manufacturer **and** a shorter-term investment in working capital)

- Funds provision (it may seem an obvious point, but not all the finance sources provided enough funds).

The requirements very clearly indicate that a combination of sources of finance is likely to be recommended.

As regards the costs:

- Equity – you are clearly given the details in the question to be able to carry out a dividend valuation calculation.

- Fixed rate loan – you need to do an IRR calculation as the debt is redeemable. Because you can draw up to £50 million, the net finance issued at time 0 after arrangement fees can match the finance required, although you have to gross up the eventual repayment. Interest payments are shown net of tax here and for the other forms of debt.

- Commercial paper – for one year, cost is interest paid, net of tax.

- Swiss Franc loan – again you need an IRR calculation which it's best to carry out in Swiss francs. Amount received at time 0 is SFr80 m – the initial costs, but you have to pay SFr 80m at time 5.

- Eurobond – interest paid is the US rate, net of tax . Again time 0 finance is taken after deducting the initial costs, and the full £42 m has to be repaid at time 10.

- US floating rate loan – easiest to estimate cost as current interest rate (3 + 3) %, net of tax.

The gearing calculation does not include other creditors. You are comparing debt with assets, so don't take into account the market value of shares. The extra debt will give rise to an asset of an equivalent amount, hence its appearance in both halves of the calculation.

As regards the rates to use, you use 1.7985 (the lower rate) to calculate the £ you will need as you will obtain fewer $ for each £ you pay to purchase the dollars you need for investment.

Easy marks. Provided you kept your answers focused on factors affecting finance, you can easily score 7-8 marks on (a). If you bore these factors in mind when answering (b), and clearly discussed the advantages and disadvantages, you can score enough on (b) to pass as well even if you didn't get any of the calculations right. Hopefully you got some right though, as you should have remembered to use an IRR calculation to calculate the value of redeemable debt.

(a)   **Foreign exchange risk**

It is possible to reduce foreign exchange risk by **matching**; using one of the dollar finance options to set against the dollar receipts.

Cost of finance

This covers not only any **annual interest payment costs,** but also arrangement fees, issue costs etc.

Availability

If the purchase is to take place rapidly, the finance should be **available quickly,** or (expensive?) **short-term bridging finance** will be required.

Flexibility

If the directors are expecting to use **different sources of finance,** they will prefer to use sources that can be changed without significant cost.

Period of investment

The length of time the finance is available should **match** the length of the investment period.

Tax

The **tax consequences** of the different sources of finance must be considered, as these may significantly affect their costs.

Desired debt-equity finance mix

The maximum amount of debt is limited by a covenant in any event, but the directors may have their own views about the **desired balance** and hence the **desired level** of **finance risk**. It will be determined by whether they believe that there is an **optimal level of gearing,** at which the company's **weighted average cost of capital** will be at its lowest.

Signalling

By issuing the maximum amount of debt, the directors may wish to demonstrate to the stock market their **confidence in the future**.

Interest rate expectations

The directors will **prefer floating rate finance** if interest rates are expected to **go down, fixed rate finance** if interest rates are expected to **increase**.

Maturity of debt

Directors will be concerned about when the debt is **due to mature**, and McTee's **likely cash position** around that date.

Security

Directors will be concerned about the **amount** of security required, also how any **restrictions over assets secured** might limit business decisions including the ability to raise loan finance in the future

Other sources

Other sources of finance such as **convertible** and **deep-discount bonds** may be appropriate.

(b) To: Directors, McTee
    From: Accountant
    Date: 15 December 20X5
    Subject: **Sources of finance**

Finance required

Amount required = $80 m = £80/1.7985 m = £44.48 m

If all raised by debt, gearing = $\dfrac{38 + 30 + 18 + 44.48}{117.8 + 8.1 + 98.1 + 44.48}$ = 48.6%

This would still be within the **terms of the covenant**, although it would not allow much scope for further investments to be financed solely by debt. There is also no indication that this is the **optimal mix of gearing** and hence **cost of capital** is at its **lowest.**

Rights issue

Amount raised = (80 × ¼ × 2.80)0.95 = £53.2 m

Cost of equity = $\dfrac{22.2(1.04)}{302}$ + 0.04 = 11.6%

Advantages

(i)   The proposed rights issue would comfortably **exceed the amount required.**
(ii)   The company's **gearing**, and thus **financial risk**, would decrease.
(iii)   There would be **no change in control** if the current shareholders took up the rights issue.
(iv)   McTee would not have a commitment to make **interest payments.**
(v)   McTee would not face **exchange risk** on payments to providers of finance.

Disadvantages

(i)   The **arrangement costs** are **higher** than for some of the other alternatives.

(ii)   A **rights issue** is likely to take **longer to arrange** than the other alternatives.

(iii)   The **cost of equity** is **higher** than the cost of debt because of the greater risk to equity shareholders and the company does not obtain the benefit of **tax relief.**

(iv)   The **exchange risk** on the **income from the US investment** remains, as it cannot be matched against the payments to finance providers.

Fixed rate sterling loan

Amount issued = 44.48 × 100/99 = £44.93 m

Cost of debt

Year		Cash flow £m	Disc factor 7%	DCF £m	Disc factor 5%	DCF £m
0	Issue net of issue costs	(44.48)	1.000	(44.48)	1.000	(44.48)
1–5	Interest					
	44.93 × 7% × (1 – 0.3)	2.20	4.100	9.02	4.329	9.52
5	Repayment	44.93	0.713	32.04	0.784	35.23
				(3.42)		0.27

Cost of loan= 5 + [$\dfrac{0.27}{0.27 - (3.42)}$][7 – 5] = 5.1%

Advantages

(i)   Cost is **lower** than some of the other options.
(ii)   There is a **further facility** available which has not been drawn.

Disadvantages

(i)   Because the loan is in sterling, there will be **foreign exchange risk** as the finance is not matched with the dollar income.

(ii)   Conditions may be attached to the security that impose **restrictions** over and above the debt limit.

Commercial paper

Amount issued = $15m   **Cost** = 0.7 (3.0 + 1.5 + 0.5) = 3.5%

Advantages

(i)   McTee will be able to take advantage of **short-term falls in interest rates.**

(ii)   The cost looks **low** compared with other sources.

Disadvantages

(i)   The commercial paper provides **less than 20%** of the finance required.

(ii)   The **maturity** is wrong for the majority of the requirement; commercial paper is a short-term source to finance a long-term requirement of $72 m.

(iii)   There are likely to be some **issuing costs.**

(iv)   The **floating rate** is not attractive if interest rates are **expected to rise.**

Swiss franc loan

Amount raised = 80 (1 − 0.03)/2.298 = £33.77m

Cost of loan

Year		Cash flow SFrm	Disc factor 5%	Disc cash flow SFrm	Disc factor 3%	Disc cash flow SFrm
0	Issue net of issue costs (80 (1 − 0.03))	(77.60)	1.000	(77.60)	1.000	(77.60)
1–5	Interest: 80m × (2.5 + 2.3) % × (1 − 0.3)	2.69	4.329	11.65	4.580	12.32
5	Repayment	80.00	0.784	62.72	0.863	69.04
				(3.23)		3.76

$$\text{Cost of loan} = 3 + \left[\frac{3.76}{3.76 - (3.23)} \right][5 - 3] = 4.1\%$$

Advantages

(i)   The **cost of finance** is still **low** even after the swap fees.

(ii)   McTee can pay interest in the currency in which it is obtaining returns, and thus **reduce exchange risk** by gearing.

Disadvantages

(i)   The loan will not be enough to cover the **whole US investment**; approximately £10 million further finance will be required.

(ii)   McTee would still be exposed to **foreign exchange risk** on the Swiss franc loan itself as against sterling.

(iii)   McTee may be subject to **counterparty risk** although this will be minimal if it uses an intermediary such as a bank.

Eurobond

Assume the Eurobond is denominated in sterling as McTee has a relative price advantage in sterling.

Amount raised = £42m (1 − 0.02 − 0.017) = £40.45 million

Cost

Year		Cash flow £m	Disc factor 5%	Disc cash flow £m	Disc factor 3%	Disc cash flow £m
0	Issue net of issue costs (42m × (1 − 0.037))	(40.45)	1.000	(40.45)	1.000	(40.45)
1–10	Interest: 42m × 4.95 % × (1 − 0.3)	1.46	7.722	11.27	8.530	12.45
10	Repayment	42.00	0.614	25.79	0.744	31.25
				(3.39)		3.25

$$\text{Cost of bond} = 3 + [\frac{3.25}{3.25 - (3.39)}][5 - 3] = 4.0\%$$

Advantages

(i) The interest payment can be **matched against the income** from the investment, reducing foreign exchange risk.

(ii) The cost is **reduced by undertaking** the **swap arrangement.**

(iii) **No security** is required, and McTee's assets could be used as security for additional loans.

(iv) The loan is for a **longer term** than the other financing.

Disadvantages

The Eurobond only raises $80m × 40.45/44.48 = $72.8 million, which is enough to cover the **longer-term financing requirement**, but not enough to cover the shorter term.

Floating rate loan

Amount provided = $40 million

LIBOR = 3%

Cost = (3 + 3) (1 − 0.3) = 4.2%

Advantages

(i) The loan **matches** with dollar income, **reducing exchange risk.**
(ii) If **interest rates fall** during the duration of the loan, the **cost of the loan** will also **fall.**

Disadvantages

(i) The loan only provides **half of the finance** required.
(ii) The loan requires **security.**
(iii) The cost is **higher** at present than some of the other sources of loan finance.
(iv) If **interest rates rise** during the duration of the loan, the **cost of the loan** will also **rise.**

Recommendation

The rights issue should be used if the directors are very concerned about gearing levels, and are prepared to accept a much higher cost of capital than is likely for any of the loan finance.

Of the longer term sources of debt finance, the Eurobond is recommended to cover the $72 million as it has the **lowest cost at present,** will **cover all of the long term investment**, does **not require security** and **matches foreign exchange. Commercial paper**, as the cheapest and best short-term source of finance, can be used to fund the shorter term working capital requirement of $8 m.

29 Kulpar

(a) **Existing position**

The company's existing gearing and value are:

	$m	%
Equity	458	60
Debt	305	40
Company value	763	100

$\beta_e = 1.4$

$$Ke = r_f + [E(r_m) - r_f] \beta_e$$
$$= 5.5 + [14 - 5.5] 1.4$$
$$= 17.4\%$$

Credit rating is A and so pre-tax cost of debt is 9%.

After tax cost of debt $= 9\% (1 - 0.3)$
$\qquad\qquad\qquad\quad = 6.3\%$

WACC $=$ (Equity proportion $\times$ Ke) + (Debt proportion $\times$ (Kd $(1 - t)$))
$\qquad\quad = (0.6 \times 17.4) + (0.4 \times 6.3)$
$\qquad\quad = 13.0\%$

Effect of changes of gearing on cost of capital

$$\beta_a = \beta_e \frac{E}{E + D(1-E)} + \beta_d \frac{D(1-t)}{E + D(1-t)}$$

Assume β_d is zero

$$\beta_a = 1.4 \frac{458}{458 + 305(1 - 0.3)}$$

$$= 0.955$$

We can use this ungeared beta to assess the effect of different capital structures.

80% equity 20% debt

$$\beta_e = \beta_a \frac{E + D(1-t)}{E}$$

$$= 0.955 \left(\frac{0.8 + (0.2(1-0.3))}{0.8} \right)$$

$$= 1.122$$

$$Ke = 5.5 + (14 - 5.5)\ 1.122$$
$$= 15\%$$

Cost of debt depends on interest cover. Assuming value of company is unchanged,

Debt = 20% × $763m
  = $152.6m

If credit rating improves to AA, annual interest would be at maximum 8% × $152.6m = $12.21m.

Earnings before interest and tax = $90m

$$\text{Interest cover} = \frac{90}{12.21}$$

$$= 7.37$$

This confirms credit rating AA and interest cost of 8%.

$$\text{WACC} = (0.8 \times 15) + (0.2(8(1 - 0.3)))$$

$$= 13.1\%$$

40% equity 60% debt

$$\beta_e = 0.955 \left(\frac{0.4 + (0.6(1.03))}{0.4} \right)$$

$$= 1.958$$

$$Ke = 5.5 + (14 - 5.5)\ 1.958$$
$$= 22.1\%$$

Assuming value of company is unchanged:

Debt = 60% × $763m
  = $457.8m

If credit rating worsens to BB, annual interest would be at maximum 11% × $457.8m = $50.36m

Earnings before interest and tax = $90m

$$\text{Interest cover} = \frac{90}{50.36}$$
$$= 1.79$$

This confirms credit rating BB and interest cost of 11%.

$$\text{WACC} = (0.4 \times 22.1) + (0.6 (11(1 - 0.3)))$$
$$= 13.5\%$$

Effect of gearing changes on WACC

The existing capital structure gives the lowest WACC, 13%. If gearing is decreased, some of the benefit of the tax shield on debt is lost. If gearing is increased, the increased financial risks causes an increase in the cost of debt.

Effect of gearing changes on company valuation

Free cash flow this year, CF_0 = EBIT $(1 - t)$ + depreciation − capital spending
$$= 90 (1 - 0.3) + 20 - 20$$
$$= \$63m$$

Free cash flow next year, CF_1 = $63 (1 + g)$

Current valuation, 763 = $\dfrac{CF_1}{(k - g)}$

$$= \dfrac{63 (1 + g)}{(k - g)}$$

$$= \dfrac{63 (1 + g)}{(0.13 - g)}$$

Therefore

$$763 (0.13 - g) = 63 (1 + g)$$

Rearranging

36.19 = $826g$

g = 4.38%

Capital structure 80% equity 20% debt

WACC is 13.1%

Valuation = $\dfrac{63 \times 1.0438}{0.131 - 0.0438}$

$$= \$754m$$

Capital structure 40% equity 60% debt

WACC is 13.5%

Valuation = $\dfrac{63 \times 1.0438}{0.135 - 0.438}$

$$= \$721m$$

The existing capital structure therefore gives the highest valuation.

(b)   The estimates of corporate value based on the formulae used depend on a number of simplifying assumptions which are not true in practice and may cause significant valuation errors. For example:

(i)   **Assumptions**

Various factors which are **assumed** to be **constant** are likely to vary: these include the **growth rate** g, **capital expenditure**, and the **tax rate**, t. The formulae also assume that changes in capital structure can be achieved at **current market values**, **without transaction costs** and **without changing assets** or earnings. In practice, this is not possible.

(ii)   **Formula for free cash flows**

The formula for free cash flow could be improved by **charging tax on earnings after interest** rather than before interest, and by including estimates of **changes in working capital**, which have been omitted.

(iii) **Credit rating**

The company's credit rating will depend on more factors than just interest cover, for example assets available for **security**, **cash flow volatility** and perceived **management ability**. Also a change in credit rating may **affect** the company's **operating income**, by altering its attractiveness to customers and suppliers.

(iv) **Risk of debt**

The company's debt has been assumed to be risk free. In practice this risk, which can be measured by the debt beta, is likely to **increase with gearing** and will affect the cost of capital.

(v) **Effect of high gearing**

Other factors affect the cost of capital at high gearing: for example direct and indirect **bankruptcy costs**, and **'tax exhaustion'** (insufficient profitability to get the full benefit of tax relief on interest).

30 Semer

> **Text references.** The cost of capital calculations are covered in Chapter 7 and free cash flows in Chapter 6; Chapters 2 and 7 discuss determination of capital structure.
>
> **Top tips.** (a) asks you to identify and correct the mistakes, so you need to say what you've done as well as carrying out the calculations. Given that 5% shows a negative value when you do the IRR calculation, there's no reason why you can't use 0% as the second rate.
>
> In (b) (656 – 416.5) is both the decrease in equity, used to calculate the decrease in dividends, and the increase in debt, used with the cost of debt in (a) to calculate the extra cost of debt. One trap in (b) is to adjust free cash flows valuation by interest and dividends; neither affect free cash flows which therefore remain unchanged.
>
> The main points in (c) are that in practice the amount of debt that can be issued is likely to be limited as first the cost of equity and also the cost of debt will increase. In addition purchase of that many shares must have consequences for the market price.
>
> **Easy marks.** The WACC calculation in (a) should have been fairly straightforward if you realised the comment about the historic cost of debt was incorrect. The discussion about issuing debt in (c) should have been fine as it does represent basic knowledge of finance sources.

(a) **Cost of equity**

Correctly calculated.

Cost of debt

The cost of debt is not the coupon rate, but the marginal cost of issuing the new debt.

Year		Cash flow $	Discount factor 5%	Discounted Cash flow $	Discount Factor 0%	Discounted Cash flow $
0	Market value	(112.0)	1.000	(112.0)	1	(112.00)
1–5	Interest, net of tax 8 (1 – 0.3)	5.6	4.329	24.24	5	28.00
5	Redemption	100.0	0.784	78.40	1	100.00
				(9.36)		16.00

$$\text{Cost of debt} = \left(\frac{16.00}{16.00 - (9.36)} \right) \times 5$$

$$= 3.2\%$$

Weighted average cost of capital

WACC should be calculated using **market values**, not **book values**, as weighting.

$$WACC = Ke_g \frac{E}{E+D} + Kd(1-t)\frac{D}{E+D}$$

E = 160 million × $4.10 = $656 million
D = $119 million + ($50 million × 1.12) = $175 million

$$WACC = 11.8 \left(\frac{656}{656+175} \right) + 3.2 \left(\frac{175}{656+175} \right)$$

$$= 10.0\%$$

Company value

Both halves of the equation should be adjusted by the **expected growth rate**.

$$Value = \frac{Free\,cash\,flow\,(1+g)}{WACC - g}$$

$$= \frac{60(1.03)}{0.1 - 0.03}$$

$$= \$883 \text{ million}$$

(b)　New WACC = (11.8 × 0.5) + (3.2 × 0.5)
　　　　　　　= 7.5%

Revised valuation

$$Valuation = \frac{60 \times 1.03}{0.075 - 0.03}$$

$$= \$1,373 \text{ million}$$

(c)　(i)　**Advantages of increasing gearing**

Tax relief

Semer will be able to claim **tax relief on interest paid** and thus reduce the cost of debt.

Lower cost of debt

Because payment of income is more certain than for equity, debt providers are likely to require a lower rate of return, and hence the **cost of debt** will be **lower**.

Sign of confidence

The market may see the issue of debt as a **sign of confidence**, that Semer feels able to service the requirements of debtholders, and this may boost its market price.

Disadvantages of increasing gearing

Increased cost of equity

The **increased financial risk** to equity shareholders brought about by use of **gearing** will mean that the **cost of equity increases**.

Increased cost of debt

If a high proportion of debt is employed, the debtholders will feel that their income is threatened and their **financial risk increased**. This will mean that the cost of debt rises as well as the cost of equity, **pushing up the weighted average cost of capital**, even if it did fall initially when cheaper debt was used.

Bankruptcy

Ultimately Semer will face the risks of the **costs and consequences of bankruptcy** if it cannot meet its **debt commitments**.

Risk aversion of directors

The managing director may not be the only director who is averse to increasing financial risk and also making the **commitments** use of debt requires (payment of interest each year, charges on property leading to loss of control).

Market reaction

The market may not place a generous interpretation on Semer's actions. It may in fact see the issue of debt as a **sign of lack of confidence**, that Semer is issuing debt because it believes the cost of debt is low due to the market undervaluing the risk premium. It may also see the purchase of its own shares as a sign of lack of confidence, that debt raised should be used for **more profitable investments**. These interpretations are likely to increase the cost of debt.

Market efficiency

In any case, if the market is efficient, it will view the company's attempts solely in terms of desiring to **decrease the cost of finance**.

(ii)   **Accuracy of estimates**

Market price

Semer will not be able to purchase all the shares at the current market price. The shareholding to be repurchased amounts to more than **one third of current shares** and such a high level of purchase will increase the market price. The eventual market price of equity and debt is likely to be difficult to forecast.

Weighted average cost of capital

As indicated above, as gearing increases, the cost of equity and debt will ultimately rise, meaning that **WACC will rise**.

Free cash flow

Increases in WACC will **decrease the value of free cash flow** and hence the **value of the company**.

31 Global financial markets

(a)   **The global debt problem**

The 'global debt problem' which has affected some developing countries for nearly thirty years is essentially the result of **domestic economic deficit** in these countries, necessitating the borrowing of money to meet basic requirements such as the import of food and fuel. This was combined with an **overoptimistic risk assessment** on the part of international banks. As a result, the level of debt in these developing countries rose and their ability to repay decreased as increasing amounts of the GDP were absorbed in servicing the debt rather then financing development.

Causes of global debt problem

The deficits of developing countries were caused by the considerable **price increases of fuel** and other commodities in the 1970s and 1980s, **widespread recession**, **reduction in import demand** from more developed countries, relatively **high international interest rates** and the propensity for such perceived financial crises to encourage **capital flight**. All this led to levels of expenditure impossible to sustain without borrowing internationally.

Bank lending

The willingness of major banks to lend vast amounts of money, based on the historical premise that sovereign nations are unlikely to default, meant that many countries in South America and Sub Saharan Africa were able to borrow to the extent that **debt servicing payments exceeded 50%** of total export earnings. Insufficient domestic savings made debt repayment impossible.

Financial contagion

The term 'financial contagion' is used to describe the **potential international proliferation** of **financial and economic problems**, a phenomenon made more prevalent by the easing of investment restrictions, lifting of trade barriers and the general trend towards globalisation. It is possible that problems affecting even a small economy can have a critically damaging effect on the economies of its neighbouring countries, as was seen with the spreading South East Asia crisis in 1997, which started in Thailand.

Interaction of global debt and financial contagion

The financial problems that countries contract from their neighbours can prove crippling where those countries are already in debt, increases in deficit making **debt servicing conditions** progressively **more difficult to meet**.

(b)   **Resolution of global debt crisis**

A number of attempts at resolving global debt have been made, some seeking primarily to **alleviate the difficulties** of the **countries in debt**, some providing a **solution for the lender** alone and some endeavouring to **address the problems faced by both parties**.

(i)   **Write-off of debt**

One solution, for example, is the partial or complete writing off of debt, an approach which clearly **aids borrower nations**, at least in the short term, but involves considerable **cost to lending institutions**. The write-offs are normally combined with conditions imposed by the IMF and by the World Bank on channelling funds towards poverty alleviation.

(ii)   **Sale of debt**

Another method of resolution is the **sale of debt** from one institution to another for less than face value, a means which ensures that the original lender sees at least some return on its loan but which offers no relief to indebted states given that the debt remains intact.

(iii)   **Macroeconomic reforms**

Capital flight can be reduced by creating an economic climate in which investors can see that **funds invested** are **secure** and **produce real returns**. This implies **reforming property** laws and **controlling the macro-economy**, using appropriate fiscal and monetary policies. **The supply side** of the economy can also be improved by methods such as introducing a more flexible market and making the country more internationally competitive.

(iv)   **Other methods**

Attempts to tackle the problems of both borrower and lender have included:

- The **extension of repayment periods** in order to moderate cash outflow
- The **lending of further funds** to countries unable to meet interest payments in order to prevent default, such loans in the main being conditional upon IMF provisos for economic reforms
- **Swapping of debt** into alternative types of commitment, ranging from the equity of local companies to the securing of promises that steps will be undertaken to reduce pollution

(v)   **Limitation of financial contagion**

Given that economic crises commonly arise in countries with fixed exchange rates and subsequently overvalued currencies, it is apparent that the risk of such occurrences and their possible contagion could be significantly lowered if governments implemented **floating exchange rates**.

(c)   The **globalisation** of the financial markets has been **buoyed** by the **creation of the Euro** and the **expansion of the European Union**.

When the European Union began the process of monetary union in the 1990s, the performance of the various member states' economies was noticeably different and there were marked differences in bond yields. However, since that time, many of the disparities have been removed, with the result that **yields have converged significantly**.

The Eurozone bond markets are now highly correlated and, at present, react very much like a homogeneous unit. For example, if the yield on the 10-year German bond rose 100 basis points, then we would expect yields on 10-year bonds from France, Spain, Italy and elsewhere to also rise by around 100 basis points. If this were not the case, then investors would not be indifferent to the investment opportunities available in the Eurozone bond market. Thus, investors would move out of the Italian bond market into Euro Government bonds of countries with stronger economics. It should be noted, however, that this cohesion may come under pressure if the Italian government bond suffers any further downgrades. The strongest core markets in the Eurozone are currently those of German, France, the Netherlands and Spain and the weakest is Italy.

32 Question with answer plan: Noifa Leisure

Text references. Chapter 15.

Top tips. In (a) you do not need to quote any version of the Z-score weightings. (b) has a fairly brief requirement, not divided into sections, and so careful planning of your answer is vital. Several different answers could be equally good, but any reasonable answer will make use of the detailed information given in the question, supporting general conclusions with specific calculations. Weaker candidates will tend to focus on ratio analysis of the group only, and not use the data about the group's various activities, in particular stripping out the investment income.

In a question like this, it is generally best to include the ratio calculations in an appendix rather than have them break up the discussion. The ratios are split into the three main categories of profitability, liquidity (short-term stability), debt and gearing (longer-term stability). The list of additional factors emphasises a number of important points, including the need for a detailed breakdown of operations, the impact of changing accounting policies or bases (revaluation), and the limitations of accounting information (several months old). A conclusion is needed although not specifically requested in the question.

Easy marks. Although the vagueness of the question requirements may appear offputting, there are a number of ways of ensuring you score well. You should be familiar from other papers with the limitations of accounting information, and being able to discuss these will always earn you a number of marks, particularly in the context of corporate problems.

For questions like (b) where you're asked to analyse a company, a balanced answer will always score well. That means comments on the key areas of profitability/returns to shareholders, liquidity and gearing, supported by some calculations, but not so many so that you leave yourself inadequate time for discussion. Here planning your answer should indicate what your discussion has to cover, and give you an idea of how much time you need for it.

Answer plan

(a)   **Corporate failure models**

Financial signs

- Ratios
- Z-scores
- Problems with accounting measures

Non-financial models

- Poor management, lack of control systems

(b) **Strategic objectives**

Group analysis

- Profitability
- Gearing
- Liquidity
- Shareholders

Additional factors

- Investment income
- Fixed asset revaluation
- Involvement in other businesses
- Post balance sheet events

Appendix

Calculations only for 20X6 and 20X9

Basic ratios

Profitability

- ROCE
- PBIT%
- Asset turnover

Debt and gearing

- Gearing
- Debt ratio
- Interest cover

Liquidity

- Current ratio
- Quick ratio

Shareholders

- P/E ratio

Ratios without investment income

- Profitability ratios

Ratios without investment income and revaluation

- ROCE
- Asset turnover
- Gearing

Sector analysis

- Net profit
- % of total turnover

(a) **Corporate failure models**

Ratios

Many corporate failure models are based on the idea that certain financial measures give a good indication of probable troubles. **Liquidity ratios**, the current and quick ratios, are often argued to be good indicators. A company with a current ratio well below 2:1 or a quick ratio well below 1:1 might be considered illiquid and in danger of failure. Research seems to indicate, however, that the current ratio and the quick ratio and trends in the variations of these ratios for a company, are often poor indicators of eventual business failure.

Z scores

Z score models calculate and weight a number of relationships between the figures in the accounts. These indicators are then used to derive a **Z score**. Firms with a Z score above a certain level are predicted to be financially sound, and firms with a Z score below a certain level are categorised as probable failures.

Problems with accounting measures

Using financial information to calculate Z scores or predict failure by another method has the following drawbacks.

(i) The information is essentially **backward-looking** and takes no account of current or future situations. The time lag between the year-end and the publication of the accounts means that **post balance sheet events** may have had a significant impact upon the business since the date to which the accounts were prepared.

(ii) The use of **creative**, or even **fraudulent**, **accounting** can be significant in situations of corporate failure.

(iii) Some financial information may not be easy to analyse by means of ratio analysis, but may still be a good indicator of future difficulties, such as a **worsening net liquid funds position or contingent liabilities**.

(iv) **Other information**, often non-financial, may be needed to give a **reliable assessment** of a company's prospects. This includes information in the chairman's or the directors' report, press comment, or other information relating to significant external matters such as **changes in legislation, competitor activity, or changes in interest or exchange rates**.

Other models

Some failure models such as Argenti's, treat financial indicators as one of a number of indicators of problems. Other signs include defects in management such as an inactive board and lack of budgetary control, or fundamental mistakes such as over-trading, too high a proportion of debt finance, or too great a dependence on a single project. The main problem with this sort of model is giving a **weighting** to each factor. Attempts at giving weightings are likely to be subjective and not be relevant for all companies. However it is difficult to use the model as a predictor if no weightings are given.

(b) **Strategic objective**

The Chairman appears to be emphasising **growth as the primary company objective**. The annual growth in turnover over the past four years has been impressive (averaging $\sqrt[3]{(680/325)} - 1 = 28\%$). However, the primary objective of the company should be **shareholder wealth maximisation**. Although growth may be compatible with this objective, it can be detrimental to shareholder wealth maximisation if it is achieved either by excessive increases in financial risk or at the cost of the efficient utilisation of assets.

Analysis at the level of the group

The following ratios are significant.

(i) From the drop in **ROCE** it can be seen that the group's apparent strategic objective has been achieved at the expense of profitability. This drop in profitability is apparently due to a fall in net profit before tax rather than asset turnover.

BPP
LEARNING MEDIA

(ii)   **Gearing** has increased on the above figures, indicating higher levels of financial risk, while interest cover has decreased markedly.

(iii)   **Current and quick ratios** have deteriorated from what appeared to be an inadequate base in the first place. It is usual to expect at least a ratio of 1 for the quick ratio to ensure continued solvency. However, given that hotels presumably have a high cash element to their turnover, this might not be significant. In addition, the inclusion of the bank overdraft as a current liability, while legally correct, may disguise the fact that this overdraft is available on a long-term basis.

(iv)   The **price earnings ratio** has indeed increased, by approximately 1.41 times. However, P/E ratios in the industry as a whole have increased by 2.5 times, so the group appears to be underperforming relative to its sector. Similarly the share price has increased by approximately 159/82 = 1.94 times, whereas the sector-wide increase has been 394/178 = 2.21 times.

Additional factors

This analysis ignores several additional factors.

(i)   The company originally derived a **substantial amount of income** from investments, which represented a significant asset in 20X6.

(ii)   There has been a **revaluation** of the fixed assets.

(iii)   The company is involved in a **number of businesses** other than the hotel industry.

(iv)   Since the end of the financial year, **significant developments** have occurred, which might impact significantly on the above ratios, especially via share price.

Analysis after allowing for investment income and investment assets

This analysis reveals a substantial drop in **ROCE**. The drop could be due to a deterioration in the profitability of existing assets, the acquisition of under performing assets or subsidiaries, or a combination of both.

Net profit percentage has also dropped, although not by as large a percentage. The problem appears to be due to a lack of growth in turnover to match the assets acquired. This is demonstrated by the fall in asset turnover.

Revaluation of fixed assets

The revaluation of the group's assets has altered the ratios significantly, especially the **gearing ratio**. Whether this alteration makes the ratios more or less comparable with 20X6 it is difficult to say. It depends on how close to market values the 20X6 values are, and whether the revaluation made was to a realistic market value. This in turn depends on the basis of the revaluation, and whether it was carried out by an independent person.

Involvement in other businesses

The company is involved in a number of businesses other than the hotel industry.

From the analysis it can be seen that the drop in group profitability can be attributed to a change in the mix of turnover to the hotel business, with its lower profit percentage. This was exacerbated by a drop in the actual level of profitability achieved by this business.

It is impossible to say which business caused the deterioration in the **asset turnover** figure without information on the breakdown of assets by business.

Post balance sheet events

The managing director has indicated that the company has expanded further into the hotel industry via the acquisition of Beddall Ltd. This is likely to **further depress group profitability** (because of the greater emphasis on this sector). The actual effect of the deal will depend on the levels of profitability achieved by Beddall's assets and business.

This deal has been **financed by debt**, which will further increase gearing levels, something of major concern. The debt is in the form of euros, exposing the group to potential losses due to the fluctuation of the euro against the pound. If the reason for taking out the loan in euros was purely to take advantage of the lower interest rate, then this was unwise, since it is likely to be compensated for by currency depreciation in the future.

However, it is possible that the group's business is associated with the **strength** of **other European currencies** (perhaps a large proportion of business is with EU countries), in which case the loan could act as a hedge against company profit fluctuations. Whether it is wise for the company to remove this risk depends on the ability of the company's shareholders to achieve this objective individually at lower cost.

Conclusion

From the information given, the company is performing worse than would be expected in comparison with other companies in the same sector. There has been a **significant deterioration in profitability, liquidity and stability**. The company appears to have expanded in the area in which it has the lowest level of profitability (hotels), and has not maintained the profit margins in this area. The assets it has acquired, and/or the profitability of its existing assets, have fallen dramatically.

I would disagree with the Chairman's statement, and advise the company to concentrate on fundamental improvements to existing business assets before further growth is pursued.

Appendix

Basic ratio analysis

	Formula	20X6		20X9	
Profitability					
Return on capital employed	$\dfrac{\text{PBIT}}{\text{Capital}}$	$\dfrac{67}{268}$	25%	$\dfrac{93}{603}$	15.4%
Net profit % before interest and tax	$\dfrac{\text{PBIT}}{\text{Turnover}}$	$\dfrac{67}{325}$	20.6%	$\dfrac{93}{680}$	13.7%
Asset turnover	$\dfrac{\text{Turnover}}{\text{Assets}}$	$\dfrac{325}{285+98}$	0.85 ×	$\dfrac{680}{700+209}$	0.75 ×
Debt and gearing					
Gearing	$\dfrac{\text{Total loans}}{\text{Equity}}$	$\dfrac{42+80}{146}$	83.6%	$\dfrac{68+102+180}{321}$	109%
Debt ratio	$\dfrac{\text{Total debt}}{\text{Total assets}}$	$\dfrac{115+42+80}{285+98}$	61.9%	$\dfrac{306+102+180}{700+209}$	64.7%
Interest cover	$\dfrac{\text{PBIT}}{\text{Interest payable}}$	$\dfrac{67}{14}$	4.8	$\dfrac{93}{36}$	2.6
Liquidity					
Current ratio	$\dfrac{\text{Current assets}}{\text{Current liabilities}}$	$\dfrac{98}{115}$	85.2%	$\dfrac{209}{306}$	68.3%
Quick ratio	$\dfrac{\text{CAs less stock}}{\text{Current liabilities}}$	$\dfrac{58}{115}$	50.4%	$\dfrac{99}{306}$	32.4%
Shareholders					
P/E ratio	$\dfrac{\text{Share price} \times \text{issued shares}}{\text{Earnings}}$	$\dfrac{0.82 \times 500}{30}$	13.7	$\dfrac{1.59 \times 500}{41}$	19.4

Adjusting ratios to remove the 'business' of investments from the company

	Formula	20X6		20X9	
Profitability					
Return on capital employed	$\dfrac{\text{PBIT}}{\text{Capital} - \text{investments}}$	$\dfrac{49}{268-120}$	33.1%	$\dfrac{92}{603-4}$	15.4%
Net profit % before interest and tax	$\dfrac{\text{PBIT}}{\text{Turnover}}$	$\dfrac{49}{325}$	15.1%	$\dfrac{92}{680}$	13.5%
Asset turnover	$\dfrac{\text{Turnover}}{\text{Assets}}$	$\dfrac{325}{383-120}$	1.24 ×	$\dfrac{680}{909-4}$	0.75 ×

Adjusting ratios for both the investment income and the valuation of fixed assets

	Formula	20X6	20X9	
Profitability				
Return on capital employed	$\dfrac{\text{PBIT} - \text{interest rec'd}}{\text{Capital} - \text{invmts.} - \text{revaln.res}}$	33.1%	$\dfrac{92}{603-4-100}$	18.4%
Asset turnover	$\dfrac{\text{Turnover}}{\text{Assets} - \text{invmts.} - \text{revaln.res}}$	1.24 ×	$\dfrac{680}{909-4-100}$	0.84 ×
Debt and gearing				
Gearing	$\dfrac{\text{Total loans}}{\text{Equity} - \text{revaln. res.}}$	83.6%	$\dfrac{68+102+180}{321-100}$	158%

Analysis of figures given for other businesses

Net profit percentage

		20X6 %		20X9 %
Hotels	36/196	18.4	45/471	9.6
Bus company	6/24	25.0	18/46	39.0
Car hire	7/43	16.0	15/62	24.0
Waxworks	1/10	10.0	5/14	36.0
Publications	3/32	9.0	5/43	12.0

Percentage of total turnover

		20X6 %		20X9 %
Hotels	196/325	60	471/680	69
Bus company	24/325	7	46/680	7
Car hire	43/325	13	62/680	9
Waxworks	10/325	3	14/680	2
Publications	32/325	10	43/680	6

33 Snowwell

> **Text references.** Chapter 7 for the WACC calculation and Chapter 15.
>
> **Top tips.** The calculations require knowledge of ratios that you should have from lower level papers. It's important to suspend any doubts you have when doing the calculations; (b) and (c) give you a chance to discuss your misgivings.
>
> Knowledge from lower level papers on how to tackle cash shortages is also relevant for (d), although your suggestions have to be relevant. Note the emphasis in (e) on market efficiency; bring this topic into discussions, even if you are not prompted to do so in the question requirements.
>
> **Easy marks.** (d) discusses points that will often be relevant to companies in financial difficulties.

(a) $S1 = \dfrac{43}{2.32 \times 2 \times 75} = 0.124$

$S2 = \dfrac{193 - 215}{150 + 94 + 192} = -0.050$

S3

Market value of equity = $75 \times 2 \times 2.32 = \$348$ million

Market value of debt

Time		Cash flow $	Discount factor 8%	Discounted cash flow $
1-3	Interest	14	2.577	36.08
3	Redemption value	100	0.794	79.40
				115.48

Market value of debt = $94 + (150 \times 1.1548) = 267.22$

$S3 = \dfrac{348}{267.22} = 1.302$

S4

	$ million
Profit before tax	23
Depreciation	38
Interest, net of tax	14
Taxation	(7)
Replacement capital expenditure	(35)
Increase in working capital (22 − 24)	(2)
Free cash flows	31

Weighted average cost of capital $= 12\,\dfrac{348}{348 + 267.22} + 8(1 - 0.3)\,\dfrac{267.22}{348 + 267.22} = 9.22\%$

Free cash flows to infinity $= 31/0.0922$
$\qquad\qquad\qquad\qquad\qquad = 336.23$

$S4 = \dfrac{336.23}{620} = 0.542$

$S0 = (3.5 \times 0.124) - (1.8 \times 0.05) + (0.25 \times 1.302) + (0.69 \times 0.542) = 1.043$

(b)   **Significance of figure**

The score appears to suggests that Snowwell needs to take some remedial action urgently, as it is approaching the point where failure appears to be probable.

Limitations of model

However there are a number of reasons for doubting the calculations.

(i)   The calculation is based on a single year's data, possibly **out-of-date**, whereas a trend figure showing a fall over a number of years may be a **more reliable indicator of approaching difficulties**.

(ii)   There is no evidence available as to why the business's school's model used the **ratios selected** (and not others), and very importantly why those particular weightings were chosen.

(iii)   The business school's model may have based on companies in industries that have **very different characteristics** to the high quality jewellery industry.

(iv)   The business's school's model has only been **developed recently**, and thus evidence of how effective the model has been as a predictor since it was developed will be limited.

(c)   **Other financial models**

Snowwell may use models with a longer history than the SO model, models that have proved to be reliable predictors in the jewellery and similar industries. However the problem with all financial models is that they are essentially backward-looking and do not take account of events that have happened since the **year-end or future conditions**. The models are also only as reliable as the accounting information used within them.

Ratios

Careful use of **key ratios** may be a more reliable method of predicting corporate failure than more sophisticated failure models.

Important ratios for Snowwell include:

Current and quick ratios

The current and particularly the quick ratios of Snowwell appear to be much lower than would be considered desirable in most industries. Although Snowwell's inventory should not deteriorate because of age, the company is very dependent on being able to **sell that inventory and generate profits**.

Gearing

Gearing analysis will demonstrate whether Snowwell is **matching long-term assets with long-term funds** and how **dependent** the company is on **debt finance**. In addition the **redemption date of loan stock** will indicate how near in the future Snowwell will have a heavy cash commitment.

Non-financial analysis

The managing director may also consider using models that take into account non-financial factors, such as Argenti's model, as an **indicator of financial uncertainties**. The main difficulty of this model is that the assessments required are subjective and involve judgement on delicate issues. It will be difficult for the Chief Executive to assess whether he himself is autocratic or whether the board is too passive (both factors in Argenti's model).

(d)   **Implications of report**

Whether or not the model is an accurate predictor, it does highlight potential weaknesses in Snowwell's balance sheet about which action should be taken:

Working capital

	20X3	20X2
Current ratio	$\dfrac{193}{215} = 0.90$	$\dfrac{164}{188} = 0.87$
Quick ratio	$\dfrac{193 - 156}{215} = 0.17$	$\dfrac{164 - 127}{188} = 0.20$

Snowwell's major problem is that inventory has increased at a significantly faster rate than revenue (23% compared with 7%) and payables have also increased by 18%. The low quick ratio indicates that Snowwell's **current liabilities** are **greatly in excess of receivables and cash**, so it could be in great difficulty if major payables enforced payment, as inventory may not be easily realisable. Snowwell should consider raising more long-term finance to overcome this weakness. Alternatively it may be able to reduce amounts owed by cutting down on lines of inventory held, concentrating on lines with shorter turnover periods.

Long-term finance

	20X3	20X2
Gearing (book values)	$\frac{244}{192} = 127.1\%$	$\frac{214}{193} = 110.9\%$
Gearing (market values)	$\frac{267.22}{348} = 76.8\%$	
Interest cover	$\frac{43}{20} = 2.15$	$\frac{52}{18} = 2.89$

Gearing has increased over the last year, with the increase in book gearing matching the increase in non-current assets. **Interest cover** has decreased, and seems now to be quite low.

The directors thus need to be careful in choosing the right source of long-term finance. Gearing is already in excess of industry average, but funds have recently been raised by floating rate loans, which are on potentially disadvantageous terms if interest rates rise. Given the need to reduce current liabilities, and given the need to invest $35 million each year, Snowwell should consider an equity issue as the next major source of long-term finance.

Profitability

Although revenue has increased, EBIT has deteriorated suggesting industry pressures on profit margins or **cost problems**. Snowwell may be able to improve cash flow by **tighter controls over costs**.

Dividends

Snowwell appears to be **maintaining its dividend levels** despite falling profits, and the directors should consider reducing these. However this may have the feared adverse impact on market prices.

(e) **Market efficiency**

If the stock market is showing strong efficiency, then the stock market will have already taken into account the information the report will contain. Thus there will be no impact on share price if the report does become public knowledge. Snowwell would therefore only wish to purchase the report if the market showed **weak or no efficiency**.

Value of report

Assuming limited market efficiency, whether Snowwell purchases the report will depend on how reliable it thinks the report will be. The organisation has a good reputation, and if Snowwell can find out how accurate its predictions have been, it may have a reason to purchase. Snowwell's decision may depend on why it thinks the **organisation's view is superior to the stock market** (which clearly does not expect Snowwell to fail, given a market price of 232p) and whether the organisation is able to carry out **analysis that is much better** than could be carried out by Snowwell itself. Snowwell should also consider whether the report might contain information that the directors should not withhold from the market even if they obtained it privately.

34 Vadener

Text references. Chapter 15 covers performance analysis, Chapter 9 covers translation risk.

Top tips. To score well in (a) you needed to calculate for three years ratios under all the headings we use, though not necessarily all the ratios we have calculated. We have asterisked the ratios we think you should have included as a minimum, but have included other calculations as a check for you if you calculated those ratios as well. As these are simple calculations the examiner expects them to be done quickly.

Although it is unclear precisely how much time to spend on calculations and discussion, when planning your answer you should have allowed enough time to write a paragraph on each of the major areas of performance, plus one on the divisions – and enough time to make worthwhile comments in each paragraph about what the figures could signify.

The only calculation that can be done with the divisions is the required v actual return calculation (alpha values), and hopefully you picked up that you needed to do this (being given CAPM information and actual return is always a sign). (c) emphasises the importance of market efficiency– will the market be 'fooled' by translation losses or gains.

Easy marks. It should be possible to gain full marks in (b) by asking yourself certain questions when planning.

- Are there any figures in the group accounts that could usefully be broken down further? (operating costs)

- What information do we have for the group that we don't have for the divisions?

- What information do we need to carry out a fair valuation of the group?(cash flow data to assess its ability to generate cash flows)

- What other comparisons would it be useful to make? (competitor)

- What information do we need to assess financial performance in the light of Vadener's business strategy? (competitor, market and product information)

(a)   **Group performance**

Profitability

The company has expanded over the last two years, and the increase in turnover (23.1%) has outpaced the increase in operating costs (16.3%). It certainly appears as if there has been some expansion of business; the increase may also be due to Vadener being able to charge **higher prices**, but this raises the question of whether it can increase prices further. Alternatively the increase in profit margins could be due to better purchasing terms or improved control of operating costs. However the explanation of improved operating cost control appears to be inconsistent with deteriorating working capital management discussed below.

Debt and gearing

The **gearing ratios** do not appear to be excessively high, although it would be helpful to know what the normal figure was for conglomerates like Vadener. However an interest cover of 8.6 times does not suggest that the group is over-geared.

Liquidity and working capital management

Working capital levels appear high, although Vadener's involvement in the construction sector may mean that levels are higher than if it was just involved in leisure or pharmaceuticals. Certainly all of the three measures have increased over the last two years, indicating **poorer control** over stock and debtors, and possibly an increased reliance on short-term funding. The acid test ratio appears quite low at 0.7, possibly indicating cash flow difficulties, particularly if creditors tighten up on the terms offered.

Stock market performance

Vadener's **share price** appears to be underperforming. Its rate of increase of 12% in recent years is below the market average of almost 16% ($(4,960/3,700)^{0.5} - 1$), when its equity beta of more than 1 suggests it should be greater than the market average. Vadener's P/E ratio of 13 is lower than the similar company's ratios of 15. The market may not view Vadener's recent expansion in business and price rises as sustainable. Alternatively Vadener's **dividend cover** may be viewed as **too low**, either because investors do not wish to receive large dividends because of poor tax efficiency, or because the market may view high dividend levels as signifying that there is a lack of opportunities to invest surpluses earned in profitable projects.

Divisions

The only comparison that can be made with the divisional information available is the **alpha value** calculation of **actual return** versus **required return** as calculated by the capital asset pricing model. This suggests that the construction and leisure are doing better than expected, and the pharmaceutical division less well. The pharmaceutical division's position is also complicated by the translation loss, and its possible greater **economic exposure** (although the other divisions may have some vulnerability to economic exposure as well, despite being based in the UK).

On the basis of the information available, Vadener should **not divert equal resources to each division**, but the information is inadequate for an informed decision to be made. We need more detailed information, data about future market prospects, and indications of the board's strategy, particularly as regards foreign expansion (see (b)).

		20X5	*20X4*	*20X3*
Profitability				
* Profit margin	$\dfrac{\text{Operating profit}}{\text{Turnover}}$	$\dfrac{560}{1,490} = 38\%$	$\dfrac{540}{1,410} = 38\%$	$\dfrac{410}{1,210} = 34\%$
Asset turnover	$\dfrac{\text{Turnover}}{\text{Long-term capital employed}}$	$\dfrac{1,490}{1,876} = 0.8$	$\dfrac{1,410}{1,665} = 0.8$	$\dfrac{1,210}{1,486} = 0.8$
* Return on capital employed	$\dfrac{\text{Operating profit}}{\text{Long-term capital employed}}$	$\dfrac{560}{1,876} = 30\%$	$\dfrac{540}{1,665} = 32\%$	$\dfrac{410}{1,486} = 28\%$
Debt and gearing				
Debt ratio	$\dfrac{\text{Current liabilities + Long-term liabilities}}{\text{Total assets}}$	$\dfrac{1,269}{2,675} = 47\%$	$\dfrac{1,138}{2,383} = 48\%$	$\dfrac{965}{2,051} = 47\%$
* Gearing (*BPP LM note.* Gearing could have been calculated excluding short-term loans)	$\dfrac{\text{Long-term liabilities + Short-term loans}}{\text{Long-term liabilities + Short-term loans + Equity}}$	$\dfrac{671}{2,077} = 32\%$	$\dfrac{580}{1,835} = 32\%$	$\dfrac{535}{1,621} = 33\%$
Interest cover	$\dfrac{\text{Operating profit}}{\text{Net interest}}$	$\dfrac{560}{65} = 8.6$	$\dfrac{540}{56} = 9.6$	$\dfrac{410}{40} = 10.3$
Liquidity				
* Current ratio	$\dfrac{\text{Current assets}}{\text{Current liabilities}}$	$\dfrac{1,015}{799} = 1.3$	$\dfrac{863}{728} = 1.2$	$\dfrac{728}{565} = 1.3$
* Acid test ratio	$\dfrac{\text{Current assets} - \text{Stock}}{\text{Current liabilities}}$	$\dfrac{525}{799} = 0.7$	$\dfrac{453}{728} = 0.6$	$\dfrac{388}{565} = 0.7$
Stock days	$\dfrac{\text{Stock} \times 365}{\text{Operating costs}}$	$\dfrac{490 \times 365}{930}$ $= 192$ days	$\dfrac{410 \times 365}{870}$ $= 172$ days	$\dfrac{340 \times 365}{800}$ $= 155$ days

		20X5	*20X4*	*20X3*
Debtor days	$\dfrac{\text{Debtors} \times 365}{\text{Turnover}}$	$\dfrac{510 \times 365}{1,490}$	$\dfrac{438 \times 365}{1,410}$	$\dfrac{378 \times 365}{1,210}$
		= 125 days	= 113 days	= 114 days
Creditor days	$\dfrac{\text{Creditors} \times 365}{\text{Operating costs}}$	$\dfrac{430 \times 365}{930}$	$\dfrac{401 \times 365}{870}$	$\dfrac{302 \times 365}{800}$
		= 169 days	= 168 days	= 138 days

Market ratios

		20X5	*20X4*	*20X3*
* Dividend yield	$\dfrac{\text{Dividend per share}}{\text{Market price}}$	$\dfrac{61.7}{1,542} = 4\%$	$\dfrac{56.7}{1,417} = 4\%$	$\dfrac{48.7}{1,220} = 4\%$
* Earnings per share	$\dfrac{\text{Profit after tax}}{\text{Number of shares}}$	$\dfrac{346}{300} = 115.3p$	$\dfrac{339}{300} = 113.0p$	$\dfrac{259}{300} = 86.3p$
* Price earnings ratio	$\dfrac{\text{Market price}}{\text{Earnings per share}}$	$\dfrac{1,542}{115.3} = 13$	$\dfrac{1,417}{113} = 13$	$\dfrac{1,220}{86.3} = 14$
* Dividend cover	$\dfrac{\text{Profit after tax}}{\text{Dividends}}$	$\dfrac{346}{185} = 1.9$	$\dfrac{339}{170} = 2.0$	$\dfrac{259}{146} = 1.8$

Required return

Return = $r_f + [E(r_m) - r_f]\beta_j$

Group

Return = 5 + (12 − 5) 1.1 = 12.7%

Actual return = Dividend yield + Increase in share price
= 4 + 12
= 16%

Divisions

	Required return	*Actual return*
Construction	5 + (12 − 5) 0.75 = 10.25%	13%
Leisure	5 + (12 − 5) 1.1 = 12.7%	16%
Pharmaceuticals	5 + (12 − 5) 1.4 = 14.8%	14%

(b) **Divisional data**

It would be helpful to have the same level of detail about divisions as is available about the group as a whole, in particular:

- How divisional turnover and profitability have changed over the last few years

- Divisional asset utilisation

- Recent investments in each division and the actual and expected returns on these

- Divisional working capital management (particularly as optimum working capital levels are likely to differ significantly between divisions)

- Economic exposure of the pharmaceutical division

Turnover

Helpful data for group turnover would be how much the increase was **due to increased volume of business**, and how much **due to higher prices**.

Cost data

A breakdown of operating costs between cost of sales and other costs would provide more information on whether Vadener was benefiting from **better supply terms**, or was more profitable because of **tighter control** over other operating costs.

Comparative data

It would be helpful to have data for other companies as a point of comparison, although comparisons on a group-wide basis might be of limited use given the diversified nature of Vadener's activities. It would be more useful to have comparative sector information so that the performance of each **division** could be compared.

Other market information

Other useful information would be the strength of **competition** that each division faces, and **expected market growth rates** in those sectors.

Forecast figures

Forecast figures, particularly **cash flow forecasts**, would assist in a realistic valuation of the company, as in an efficient market, valuation ought to equal the sum of expected cash flows.

Strategic information

Useful information about the group's strategy would include future **product and investment plans**, and what might change the **equal resources strategy.**

(c) **Translation loss**

A loss on translation is a loss on restatement of assets; it does not affect cash flows unless the assets are realised. If the assets continue in the business, a translation loss has no impact on their ability to generate economic value.

Implications of market efficiency

If the stock market is **efficient**, a translation loss should not have any impact on share price, since share price will be dependent on Vadener's ability to generate cash flows. However if the stock market is inefficient, and therefore **accounting profits do impact** upon share price, then translation losses may depress share prices and they should therefore be kept to a minimum.

Need for hedging

If the directors believe that translation losses may impact upon share prices, they may undertake **internal hedging**, for example matching the asset with a liability in the same currency. However such internal hedging should fit in with hedging of more significant risks, for example transaction risk on significant receipts or payments. It should also be compatible with Vadener's strategy in other respects, for example raising a loan abroad to match the assets may conflict with financial strategy because it raises gearing or because the cost of the loan is too high.

35 Stanzial

(a)   We need to value Besserlot's equity since Stanzial will need to acquire a majority of it to gain control.

   (i)   **Asset-based valuation**

   This can be done on the basis of historic book values, replacement cost values or disposal values. The information provided allows for a book value-based valuation with adjustments made for some items.

	£'000
Net assets	6,286
Patent	10,000
Stock adjustment (30% × 3,400)	(1,020)
	15,266

   This implies a valuation of around **£15.3 million.**

   Problems with asset-based valuation

   There are a number of problems with this method that means it is unlikely to produce a realistic valuation.

   (1)   Book valuations depend on Besserlot's **amortisation and depreciation policy**.

   (2)   The book valuation of assets does **not necessarily reflect their future economic earnings power**, which will interest potential purchasers more.

   (3)   A book values based valuation takes **no account** of **significant intangible assets** that are not in the balance sheet such as the value of human capital.

   (4)   The adjustments relate to the **disposal value of individual assets**; however Besserlot is not being sold on an asset-by-asset basis, but as a going concern.

   (5)   The valuation above is a **hybrid method** that does **not value assets on a consistent basis**.

   Overall an asset-based valuation can be used as the minimum bidding price; shareholders of Besserlot may be reluctant to sell for less than this value.

   (ii)   **P/E ratios**

   This method is based on applying **a fair P/E ratio** to Besserlot's earnings. As Besserlot is unlisted, it does not have a published P/E ratio, and so the calculation is based on **industry figures**.

   If we are using the 20X6 earnings as the basis for the valuation of Besserlot's shares, these need to be adjusted for the exceptional items.

	£'000
Loss before taxation	(983)
Add back: Exceptional items	2,005
Adjusted profit before tax	1,022
Taxation 30%	(307)
Adjusted profit after tax	715

   Besserlot is expected to do better than the industry average, but it is an unlisted company whose shares are not as marketable. Therefore the P/E ratios used will be 30-40 adjusted by multiplying by 0.75 to reflect Besserlot's unlisted status; we shall therefore multiply 715 by 22.5 and 30, giving a range of values of between **£16.1 million and £21.5 million.**

   However as Besserlot is being purchased for its future earnings potential, it is perhaps better to use the forecast figures for 20X7.

	£'000
Turnover (22,480 × 1.25)	28,100
Operating profit (28,100 × 0.08)	2,248
Interest paid (280 × 1.25)	(350)
Profit before tax	1,898
Taxation 30%	(569)
Profit after tax	1,329

Applying the same P/E ratios gives a range of values of between **£29.9 million** and **£39.9 million.**

Problems with P/E ratio valuation

(1)   Industry P/E ratios averages hide a **wide range of variations** within an industry, so using the average may not be appropriate. Besserlot's earnings are expected to grow faster than the rest of the industry. This method is therefore better at establishing a range of values within which negotiations can take place.

(2)   When this method is used to **value unlisted companies**, a downwards adjustment is normally made as above. However the **choice of adjustment** to use is quite **subjective.**

(3)   Using historic earnings figures may **not be a fair reflection** of future potential, particularly if significant synergies are expected from a merger or the year chosen has earnings that deviate from recent trends. However historical figures may be more reliable than forecast figures which may have been prepared on the **basis of unrealistic assumptions**, or which fail to reflect **significant uncertainties** about future earnings.

(4)   The methods uses profit figures which may be **distorted by accounting policies** and **do not reflect the cash** that can be distributed to shareholders.

(iii)   **Dividend valuation model**

This bases the valuation on the present value of future dividends. As dividend growth rates differ, this calculation is in two parts.

	20X7	20X8	20X9
	£'000	£'000	£'000
Expected dividend (25% rise)	250	313	391
Discount factor 14%	0.877	0.769	0.675
Present values	219	241	264

Present value 20X7-20X9 = £724,000

Valuation post 20X9 using the dividend growth model and discounted 20X9 figure

$$P_0 = \frac{D_0(1+g)}{Ke-g}$$

$$= \frac{264(1+0.1)}{0.14-0.1}$$

$$= £7.3 \text{ million}$$

Valuation = 7.3 + 0.7 = £8 million

Problems with dividend valuation model

There are a number of issues with this valuation.

(1)   The model is based on the assumptions that Besserlot's **current dividend policy** is continued. However if Besserlot becomes part of the Stanzial group, the dividends will reflect Stanzial's policy that may be different.

(2)   The **cost of capital** used should reflect changes in financial and business risk that may occur if Besserlot becomes part of the Stanzial group.

(3)   If Besserlot has a **low dividend payout ratio**, which it appears to have as the valuation is much lower than the 'floor' value suggested by the asset valuation model, the dividend valuation model may not provide a fair indication of future earnings potential.

(4)   The model assumes that all shareholders view dividend levels in the same way. Shareholders may have **differing preferences between dividends and capital gains,** depending for example on their tax position.

(iv)   **Present value of free cash flows model**

This model bases the valuation on the present values of the future free cash flows to equity. As with the dividend valuation model, the differing growth rates mean that the calculation has to be done in two parts.

For the years 20X7 – 20X9, the assumption that all figures increase by 25% each year means that we can calculate the free cash flows for 20X7 and just increase that figure by 25% for years 20X8 and 20X9.

	20X7	20X8	20X9
	£'000	£'000	£'000
Turnover	28,100		
Operating profit	2,248		
Interest paid	(350)		
Profit before tax	1,898		
Taxation	(569)		
Profit after tax	1,329		
Add non-cash expenses (820 × 1.25)	1,025		
Less: working capital increase (W)	(172)		
capital investment (1,000 × 1.25)	(1,250)		
Free cash flow to equity			
(× 1.25, 20X8 and 20X9)	932	1,165	1,456
Discount factor 14%	0.877	0.769	0.675
Present values	817	896	983

Present values 20X7–20X9 = £2,696,000

Working

20X7 increase = 686,000 × 0.25 = £171,500

Valuation post 20X9 using the earnings growth model and discounted 20X9 figure

$$P_0 = \frac{FCF(1+g)}{Ke-g}$$

$$= \frac{983(1+0.1)}{0.14-0.1}$$

= £27.0 million

Valuation = 2.7 + 27.0 = £29.7 million

Problems with free cash flows model

Investors are particularly interested in free cash flows, but this model does have some limitations.

(1)   The **assumptions** that **all revenues and costs will increase by the same amount** each year, and that **growth rates will only change once** in the future are clearly **too simplistic**.

(2)   As with the dividend valuation model, the **cost of capital** used should reflect changes in financial and business risks that may occur if Besserlot becomes part of the Stanzial group.

(3) Stanzial is unlikely to be able to **access detailed cash flows forecasts** by Besserlot before it makes its initial bid.

(4) The valuation fails to consider any **real options** such as abandonment.

Conclusions

The models provide very different suggestions, so recommendations on offer terms cannot be very strong. The dividend valuation model is out of step with the other models and should be ignored. The asset valuation of about £15 million could be used as the minimum price, and the most optimistic price-earnings calculation of around £40 million is the maximum recommended offer. An offer in the middle of these two figures of around £27.5 million might be the amount accepted.

(b) **Obtaining control**

Assuming there are no special clauses in Besserlot's constitution making it difficult for an acquirer, Stanzial has to acquire a **majority of shares** to gain control. The arithmetic is that the venture capital company owns 30%, the other large single shareholder 25% and senior managers 35% between them. Therefore obtaining the venture capital and large single shareholder's shares will mean Stanzial achieves a majority of shares, as will obtaining one out of these two shareholdings plus the great majority of the shares held by the senior managers.

Magnitude of offer

Stanzial may assume that all shareholders will sell if the offer is high enough. The question is whether the **shareholders' position** will be **solely determined by price,** or whether the shareholders have other concerns which, if they are addressed, will mean that they are prepared to accept a lower price.

Venture capitalists

The venture capitalists may well see the offer as a **natural exit point** for them, so may well only be concerned with price. What price they accept may depend on what price they think they can obtain from other exit methods, for example sale to another purchaser or Besserlot obtaining a listing. If they are looking for continued involvement, Stanzial may have to fulfil the conditions that Besserlot has had to meet, for example continued venture capitalist involvement in senior management.

If the venture capitalists are looking for an exit, it would seem **logical to accept a cash offer** rather than to substitute shares in Stanzial, although the decision might alternatively depend on the venture capitalists' expectations of the future price movements of Stanzial's shares.

Single shareholder

Like the venture capitalists, the single shareholder may see the offer as a chance to liquidate his investment. However the shareholder's stance may be complicated by his **tax position** that means that he prefers to accept shares rather than suffer capital gains tax on a tax receipt. The single shareholder may also accept shares if he expects the shares to increase significantly in value or provide a **certain level of dividend income**, and may be more likely to accept shares if he can **retain his position on Besserlot's board** (or better still perhaps, obtain a seat on Stanzial's board).

Managers

Managers may have similar concerns to the single shareholder and their decision be determined by the **magnitude of the offer**, and their preference for cash or shares by their **tax position.**

However managers' primary concern may not be the income or capital gain from the shares, but the **security** of their jobs or **retaining the same say** over Besserlot's affairs as they have had before the takeover. Stanzial may therefore have to provide guarantees about **job security or continuing positions** on Besserlot's board; if it prefers to have its own people managing Besserlot it may have to offer the managers good opportunities elsewhere in the Stanzial group.

36 Evertalk

> **Text references.** Mainly Chapter 16, though Chapter 6 (free cash flow) and Chapter 7 (cost of debt) are also relevant.
>
> **Top tips.** The question takes you through in logical stages what you need to consider in a reconstruction; firstly the base position if the company is liquidated and then the restructuring proposal. The key is working out what calculations to do, as the calculations mostly take figures straight from the scenario detail or require little adjustment.
>
> The hint about replacement investment in the question details should have alerted you to the need to consider free cash flows when assessing whether continuation is viable. Free cash flows require a cost of capital and the details given about equity beta should have hinted to you that you are expected to use CAPM. It's fundamental to (b) that your answer should contain discussion of the position of all interested parties. Note how (c) considers different possibilities in terms of the number of years' cash flows to take and what sales, if any, will be cost if the network division is closed. Globtalk wishes to close the network division because it has already has its own network, it wants to buy Evertalk to acquire a manufacturing division (vertical integration).
>
> **Easy marks.** It's easier to make comments about the position of the various stakeholders and reasonable consideration of their interests should have earned you good marks even if you struggled with the calculations.

Report on the restructuring of Evertalk

Introduction

The decision has to be in the best interest of shareholders; it also has to take account of other stakeholders' interests.

(a) **Closure of the company**

The estimated liquidation values of assets are:

	$m
Land and buildings	140
Other non-current assets	50
Inventory	100
Receivables	70
Cash	5
Less: redundancy and closure costs	(100)
	265

Payables are:

	$m
Bank loan	40
Bond	300
Other payables	209
	549

If the company is liquidated, payables will receive (265/549) = 48% of funds due to them; ordinary shareholders will receive nothing. Thus any proposal which results in a positive outcome for ordinary shareholders is better than closure, and these figures perhaps give scope for an alternative that offers a better arrangement for payables.

(b)   **Restructuring**

Consideration of stakeholders' interests particularly applies to a reconstruction, where the company must present proposals that leave stakeholders with financial interests in the company in a **better situation** than in a **liquidation**.

Bondholders

The bondholders are expected to swap $300 million of loans for 95 million shares. The **effective price** of these shares is $(300/95) = \$3.16$ per share compared with a current value of 10p and a two-year high of $1.80. Bondholders are also expected to subscribe $100 million extra loans.

The benefits for bondholders are that they would stand to lose approximately $156 million ($300 million × 52%) if the company was liquidated. In addition they would **gain control** of the company.

Therefore whether this package is acceptable to bondholders depends on whether the company is expected to survive and do well enough for the shares to increase in value. To judge this, we should examine the **free cash flows** of the company if the bondholders accept the proposal, and assuming also that the surplus assets of $40 million are disposed of and used to pay off the bank loan.

	Free cash flows $m
Current income from operations	(60)
Interest savings – bond (300 × 12%)	36
Interest savings – bank loan (40 × 8%)	3
Rationalisation gains	30
Depreciation (60 × (140 − 40)/140)	43
Replacement investment required	(100)
	(48)

Evertalk's free cash flows remain negative and the company continues to appear unviable. On this evidence it is **not worth the bondholders accepting the proposals**, as they could stand to lose all the $300 million invested in shares, plus at least some of the $100 million extra loans. However the bondholders might decide differently if the company closed its network division rather than rationalising it.

Shareholders

The best shareholders can do at present is to realise 10p per share on their holdings, though if many of them sell, this price will reduce towards zero. Taking the debenture means that they will **receive a guaranteed income** if the company survives. Against this, they would lose control of the company and the conversion terms imply a price of 100/50 = 200 pence that Evertalk's shares may well not reach over the next five years.

Share option participants

Share options will have **little or no value**, as the current share price is so low. The offer made appears to be very, perhaps **excessively, generous** to probably the directors and the senior managers.

Other payables

Whether the other payables gain from these proposals is unclear. They may stand more chance of being repaid if the **proposals are accepted** and the **company's prospects improve**, although as currently forecast this seems unlikely. If the company is liquidated, the payables will benefit from the bond finance having been converted into shares, meaning that the former bondholders will no longer have first call on the proceeds from liquidation. However the bondholders may obtain priority on the extra $100 million they are lending if they obtain **security** and this could jeopardise the position of the other payables.

(c)   **Sale to Globtalk**

Disposal of network division

	$m
Land and buildings $((140 - 40) \times 0.5)$	50
Other non-current assets (50×0.5)	25
Inventory (100×0.1)	10
Receivables (70×0.5)	35
Cash (5×0.5)	3
Payables (209×0.5)	(105)
Bonds	(300)
Closure costs (100×0.5)	(50)
	(332)

The deficit on disposal of the network division if bonds are excluded would be $32 million.

Projected free cash flow of manufacturing

	$m
Current pre-tax income $(320 - 230)$	90
Interest on bank loan	3
	93
Tax at 30%	(28)
Depreciation $(60 \times {}^{20}/_{100})$	12
Replacement investment	(20)
	57

Weighted average cost of capital

Cost of equity

$Ke = r_f + [E(r_m) - r_f]\beta_i$

$\quad = 5 + (14 - 5)\,0.9$

$\quad = 13.1\,\%$

Cost of debt

Cost of loan stock

Year		Cash flows $	Discount factor 10 %	Discounted cash flow $	Discount factor 5%	Discounted cash flow $
0	Market value	(121.00)	1.000	(121.00)	1.000	(121.00)
1–7	Interest	12.00	4.868	58.42	5.786	69.43
7	Redemption	100.00	0.513	51.30	0.711	71.10
				(11.28)		19.53

$Kd = 5 + \left(\dfrac{19.53}{19.53 - -11.28}\right)(10 - 5) = 8.2\%$

WACC $= (0.6 \times 13.1) + (0.4 \times (1 - 0.3) \times 8.2) = 10.2\%$, say 10%

Value of free cash flows to infinity $= 57/0.1 = \$570$ million
Value of free cash flows for the next ten years $= 57 \times 6.145 = \$350.3$ million

Other factors

In practice the value of free cash flows could be reduced by the sales lost to the network division of Evertalk. This would be an annual loss of $(90 \times 0.25 \times (1 - 0.3)) = \$15.75$ million. In these circumstances:

Value of free cash flows to infinity $= (57 - 15.75)\,/0.1 = \$412.5$ million

Value of free cash flows for the next ten years $= (57 - 15.75) \times 6.145 = \$253.5$ million

However this is likely to be a very pessimistic view as some or all of these losses could be recouped by Globtalk using the manufacturing division to supply its own customers. In addition some of Evertalk's current subscribers may transfer to Globtalk, so in fact the free cash flow gains may be higher than $57 million per annum.

It therefore seems that there is a good chance that the value gained by Globtalk will be above the value of consideration plus loans (50 + 332 = $382 million), and is certainly a long way above the $50 million purchase consideration. **Stakeholders** should consider **this issue carefully**.

Closure of the network division

Evertalk could itself close its network division, sell its subscriber base and concentrate on manufacturing operations. However the manufacturing division would then have to make up the shortfall of $332 million which will not be easy.

Recommendation

The best solution for Evertalk's stakeholders may be negotiating **better acquisition terms** with Globtalk, so that Globtalk takes over the bond liability.

37 Romage

Text references. Chapter 17 on sell-offs and demergers, Chapters 7 and 8 cover the more complicated calculations.

Top tips. It is easy to confuse sell-offs and demergers in (a). (b) is quite a thorough test of your financial appraisal skills, involving relevant cash flows, the correct risk, discounting over nominal cash flows and how real and nominal cash flows are used in investment appraisal.

In the workings, before going into the ungearing and regearing betas stage, you first have to confirm whether it is necessary by checking whether the capital structure of the divisions differs from the industry structure. Remember that you have to carry out IRR analysis to determine the cost of debt if it is redeemable.

Easy marks. The key to success in tackling this question is to make sure you score well on part (a). You can get a few easy marks on the calculations in (b) (central costs, correct treatment of depreciation, taxation) but the marking on the calculations is weighted towards getting the costs of capital right. However if you make a reasonable attempt at these you should be able to gain 3 or 4 marks for using the right techniques and getting the easier numbers even if your final answers are incorrect.

(a) Demergers and sell-offs are both means of **restructuring businesses**.

    (i) **Sell-offs**

        A **sell-off** involves the sale of part of a company to another company. A sell-off can act to **protect the rest of a business from a take-over,** by selling off a part that is particularly attractive to a buyer. It can also **provide cash**, enabling the remaining business to invest further without the need for worsening its gearing by obtaining more debt finance. It would also enable Romage to **concentrate** on what it perceives to be its core business, and **dispose of the more peripheral areas**.

    (ii) **Demergers**

        A **demerger** is the splitting up of a corporate body into two or more separate and independent bodies. It is **not** a **sale** of the separate bodies themselves, as the original shareholders have shares in both companies. The split does **enable analysts** to **understand** the two businesses fully, particularly when, as here, the two main divisions are in different fields. The two divisions are likely to have different risk profiles, and splitting them up enables **shareholders** to **adjust** the **proportion of their holdings** between the two different companies.

Improvements in management

Both **methods** can lead to improved **management and control**, and can enable management to **focus** on the **competencies** of the individual divisions rather than the varying considerations of both. These improvements may result in **reverse synergy**, where the combined value of the split-off divisions is more than the company would be worth if the divisions were still together.

Romage's position

The choice for Romage's management is therefore whether they wish to **retain control** of both divisions, or to relinquish control of one and just concentrate on the other division.

(b)   **Manufacturing**

	1	2	3	4	5	6
	$m	$m	$m	$m	$m	$m
Net operating cash flow	45.0	48.0	50.0	52.0	57.0	60.0
Central costs	(6.0)	(6.0)	(6.0)	(6.0)	(6.0)	(6.0)
Taxable cash flows	39.0	42.0	44.0	46.0	51.0	54.0
Tax at 31%	(12.1)	(13.0)	(13.6)	(14.3)	(15.8)	(16.7)
Post tax cash flows	26.9	29.0	30.4	31.7	35.2	37.3
Tax credit on depreciation (depreciation charge × 31%)	3.1	2.5	2.2	2.5	2.5	2.5
One-off cost	(8.0)					
Net cash flow	22.0	31.5	32.6	34.2	37.7	39.8
Discount factors (10%) (W1)	0.909	0.826	0.751	0.683	0.621	
PV cash flow	20.0	26.0	24.5	23.4	23.4	

PV to infinity   = PV years 1–5 + PV years 6–infinity

$$= 117.3 + \left(\frac{39.8}{0.1} - (39.8 \times 3.791) \right)$$

= $364.4 million

PV years 1 to 15   = 117.3 + (39.8 × (7.606 − 3.791))
= $269.1 million

Property

	1	2	3	4	5	6
	$m	$m	$m	$m	$m	$m
Net operating cash flow	32.0	40.0	42.0	44.0	46.0	50.0
Central costs	(6.0)	(6.0)	(6.0)	(6.0)	(6.0)	(6.0)
Taxable cash flows	26.0	34.0	36.0	38.0	40.0	44.0
Tax at 31%	(8.1)	(10.5)	(11.2)	(11.8)	(12.4)	(13.6)
Post tax cash flows	17.9	23.5	24.8	26.2	27.6	30.4
Tax credit on depreciation	1.6	1.6	1.6	1.6	1.6	1.6
One-off cost	(8.0)					
Net cash flow	11.5	25.1	26.4	27.8	29.2	32.0
Discount factors (8%) (W2)	0.926	0.857	0.794	0.735	0.681	
PV cash flow	10.6	21.5	21.0	20.4	19.9	

PV to infinity   = PV years 1–5 + PV years 6–infinity

$$= 93.4 + \left(\frac{32.0}{0.08} - (32.0 \times 3.993) \right)$$

= $365.6 million

PV years 1 to 15   = 93.4 + (32.0 × (8.559 − 3.993))
= $239.5 million

Working 1

Discount rate for manufacturing:

Gearing

MV debt $= \$60$ million

$$\text{MV equity} = \frac{50}{0.25} \times 0.55 \times 2.96$$

$$= \$325.6 \text{ million}$$

$$\text{Gearing level} = \frac{325.6}{325 + 60} \text{ equity, } \frac{60}{325 + 60} \text{ debt}$$

$$= 84.4\% \text{ equity, } 15.6\% \text{ debt}$$

This differs from the industry gearing levels, and so we must ungear the industry beta and must regear the asset beta to take into account the differing capital structure.

$$\beta_a = \beta_e\left(\frac{E}{E + D(1-t)}\right) \text{ (assuming debt is risk-free)}$$

$$= 1.3 \times \left(\frac{70}{70 + 30(1 - 0.31)}\right)$$

$$= 1.00$$

Regearing

$$\beta_e = \beta_a\left(\frac{E + D(1-t)}{E}\right)$$

$$P = 1.00 \times \left(\frac{84.4 + 15.6(1 - 0.31)}{84.4}\right)$$

$$= 1.128$$

$$\begin{aligned}K_e &= r_f + [E(r_m) - r_f]\beta \\ &= 5.5 + [14 - 5.5]1.128 \\ &= 15.09\%\end{aligned}$$

For Kd, calculate redemption yield on loan stock as we are told that the cost of the term loan is virtually the same.

$$131 = \frac{13(1 - 0.31)}{(1 + Kd(1-t))} + \frac{13(1 - 0.31)}{(1 + Kd(1-t))^2} + ... + \frac{13(1 - 0.31)}{(1 + Kd(1-t))^{15}} + \frac{100}{(1 + Kd(1-t))^{15}}$$

Year		Cash flow $	Discount factor 5%	PV $	Discount factor 6%	PV $
0	Market value	(131.00)	1.000	(131.000)	1.000	(131.00)
1–15	Interest	8.97	10.38	93.11	9.712	87.12
15	Capital repayment	100.00	0.481	48.10	0.417	41.70
				10.21		(2.18)

$$\text{Kd}(1-t) = 5\% + \left(\frac{10.21}{10.21 + 2.18} \times (6 - 5)\right)$$

$$= 5.82\%$$

$$\begin{aligned}\text{WACC for manufacturing division} &= Ke_g\left(\frac{E}{E + D}\right) + Kd(1-t)\left(\frac{D}{E + D}\right) \\ &= 15.09\left(\frac{325.6}{60 + 325.6}\right) + 5.82\left(\frac{60}{60 + 325.6}\right) \\ &= 12.74 + 0.91 \\ &= 13.65\%\end{aligned}$$

$$\text{Real rate} = \frac{(1 + \text{money rate})}{(1 + \text{inflation rate})} - 1$$

$$= \frac{1.1365}{1.03} - 1$$

$$= 10.34\%, \text{ say } 10\%$$

Working 2

Discount rate for property

$$\text{MV equity} = \frac{50}{0.25} \times 0.45 \times 2.96$$

$$= \$266.4 \text{ million}$$

$$\text{MV debt} = 50 \times 1.31$$
$$= \$65.5 \text{ million}$$

$$\text{Gearing level} = \frac{266.4}{266.4 + 65.5} \text{ equity} + \frac{65.5}{266.4 + 65.5} \text{ debt}$$

$$= 80.3\% \text{ equity} + 19.7\% \text{ debt}$$

These are near enough industry averages (80 + 20) and thus there is no need to ungear and regear.

$$\text{Ke} = r_f + [E(r_m) - r_f]\beta$$
$$= 5.5 + [14 - 5.5]0.9$$
$$= 13.15\%$$

$$\text{Kd}(1 - t) = \text{same as above, } 5.82\%$$

$$\text{WACC for property division} = \text{Ke}_g\left(\frac{E}{E + D}\right) + \text{Kd}(1 - t)\left(\frac{D}{E + D}\right)$$

$$= 13.15\left(\frac{266.4}{266.4 + 65.5}\right) + 5.82\left(\frac{65.5}{266.4 + 65.5}\right)$$

$$= 10.55 + 1.15$$

$$= 11.70\%$$

$$\text{Real rate} = \frac{(1 + \text{money rate})}{(1 + \text{inflation rate})} - 1$$

$$= \frac{1.1170}{1.03} - 1$$

$$= 8.44\%, \text{ say } 8\%$$

Conclusion

$$\text{Total of two divisions to infinity} = 364.4 + 365.6$$
$$= \$730.0 \text{ million}$$

$$\text{Total of two divisions to year 15} = 269.1 + 239.5$$
$$= \$508.6 \text{ million}$$

Current market value is \$592 million (equity) plus \$125.5 million (debt), \$717.5 million.

The total of the two separate divisions to infinity is just higher than the current market value, but using a 15 year time horizon the total of the two separate divisions is lower.

As no replacement capital investment has been included in the calculation, it does not appear that Romage should float the two divisions separately.

38 Reflator

Text references. Chapter 17.

Top tips. Most of the advantages in (a) are for the investing company, although discussion of the other parties as well enhances your chances of scoring marks. Note in (b) the method for calculating the annual payment if a mix of interest and capital repayment is being made each year. The point of (c) is to focus on the number of shares being issued under the warrant in exchange for the loan stock, and not the price.

Easy marks. If you revised management buyouts, discussing their advantages in (a) should be straightforward.

(a) (i) **Disposing company's position**

Convenient disposal method

A management buyout is a means of obtaining consideration for a subsidiary that is **peripheral** to the company's activities or is **loss-making**.

Liquidation avoidance

Disposal to managers will avoid the **costs and administration** involved in liquidating a subsidiary.

Speed of disposal

It may be **quicker** to dispose of a subsidiary to managers than to an external party.

Greater co-operation

If a parent company has decided to dispose of a subsidiary, it will probably get **more co-operation** from the managers and employees of the subsidiary if the sale is a management buyout.

Future links

The selling organisation is more likely to be able to **maintain beneficial links** with a segment sold to managers than to a third party.

(ii) **Managers' position**

Because of their **expertise and knowledge of the company**, managers may have a better chance of making their acquisition succeed than an external party would. They may also be more **motivated** because of the possibility of the gains that they can earn.

(iii) **Venture capitalists' position**

Although venture capitalists may take **high risks** when investing in management buyouts, they will do so because of the possibility of **high returns** and the possibility of eventually being able to **realise their investment** by sale when the company is listed on the **stock market**.

(b) **Assume maximum dividend of 15% is paid.**

	Working	1	2	3	4
		$'000	$'000	$'000	$'000
EBIT		320.0	410.0	500.0	540.0
Interest 8.5% loan		(170.0)	(170.0)	(170.0)	(170.0)
Interest 9% loan	1	(27.0)	(23.4)	(19.5)	(15.2)
EBT		123.0	216.6	310.5	354.8
Tax 30%		(36.9)	(65.0)	(93.2)	(106.4)
EAT		86.1	151.6	217.3	248.4
Dividends 15%		(12.9)	(22.7)	(32.6)	(37.3)
Retained earnings		73.2	128.9	184.7	211.1
Book value of equity		873.2	1,002.1	1,186.8	1,397.9

Working

Annual payment required = 300,000/Cumulative 6 yr factor 9%

$\qquad$ = 300,000/4.486

$\qquad$ = $66,875, say $66,900

	1	2	3	4
	$'000	$'000	$'000	$'000
Remaining value	300	260.1	216.6	169.2
Interest 9%	27	23.4	19.5	15.2
Capital	39.9	43.5	47.4	51.7

Annual growth rate in book value of equity = $4\sqrt{(1,397.9 \div 800)} - 1 = 15.0\%$

This is below the 20% claimed; however this growth rate is likely to be less significant to the investor than the growth rate of the **market value of equity**.

(c) **Original position**

Under the original suggestion managers would have 1 million shares and the venture capitalists 600,000. The warrants would give the venture capitalists 100/100 × 300,000 = 300,000 extra shares, bringing their total to 900,000, but still meaning that the managers owned the majority of shares.

Revised position

However on the revised terms suggested by the venture capitalists, they would gain 150/100 × 300,000 = 450,000 extra shares, bringing their total to 1.05 million and giving them **effective control** of the company if the warrants are exercised. The managers may not be prepared to accept this, unless they too have chances to increase their shareholdings.

(d) **Memorandum: The role of a venture capitalist**

Venture capitalists are organisations, such as 3i, willing to **provide venture (ie risk) capital** to a business organisation **normally in return for an equity stake in the organisation**. Venture capitalists are more inclined to **fund management buyouts**, as in this case, rather than the relatively riskier start-up situations. The minimum investment considered will normally be around $100,000 with the **average investment of $1 million to $2 million**, and so the additional finance requirements should present no problems to the venture capitalist.

The return required on venture capital for a well-established business with sound management (as in this case) is likely to be around the 25% – 30% mark. Clearly not all investments made by venture capitalists are successful and the **overall returns** on venture capital **average** out at around **10% – 15%**.

As in this case, the venture capitalist will not necessarily provide the majority of the finance. The **buyout** may be **funded by $300,000 venture capital, $2 million debt finance** and **$300,000 subordinated debt finance**.

The venture capitalist must **protect the interests of the investors** providing the venture finance. As a result, the venture capitalist will normally require an **equity stake**. This is normally between a 20% to 30% shareholding in the management buyout company. They may also wish to have **special rights** to be able to appoint an agreed number of directors. These directors will act as their representatives on the board and look after the interests of the venture capital organisation. The venture capitalist may require the company to seek their prior approval for any new issues or acquisitions. The venture capitalists will want the **managers** to be **financially committed**. This is not an issue in this situation as the management will hold 1,000,000 equity shares and the venture capitalists 600,000 equity shares.

The venture capitalist are generally likely to want a **predetermined target exit date**, the point at which they can recoup some or all of their investment in the management buyout. At the outset the venture capitalist will want to establish various **exit routes**. These include the sale of shares to the public or institutional investors following a flotation of the company's shares on a recognised stock market. Other exit strategies include the sale of the company to another firm, or the repurchase of the venture capitalist's shares by the company or its owners, or the sale of the venture capitalist's shares to an institution such as an investment trust.

39 Airgo

(a)   To: The Managers of the proposed Airgo Co
        From: Management Consultant
        Date: 12 January 20X2
        Subject: **Report on the financing mix for the proposed leveraged buy-out of the regional airport**

If the airport can be purchased for $35 million, **the financing mix** is proposed as:

	$m
Equity: 50 pence ordinary shares	
8 million purchased by managers and employees	4
2 million purchased by ASTER Co	1
Debt	
EPP Bank: secured floating rate loan at LIBOR + 3%	20
Allvent Co: mezzanine debt with warrants (balancing figure)	10
Total finance	35

Up to $15 million of the mezzanine debt is available, which could be used to replace some of the floating rate loan. However, this possibility has been rejected because its cost is 18% compared with 13% and the warrants, if exercised, could dilute the manager/employee shareholding.

Leveraged buyout

A **leveraged buyout** of the type proposed allows managers and employees to own 80% of the equity while only contributing $4m out of $35m capital (11%). However, it is important that the managers and employees agree on the company's strategy at the outset. If the shareholders break into rival factions, control over the company might be difficult to exercise. It would be useful to know the disposition of shareholdings among managers and employees in more detail.

Gearing

The initial **gearing** of the company will be extremely high: the debt to equity ratio is 600% ($30 million debt to $5 million equity). Clearly one of the main medium-term goals following a leveraged buyout is to reduce gearing as rapidly as possible, sacrificing high dividend payouts in order to repay loans. For this reason EPP Bank, the major creditor, has imposed a covenant that capital gearing (debt/equity) must be reduced to 100% within four years or the loan will be called in.

Reduction of gearing

The gearing will be reduced substantially by **steady repayment** of the unsecured mezzanine finance. This carries such a high interest rate because it is a very risky investment by the venture capital company Allvent Co. A premium of 5% over secured debt is quite normal. The debt must be repaid in five equal annual instalments, that is $2 million each year. If profits dip in any particular year, Airgo might experience cash flow problems, necessitating some debt refinancing.

Warrants

If the **warrants** attached to the mezzanine debt are exercised, Allvent Co will be able to purchase 1 million new shares in Airgo Co for $1 each. This is a cheap price considering that the book value per share at the date of buyout is $3.50 ($35m/10 million shares). The ownership by managers and staff will be diluted from 80% to approximately 73%, with ASTER Co holding 18% and Allvent Co holding 9%. This should not affect management control provided that managers and staff remain as a unified group.

Forecast income statements

The forecast income statements for the first four years of the company's operations are shown in the appendix to this report, together with estimates of gearing for each year, measured as total book value of debt divided by book value of shareholders' funds. A key assumption behind these predictions is that **no dividends are paid** over this period. This may not be acceptable to managers or employees. It is also assumed that cash generated from operations is sufficient to repay $2 million of mezzanine debt each year, which is by no means obvious from the figures provided.

Predicted gearing

Using these assumptions and ignoring the possible issue of new shares when warrants are exercised, the **gearing at the end of four years** is predicted to be 132%, which is significantly above the target of 100% needed to meet the condition on EPP's loan. If warrants are exercised, $1 million of new share capital will be raised, reducing the year 4 gearing to 125%, still significantly above the target.

Effect of rise in LIBOR

Results will be worse if LIBOR rises above 10%, over the period. However the purchase of the cap will stop interest payments on EPP's loan rising above 15%. Conversely if LIBOR falls, the increase in profit could be considerable, but it is still very unlikely that the loan condition will be met by year 4.

Meeting loan condition

There will therefore definitely be a **problem in meeting** the EPP's loan condition. However, if the company is still showing steady growth by year four, and there have been no problems in meeting interest payments, EPP bank will probably not exercise its right to recall the loan.

Measures by directors

If the loan condition is predicted to be a problem, the directors of Airgo could consider:

(i)   Aiming for **continuous improvement** in **cost effectiveness**

(ii) **Renegotiating the central services contract** with ASTER, or providing central services in-house, in order to save costs

(iii) **Renegotiating the allowed gearing ratio** to a more realistic figure

(iv) Going for **further expansion after**, say, one or two years (eg extension of a runway in order to handle long-haul flights); financing this expansion with an issue of equity funds. However, this may affect control of the company

(v)   **Looking for possible alternative sources of debt or equity finance** if the EPP loan is recalled, including the possibility of flotation on the stock market

APPENDIX

Airgo Co: forecast income statements for the first four years and computation of debt/equity gearing ratios

	Estimates from Year 0 $'000	Year 1 $'000	Year 2 $'000	Year 3 $'000	Year 4 $'000
Landing fees	14,000				
Other revenue	8,600				
	22,600				
Labour	5,200				
Consumables	3,800				
Other expenses	3,500				
	12,500				
Direct operating profit growing at 5% pa	10,100	10,605	11,135	11,692	12,277
Central services from ASTER		(3,000)	(3,150)	(3,308)	(3,473)
EPP loan interest at 13% on $20m		(2,600)	(2,600)	(2,600)	(2,600)
Mezzanine debt interest at 18%					
On $10m		(1,800)			
On $8m			(1,440)		
On $6m				(1,080)	
On $4m					(720)
Profit before tax		3,205	3,945	4,704	5,484
Tax at 33%		1,058	1,302	1,552	1,810
Profit after tax		2,147	2,643	3,152	3,674
Reserves b/f		0	2,147	4,790	7,942
Reserves c/f		2,147	4,790	7,942	11,616

	Estimates from Year 0 $'000	Year 1 $'000	Year 2 $'000	Year 3 $'000	Year 4 $'000
Share capital + reserves c/f (5,000 + reserves c/f)		7,147	9,790	12,942	16,616
Total debt at end of year (20,000 + 10,000 – 2,000 more each year)		28,000	26,000	24,000	22,000
Gearing: debt/equity		392%	266%	185%	132%

If warrants are exercised, $1 million of new share capital is issued, reducing the gearing at year 4 to 22,000/17,617 = 125%.

Assumptions

The central services will be provided by ASTER for the full 4-year period.

No dividend will be paid during the first four years.

Sufficient cash will be generated to repay $2 million of mezzanine finance each year and to fund increased working capital requirements.

LIBOR is assumed to remain at 10%.

(b) In order to decide whether the management buy-out can be considered for a $10 million loan, the venture capital company would need the following information:

(i) The **purpose** of the buy-out

(ii) Full **details of the management team**, in order to evaluate expertise and experience and to check that there are no 'gaps' in the team

(iii) The company's **business plan**, based on a realistic set of strategies (apparently most approaches to venture capital companies fail on this criterion)

(iv) **Detailed cash flow forecasts** under different scenarios for economic factors such as growth, and interest rates. Forecasts of profit and balance sheets

(v) Details of the **management team's investment** in the buy-out. Venture capital companies like to ensure that the team is prepared to back their idea with their own money

(vi) Availability of **security** for the loan, including personal guarantees from the management team. Any other **'sweeteners'** that could be offered to the lender, such as warrants

(vii) The possibility of **appointing a representative of the venture capital company as a director** of Airgo

40 Troder

Text references. Chapter 19.

Top tips. Remember in (a) that a cap is designed to benefit a lender, but a collar is used by both borrowers and lenders. The hint about not calculating the number of contracts in (b) indicates that you are meant to carry out the main calculations in terms of net interest rates rather than monetary amounts. Hence the first stage is to calculate the net interest rate that corresponds to receiving £6.75 million. The difference between (b)(i) and (ii) is that (b)(i) calculates the amount Troder is guaranteed to receive whereas (b)(ii) indicates how much leeway Troder has by letting its call option lapse, before the buyer of the put option exercises his rights.

Easy marks. Good discussion in (a) could earn you 6 of the 8 marks you need to pass this question.

(a) **Advantages of caps**

(i) For payment of a **premium**, caps provide an **insurance policy**, determining the **maximum level of interest** that a borrower will have to pay. By **buying a put option**, a borrower can deal in an agreed interest rate at a future date and will not need to go above that interest rate. Caps can provide **long-term protection** for up to ten years.

(ii) If interest rates fall, the purchaser of the cap will not exercise the option and will thus take advantage of the **lower interest rates**.

Advantages of collars

(i) Using a collar, a borrower can **buy** an **interest rate cap (put option)** and **sell** an **interest rate floor (call option)** at a lower strike rate. The main advantage compared with a **pure cap** is that the cost will be lower, since the borrower will **receive a premium** for **selling a call option**. However this advantage is tempered by the **borrowing company foregoing the benefit of movements in interest rates** below the floor.

(ii) A collar for a lender would be **buying an interest rate floor (call option)** and **selling an interest rate cap (put option)**. The cost again would be **lower** than for a one-way option, and the lender would receive a **guaranteed minimum rate of interest**. However the lender would not be able to enjoy the benefit of receiving interest above the level at which the cap is set.

(b) (i) To earn $6.75 million, annual interest rate after premium costs would have to be:

$$\frac{\$6.75\,\text{million}}{\$400\,\text{million}} \times \frac{12}{5} = 4.05\%$$

Three possible collar combinations, using **December** options:

Call strike price	Put strike price	Interest rate %	Less 0.25% %	Less Call premium %	Add Put premium %	Net receipt %
95750	95500	4.25	(0.25)	(0.165)	0.170	4.005
95750	95250	4.25	(0.25)	(0.165)	0.085	3.920
95500	95250	4.50	(0.25)	(0.280)	0.085	4.055

Of the three the only combination that guarantees an interest rate above 4.05% is buying a call option at 95500 and selling a put option at 95250. The minimum return will be:

$$\$400,000,000 \times \frac{5}{12} \times 4.055\% = \$6,758,333$$

(ii) The maximum interest rate that is possible under the selected hedge is 4.75%, equivalent to the put option exercise price of 95250. Troder will not have exercised its option, but taken advantage of the rate being above 4.5%.

Net return = 4.75 − 0.25 − 0.280 + 0.085 = 4.305%.

$$\text{Maximum return} = \$400,000,000 \times \frac{5}{12} \times 4.305\% = \$7,175,000.$$

(c) **Definition**

A currency swap is the exchange between two parties of streams of cash flows denominated in different currencies. In this example the swap takes place as follows:

(i) A **principal amount** is **exchanged** at an **agreed exchange rate**: 1,500 million EE marks for $100 million pounds.

(ii) **Interest** is **paid** by the **party** which **received** the **currency** in the swap: BB Co pays 20% pa on the EE marks and the EE based company pays 12% on the pounds.

(iii) The **principal amounts** are **swapped back** on agreed terms: in this case it is a straight repayment of the original amount received.

Initial workings

Cash flows occur at three points in time: now, in 6 months and in one year. The spot rate today is EE 18 = $1. Using **purchasing power parity**, which assumes freely floating currencies and bases currency predictions on relative inflation rates, the exchange rate in one year will be 18 × 1.25/1.03 = 21.84 EE marks to the pound.

Assuming a uniform depreciation of the currency, the exchange rate after 6 months would be approximately (21.84 + 18)/2 = 19.92. (Alternatively 18 × (1.25/1.03)$^{1/2}$ = 19.83).

In the computations, account will be taken of the interest cost of funds by compounding cash flows forward to the end of year 1.

Investment project without the swap

Time		EEm	Exchange rate	$m
0	Outlay 1	(750)	18.00	(41.67)
6 months	Outlay 2	(750)	19.92	(37.65)
1	Project sales receipt from EE govt.	2,000	21.84	91.58
	Surplus from project at end of year 1:			12.26

However, this is highly risky as the full amount of project receipts depends on the exchange rate in one year.

Investment project financed by currency swap

Time		EEm	Exchange rate	$m
0	Receive/pay: swap	1,500	15.00	(100.00)
0	Outlay	(750)		
6 months	Outlay	(750)		
1	Interest paid /received on swap: EE 20%, $ 12%	(300)		12.00
1	Project sales receipt from EE govt.	2,000		
1	Repay swap	(1,500)		100.00
	Net surplus in EE, converted to $	200	21.84	9.16
	Surplus from project:			21.16

The use of the swap increases the **expected value** of the investment.

41 FNDC

(a) **Interest rate futures**

Hedging

Hedging with futures offers protection against **adverse movements in the underlying asset market** (here the cash market and therefore changes in interest rates); if these occur they should be approximately offset by a gain on the futures market.

Basis risk

The person hedging may be affected by **basis risk**, the risk that the futures price may move differently from the amount that would be forecast from the change in interest rates.

Terms

The **terms, sums involved and periods** are **standardised** and hedge inefficiencies will be caused by either having too many contracts or too few, and having to consider what to do with the unhedged amount. Also the terms of the future may be based on **LIBOR**, which may not match with the basis of calculation of the interest rate being hedged.

Deposit

Futures require the payment of a **small deposit**; this transaction cost is likely to be lower than the premium for a tailored forward rate agreement or any type of option. However further payments of **variation margin** could be demanded if prices move in an adverse direction.

Interest rate options

Guaranteed amounts

The main advantage of options is that the buyer cannot lose on the interest rate and can take advantage of any favourable rate movements. An interest rate option provides the **right to borrow a specified amount** at a **guaranteed rate of interest**. On the date of expiry of the option the buyer must decide **whether or not to exercise his right to borrow**. He will only exercise the option if actual interest rates have risen above the guaranteed option rate.

Premium cost

However a premium must be paid regardless of whether or not the option is exercised, and the **premium cost** can be quite **high**, high enough not to make an option worthwhile if interest rate movements are expected to be marginal.

Choice of interest rates

Options offer a **wider choice of rate** to protect against adverse movements; the rate chosen may depend on **expectations of interest rate movements** and the **premium** for each option.

(b)   **Hedging the borrowing rate using futures**

Setup

(i)   June contracts as looking to borrow in five months time
(ii)   Sell June futures as borrowing
(iii) Number of contracts

$$\frac{\text{Exposure}}{\text{Contract size}} \times \frac{\text{Inv period}}{\text{Length of contract}}$$

$$\frac{£45,000,000}{£500,000} \times \frac{2}{3} = 60 \text{ contracts}$$

(iv)   Tick size

£12.50

Estimate closing futures price

June contract expires in 7 months

LIBOR is currently 4.0% (96.00)

June contract basis risk 96.00 − 95.55 = 45 ticks, difference between current and futures price

1 May 2 months to expiry: $45 \times \frac{2}{7} = 13$ ticks

If LIBOR rises to 4.5% (95.50), 95.50 − 0.13 = 95.37

If LIBOR falls to 3.5% (96.50), 96.50 − 0.13 = 96.37

Outcome

The results of the hedge under cases (i) and (ii) are shown below.

(i)   **Futures market**

	0.5% rise	0.5% fall
1 Dec: Sell 60 @	95.55	95.55
1 May: Buy 60 @	95.37	96.37
Tick movement: $\dfrac{\text{Opening rate} - \text{closing rate}}{0.01}$	18	82
Profit/ (Loss): 60 contracts × £12.50 × tick movement	13,500	(61,500)

(ii)   **Net outcome**

	£	£
Payment in spot market (4 ± 0.5 + 1.25)% × £45m × 2/12	(431,250)	(356,250)
Profit/(Loss) in futures market	13,500	(61,500)
Net cost of loan	(417,750)	(417,750)

Effective interest cost is 417,750 × 6 /45,000,000 = 5.57%

However this rate is dependent on the assumption that **basis declines linearly**; this may not be the case if **basis risk exists**.

Hedging the borrowing rate using options

Setup

(i)   June as above

(ii)   Buy put options

(iii)   Consider all three possible prices

(iv)   Number of contracts 60

(v)   Tick size £12.50

(vi)   Option premium

9500: 60 × 1.5 × 12.50 = £1,125
9550: 60 × 16.5 × 12.50 = £12,375
9600: 60 × 71 × 12.50 = £53,250

Closing prices

95.37 and 96.37 as above

Outcome interest rates rise

(i)   **Option market outcome**

	9500	9550	9600
Put option strike price (right to sell)	95.00	95.50	96.00
June futures price	95.37	95.37	95.37
Exercise option? (prefer to sell at highest price)	No	Yes	Yes
Gain (ticks)	–	13	63
Option outcome (60 × 12.50 × tick movement)	–	9,750	47,250

(ii) **Net position**

	9500 £	9550 £	9600 £
Actual interest cost (as above)	(431,250)	(431,250)	(431,250)
Value of option gain	–	9,750	47,250
Premium	(1,125)	(12,375)	(53,250)
Net cost of loan	432,375	433,875	437,250
Effective interest cost (Cost × 6/45m)	5.77%	5.79%	5.83%

Outcome interest rates fall

At a closing futures price of 96.37 none of the options will be exercised

Net position

	9500 £	9550 £	9600 £
Actual interest cost (as above)	(356,250)	(356,250)	(356,250)
Premium	(1,125)	(12,375)	(53,250)
Net cost of loan	(357,375)	(368,625)	(409,500)
Effective interest cost (Cost × 6/45m)	4.77%	4.92%	5.46%

Options will produce a better result if **interest rates fall**; the 9500 option appears to be the best choice whether rates fall or rise.

However if **interest rates rise**, as expected, the futures will produce a lower interest cost than the best option (the 9500).

(c)   **Exercise prices**

If the company is seeking a **maximum rate** of 5.75%, this implies LIBOR of (5.75 – 1.25) = 4.5%, and a put option exercise price of 9550.

If the company is seeking a **minimum rate** of 5.25%, this implies LIBOR of (5.25 – 1.25) = 4.0%, and a call option exercise price of 9600.

FNDC will **buy put** and sell **call options**.

Premium

60 × (16.5 – 7) × 12.50 = £7,125

If interest rates rise

Put option will be exercised, and calculation of outcome will be as in (b) with a different premium.

	£
Actual interest cost	(431,250)
Value of option gain	9,750
Premium	(7,125)
Net cost of loan	(428,625)
Effective interest cost (Cost × 6/45m)	5.72%

If interest rates fall

The put option won't be exercised, but the gain will be limited by the call option. Interest will be payable at LIBOR of 4% + 1.25%.

	£
Actual interest cost (4 + 1.25)% × £45m × 2/12	(393,750)
Premium	(7,125)
Net cost of loan	(400,875)
Effective interest cost (Cost × 6/45m)	5.35%

The collar **saves premium cost**, but again it interest rates rise as expected the outcome is worse than **hedging with the futures**.

(d)   Writing options will produce an income for the company. However option writers are **exposed to unlimited loss** unless the writer takes out a hedging transaction. Writing options is speculative and requires specialist financial expertise; it is not something that a manufacturing company such as FNDC would normally undertake.

42 HYK

Text references. Chapter 20.

Top tips. Remember that the contracts are required for four months, and the fact that they're needed in two months time is irrelevant for calculating the number of contracts. In (a) the question does not give a suggested figure for the movement in the price of the futures contract. It is better to assume that basis risk narrows evenly over the life of the contract. Alternatively you may assume that there is no change in basis risk. In either case, state your assumption. Transparency, speed and flexibility are key considerations in (b).

Easy marks. Make sure you get the easiest 5 marks first, for the basic interest rate calculations at the start of answers and the type and number of contracts in (a) and also leave enough time to earn the marks available in (b).

(a) The cost for HYK plc of borrowing £18 million for 4 months at today's rate of LIBOR + 0.75% (6.5% + 0.75% = 7.25%) is £18m × 4/12 × 7.25% = £435,000.

Maximum interest desirable = £18m × 4/12 × 7.5%
$$= £450,000$$

Hedging the borrowing rate using futures

Setup

(i) Either March or June contracts; use March

(ii) Sell March futures

(iii) Number of contracts

$$\frac{£18 \text{ million}}{£500,000} \times \frac{4}{3} = 48 \text{ contracts}$$

(iv) Tick size

$$(0.01\% \times \frac{3}{12} \times 500,000) = £12.50$$

Estimate closing futures price

March contract expires in 4 months

LIBOR is 6.5% (93.50)

March contract basis risk 93.50 − 93.10 = 40 ticks

1 February 2 months to expiry $40 \times \frac{2}{4} = 20$ ticks

$\Rightarrow$ If LIBOR rises to 8% (92.00) future price will be 92.00 − 0.20 = 91.80.

If LIBOR falls to 6% (94.00) future price will be 94.00 − 0.20 = 93.80.

Outcome

The results of the hedge under cases (i) and (ii) are shown below.

(i) **Futures market**

	Rises	Falls
1 Dec: Sell 48 @	93.10	93.10
1 Feb: Buy 48 @	91.80	93.80
Tick movement: $\frac{\text{opening rate} - \text{closing rate}}{0.01}$	130	(70)
Profit/(Loss) 48 contracts × £12.50 × tick movement	78,000	(42,000)

(ii) **Net outcome**

	£	£
Payment in spot market (LIBOR + 0.75%) × £18m × 4/12	(525,000)	(405,000)
Profit/(Loss) in futures market	78,000	(42,000)
Net cost of loan	(447,000)	(447,000)
As annual % (Cost/£18m × 12/4)	7.45%	7.45%

In both cases the net interest cost after hedging is below the target maximum of £450,000 (or 7.50%).

In practice **basis risk** may **not move evenly**. Potential futures gains or losses between December and February may be large if interest rates are volatile, because they are computed on a daily basis.

Hedging the borrowing rate using traded options

Setup

(i) March or June contracts can be used. Assume March, since this will have a lower time premium at close out on 1 March.

(ii) Buy put options

(iii) A strike price of 93.50 will be used since this is closest to today's LIBOR. (100 − 6.5 = 93.50)

(iv) Number of contracts 48

(v) Tick size £12.50

(vi) Option premium March Put 0.60, 60 ticks

Total premium = 48 × 60 × 12.50 = £36,000

Closing prices

	(i)	(ii)
Spot	8.75%	6.75%
Futures	91.80	93.80

Outcome

(i) **Option market outcome**

On 1 February, the possibilities are:

	(i)	(ii)
	Rises	Falls
LIBOR		
Put option strike price (right to sell)	93.50	93.50
March futures price	91.80	93.80
Exercise option? (prefer to sell at highest price)	Yes	No
Gain (ticks)	170	nil
Option outcome (170 × 12.50 × 48)	£102,000	nil

(ii) **Net position**

	£	£
Actual interest cost	(525,000)	(405,000)
Value of option gain	102,000	nil
Premium	(36,000)	(36,000)
Net cost of loan	(459,000)	(441,000)
Effective interest cost (cost/18m × 12/4)	7.65%	7.35%

Similarly, the results of using options with the other two strike prices are shown below.

Strike price	94.00		93.00	
Premium on setup	135 ticks × 48 × 12.50 = 81,000		20 ticks × 48 × 12.50 = 12,000	
	(i)	(ii)	(i)	(ii)
LIBOR	Rises	Falls	Rises	Falls
Put option exercise price	94.00	94.00	93.00	93.00
March futures price	91.80	93.80	91.80	93.80
Exercise option?	Yes	Yes	Yes	No
Buy 48 @	91.80	93.80	91.80	No action
Sell 48 @	94.00	94.00	93.00	No action
Gain (ticks)x	220	20	120	–
Option outcome	132,000	12,000	72,000	–
	£	£	£	£
Actual interest cost	(525,000)	(405,000)	(525,000)	(405,000)
Value of option gain	132,000	12,000	72,000	–
Premium	(81,000)	(81,000)	(12,000)	(12,000)
Net cost of loan	(474,000)	(474,000)	(465,000)	(417,000)
Effective interest cost	7.90%	7.90%	7.75%	6.95%

If LIBOR rises, none of the options **allow** the **required maximum** of 7.50%. If LIBOR falls, the cheapest option (the 93.00 option) is the best, but this is, of course the situation where no hedge is needed. The futures hedge appears to be better.

However, the time value of the options sold, which still have 2 months to expiry, has been ignored in these calculations. This is likely to have a significant impact on the calculations.

(b)   **Advantages of traded interest rate options**

   (i)   The **prices** are **clearly visible** and no negotiation is required.

   (ii)   The market place gives **quick access** to buyers and sellers.

   (iii)   The **options** can be **sold** if not required and there is still time to expiry.

   (iv)   **Gains or losses** are **computed** ('marked to market') on a **daily basis** and ability of counterparties to meet obligations is monitored.

   (v)   **Traded options** are **normally American-style** (ie can be exercised at any time). They are more flexible than many OTC options which are European-style (ie can only be exercised on maturity date).

   (vi)   The market is **more highly regulated** than the OTC market.

   Advantages of OTC options

   The main advantage of **OTC options** is that they can be **tailored more exactly** to the **needs** of the purchaser, in terms of maturity date, contract size, currency and nature of interest. **Contract sizes** are **larger** than on the traded markets and longer times to expiry are available. These complexities tend to mean that they are more expensive.

43 Pondhills

Text references. Chapters 9, 10.

Top tips. An illustration that questions about the risks of international exposure can cover risks other than transaction risks, although translation risk should only be a problem if stock markets are not very efficient. Remember that translation and transaction risks are different, and transaction risk is part of the wider category of economic risk.

Translation risk will only be a problem if market efficiency is limited and investors don't understand the impact on the accounts. Note that the main economic risks involve long-term factors and hence have consequences for strategic decisions.

The most important aspect of (b) is identifying which assets and liabilities are exposed. If you worked on the principle that all assets and liabilities were exposed unless question details indicated otherwise (receipts or payments in dollars or sterling) you should have gained the necessary marks. The shareholders' equity is the balancing figure.

Easy marks. (a) is a good test of your knowledge of translation and economic exposures; if you struggled our discussion covers the key points. You need to discuss the significance (ie the implications).

(a)   **Translation exposure**

   Translation exposure arises from **differences in the currencies** in which assets and liabilities are **denominated.** These effects are most obvious when **consolidated group accounts** are prepared and the values of assets and liabilities denominated in a foreign currency are translated into the home currency.

Implications of translation exposure

(i) **Effect on accounts**

The exact effect translation exposure has on the accounts will depend on the methods of translation used. **Legislation** or **accounting standards** will prescribe which methods should be used.

(ii) **Effect on cash**

Translation exposure is essentially an **accounting measure** and does not involve actual cash flows.

(iii) **Investors' and payables' attitudes**

However if markets are not strongly efficient, investors and payables may interpret losses on translation as a **reduction** in the **financial worth** and **creditworthiness** of the company. This risk can be reduced if assets and liabilities denominated in particular currencies are held in **balanced amounts**.

Economic exposure

Economic exposure is the risk that the **present value** of a company's future cash flows might be **reduced** by **unexpected adverse exchange rate movements**. Economic exposure includes **transaction exposure**, the risk of adverse exchange rate movements occurring in the course of **normal international trading transactions**.

Implications of economic exposure

(i) **Effect on international competitiveness**

This can affect companies through its **purchases** (where raw materials from abroad become more expensive because of a devaluation of the home currency) or its **sales** (where an appreciation in the home currency will mean that sales priced in foreign currencies will be worth less in home currency terms).

(ii) **Effect on remittances from abroad**

If a subsidiary is set up in an overseas country, and that country's exchange rate **depreciates** against the **home exchange rate,** the remittances will be worth less in home currency terms each year.

(iii) **Effect on accounts**

Investors will identify economic exposure as having an **adverse effect** on **accounts** if the markets are efficient.

(iv) **Effect on operations and financing**

In order to hedge the adverse effects of economic exposure, companies will consider **diversification** of operations, so that sales and purchases are made in a number of different currencies. The financing of operations can also be done in a **large number of currencies**.

(b) (i)

	Dinars m	Exposed	$'000 at current rate	$'000 if dinar devalues
Non-current assets	510	Yes	2,071	1,801
Current assets				
Cash	86	Yes	349	304
Receivables	410	No	1,665	1,665
Inventory	380	Yes	1,543	1,342
	876		3,557	3,311
Short-term payables	(296)	50%	(1,202)	(1,123)
Long-term loan stock	(500)	Yes	(2,030)	(1,766)
	590		2,396	2,223
Shareholders' equity	590	Residual	2,396	2,223

Rate if dinar devalues = 246.3 × 1.15 = 283.2

Balance sheet exposure = 510 + 86 + 380 − 148 − 500
                                        = 328 m dinars

Expected loss on translation = 2,396 − 2,223
                                            = $173,000

Alternative working

Loss = 328 × (1/283.2 − 1/246.3)
        = $174,000 difference due to rounding

(ii)

	Dinars m	Exposed	$'000 at current rate	$'000 if dinar devalues
Revenue	2,300	No	9,338	9,338
Cost of goods sold and operating expenses				
Dinars (2,300 × 60% × 70%)	966	Yes	3,922	3,411
Overseas (2,300 × 40% × 70%)	644	No	2,615	2,615
Interest (500 × 12%)	60	Yes	244	212
Net cash inflows	630		2,557	3,100

Gain in cash flow = 3,100 − 2,557
                            = $543,000

(c)   **Translation exposure**

There should in theory be no need to hedge against the translation exposure in (b) (i) as it does not represent actual cash flows. Hedging might be undertaken if markets are **not efficient,** and transaction exposure has a detrimental effect on share price.

Economic exposure

(b) (ii) demonstrates that Pondhills is expected to make a gain based on the current predictions of exchange rates. However Pondhills should consider the **likelihood** of the dinar strengthening against the US dollar. Pondhills might also **settle hard currency cash liabilities** by **reducing dinar cash holdings** before devaluation.

(d)   **Examples of long-term consequences**

  (i)   **Effect on production factor prices**

          A devaluation of the exchange rate might be accompanied by an **increase in inflation,** increasing the cost of sales of Ponda.

  (ii)   **Effect on sales in Africa**

          The devaluation should give Ponda scope to reduce its prices without decreasing its overall sales revenues. The extent to which Ponda can do this will depend on its **elasticity of demand.**

  (iii)   **Pricing**

          Pondhills may use the devaluation to consider its overall pricing strategy, to decide whether **different prices** should be **charged** in **different markets**.

44 Somax

(a) **Use of WACC**

The discount rate that should be used is the **weighted average cost of capital (WACC)**, with weightings based on market values. The cost of capital should take into account the **systematic risk** of the new investment, and therefore it will not be appropriate to use Somax's existing equity beta. Instead, the estimated equity beta of the main Swiss competitor in the same industry as the new proposed plant will be ungeared, and then the capital structure of Somax applied to find the WACC to be used for the discount rate.

Ungearing of Swiss beta

Since the systematic risk of debt can be assumed to be zero, the Swiss equity beta can be **ungeared** using the following expression.

$$\beta_a = \beta_e \frac{E}{E + D(1-t)}$$

where: β_a = asset beta
β_e = equity beta
E = proportion of equity in capital structure
D = proportion of debt in capital structure
t = tax rate

For the Swiss company:

$$\beta_a = 1.5 \times \frac{60}{60 + 40(1 - 0.33)}$$

$$= 1.037$$

This can now be **substituted** into the **capital asset pricing model (CAPM)** to find the cost of equity.

$$Ke = r_f + [E(r_m) - r_f] \beta_a$$

where: Ke = cost of equity
r_f = risk free rate of return
$E(r_m)$ = market rate of return
Ke = 7.75% + (14.5% − 7.75%) × 1.037 = 14.75%

The next step is to **calculate the debt and equity of Somax** based on market values.

		£m
Equity:	2 × 225m = 450m shares at 376p	1,692.00
Debt:	Bank loans	135.00
	Bonds (75m × 1.195)	89.63
	Total debt	224.63

Then, re-gear at the company's gearing ratio, using MM:

$$WACC_g = Ke_u\left[1 - \frac{Dt}{E+D}\right]$$

$$= 14.75 \times (1 - (224.63 \times 0.33)/(1,692 + 224.63)) = 14.18\%$$

(b)   (i)   **Annual interest cost**

The **annual interest cost** to Somax of issuing a five year sterling fixed rate bond is not known. It can probably best be estimated by comparison with the existing 14% fixed rate bonds due to mature in five years time and redeemable at £100. The effective interest rate on this bond is that at which the cost of the remaining interest payments and redemption equals the current market price of £119.50. This can be calculated as follows:

	£14 × 5 year annuity at n%
plus	£100 discounted at n% in five years time
equals	£119.50

This can be estimated by trial and error from present value and annuity tables. (Alternatively, the internal rate of return of the cash flows relating to the bond can be calculated.)

		£
At 9%:	£14 × 3.890	54.46
	£100 × 0.650	65.00
		119.46

This is very close to £119.50, and therefore the cost of the five year fixed rate bond is approximately 9%.

Summary of swap transactions

	Somax	*Swiss co*
Borrowing (actual)	(9.0%)	(SFr LIBOR + 1.5%)
Payments		
Somax to Swiss co.	(SFr LIBOR + 1.0%)	SFr LIBOR + 1.0%
Swiss co. to Somax	9.5%	(9.5%)
Net payment after swap	(SFr LIBOR + 0.5%)	(10%)

Somax's viewpoint

If Somax were to enter into the swap, it would receive a fixed rate of interest from the Swiss company of 9.5% per year, which represents a net benefit of 0.5% (9.5% − 9%). At the same time it would pay the Swiss company at SFr LIBOR + 1.0% per year, making a net cost of SFr LIBOR + 0.5% per year. The alternative would be to borrow directly at SFr LIBOR + 0.75% per year (5.75% − 5.0%). Thus the swap offers Somax a gain over direct borrowing of 0.25% per year. Against this must be offset the annual fee to the bank of 0.20%, giving Somax a net gain of 0.05% per year.

Swiss company's viewpoint

From the point of view of the Swiss company, it can borrow directly at SFr LIBOR + 1.5%. Against this can be offset the annual interest payments from Somax of SFr LIBOR + 1.0%, making a net cost of 0.5% per year in addition to the 9.5% interest payment to Somax. This equates to an annual cost of 10%, to which must be added the bank fee of 0.2% giving a total cost of 10.2%. This compares with the cost to the Swiss company of borrowing fixed rate sterling at 10.5% per annum – a net annual benefit of 0.30%.

Thus both parties will benefit from the swap, although the Swiss company stands to gain more than Somax. However, if the SFr strengthens against the pound, then the benefits to Somax could be further reduced since the value of the sterling interest payments will fall relative to those denominated in SFr.

(ii) **Benefits of swaps**

(1) **Timing**

The companies may be able to **structure** the **timing of payments** so as to improve the matching of cash outflows with revenues.

(2) **Increased access to debt finance**

The companies gain **access to debt finance** in another country and currency where it is little known, and consequently has a poorer credit rating, than in its own country.

(3) **Hedging**

The swap provides a **hedge against currency risk** for the full five year period.

(4) **Restructuring interest rate liabilities**

Swaps give the companies the opportunity to **restructure their interest rate liabilities** in terms of the relative proportions of fixed rate and floating rate debt, without the need to restructure the debt base itself.

(5) **Bank benefits**

The bank **benefits from the fees** from the swap; it may also gain the opportunity to undertake further business with the two parties if it is not already their first line bank.

Risks of swaps

(1) **Default**

There is the **risk** of one of the parties **defaulting**.

(2) **Adverse movements**

There is the **risk** that **interest rates** and **exchange rates** could **move** in such a way that the net payments arising as a result of the swap are higher than they would have been had the swap not been undertaken.

(3) **Bank risks**

If the bank takes on a temporary role in the financing during the arrangement of the swap, it runs the risk that rates could **move during the delay** involved in completing the transactions.

45 Galeplus

Text references. Mainly Chapter 19.

Top tips. As well as reducing borrowing costs, your answer to (a) needs to bring out other uses, effectively changing finance structure and hedging. (b) (i) is a starting point for all swap calculations. Note in (b) (ii) that the examiner regards purchasing power parity as a core technique and is pained by the number of students who don't use it.

The other key point was making sure to use different rates for the payment on which the swap was based and the rest of the monies. The key in (c) is expectations; do current economic indicators suggest that there will be a good enough chance that the option will be exercised for it to be worth paying the premium.

Easy marks. (a) should have been the easiest part and the answer is worth learning if you couldn't come up with many suggestions.

(a)   **Currency swaps**

Currency swaps are agreements between two parties to **swap payments on each other's loans**, those loans being in different currencies. For example, a company may arrange to make the payments on a counterparty's US dollar loan, while the counterparty makes payments on the company's euro loan. The effect is to enable the company to **switch its effective interest payments from euros to dollars**. An equivalent effect could be achieved by terminating the company's euro loan and taking out a new loan in US dollars.

Advantages of swaps

(i)   Companies may have a **comparative advantage borrowing in their own currency**. Doing this and agreeing a currency swap may produce a cheaper interest rate than trying to borrow directly in a foreign currency.

(ii)   **Termination costs** for an existing loan may make it **prohibitively expensive** to change finance. A bank's service fee to arrange a swap may be lower than the termination charge. Also, if a company has long term borrowings in one currency but needs to switch to paying interest in another currency for a shorter period, a swap can enable this without having to terminate the original loan.

(iii)   In some countries it is difficult or impossible for foreign registered companies to **borrow in the local currency**. A currency swap gets round these restrictions.

(iv)   Borrowing in a foreign currency is an **effective method of hedging income** in that currency, and currency swaps are one way of achieving this. The **cost is often cheaper** than using the market for long term forward contracts. Currency swaps have also been used as a method of avoiding **exchange control restrictions**.

Problems of swaps

(i)   The **counterparty** to the swap arrangement may **default** if it gets into financial difficulties. In this case the company is still liable to pay the interest on the original loan. In general, banks make less risky counterparties than many corporates.

(ii)   If the swap is into a developing country's currency, there may be **significant risk of adverse government restrictions** being introduced.

(iii)   If the swap has been entered into to **reduce currency risk** as with any hedging instrument, the exchange rate may move in a direction that means it would have been better **not to have undertaken the hedge**.

(iv)   A swap between two floating rate loans may introduce **basis risk** if the interest rates are not referenced to the same base rate.

(b)   (i)   The borrowing rates for Galeplus and its counterparty can be summarised as follows:

	Galeplus Floating	Counterparty Fixed	
Wants			
Pays with Swap	6.25%	PIBOR + 1.5%	PIBOR + 7.75%
Pays without Swap	PIBOR + 2%	8.3%	PIBOR + 10.3%
Potential gain			2.55%
Bank fee			− 0.75%
Potential gain			1.8%
Split 75:25	1.35%	0.45%	

(ii)   Future currency exchange rates may be estimated using **purchasing power parity theory**.

Assuming the inflation rate in UK is zero the formula $(i_f - i_{uk})/(1+i_{uk})$ reduces to i_f. In other words the percentage increase in the exchange rate each year is the Perdian inflation rate, at best 15% and at worst 50%, as follows:

259

Estimated exchange rates, rubbits/£

	Inflation	Spot	Year 1	Year 2	Year 3
Best case	15%	85.40	98.21	112.94	129.88
Worst case	50%	85.40	128.10	192.15	288.23

The cash flows of the telecommunications centre are:

Million rubbits

Year	0	1	2	3
Purchase cost	(2,000)			
Fees		40	40	40
Sale price				4,000
	(2,000)	40	40	4,040

If the currency swap is used, 2,000 million of the year 3 cash flows will be translated at the current spot rate of 85·40 rubbits/£, giving £23.42 million and the remainder (2,040 million) will be translated at the year 3 rate. The net present values of the best and worst cases can be calculated using the 15% risk adjusted discount rate.

Cash flows £m

Year	0	1	2	3
Purchase cost	(2,000)	40	40	4,040
Best case rate	85.40	98.21	112.94	
Best case £m	(23.42)	0.41	0.35	39.13
15% factors	1.000	0.870	0.756	0.658
Present values	(23.42)	0.36	0.25	25.75
NPV	2.95			
Worst case rate	85.40	128.10	192.15	
Worst case £m	(23.42)	0.31	0.21	30.50
15% factors	1.000	0.870	0.756	0.658
Present values	(23.42)	0.27	0.16	20.07
NPV	(2.92)			

$$\text{Year 3 cash flows} = 23.42 + \frac{2{,}040}{\text{Best/worst rate}}$$

$$\text{Best} = 23.42 + \frac{2{,}040}{129.88}$$

$$= 39.13$$

$$\text{Worst} = 23.42 + \frac{2{,}040}{288.23}$$

$$= 30.50$$

Results

Because the project receipts are fixed in Perdian rubbits, the net present value of the project depends entirely on the **rubbit exchange rate against the pound becoming worse** the **more the rubbit depreciates**. The currency swap provides some hedging, but this is for less than half the sum at risk in year 3. Galeplus should consider the availability of other hedging techniques to cover a greater proportion of the cash flows.

On the basis of the figures used the expected value is approximately **break even**, but the **risk** of a **negative result** is high and on balance the investment does not appear to be worthwhile Other factors that also need to be considered include **default risk** of the Perdian government and liability of the project receipts to **taxation** in the UK.

(c) (i) **Swaptions**

A swaption is an **option to enter into a swap**. In this case Galeplus would exchange 2,000 million rubbits for pounds at today's spot rate and, on payment of a premium of £300,000, would have the option of swapping the money back at the same exchange rate. This option would be exercised if the rubbit depreciated against the pound over the next three years, but if it strengthened, the swaption would be abandoned and the pounds purchased on the prevailing spot rate.

Recommended course of action

The inflation rate in Perdia is so high compared with the UK's that it is highly unlikely that the rubbit would strengthen against the pound. The payment of £300,000 for the swaption's protection would therefore be unwise.

(ii) The European put option enables Galeplus to **sell the whole cash flow** at (and not before) the end of year 3 (4,040 rubbits) at 160 rubbits/£. On the basis of the forecasts provided, the option would be exercised under the worst case scenario (spot rate 288.23 > 160) but abandoned under the best case (spot rate 129.88 < 160).

Worst case scenario

Year 3 cash is 4,040 million rubbits, exchanged at the option rate of 160 r/£ giving £25.25 million. Discounted at 15% gives £25.25m × 0.658 = £16.61 million.

Years 0 to 2 present values are the same (see above, worst case), so discounted cash flows are – (23.42) + 0.27 + 0.16 +16.61 = (£6.38 million), less the option premium of £1.7 million gives **(£8.08 million)**.

Best case scenario

Spot rate of 129.88 r/£ is used: 4,040/129.88 = £31.11 million. Discounted at 15% gives £31.11 million × 0.658 = £20.47 million.

Discounted cash flows (best case) are (23.42) + 0.36 + 0.26 + 20.47 = (£2.33 million), less the option premium of £1.7m gives (£4.03 million).

Results

On the basis of these figures, the option **does nothing to protect Galeplus's investment** and should not be used.

In comparison with the swap its potential **advantage** is that it **covers the whole of year 3 proceeds**; the swap covers less than one half of this.

Its **disadvantages** are:

*   It offers a **significantly inferior maximum exchange rate** (160 compared with 85.4).
*   It has an expensive premium cost.

46 Polytot

> **Text references.** Chapter 19 on hedging techniques, Chapter 9 on raising capital overseas and Chapter 23 on international trade.
>
> **Top tips.** With the futures and options contracts, calculating the outcome is slightly different from some other questions:
>
> (i)   With futures you are told enough about basis to work out the price in four months time, and you have to use that in this question to find the number of contracts. Strictly you should also take into account the over-hedge and take the difference to the forward market to make the results strictly comparable with the forward market result; however you are unlikely to be penalised for not doing so.
>
> (ii)   With the options you use the 1.5250 to calculate the number of contracts but again should calculate the over-hedge. Remember the premium is translated at the opening rate. It would also be possible (although it would give you an extra calculation) to calculate the outcome using an option price of $1.55 as it is not that much worse than the forward market, and does mean the company can choose not to exercise the option if necessary.
>
> (b) requires imagination as much as anything, but also note that it brings in government rules and reaction (tax).
> (c) is a discussion of the key factors involved in the decision to borrow on the Euromarkets.
>
> **Easy marks.** Hopefully the forward calculations and (c) if you have a good understanding of the Euromarkets.

(a)   **Currency hedges available to Polytot**

Polytot's receipt will be in four months' time, on 31 October.
60% of the sales price is 675 × 60% = 405 million pesos.
Converted to dollars at the spot rate this is worth 405/98.20 = $4,124,236

From the information given, the company could try a forward market hedge, a currency futures hedge or a currency options hedge for this receipt of dollars.

The remainder of the sales price will in each case be converted at the unofficial rate of 1.15 × 156.30 pesos to the £, ie 179.745 peso/£, $\dfrac{675 - 405}{179.745}$ giving £1,502,128.

Forward market hedge

On 1 July, Polytot will enter into a contractual obligation to sell $4,124,236 for £ on 31 October at a rate to be agreed on 1 July.

The 4 months $/£ forward rate will have to be interpolated between the 3 month and the one year rates.

Interpolating, the rate for 4 months forward   = 1.5398 − ((1.5398 − 1.5178)/9)
                                              = 1.5398 − 0.0024
                                              = 1.5374

$4,124,236/ 1.5374 = £2,682,604.

Futures hedge

Setup

(i)   December £ futures

(ii)   Buy futures

(iii)   Number of contracts

The basis now is:

	1.5510
	1.5275
	235 ticks

If basis reduces evenly over the six month life of the contract, in 4 months' time basis will be 1/3 × 235 ticks = 78 ticks.

1.5275 + 78 ticks = 1.5353 (lock-in rate)

$$\frac{4,124,236/1.5353}{62,500} = 42.98, \text{ say 43 contracts}$$

(iv)   Amount to be hedged on forward market = (43 × 62,500 × 1.5353) − 4,124,236
                                                                      = 4,126,119 − 4,124,236
                                                                      = $1,883

Use interpolation to find rate (different forward rate to rate used above, as over-hedge).

1.5362 − ((1.5362 − 1.5140)/9 = 1.5337

(v)   Tick size 0.0001 × 62,500 = $6.25

Closing futures price

As an example, use forward rate of 1.5374 as predicted spot rate

Using basis of 78 ticks as above, closing futures price = 1.5374 − 0.0078 = 1.5296

Hedge outcome

(i)   **Outcome in futures market**

Opening futures price	1.5275 Buy
Closing futures price	1.5296 Sell
Movement in ticks	21 ticks profit

Futures profit 43 × $6.25 × 21 = $5,644

(ii)   **Net outcome**

	£
Spot market receipt ($4,126,119/1.5374)	2,683,829
Futures profit, translated at closing rate ($5,644/1.5374)	3,671
Over-hedge on forward market ($1,883/1.5337)	(1,228)
	2,686,272

Basis risks

The basis calculation is subject to **basis risk**, which means that the basis of 0.78 cents is subject to a margin of error, which may give a better or worse result.

Initial margin

Unlike forward contracts, when Polytot enters into a futures contract, a deposit known as **initial margin** must be paid. Daily gains or losses on the futures market, known as variation margin, are then marked to Polytot's account and, in the case of losses, must be financed.

Impact of uncertainties

The futures market hedge aims to give the same locked-in exchange rate as is obtainable from the forward market, but a few more **uncertainties** are involved. For Polytot the exchange rate obtainable may be better than on the forward market, if it is prepared to accept the risks.

Currency options hedge

Currency options **provide protection against losses** in the event of unfavourable exchange rate movements, but allow the company to take advantage of exchange gains in the event of favourable movements. This is because an option does not have to be exercised unless it is to the investor's advantage.

Set up the hedge

(i)   December options

(ii) Call options as we need to buy £

(iii) Strike price 1.5250 as better than the forward rate

(iv) How many contracts

$$\frac{4{,}124{,}236 \div 1.525}{31{,}250} \approx 87 \text{ contracts}$$

Amount hedged on forward market = $(31{,}250 \times 87 \times 1.525) - 4{,}124{,}236 = \$21{,}858$

(v)   Premium $= \dfrac{3.35}{100} \times 31{,}250 \times 87$

$\qquad\qquad\quad$ = \$91,078 @ 1.5475

$\qquad\qquad\quad$ = £58,855

Outcome

	£
Option market (31,250 × 87)	2,718,750
Over-hedge on forward (21,858/1.5374)	(14,217)
Premium	(58,855)
	2,645,678

Effect of premium

As with all options, the **minimum guaranteed outcome** will be less than that obtainable on the forward or futures markets because of the cost of the option premium. However, if the dollar strengthens, the option can be allowed to lapse, enabling Polytot to make currency gains that would not be possible if the forward or futures contracts were used.

Recommendations

The hedge taken will depend on Polytot's **overall strategy** and **attitude towards currency gains and losses**.

Not hedging

Given that the forward markets are indicating that the dollar is likely to strengthen, Polytot may **decide not to hedge** at all, which is unwise, as an unexpected decline in the dollar could produce embarrassing losses

Forward and futures market

The forward and futures markets are effective at **eliminating losses**, which is the prime requirement for a risk averse policy. Of these two methods, the forward contract has **less risk** and requires **less administration**, though in this case it is predicted to produce slightly worse results.

Option

The option is a **compromise** between these two possible approaches, providing a degree of protection against losses but the opportunity of making a gain if the chance arises.

Conclusion

Assuming the company is reasonably risk-averse, the best hedge would probably be the simple, **risk averse forward contract**.

(b) **Sale of strawberries**

Three million kilos of strawberries could be sold at between 50 and 60 pence per kilo, providing receipts of £1.5 to £1.8 million. This is in comparison with the receipt of £1,502,128 if the pesos are exchanged on the unofficial market.

Potential problems

The strawberries therefore can potentially provide a better income. However, there are important questions to be answered before the deal can be accepted.

(i) Does the import of strawberries **contravene food quotas** set under the European common agricultural policy?

(ii) How **reliable is the offer** to provide strawberries? Is it realistically possible to organise the supply? Will they be provided all at once, or in several lots?

(iii) What is the **general quality** of Grobbian strawberries? Are they likely to be rejected by large buyers? How will the quality be determined and inspected? What are costs of this?

(iv) Strawberries are perishable goods. How will they be **transported** and **insured**? Who will bear the cost of this?

(v) What **other additional costs** might be incurred?

(vi) How will the **receipt and sale** of strawberries be **taxed**?

(c) To: Directors of Polytot plc

From: Financial advisor

Briefing note

Using Euromarkets to raise international finance

Raising finance on Euromarkets has a number of advantages compared with domestic capital markets.

Regulation

Euromarkets are subject to fewer regulatory controls than domestic markets. This results in relatively low issue costs, smaller differentials between lending and borrowing rates and hence cheaper borrowing costs. Interest is usually payable gross of tax, that is attractive to some investors.

Range of products

The Euromarkets provide a flexible range of products, including interest rate swaps and currency swaps, and there is an active secondary market in many of the securities. They are capable of handling very large loan offers within a short lead time, compared with domestic markets that have queuing processes.

Need for high rating

In order to borrow on the Euromarkets the Grobbian company would need to achieve a high rating by an international rating agency or, as an alternative, would need to have any issue of funds guaranteed by the Grobbian government. Since the loan would be in a hard currency, the market will need to be sure that the company will have access to sufficient hard currency to pay interest and repay the principal.

47 Microchip Engineering

(a)   **Memorandum: Hedging Foreign Exchange Risk**

Foreign exchange risk exposure is driven by a mismatch of currency trade flows and the variability of the exchange rates. The volatility of the Euro against sterling is 21.65% (annualised). This indicates significant value at risk in any forward commitment to Euros and must be managed carefully.

For capital flows the ultimate target must be to match assets and liability. Hedging is costly. The expenses associated with establishing a treasury function and developing the in-house expertise can be considerable. Hedging through derivative contracts can be avoided by the creation of internal hedging arrangements whereby finance is raised in the country of operations. This matches the borrowing costs with the revenue streams.

The firm's exposure to exchange rate volatility which is a market wide phenomenon can be controlled by hedging. The use of hedging would lead to a reduction in the firm's beta and its cost of capital. Another benefit of hedging through the use of derivative contracts is that it allows us to manage uncertain risk exposure through the use of options contracts.

Hedging FOREX risk using derivatives can be expensive especially when exposure is uncertain. Where the exposure is certain, the use of futures or forward contracts can eliminate a large element of the risk at a much lower cost. The policy to hedge against FOREX will depend upon:

(i)   The magnitude of the risk exposure (the high volatility and long-term exposure, as in this case, creates a high hedging cost). Value at risk may be an appropriate method for measuring the likely financial exposure.

(ii)   The materiality of the exposure in terms of the magnitude of the sums involved.

(iii)   The extent to which the risk can be mitigated by matching agreements.

(iv)   The extent to which the exposure has crystallised. If it is uncertain FOREX options allow the hedging of the downside risk but at a high cost.

A general policy concerning the hedging of foreign exchange risk should identify the principles which should be followed to cover:

(i)   **Risk assessment**

This involves the assessment of the likelihood and impact of any risk on the financial position of the firm. Derivative positions can be highly geared and this may expose the firm to high liabilities. It is recommended that derivatives should only be used for the management of specific risks and that no speculative or uncovered position should be taken.

(ii)   **Cost of hedging**

This includes all direct costs as well as costs related to management time in establishing positions and operating the internal control procedures required when derivatives are used to hedge against risk. It is recommended that hedging costs are minimised to an agreed percentage of the value of risk through the unhedged position.

(iii)   **Contract and approval procedures**

For both OTC and exchange traded products it is necessary to establish a clearly defined approval process with clear lines of responsibility and sign off on contracts (up to and including board level). It is recommend that the board appoint a risk management committee to review and monitor all hedging contracts where the value at risk is in excess of an agreed amount. The firm will also need to establish policies with respect to the legal aspects of the contracting process.

(iv) **Hedging monitoring**

It is necessary to establish a policy relating to the monitoring of all derivative positions and to stipulate the conditions under which any given position will be reversed. It is recommended that the risk management committee actively monitor all open positions.

(b) (i) **The likely price for the at the money option**

	3 months	9 months
Sterling Euro spot	0.6700	0.6700
Sterling Euro (indirect)	1.4925	1.4925
Euro LIBOR	2.6765	3.0195
Sterling LIBOR	4.2613	4.3701
Sterling Euro forward (indirect)	1.4867	1.4779
Sterling Euro forward (direct)	0.6726	0.6766
Annual volatility of £/Euro	21.65%	21.65%
d_1	0.0904	0.1147
d_2	-0.0178	-0.0728
$N(d_1)$	0.5360	0.4543
$N(d_2)$	0.4929	0.5290
3 month call and 9 month put price (pence per Euro) (ie the price of a call or put to buy or sell one Euro at spot)	2.9969	4.7276
Contract value (Euro equivalent)	2997	4728

The values for d_1, and d_2 have been calculated as follows:

$$d_1 = \frac{\left(Ln \left(\frac{F}{S} \right) + \sigma^2 \frac{t}{2} \right)}{\sigma \sqrt{t}}$$

$$d_1 = \frac{\left(Ln \left(\frac{0.6726}{0.6700} \right) + 0.2165^2 \frac{0.25}{2} \right)}{0.2165 \sqrt{0.25}}$$

$d_1 = 0.0904$

$d_2 = d_1 - \sigma \sqrt{t}$

$d_2 = 0.0904 - 0.2165 \sqrt{0.25}$

$d_2 = 0.0178$

where F = forward rate
  S = spot rate
  σ = volatility
  t = time to maturity

$N(d_1)$ and $N(d_2)$ are derived from the tables from the normal density function for situations $N(x) \geq 0$ and $N(x) \leq 0$.

The value of the currency call and the currency put are as follows.

$C = e^{-rt}[FN(d_1) - SN(d_2)]$

$C = e^{-0.042613 \times 0.25}[0.6726 \times 0.5360 - 0.6700 \times 0.4929]$

C = 2.9969 pence per Euro, or £2,996.90 per contract (€100,000)

and

$P = e^{-rt}[SN(-d_2) - FN(-d_1)]$

$P = e^{-0.043701 \times 0.75}[0.6700 \times 0.5290 - 0.6726 \times 0.4543]$

P = 4.7276 pence per Euro, or £4,727.60 per contract (€100,000)

The call should be exercised if the exchange rate rises above 0.6700 (thus making the sterling equivalent more expensive) and the nine month put should be exercised if the spot should be below 0.6700 at the exercise date.

Note: the rates in the formula must all be direct, the volatility and interest rates are employed on an annual basis.

(ii) The **number of contracts required to hedge the exposure** are as follows.

	3 months	9 months
Number of contracts	4,664	5,503
Cost of hedge	13,977,542	26,015,983
As percentage of value	0.0559	0.1041

$$\text{Number of contracts} = \frac{\text{Capital required}}{\text{Contract size}} \times \frac{1}{N(d_1)}$$

$$\text{Number} = \frac{250,000,000}{100,000} \times \frac{1}{0.5360}$$

$$= 4,664.179$$

$$\text{Number} = 2,500 \times \frac{1}{0.4543}$$

$$= 5,502.97$$

Cost of hedge (3 mth)   = Cost/contract × No of contracts
= £2,996.90 × 4,664
= £13,977,541.60

Cost of hedge (9 mth)   = £4,727.60 × 5,503
= £26,015,982.80

(iii) The **issues to be considered** when reviewing the hedging proposal are:

(1) Hedging with options **eliminates downside** risk and are **useful when the exposure is uncertain**.

(2) The **cost** of this type of hedge can be high (especially for the long dated put). The company may reduce the cost by purchasing out of the money options. This will not eliminate the downside risk completely but will allow the board to hedge a known exposure.

(3) An **alternative approach** would be to hedge the three-month exposure which is where the option is most valuable given the uncertainty over whether the bid will be accepted. If the bid is accepted then the company can enter into a future contract at that date to lock in the prevailing spot rate. Alternatively, purchasing the put option may be held back until the contract is won.

(4) Given set contract sizes it is **not possible to create a perfect hedge**. The position would need continual monitoring and adjustment to offset gamma risk which is likely to be high for near the money options.

(5)   There is **timing risk** given that currency options are quoted as Europeans. Early sale of the option if the requirement materialised early will create basis risk. If the requirement materialises late the residual time delay will be unhedged.

48 Exchange rates

Text references. Chapter 19.

Top tips. By using headers our answer emphasises that we are discussing the key points required in the question. Stability is a key factor; not only does a stable currency remove exchange uncertainty, it also should lead to a better economic environment. The caveat is that in order to achieve stability, deflation may be required which may damage the subsidiary's business.

(a)   **Managed floating exchange rate**

Foreign exchange risk

A managed foreign exchange rate will mean that there is **foreign exchange risk**, Uncertainty is caused by:

(i)   The **factors affecting market supply and demand** and whether markets may be vulnerable to unpredictable events.

(ii)   **Uncertainty over government intervention**. Fluctuations can occur within **limits** set down by the government and enforced by government intervention to sell or buy the currency on the market. The government may not publicise when it will intervene, and so there is the further uncertainty of how great the fluctuations could be before government does intervene.

The multinational may try various hedging methods to limit risk. For example it may try to **invoice in its own currency** to **safeguard its receipts**, although this is dependent upon customers being **willing to pay** in **that currency.**

Economic implications

(i)   **Investments** made in the foreign country may **not be as profitable** as planned, if the receipts are less than expected due to exchange rate fluctuations.

(ii)   Uncertainty over exchange rates may limit the **level of investment** in that country and hence **depress demand**, threatening the value of the subsidiary if it was expected to generate significant local sales.

(iii)   In the long-term however managed floating exchange rates should result in **equilibrium**. The multinational should not have to worry about exchange rate distortions impacting adversely upon the subsidiary's competitiveness and the pressures on a country's economy caused by speculation in its currency.

(b)   **Fixed exchange rate linked to a basket of currencies**

Foreign exchange risk

Foreign exchange risk for the multinational should be limited under the system of linking to a number of weighted currencies. The link to a basket of currencies means that the rate will **not be distorted** by pressures on the currency to which it is linked. However if the basket is weighted according to international trade, the distortion may occur if one country is a dominant trading partner and hence its currency has a major impact upon the basket's value.

Economic implications

(i)   If the currency is overvalued, demand for the **subsidiary's products** may be depressed. When exporting it will be **less competitive**, whilst it may be undercut in its home market by underpriced imports (although this may benefit the multinational parent).

(ii) The **economic measures** taken by the government to maintain the exchange rate such as keeping interest rates high and reducing demand by raising taxes may depress demand for the subsidiary's products in its local market.

(iii) However the removal of uncertainty over exchange rates may encourage investment, and **boost demand** in the country's economy.

(iv) The multinational should find **pricing and investment planning easier** if uncertainty is minimised.

(v) If the levels of inflation in the local economy remain high compared with the countries in the basket, eventually the country will be **forced to devalue** to maintain competitiveness. The level and timing of devaluation may be difficult to forecast, particularly if influenced by currency speculation.

(c) Currency board

Foreign exchange risk

This is a type of fixed exchange rate where the local currency is **backed** by a major world currency such as the dollar. Currency issues are equalled by corresponding amounts of the major currency; thus the local currency is convertible into the backing currency at a fixed exchange rate. Foreign exchange risk should be **minimised** if the major currency is the multinational's **own currency**, and will otherwise be limited to the risk of adverse movements against the major currency.

Economic implications

(i) The local currency should achieve **stability** as it is tracking a major currency.

(ii) Currency stability should lead to **economic stability**, with lower inflation and less uncertainty for investors.

(iii) However a multinational's subsidiary may suffer from **higher interest rates** and **lower demand** because of limitations in the money supply that result from a currency board system.

(d) Adjustable peg systems

An adjustable peg system is a system of **fixed exchange rates** but with a **provision** for **either** the **devaluation** or **revaluation** of a currency.

Economic implications

(i) Countries with a balance of payments surplus may not wish to revalue their currency and to pursue inflationary policies. Conversely, countries with a balance of payments deficit may be reluctant to devalue their currency as it may be perceived as a failure. Clearly, if not all countries apply the rules by this system then the resulting exchange rate will not be accurate.

(ii) Fixing the nominal value of exchange rates would not necessarily protect real values due to differences in the rate of inflation from one country to another. The problem of inflation may need exchange rates to be adjusted more frequently thereby removing a major reason for having an adjustable peg system.

(iii) Speculation could put excessive pressure on a currency and may force a devaluation. The gains of speculators would effectively need to be paid out of the countries central bank's reserves.

(iv) If the level of speculative capital exceeds the official reserves the governments would be unable to prevent successful, co-ordinated speculation and thereby fail to control the fluctuation in the country's exchange rate.

49 Gitlor

Text references. Chapters 19 and 20.

Top tips. The question clearly implies that you should use the parity formulae to produce calculations illustrating your arguments. What is less clear is what is meant by mechanisms influencing exchange rates; the answer required concentration on factors affecting currency markets, although you could also discuss other mechanisms such as political state. Politics is also important in the last part of the question as the extent and timing of government management will often be determined by the political state and cycle.

Report

To: Managing Director, Gitlor plc
From: Accountant
Date: 5 January 20X5
Subject: **Exchange rate forecasts**

(a) **Reasons why exchange rate forecasts differ**

Interest rate and purchasing power parity

Comparisons of the results of interest rate parity and purchasing power parity illustrate why the banks' forecasts may differ.

Interest rate parity is based on the assumption that differences in interest rates will cause changes in exchange rates, since they will cause flows of capital between countries and hence increased demand for currencies which will be reflected in changes in exchange rates.

The formula for interest rate parity can be expressed as:

$$\text{Forward rate a/b} = \text{Spot rate a/b} \times \frac{(1 + \text{interest rate in country a})}{(1 + \text{interest rate in country b})}$$

Purchasing power parity theory suggests that changes in exchange rates are caused by differences in the rate of inflation between countries, that the exchange value of a foreign currency depends on its **relative purchasing power**.

The formula for purchasing power parity can be expressed as:

$$\text{Forward rate a/b} = \text{Spot rate a/b} \times \frac{(1 + \text{interest rate in country a})}{(1 + \text{interest rate in country b})}$$

Using the two formulae produces the following predictions for forward rates:

	Interest rate parity	Purchasing power parity
$/Euro	0.872	0.880
£/Euro	0.623	0.614
Yen/$	121	120
$/£	1.400	1.434

Not only do the exchange rate movements differ whatever the formula, in some cases the **movement** has been in **different directions**. This is because for example American inflation rates are higher than UK inflation rates, but UK interest rates are higher than American rates.

Further differences will have been caused by banks using predicted exchange or interest rates rather than current rates.

Different models

In practice also the forecasts made by banks will be the results of calculations using models that **incorporate several factors**, not just simple exchange or inflation rates. This will inevitably result in different forecasts, as the **weightings** given to each factor will differ between models, and the **assumptions** made about each factor may also differ.

(b) **Mechanisms influencing exchange rates**

Market efficiency

A key determinant will be the degree of efficiency of the foreign exchange markets. If markets are **strongly efficient**, exchange rates will only change if random events occur which cannot be anticipated by the market. This includes political or natural events, but may also include movements in economic variables that cannot be predicted. If markets are not strongly efficient, exchange rates may be influenced by subjective **market sentiment** or possibly **speculation**.

Market contagion

The degree of market contagion may also influence how **exchange rates are affected**, by determining when and by how much a country's exchange rate is affected by developments elsewhere in the world's financial system.

Reserve currencies

If a currency is being held as a **reserve currency, as part of the reserves** of another country, then its exchange rate will depend on the actions not just of its own government but the other countries that hold it in their reserves.

(c) **Forecasting exchange rates**

Floating rates

It is thus extremely difficult to forecast exchange rates especially if movements are dependent on **unpredictable future events**. In theory freely floating rates will be exposed to the full impact of these random events.

Managed rates

Exchange rates may be more **predictable** if their level is managed by governments buying and selling currency in the markets. The degree of predictability will depend on **how well government criteria for intervention** are understood. However sometimes **market pressures** can **overwhelm government attempts at intervention**.

Fixed rates

Fixed rates should be the **easiest to predict**, at least in the short-term. However in the longer-term **changes in economic variables** will put pressure on exchange rate levels that will eventually cause realignments. Knowledge of economic indicators can be used to predict the likely direction of any revaluation, but not necessarily its timing or amount; these may depend on non-financial factors such as **political pressures**.

(d) **Factors governing exchange rates**

In the shorter term, the exchange rate is determined by reference to interest rate differential between the two currencies which in turn will depend on relative supply and demand for those currencies. The longer term exchange rates are determined by purchasing power parity and the inflation differential between two currencies. The interest rates, inflation and the foreign exchange markets are linked by the International Fisher Effect.

Fisher states that the nominal rate of return (r), ie the interest rate charged is equal to the real rate of return (R) adjusted to compensate for the effect of inflation (i) as follows:

$$(1 + r) = (1 + R)(1 + i)$$

the above relationship applies in all economies and can be extrapolated to mean that the interest rate differentials in the long-term equate to inflation rate differentials over the same period. Taking this to its logical conclusion it is possible to state that the exchange rate differentials in the long-term are driven by inflation rate differentials between the two economics concerned.

(e) **Controlling foreign currency risk**

Movements in exchange rates causing variability in returns, either in the forms of cash flows or asset values can be reduced or eliminated by use of various foreign currency hedging techniques. These can be summarised as follows:

(i) **Forward contracts**

The risk of the exchange rate moving in an adverse manner compared to the forecast can be removed by taking out a forward contract. This fixes the rate today for delivery at a specified future date. The relevant rate for the forward contract is the forward rate. The problems with this method of hedging is that it assumes all flows are known with certainty. Significant changes in flows would require separate forward contracts, thereby increasing costs and administration. In addition, the company will not be able to take advantage of any favourable movements. The forward market is most active in the three to six month period. It becomes more difficult to obtain competitively priced forward contracts for periods exceeding six months; hence they tend to be more expensive and illiquid.

(ii) **Borrowing and depositing**

An alternative means of hedging an expected receipt in another currency would be through borrowing and depositing. That is to borrow now in that other currency, convert the money received now into sterling at today's spot rate and place this sterling on deposit, then to use the expected receipt in the other currency to repay the borrowing on maturity. The key problem with borrowing is that, as with the forward contract, it creates an exposure to foreign currency which will still be there if the expected receipts from the investment do not flow through.

(iii) **Options**

The currency options avoids many of the problems noted above for borrowing and use of forward contracts. The currency option gives the buyer of the option the right, but not the obligation to buy or sell foreign currency at a specified rate and a specified date in the future. The cost of the option is the premium.

The key benefit of the option is that it enables the company to benefit from favourable exchange rate movements but protects it from adverse movements. The option need only be exercised if it is in the interests of the company to do so. The problem with this method of hedging is the cost. A premium needs to be paid on the option irrespective of whether the option is exercised or not. The larger the amount to which the option relates or the greater the chance the option can be exercised profitably then the higher the premium.

50 MJY

> **Text references.** Chapter 19.
>
> **Top tips.** Provided you recognised the importance of netting off transactions, part (a) is not as time-pressurised as many derivative questions. It is necessary to net off inter-group as well as external transactions though.
>
> Possible problems are:
>
> - Using the right forward rates; you wish to obtain dollars to settle the payment, so use the lower rate as you will obtain fewer dollars for each £ you spend. By contrast you need to use the higher rate on the € receipt as you will be sacrificing more of the € you have received to obtain the £ you ultimately want.
>
> - Purchasing a put option as you have to **sell** £ contracts to obtain the dollars you require
>
> - Translating the premium at the **opening** spot rate
>
> - Because this is a single contract, and being compared with a forward contract, you should calculate the over-hedge and hedge the difference on the forward market.

(a)   **Netting off**

We need to net off $ and € receipts and payments as far as possible inside and outside the group before hedging (ignore £ as MJY based in UK)

$ hedged amount = 90 + 50 + 40 + 20 + 30 − 170 − 120 − 50 = $110,000 payment
€ hedged amount = 75 + 85 + 72 + 20 + 52 + 35 − 72 − 35 − 50 − 20 − 65 = €97,000 receipt

Forward contract

Buy $ 3 months $\dfrac{110,000}{1.7835}$ = £61,676

Sell € 3 months $\dfrac{97,000}{1.4390}$ = £67,408

Option

Set up

(i)   Contract date May

(ii)   Option type Put as sell £ to buy $

(iii)   Price Try $1.78 and $1.80

(iv)   No of contracts Price 1.78

110,000 ÷ 178/62,500 = 0.99, say 1 contract

Over-hedge in forward market = (62,500 × 1.78) − 110,000 = $1,250

No of contracts Price 1.80

110,000 ÷ 1.80/62,500 = 0.98, say 1 contract

Over-hedge in forward market = (62,500 × 1.80) − 110,000 = $2,500

(v)   Premium

1.78: 0.0420 × 62,500/1.7982 = £1,460
1.80: 0.0534 × 62,500/1.7982 = £1,856

Outcome

Assuming option exercised:

	1.78	1.80
	£	£
Amount paid through option	62,500	62,500
Premium	1,460	1,856
Forward market receipt 1,250/2,500÷ 1.7861	(700)	(1,400)
	63,260	62,956

Both options offer a worse outcome than the forward contract. However they will enable the company to use the spot market if the dollar weakens and hence the option be allowed to lapse.

However given that this is a small hedge for a multinational company, a forward contract would probably be used to **save time and costs**.

(b) **Hedging strategy for the MJY Group**

Netting inter-company transfers is a **common international cash management strategy** to **manage foreign currency risk**. The basis of netting is that, within a closed group of related companies, total payables will always equal total receivables. The **advantages** of netting are reduction in foreign exchange conversion fees and funds transfer fees and a quicker settlement of obligations reducing the group's overall exposure.

In the case of MJY Group it will be necessary to arrange for **multilateral netting** as it involves more than two companies. The arrangement can be co-ordinated either through the group's central treasury function or alternatively through the company's bankers. Given, that a group treasury function already exists it would be sensible to **use the in-house expertise** to carry out the multilateral netting.

It is also necessary to determine the **common currency** in which netting needs to be effected as well as the method of establishing the exchange rates to be used for netting purposes. In order to agree the outstanding amounts in time, but with minimum risk of exchange rate fluctuations, it may involve using exchange rates applying a few days before the date at which payment is to be made.

The **benefits** of netting are:

(i) Reduced foreign exchange costs including commission and the spread between selling and buying rates as well as reduced money transmission rates.

(ii) Less loss in interest from having money in transit.

However, it will be necessary to **check local laws and regulations** for these foreign countries to ensure multilateral netting is permitted.

It should be noted, however, that once netting has been accomplished then the **foreign exchange exposure** will need to be **hedged** in the normal way, ie through the use of:

- Forwards contracts
- Matching of receipts and payments within the individual company
- Currency options

51 KYT

(a) (i)   KYT can **hedge using futures** as follows:

- Use September futures, since these expire soon after 1 September, price of 1/0.007985 = 125.23 ¥/$.

- **Buy** futures, since it wishes to acquire yen to pay the supplier, and the futures contracts are in Yen.

- Number of contracts 140m/12.5m = 11.2 contracts ~ 11 contracts.

- Tick size

  $0.000001 \times 12.5m = \$12.50$

(ii)   **Basis risk** arises from the fact the price of a futures contract may not move as expected in relation to the value of the instrument being hedged. Basis changes do occur and thus represent potential profits/losses to investors. Typically, this risk is much smaller than the risk of remaining unhedged.

Basis risk is the **difference between the spot and futures prices**.

Spot price = 1/128.15

           = 0.007803

Basis   = 0.007803 − 0.007985

           = 182 ticks with 3 months to expiry

Basis with one month to expiry, assuming uniform reduction = $\frac{1}{3} \times 182$

                                                = 61 ticks

Spot price on 1 Sept = 1/120 = 0.008333

Therefore predicted futures price = 0.008333 + 0.000061

                                       = 0.008394

(iii) **Outcome**

Futures market

Opening futures price	0.007985
Closing futures price	0.008394
Movement in ticks	409 ticks

Futures market profit 409 × 11 × $12.50 = $56,238

Net outcome

	$
Spot market payment (¥140m ÷ 120)	(1,166,667)
Futures market profit	56,238
	(1,110,429)

Hedge efficiency

$$\frac{56,238}{74,197} = 76\%$$

This hedge is not perfect because there is **not** an **exact match** between the exposure and the number of contracts, and because the **spot price** has moved more than the futures price due to the reduction in basis. The actual outcome is likely to differ since basis risk does not decline uniformly in the real world.

(b) **Foreign exchange exposure risks resulting from overseas subsidiary**

If a wholly owned subsidiary is established overseas then KYT Inc will face exposure to foreign exchange risk. The magnitude of the resulting risk can, if not properly managed, eliminate any financial benefits we would be hoping to achieve by setting up the overseas subsidiary.

The **foreign exchange risks resulting from a wholly owned overseas subsidiary** are as follows:

(i)   **Transaction risk**

This is the risk of adverse exchange rate movements occurring in the course of normal trading transactions. This would typically arise as a result of exchange rate fluctuations between the date when the price is agreed and the date when the cash is paid.

This form of exposure can give rise to real cash flow gains and losses. It would be necessary to set up a treasury management function whose role would be to assess and manage this risk through various hedging techniques.

(ii)   **Translation risk**

This arises from fluctuations in the exchange rate used to convert any foreign denominated assets or liabilities, or foreign denominated income or expenses when reporting back to the head office and thereby impacting on the investment performance.

This type of risk has no direct cash flow implications as they typically arise when the results of the subsidiary denominated in a foreign currency are translated into the home currency for consolidation purposes. Although there is no direct impact on cash flows, it could influence investors' and lenders' attitudes to the financial worth and creditworthiness of the company. Given that translation risk is effectively an accounting measure and not reflected in actual cash flows normal hedging techniques are not normally relevant. However, given the possible impact the translated results have on the overall group's performance and the possible influence on any potential investment decision making process it is imperative that such risks are reduced by balancing assets and liabilities as far as possible.

52 Ethnic Designs

(a)   **Calculation of the expected WACC**

	Current		New
Debt	0.5	(0.5 + 0.3)	0.8
Equity (4.5 − 0.5)	4.0		4.0
	4.5		4.8

	D/E	D/(D+E)
Current Gearing	0.125	0.1111
New Gearing	0.2	0.1667

Cost of debt

		Risk free	Spread	Total
Current yield on debt		0.04000	0.00300	0.04300
New yield on debt	5 years	0.04000	0.00340	0.04340
	10 years	0.04200	0.00524	0.04724

Spread

0.6×50 bp $+ 0.4 \times 56$ bp $= 0.00524$

Combined rate

	MVd	Rd	
Market value of 5 year debt	0.5	0.43400	0.021700
Market value of new debt	0.3	0.04724	0.014172
Total Market value of debt and combined rate	0.8		0.035872

Existing cost of equity

Rearrange WACC as follows

$$r_e = \frac{WACC - w_d r_d \,(1 - T)}{1 - w_d}$$

$$\frac{7\% - 0.1111 \times 0.043 \times 0.7}{(1.0 - 0.1111)} = 0.06624$$

Existing cost of equity = 6.624%

Ungeared cost of equity

$$r_e = r_e{}^1 + (r_e{}^1 - r_d)\,\frac{D}{E}\,(1 - T)$$

$$r_e = r_e{}^1 + (r_e{}^1 - r_d)\,\frac{D}{E}\,(1 - T) - r_d\,\frac{D}{E}\,(1 - T)$$

$$r_e{}^1 = \frac{r_e + r_d \,{D}\!/\!{E}\,(1 - T)}{1 + {D}\!/\!{E}(1 - T)}$$

$$r_e{}^1 = \frac{6.624\% + 0.043 \times 0.125 \times 0.7}{1 + 0.125 \times 0.7} = 0.06437$$

Regeared cost of equity assuming cost of debt remains unchanged

$$r_e = r_e{}^1 + (r_e{}^1 - r_d)\,\frac{D}{E}\,(1 - T)$$
$$r_e = 0.06437 + (0.06437 - 0.043) \times 0.2 \times 0.7$$
$$r_e = 0.067362$$

This assumes that the equity cost of capital is unaffected by the change in level of default risk. This is a reasonable assumption at modest levels of gearing but would not be expected to hold at very high gearing levels.

New weighted average cost of capital is calculated using revised equity cost and the revised debt cost.

$$WACC = (1 - w_d)\,r_e + w_d\,r_d\,(1 - T)$$
$$= (1 - 0.1667) \times 0.06736 + 0.1667 \times 0.035872 \times 0.7$$
$$= 0.06032$$

This shows a 97 basis point fall in the weighted average cost of capital.

Summary

Existing weighted average cost of capital	7.0%
Existing cost of debt	4.3%
Existing cost of equity	6.624%
Ungeared cost of equity	6.437%
Regeared cost of equity	6.736%
New weight average cost of capital	6.032%

The increased cost of debt is more than offset by the impact of the tax shield. Financing the project through a bond issue has resulted in a 96.8 basis point fall in the overall weighted average cost of capital.

(b) **Briefing note on managing currency risk exposure and sources of finance available for project**

Currently, the company is expecting to finance the project through the use of existing liquid reserves ($150 million) and raising the remaining $300 million through a bond issue in the US market. The finance is to set up a wholly owned subsidiary in the UK which will seek to service and develop the UK and European business. The US $ debt capital underlying the business is in US dollars whereas the revenue streams are UK sterling, it will be necessary to hedge the foreign exchange risk. There are a number of basic **methods available in order to manage this risk**.

(i)   One way of minimising the risk would be to **invoice the UK and European customers in US dollars**. This would allow the revenue stream and underlying capital to be in the same currency and hence minimise exposure to currency fluctuation. However, costs will be incurred in UK sterling and will need to be settled in UK sterling which would necessitate the creation of a pro-active treasury function in the UK company.

(ii) Alternatively, if all revenues and costs are in sterling then it may be possible to **enter into a currency swap** and switch the US$ debt into sterling. The advantages of this method is that all cash flows relating to the swap are know with certainty and would be in the same currency as the base currency of the UK company.

(iii) A simpler option would be to **raise the capital in UK sterling for the UK operation**. This would eliminate any currency risk resulting from the creation of the UK company.

Alternative sources of finance

(i)   The proposed project currently assumes that the additional finance will be raised **through a bond issue in the US market**. Ignoring foreign exchange considerations, the weighted average cost of capital suggests that the firm should increase its gearing to capture further tax shield effects which are not currently being offset by increased default risk. Thus **debt finance should be preferred to equity finance**, raising $300 million of debt by a bond issue is at the low end of the scale for a new debt issue of this type, although it my be possible to arrange a syndicated issue. The **issue cost** in terms of commissions and underwriting fees are likely to be high. As previously discussed if the finance is raised on the US market it will be necessary to consider entering into a **swap arrangement** to hedge against the currency risk for the ten year term.

(ii) Alternatively, it may be possible to raise finance through a **bond issue in the UK market**. This has the benefit that these would eliminate the need to consider methods of hedging against currency risk. However, given that Ethnic Designs is a US based company the cost of debt finance is likely to be higher than if it was raised in the US. The issues costs associated with a UK bond issue are likely to be as high as those for the US market.

(iii) A third source available would be for the **subsidiary to take out a loan to finance the project**. Once again, this would avoid any foreign currency risk for the subsidiary. However, given the lack of business history and performance in the UK the subsidiary is likely to be charges a premium for the debt finance. In addition, the lending institution may also insist upon a guarantee from the US parent company. The last two sources have the advantage of matching the borrowing and income flows and hence eliminating foreign currency exposure risk.

(iv) The company may raise the finance through **Eurobond issue**. The advantage of this source of finance is that the company can use its good credit rating (AA+) to raise the finance at a lower cost than direct borrowing from banks. However the issue costs are likely to be high.

(v)   Another source of debt finance is on the **sale and leaseback of existing assets** in the US to raise finance for the projects. There are reporting implications for reporting under FAS 13 depending upon whether the leases are financing or operating leases.

(vi) Other sources of finance would be to **raise equity capital by a rights or new issues**. This would have the effect of increasing the weighted average cost of capital and would not provide any additional benefits of the tax shield.

(vii) Finally, the finance can be raised by **reducing the dividend payment policy and thereby using the retained cash to finance the project**. The change in the dividend policy is unlikely to be viewed favourably and could cause problems in the future.

Of course the company could raise the capital in a **combination** of debt and equity in order to maintain the gearing level.

53 NTC

Text references. Chapters 19 on hedging techniques, Chapter 18 on treasury management.

Top tips. In (b) (i) you would not have time to set out the workings of the exchange rates in full in the exam; you would have to put the figures straight in the multilateral netting table. In each case you should have divided the figure in the table in the question by the mid-market value eg $210 \div 1.4362 = 299.40$. It would be perfectly legitimate exam technique to round the answers in (b) (i) and subsequently to the nearest £'000.

In (b) (ii) about 5 out of 15 marks would be available for the forward and money market hedgings, so provided you got those right and made some sort of an attempt at the option calculation (and drew a conclusion) you would have done enough to pass that part. You would not have been told that the Hong Kong dollar was fixed to the US dollar if you were not expected to make use of the information.

In (b) (ii) we have not carried out a full option calculation. Remember that we are trying to work out whether it would be advantageous to use options rather than the next best alternative. This involves considering what happens if the options are exercised, for which we need to know (i) the effect of hedging the amounts at the option price, (ii) the premium and (iii) what happens to the amount not hedged by the option contracts. Here it's best to assume that the amount not hedged by the option contracts is hedged on the forward market. Remember though you don't know in advance whether it will be necessary to exercise the option; hence the final calculation assuming options aren't exercised and trying to find the rate at which options are the best choice.

If you were short of time on (b) (ii) you could have passed that part by getting the money market and forward market calculations correct and correctly considering one of the possible option prices. However you would not have achieved full marks on this part without considering all of the option prices. Option outcomes should be considered at different exercise prices, and you should consider alternative exercise prices.

Don't worry if you didn't take into account the financing cost of the premium, it's a small issue.

Points to stress in (c) are costs, the difficulty of negotiating how much wheat to exchange and the potential problems of disposing of wheat (although it might be easier to dispose of wheat than other commodities).

Easy marks. The discussion in (a) is a nice start to the question. You need to focus on economies of scale and expenditure, netting and enforcement of strategy, weighed against flexibility, responsiveness to local conditions and management motivation.

(a) **Advantages of centralised treasury management**

(i) Centralised management **avoids** having a **mix of cash surpluses** and **overdrafts** in different localised bank accounts. It facilitates **bulk cash flows**, so that lower bank charges can be negotiated and the subsidiaries who need to borrow can **borrow** from the **parent company** and hence **gain the benefit of lower rates**.

(ii) **Larger volumes of cash** are **available to invest**, giving better short-term investment opportunities (for example international money markets, high-interest accounts and CDs).

(iii) **Any borrowing** can be **arranged in bulk**, at lower interest rates than for smaller borrowings, and on the eurocurrency or eurobond markets. **Interest rate hedging** will be facilitated.

(iv) **Foreign currency risk management** is likely to be **improved** in a multinational group of companies. A central treasury department can match foreign currency income earned by one subsidiary with expenditure in the same currency by another subsidiary.

(v) A **specialist treasury department** will **employ experts** with knowledge of dealing in forward contracts, futures, options, eurocurrency markets, swaps and so on. Localised departments would not normally have such expertise.

(vi) The **centralised pool of funds** required for precautionary purposes will be **smaller** than the **sum of separate precautionary balances** that would need to be held under decentralised treasury arrangements.

(vii) A central function acts as a single focus, ensuring the **strategy** of the group is **fulfilled** and **group profitability** is **enhanced** by good cash, funding, investment and foreign currency management.

(viii) **Transfer prices** can be **set centrally**, thus **minimising the group's global tax burden**.

Disadvantages of centralised treasury management

(i) Local departments may find it easier to diversify sources of finance and **match local assets**.

(ii) Centralised management means that managers in subsidiaries and divisions are not motivated by being given the **autonomy to deal** with cash management and it may be **difficult to assess their performance** if the major decisions are being made centrally.

(iii) A decentralised Treasury function may be **more responsive** to the needs of individual operating units.

(iv) A decentralised operation may find it **easier to invest** its own balances quickly on a short-term basis than a centralised function would.

(v) A central function may find it difficult to **monitor remote sites**; it may be difficult to **obtain information** from those sites.

(b) (i)

			Paying subsidiaries		
Receiving subsidiaries	UK	SP	HK	U US	Total
	£'000	£'000	£'000	£'000	£'000
UK		128.96	64.27	76.59	269.82
SP	100.00		49.13		149.13
HK	35.71				35.71
USA	299.40	73.69	26.78	–	399.87
Total payments	(435.11)	(202.65)	(140.18)	(76.59)	(854.53)
Total receipts	269.82	149.13	35.71	399.87	854.53
Net receipt/(payment)	(165.29)	(53.52)	(104.47)	323.28	–

Rather than have the UK, Spain and Hong Kong settle amounts owed amongst themselves, multilateral netting ensures the procedure is simplified by having each country make net payment to the US subsidiary.

(ii) The first stage is to work out what transactions need to be hedged.

Spain

As the balances are in different currencies, the full receipt of 210,000 Euros will be hedged.

US

The receipts and payments can be netted off.

430 – 110 = $320,000 payment

Hong Kong

The receipts and payments can be netted off.

720 – 400 = HK$320,000 receipt

As $HK is pegged to $US, the $HK can be converted to $US using the cross rate 11.2050/1.4358 = 7.8040. (There is little economic pressure to unpeg, since there is only a small difference in interest rates between US and Hong Kong.)

320,000/7.8040 = $41,005

Netting off against US payment

Hedged amount = 320,000 – 41,005 = $278,995 payment

Euros

(1) **Forward contract**

NTC should sell €210,000 three months forward at 1.6166 Euro/£

210,000/1.6166 = £129,902

(2) **Money market**

Borrow sufficient Euros now for three months at 5.3% per year in order to have a balance of €210,000 in three months' time. The net trading receipts will then be used to repay this loan. The interest rate for six months will be 1.325%.

To obtain €210,000, borrow now 210,000/1.01325 = €207,254.

The euros will be converted into £ at spot: 207,254/1.6292 = £127,212

£127,212 can then be invested in the UK for three months at 6.0% per year (1.5% for three months) to yield 127,212 × 1.015 = £129,120

Dollars

(1) **Forward contract**

NTC should buy $278,995 at 1.4285$/£

278,995/1.4285 = £195,306

(2) **Money market**

Invest sufficient dollars now for three months in order to have a balance of $278,995 in three months' time. Since the annual dollar deposit rate is 5.4%, the three month rate is 1.35%.

To earn $278,995, invest now 278,995/1.0135 = $275,279.

Purchase dollars with pounds at spot rate of $/£ 1.4358

275,279/1.4358 = £191,725.

Borrow £191,725 in the UK for three months at 6.9% (1.725% for three months) to cost £191,725 × 1.01725 = £195,032.

Options

Dollars

Using currency options

Set up

(1) Date September
(2) Type of contract put as wish to buy $/sell £ with option contract in £.
(3) Exercise price 1.42/1.43/1.44
(4) Contracts and amounts hedged

	Number of contracts	Amount hedged 31,250 × 6 = £187,500	Amount not hedged, hedged on forward market
1.42	$\dfrac{278,995/1.42}{31,250} = 6.29$, say 6	187,500 × 1.42 = $266,250	$\dfrac{278,995 - 266,250}{1.4285} = £8,922$
1.43	$\dfrac{278,995/1.43}{31,250} = 6.24$, say 6	187,500 × 1.43 = $268,125	$\dfrac{278,995 - 268,125}{1.4285} = £7,609$
1.44	$\dfrac{278,995/1.44}{31,250} = 6.20$, say 6	187,500 × 1.44 = $270,000	$\dfrac{278,995 - 270,000}{1.4285} = £6,297$

(5) Tick size

$3.125

(6) Premium cost

As we are comparing the option with the money market hedge, we have to take into account the financing cost of the premium, 6.9% annual borrowing cost in the UK or 1.725% for the three months. Premium cost is translated at spot rate,

$$1.42 \text{ premium cost} = \frac{3.125 \times 215 \text{ ticks} \times 6 \times 1.01725}{1.4358} = £2,856$$

$$1.43 \text{ premium cost} = \frac{3.125 \times 312 \text{ ticks} \times 6 \times 1.01725}{1.4358} = £4,145$$

$$1.44 \text{ premium cost} = \frac{3.125 \times 435 \text{ ticks} \times 6 \times 1.01725}{1.4358} = £5,779$$

(7) Total cost of exercising option

	Amount hedged by option £	Amount hedged on forward market £	Premium £	Total £
1.42	187,500	8,922	2,856	199,278
1.43	187,500	7,609	4,145	199,254
1.44	187,500	6,297	5,779	199,576

Therefore the **money market hedge** will be **preferable** if any of the options have to be **exercised**. However we do not know in advance whether the option will be exercised. For each option price, the option will be advantageous if the option is not exercised and the dollar is weaker than a certain spot rate.

	Payment on money market £	Less: amount hedged on forward market £	Premium £	Required option cost £	Required spot rate $\dfrac{\text{Amount hedged in £}}{\text{Required option cost}}$
1.42	195,017	(8,922)	(2,856)	183,239	266,250/183,239 = 1.4530
1.43	195,017	(7,609)	(4,145)	183,263	268,125/183,263 = 1.4631
1.44	195,017	(6,297)	(5,779)	182,941	270,000/182,941 = 1.4759

For each option price, the dollar will have to **weaken to beyond the required spot rate** for the best choice to be to take out the option and then not exercise it. The cost of 1.42 and 1.43 options is similar, but the 1.42 option is preferable as the dollar will have to weaken less for that to become the best choice.

(iii) **Advantages of countertrade**

(1) Countries such as Russia **lack commercial credit** or **convertible foreign currency** to pay for imports, and so countertrade in wheat and other commodities is needed to finance imports.

(2) **Countertrade** may be the **best means** of **obtaining new business** in the Russian market.

(3)   **Countertrade** will **eliminate the risk of foreign exchange movements**.

(4)   The company may be able to take advantage of the **futures** market in wheat.

Disadvantages of countertrade

(1)   Countertrade may prove **costly** for NTC. As well as **transportation costs**, it can create **lengthy and cumbersome administrative problems** just to set up a countertrade arrangement. **NTC** might have to **increase the export price** to cover the extra costs, or it might try to **absorb the extra costs itself**.

(2)   NTC may be **pushed into agreeing** to accept large quantities of wheat without being able to dispose easily of all of it, either because **lack of access to markets** or because the **wheat is of poor quality**.

(3)   The importer may place an **unrealistically high value** on the wheat it wishes to countertrade.

(4)   It may be difficult to obtain **bank guarantees or insurance** to combat the risks of countertrade.

54 Question with analysis: Avto

Text references. Chapter 9 on overseas investment appraisal, Chapter 21 and 24 on political risks.

Top tips. Most of the calculations in (a) are fairly straightforward. However one of the most complicated workings is the PPP working. You need to attempt this fairly early on, as it affects the sales and some costs, and hence the taxable profits and all totals below.

The most likely trap on most of the other calculations is not reading the question carefully enough. Not every figure is adjusted for inflation, some cash flows are shown pre-tax and some post-tax. It is not necessary to show in workings how you adjust for inflation – we have done so to make it clear.

You can tell by carrying out the preliminary calculations that closing down the UK operations is a worse option than downsizing, so you don't need to consider the implications of not being able to meet demand.

The discussion on dealing with blocked remittances should refer to Avto's circumstances and should include calculations

Easy marks. For the calculations, the figures that just involve adjustments for inflation are easiest. You can probably about just pass the calculations by getting virtually all of the Terranian cash flows right.

There would also be some generally straightforward marks for discussing the limitations of your analysis, as there are a number of general comments that will apply on most occasions:

- Predicted growth rates of income or costs may differ in practice

- There may be relevant information that you don't have

- You may get a better picture by doing further analysis such as sensitivity calculations, or carrying the analysis on beyond the artificial time horizon

(a)   **UK investment**

Cost of closing UK factory = 35 (1 − 0.3) − 20 = £4.5 million

Cost of downsizing = 20 (1 − 0.3) − 10 = £4 million

Downsizing is the cheaper option, even before cash flows from the downsized factory and the fact that closure would mean markets couldn't be fully supplied is taken into account.

Using CAPM, discount rate = 4.5 + 1.1(11.5 − 4.5) = 12.2%, say 12%

Present value for post-tax cash flows 4 (1 – 0.3) × inflation factor (1.02 yr 1, 1.02 × 1.03 year 2)

	0 £m	1 £m	2 £m	3 £m	4 £m
Net downsizing costs	(4.0)				
Post-tax cash flows		2.9	2.9	3.0	3.1
	(4.0)	2.9	2.9	3.0	3.1
Discount factor 12%	1.000	0.893	0.797	0.712	0.636
	(4.0)	2.6	2.3	2.1	2.0

Net present value = £5.0 million

Terranian investment

	Working	0 Fm	1 Fm	2 Fm	3 Fm	4 Fm
Sales	2		659	735	785	839
German comp.	3		(41)	(47)	(52)	(57)
Labour	4		(228)	(262)	(288)	(317)
Local comp	5		(90)	(104)	(114)	(125)
Sales and distrib	6		(20)	(23)	(25)	(28)
Fixed costs	7		(50)	(58)	(63)	(70)
Tax allow deprec	8		(145)	(109)	(82)	(94)
Taxable profit			85	132	161	148
Tax at 20%			(17)	(26)	(32)	(30)
Tax allow deprec			145	109	82	94
Investment		(580)				150
Working capital	9	(170)	(34)	(31)	(23)	258
Remittable cash flows Fm		(750)	179	184	188	620
Exch rate	1	36.85	43.35	48.40	51.69	55.20
Remittable cash flows £m		(20.4)	4.1	3.8	3.6	11.2
Add UK tax	10		(0.2)	(0.3)	(0.3)	(0.3)
Net cash flows		(20.4)	3.9	3.5	3.3	10.9
Disc factor	11	1.000	0.870	0.756	0.658	0.572
Disc cash flows		(20.4)	3.4	2.6	2.2	6.2

Net present value = –£6.0 million

Present value overall = 5 – 6.0 = – £1.0 million

On these figures, the reorganisation does not appear to be worthwhile.

Workings

1   **Exchange rates**

Year	PP factor	Terranian francs/£	Terranian francs/Euros
0		36.85	23.32
1	1.20 / 1.02	43.35	27.44
2	1.15 / 1.03	48.40	30.64
3	1.10 / 1.03	51.69	32.72
4	1.10 / 1.03	55.20	34.94

2 **Sales**

50,000 × 480 × Exchange rate

3 **German component**

50,000 × 30 × Exchange rate × Inflation factor

Inflation factor = 1.03 Yr 2, 1.03 × 1.03 Yr 3 etc

4 **Labour**

Incremental cost of employing 50 extra workers

50,000 × 3,800 × (50/250) = F38 million

This is less than the F75 million a year factory rental, so the extra workers are employed.

Costs

50,000 × 3,800 × (300/250) × Inflation factor

Inflation factor 1.15 Yr 2, 1.15 × 1.1 Yr 3 etc

5 **Local components**

50,000 × 1,800 × Inflation factor for labour

6 **Sales and distribution**

50,000 × 400 × Inflation factor for labour

7 **Fixed costs**

50 m × Inflation factor for labour

8 **Tax allowable depreciation**

Year	Writing down allowance	Tax written down value
	Fm	Fm
0		580
1	145	435
2	109	326
3	82	244
4	94	0

WDA = 25% previous year's tax written down value Yr 1-3, (244 − 150) Yr 4

9 **Working capital**

(170 m × Inflation factor) − Previous year's Working Capital balance

Inflation factor 1.2 Yr 1, 1.2 × 1.15 Yr 2 etc

Assume working capital is repaid at end of year 4.

10 **UK tax**

Taxable profits × (0.3 − 0.2) × 1/exchange rate

11 **Discount factor**

k = 4.5 + 1.5 (11.5 − 4.5)
= 15%

(b) **Strategic investments**

Avto should consider whether this decision is sensible from the point of view of **business strategy**. Is there a particularly good reason for becoming involved in Terrania, potential future markets possibly? Might investing in other countries with greater market potential and/or lower costs be better? Avto should also take into account the **PEST** factors affecting the business environment including the legal and regulatory position, enforcement mechanisms, cultural influences on demand and methods of doing business.

Financial structure

The **availability of finance** could be a significant issue.

Limitations of analysis

The financial analysis has a number of possible limitations.

(i) If increases in costs are greater than expected, cash flows will be adversely affected, since Avto **cannot increase selling prices**.

(ii) Avto may wish to consider **prolonging the investment beyond year 4**. If this is so, the analysis should consider the present value of cash flows after year 4 rather than the realisable value of assets at that date, also the **rental** payable for the factory beyond year 4.

(iii) Assuming production does cease in Terrania in four years' time, the analysis fails to consider **what will happen after that or** what will happen if moving production does not prove successful because of for example **adverse effects on quality**.

(iv) **Purchasing power parity** may not be a **completely reliable predictor** of short-term exchange rates.

Therefore to gain a better picture of the desirability of this investment, **sensitivity analysis** needs to be undertaken on **key variables**, the **analysis extended** beyond four years, and the effects of **changing assumptions** investigated.

Bad publicity

Relocating to a market where labour is cheaper may lead to bad publicity for AVTO and **potential boycotts** of its goods.

Political risk

As discussed below, the investment is subject to political risk from action by the Terranian government. Given the uncertainty, it may be worth **postponing the analysis** until a year's time, and awaiting developments in the situation (will the IMF lend more money, have further restrictions on remittances been imposed).

(c) **Impact of blocked remittances**

Year	Cash flows	Investment factor	Cash flows at yr 4
	Fm		Fm
1	179	1.15 × 1.10 × 1.10	249
2	184	1.10 × 1.10	223
3	188	1.10	207
4	620		620
Amount in Terrania			1,299
Exchange rate			55.20
Amount in Terrania £m			23.5
Disc factor 15%			0.513
Discounted cash flow			12.1

This compares with discounted cash flows totalling £14.2 million if remittances are not blocked.

Dealing with blocked remittances

(i) **Invest in Terranian money market**

As above, but this leads to a shortfall of £2.1 million, and there is no guarantee of when this money can be transferred from Terrania.

(ii) **Use methods other than dividends**

Funds can be obtained by charges such as **transfer prices**, **royalties or management fees**, or making a loan and charging high interest rates. The problem with all of these methods is that they may be difficult to camouflage, and the Terranian government may try to prevent removal of funds by allegedly artificial transactions.

(iii) **Negotiations**

Ahead of investing in Terrania, Avto may try to **negotiate with the foreign government** to obtain exemptions from any block on remittances. However it may be difficult to get the government to acquiesce to a **legally-binding agreement**.

(iv) **Finance sources**

If Avto obtains funds in local markets, intervention by Terrania's government might damage local lenders, although this is **unlikely to influence the government** in the event of a **blanket ban**.

55 Beela

Text references. Chapter 24.

Top tips. We have given more points than you would need to gain full marks on this question, to indicate the variety of possible points.

Easy marks. (b) should represent fairly easy marks as it allows a general discussion on political risk.

(a) **Reasons for using the consultant's report**

(i) **Added expertise**

The consultant may have **expertise** on the situation in Africa which the finance department of Beela lack.

(ii) **Use of variety of factors**

The consultant has taken into account a variety of factors at both the **microeconomic** (eg labour supply) and **macroeconomic** (eg currency convertibility) levels and **financial** (eg inflation) and **non-financial** (eg cultural) factors.

Problems with using the consultant's report

(i) **Lack of information**

The details given do not indicate why the **scores** for **different categories** were given, the **reasons** for **double weighting economic growth** and **political stability** and why 30 is used as the **target score** for deciding whether to invest.

(ii) **Application to other countries**

The model used by the consultant may **not apply** to **other African countries**. We are not given any details about the size, recent history or location of these countries; other countries may face different conditions.

(iii) **Other factors**

The consultant's report appears to omit a number of factors that may affect the decision of whether to invest:

(1)   The **regulatory environment.** Governments might interfere in ways other than nationalisation, for example through the tax regime or by tariffs or environmental controls.

(2)   **Industry-specific factors** such as the **supply of local raw materials** may be more important for Beela.

(3)   The **availability of local capital** will be of significance, also whether there has been a significant influx or outflow of overseas capital in recent years.

(4)   The report takes no account of the **mechanisms** by which investments might take place, which may influence the risk of other factors. For example risk of nationalisation may be reduced if local investors have a **substantial share** in the investment Beela undertakes, if a joint venture is used for instance.

(iv) **Risk reduction**

The measures used do not take into account **methods for reducing** some of the risks, for example local employment to reduce cultural incompatibility.

(v) **Risk and return**

The measures take no account of Beela's attitudes towards returns. Higher levels of risk may be tolerated if investments are expected to **yield higher returns**. However Beela may apply a lower cut-off score if it has expectations of low returns.

(vi) **Strategic issues**

Ultimately investment in Africa should be determined by **Beela's longer-term strategic objectives** such as gaining new markets or diversifying sources of supply.

Conclusion

The limitations and lack of detail given of the methods the consultant has used mean that the report should not be used on its own to determine whether to invest in Africa. The directors may wish to consider using the report in conjunction with other reports or other indicators such as visits to decide on investment policy.

(b)   **Minimisation of political risks**

Beela can take the following steps to minimise the effects of political risk.

(i)   **Negotiations with host government**

Beela might be able to obtain a **concession agreement**, covering matters such as the transfer of capital, remittances and products, access to local finance, government intervention and taxation and transfer pricing. However if there is a change in government, the new government may not feel bound to honour the agreement with the previous government.

(ii)   **Insurance**

Insurance might be available against **nationalisation** and **currency conversion problems**.

(iii)   **Production strategies**

Beela could locate **key parts** of the **production process** abroad. If governments take action, they will not be able to produce the product without investment in new facilities. Alternatively risk could be reduced by local sourcing of **factors of production** or **components**.

(iv) **Distribution channels**

Control by Beela of distribution channels might limit the risk of government interference because of the **disruption** to **distribution arrangements** that interference might cause.

(v) **Patents**

Beela might protect its investment by **patents or use of trademark legislation.** These might be **difficult to enforce** in local courts however.

(vi) **Financial management**

If businesses obtain funds **in local markets,** governments might be deterred from intervening by the risks posed to local lenders.

(vii) **Ownership structure**

Instead of having a direct ownership interest, Beela might establish a presence by a **joint venture**, or ceding controls to local investors and obtaining profits by a **management contract**.

(viii) **Overcoming blocked funds**

Funds can be obtained by 'legitimate' charges such as **royalty or management charges,** or making a loan and charging **high interest rates.** Beela might also engage in **countertrade** (reciprocal or barter arrangements) rather than trade for cash.

(c) **Duty of care**

All companies have to balance the need to compete against their ethical duty of care to stakeholders. The laws of developed countries have progressively reflected voters' concerns on **ethical issues** by banning activities considered harmful to society (eg drug dealing) or to the economy (eg corruption) and by developing numerous constraints on companies' behaviour towards employees, the local community and the environment. These are intended to give companies a level playing field on which they can compete vigorously.

Adverse publicity

Where potentially unethical activities are not banned by law, companies need to make difficult decisions, weighing up **increased profitability** against the **harmful effects of bad publicity**, organisational ill-health and the knowledge that some activities are clearly wrong. Whereas in developed countries such decisions might relate to experimentation on animals or sale of arms, the laws of developing countries are far less advanced, forcing companies to make their own decisions on major issues such as the following:

(i) Provision of proper safety equipment and working conditions for employees
(ii) Use of child labour
(iii) Wage rates below subsistence level
(iv) Discrimination against women, ethnic minorities, etc
(v) Pollution of the environment
(vi) 'Inducement' payments to local officials to facilitate investment

Unethical investment

In addition, multinational companies must decide whether it is right to invest at all in some countries which are regarded as **unethical**, for example because of violation of human rights.

56 Shegdor

(a)   **Objectives of transfer pricing strategies**

   (i)   The transfer price should provide a **selling price** that enables the transferring division to earn a return for its efforts, and the receiving division to incur a cost for benefits received.

   (ii)   The transfer price should be set at a level that enables **profit centre performance** to be **measured commercially**; thus the transfer price should be a **fair commercial price**.

   (iii) The transfer price should encourage profit centre managers to **agree** on the **amounts of goods and services to be transferred**.

   (iv)   The transfer price should lead to a level **of goods and services being transferred** which is **congruent** with the **objectives** of the organisation, for example **generating retained earnings** in the most advantageous locations or **limiting remittances** of foreign currency between group members.

   (v)   **Transfer prices** can be used to **minimise the effect of import duties**; the lower the transfer price, the lower the level of import duty.

   (vi)   Transfer prices can also be used to **minimise tax levels** by ensuring that taxable income is earned in low tax economies.

   (vii) **Transfer prices** can be used as a means of **remitting income** if restrictions on dividend remittances are in place.

(b)   **Fixed plus variable cost**

	Umbaga	Mazila	Bettuna
	$000	$000	$000
Sales	8,200	16,000	14,800
Costs			
Variable costs	6,400	3,600	3,000
Fixed costs	1,800	700	900
Transfer price	–	8,200	8,200
Import duty	–	820	–
	8,200	13,320	12,100
Taxable profit	–	2,680	2,700
Tax	–	670	864
Profit after tax	–	2,010	1,836
Withholding tax	–	–	–
Remittance	–	1,206	1,101.6
UK tax on remittance (W)	–	(134)	–
	–	1,072	1,101.6
Retained (40% after tax profit)	–	804	734.4
Total profit		1,876	1,836.0

Total profit

Umbaga + Mazila 0+ 1,876 = $1,876,000

Umbaga + Bettuna 0 + 1,836 = $1,836,000

Working

UK tax = (2,680,000 × 0.3) − 670,000 = 134,000

Fixed plus variable cost plus 30%

	Umbaga	*Mazila*	*Bettuna*
	$000	*$000*	*$000*
Sales	10,660	16,000	14,800
Costs			
Variable costs	6,400	3,600	3,000
Fixed costs	1,800	700	900
Transfer price	–	10,660	10,660
Import duty	–	1,066	–
	8,200	16,026	14,560
Taxable profit	2,460	(26)	240
Tax	984	–	76.8
Profit/(Loss) after tax	1,476	(26)	163.2
Withholding tax			
(Umbaga 1,476 × 0.6 × 0.15)	132.84	–	–
Remittance			
(Umbaga 1,476 × 0.6 × 0.85)	752.76	–	97.92
UK tax on remittance	–	–	—
	752.76	–	97.92
Retained (40% after tax profit)	590.4	(26)	65.28
Total profit	1,343.16	(26)	163.2

Total profit

Umbaga + Mazila 1,343.16 − 26 = $1,317,160
Umbaga + Bettuna 1,343.16 + 163.2 = $1,506,360

Conclusion

The best plan is to charge sales at fixed plus variable costs, and manufacture in Mazila. This avoids tax in the country of highest tax, Umbaga.

(c) **Likely government attitudes**

Umbaga

The government may query whether the **transfer price** is at a **commercial rate** and, depending on the tax laws, may be able to impart an artificial profit to the transaction and hence charge tax.

Mazila

The government's attitude is likely to be **favourable** as manufacturing is taking place in the country, and hence boosting its economy. Although the import duty is lower than under the markup scenario, this is more than outweighed by the company tax that the government will be able to collect.

Bettuna

The government can take **no action** against the company as the company is not doing anything. It can try to attract the company by offering a subsidy, which would only need to be greater than $40,000 (1,876,000 − 1,836,000) for the decision to be changed.

UK

The UK government would be happy with this arrangement, since it is the only arrangement of those considered that will mean that the company pays tax.

(d) Transfer price manipulation is said to occur when multinationals use transfer prices to evade or avoid payment of taxes and tariffs, or other controls that the government of the host country has put in place.

The most common solution that tax authorities have adopted to reduce the probability of transfer price manipulation is to develop particular transfer pricing regulations as part of the corporate income tax code. These regulations are based on the concept of the arm's length standard, which states that all intra-firm activities of multinationals should be priced as if they took place between unrelated parties acting at arm's length in competitive market.

The arm's length standard is defined as the prices which would have been agreed upon between unrelated parties engaged in the same or similar transactions under the same or similar conditions in the open market. In the absence of the existence of data to allow a reasonable estimate of the arm's length standard then the alternative methods used to establish the arms length transfer price include:

(i) **Comparable uncontrolled price**

This method looks for a comparable product to the transaction in question being traded by the multinational in a comparable transaction with an unrelated party or the same or similar product being traded between two unrelated parties.

(ii) **Resale price method**

This method focuses on one side of the transaction either the manufacturer or distributor and to estimate the transfer price using a functional approach.

(iii) **Cost plus method**

This method starts with the costs of production, measured using recognised accounting principles and then adds an appropriate mark up over costs. The appropriate mark up is estimated from those earned by similar manufacturers.

(iv) **Comparable profit method**

This method is based on the premise that companies in similar industries will tend to have similar financial performance and to have similar financial characteristics. This similarity in performance will be indicated by a similarity in financial ratios.

(v) **Profit split method**

This method allocates the profit earned on a transaction between related parties.

57 Serty

(a)   **Modigliani and Miller**

In financial management theory some writers (eg Modigliani and Miller) have shown that, under perfect capital market conditions, the discussion of whether cash should be paid as dividends or reinvested is irrelevant, provided that the company accepts all its profitable opportunities. The argument is based on two main premises.

- If cash is **paid** as **dividends**, **funds for expansion** can be **raised by share issues**.
- If cash is reinvested, shareholders can achieve their returns by **selling shares** at an **increased value**.

Real world factors

However, the real world factors which affect dividend policy in practice include the following:

(i)   **Costs of share issue**

Share issues are **expensive, time consuming** and **require divulgence of information** to the general public. It is cheaper and more convenient to fund expansion by use of retained earnings. These factors would lead the company to prefer lower dividend payouts.

(ii)   **Brokerage fees**

If shareholders have to **sell shares** to achieve their returns, they suffer **brokerage fees**. This may lead them to prefer higher dividend payouts.

(iii)   **Taxation of shareholders**

Some shareholders may prefer to take their rewards as **capital gains** if there is a lower effective tax rate. These would prefer lower dividend payouts.

(iv)   **Taxation of company**

Corporate taxation treatment may also favour the payment of lower dividends.

(v)   **Dividend signalling**

In the **absence of perfect information** concerning the company's prospects, shareholders may take the dividend as a **signal**. For example, an increase in dividends may be taken as a signal of higher expected future earnings.

Dividend trends

All these factors need to be taken into consideration when formulating a dividend policy. In practice companies often aim for a **smooth trend** in dividend growth, allowing increases or decreases in borrowings to absorb the fluctuations in cash generated. In order to carry out this policy, dividend pay-out must be reasonably low, and there should be good reasons for any significant increase.

Assumption that investment opportunities exist

However, the above arguments assume that the company has **investment opportunities**. If it does not, then it is not advisable to allow cash to accumulate in the bank. A choice needs to be made between increasing dividends and buying back shares.

(b)   The company has 40 million shares (worth a total of $160 million) and a shareholder owning 1,000 shares currently has a wealth of $4,000 cum div.

(i)   **Cash dividend**

If a cash dividend of 15 pence per share is paid, the expected ex div price will drop to 385 pence. The **shareholder's wealth** will be **$3,850 in share value** and $150 in cash, with the total unchanged at $4,000.

(ii) **Scrip dividend**

If a 5% scrip dividend is paid, the company will **issue 2 million new shares** at no charge. Since the value of the company will not change, the share price will drop to 400p × 100/105 = 381 pence. The shareholder will now have 1,050 shares worth 381p each, giving a total wealth of $4,000.

(iii) **Share repurchase**

If 10% of the ordinary share capital (4 million shares) are repurchased at 400 pence each, the **value of the company** will **drop** by the $16 million cash spent to $144 million. The share price will be $144m/36m = 400 pence per share, unchanged. The shareholders wealth will be made up of 900 shares at 400 pence ($3,600) and cash of 100 × $4 ($400), giving total wealth of $4,000, as before.

Information content

These estimates may be inaccurate because they **ignore any information content** which may be contained in the company's action. For example, a share buy-back may cause investors to assume that the company has no immediate plans to expand, whereas a scrip dividend may be taken as indication of expansionary plans.

(c) **Should a company pay dividends equal to the free cash flow to equity?**

Free cash flow

Free cash flow to equity is the annual cash that the company has available to pay dividends, after net investment in fixed and working capital and net debt financing flows have been taken into account.

Preference for lower dividends

Although payment of dividends equal to free cash flow is a sensible level for maximum dividends, there are reasons why companies often prefer dividends to be lower. For example:

(i) **Retaining cash** enables the trend of **dividends** from year to year to be **smoother**; this may increase shareholder confidence

(ii) The company may be **accumulating cash** in order to make an **acquisition** or to hold as a **precautionary balance**

(iii) **Legal restraints** (eg rules on distributable profits) may prevent a company from paying out all its free cash flows as dividend

Consequences of higher dividends

When companies pay out dividends that are more than FCFE this is **financed by reducing cash reserves** or alternatively by issuing new shares.

58 World Trade Organisation

(a)   **Tariffs or customs duties**

Tariffs or customs duties are taxes on imported goods. The effect of a tariff is to **raise the price paid for the imported goods** by domestic consumers, while leaving the price paid to foreign producers the same, or even lower. The difference is transferred to the government.

Import quotas

Import quotas are restrictions on the **quantity** of a product that is allowed to be imported into the country. Both domestic and foreign suppliers enjoy a **higher price,** while consumers buy less. This should mean **domestic producers supply more** and there are **fewer imports** (in volume). The government collects no revenue.

Export subsidies

Export subsidies include **export credit guarantees** (government-backed insurance against irrecoverable debts for overseas sales), **financial help** (such as government grants to the aircraft or shipbuilding industry) and **state assistance**.

Import restrictions

Import restrictions include **complex import regulations** or **special safety standards** demanded from imported goods and so on

Bureaucratic procedures

Governments may prefer delay rather than restrictions so that importers expend resources in **supplying complex documentation** or are **forced to wait for licences** or **customs clearance**.

(b)   **Arguments in favour of and against protection**

Arguments for protection

(i)   **Imports of cheap goods**

Measures can be taken against imports of cheap goods that compete with higher priced domestically produced goods, and so preserve output and employment in domestic industries.

(ii)   **Dumping**

Measures might be necessary to counter dumping of surplus production by other countries at an uneconomically low price. Although dumping has short term benefits for the countries receiving the cheap goods, the longer term consequences would be a reduction in domestic output and employment, even when domestic industries in the longer term might be more efficient.

(iii)   **Retaliation**

Any country that does not take protectionist measures when other countries are doing so is likely to find that it suffers all of the disadvantages and none of the advantages of protectionism.

(iv) Infant industries

Protectionism can protect a country's 'infant industries' that have not yet developed to the size where they can compete in international markets. Less developed countries in particular might need to protect industries against competition from advanced or developing countries.

(v) Declining industries

Without protection, these industries might collapse and there would be severe problems of sudden mass unemployment amongst workers in the industry.

(vi) Reduction in balance of trade deficit

Due to retaliation by other countries, the success of such measures by one country would depend on the demand by other countries for its exports being inelastic with regard to price and its demand for imports being fairly elastic.

Arguments against protection

(i) Reduced international trade

Since protectionist measures taken by one country will almost always provoke retaliation by others, protection will reduce the volume of international trade. Therefore the following benefits of international trade will be reduced:

- Specialisation
- Greater competition, and so greater efficiency amongst producers
- Advantages of economies of scale amongst producers who need world markets to achieve their economies and so produce at lower costs.

(ii) Retaliation

If a country applies protectionist measures then other countries will tend to retaliate and thus protectionist measures to reverse a balance of trade deficit are unlikely to succeed. Imports may be reduced, but so too would exports.

(iii) Effect on economic growth

Widespread protection will damage the prospects for economic growth amongst the countries of the world. Thus protectionist measures ought to be restricted to special instances which have been discussed and negotiated with other countries.

(iv) Political consequences

From a nation's own point of view, protection may improve its position, protectionism leads to a worse outcome for all. Protection creates political ill-will amongst countries of the world and so there are political disadvantages in a policy of protection.

(c) The World Trade Organisation (WTO)

The **World Trade Organisation (WTO)** was formed in 1995 to continue to implement the General Agreement on Tariffs and Trade (GATT) to promote free trade. Its aims include:

(i) To **reduce existing barriers** to free trade

(ii) To **eliminate discrimination** in international trade and **distortions** such as subsidies

(iii) To **prevent the growth of protection** by getting member countries to consult with others before taking any protectionist measures

(iv) To act as a **forum** for assisting free trade by for example administering agreements and helping countries negotiate

One difference is that GATT focused mainly on goods, whereas the WTO also covers trade in services.

The most favoured nation principle

The WTO encourages free trade by applying the **'most favoured nation'** principle where one country (which is a member of GATT) that offers a reduction in tariffs to another country must offer the same reduction to all other member countries of GATT.

Impact on protectionist measures

Although the WTO has helped reduce the level of protection, some problems still remain:

(i)   Special circumstances (for example economic crises, the protection of an infant industry) have to be **admitted** when protection or special low tariffs between a group of countries are allowed.

(ii)   A country in the WTO may **prefer not to offer a tariff reduction** to another country because it would have to offer the same reduction to all other GATT members.

(iii) In spite of much success in reducing tariffs, the WTO has had **less effect** in dealing with **many non-tariff barriers** to trade which countries may set up.

(d)   **Impact on investments in that country**

Removal of barriers as a result of WTO membership may **remove the favoured status** that the multinational's investment has enjoyed. It may be more exposed to **competition** from other countries. However by promoting trade with that country, WTO membership may **improve the economic environment** within which it operates, leading to more opportunities to export and the chance to take advantage of improvements in the supply of resources.

Impact on other investments

On the other hand, the multinational's investments elsewhere may themselves be able to **take advantage** of the **reduction in barriers** and improve trade with that country.

Time lag

WTO conditions will require the removal of barriers **gradually over a period of time**, hence the multinational will have time to adjust to the new circumstances.

59 Uniglow

Text references. Chapter 26.

Top tips. Your answer to (a) needs to bring out how these measures are used. You probably wouldn't lose very many marks if you didn't interpolate in (b) and just used the value for –0.19 in the calculations. Remember you take negative values from 0.5 to arrive at N(d).

Easy marks. The comment in (ii) will always be worth a couple of marks in delta hedging questions.

(a)   **Delta**

$$\text{Delta} = \frac{\text{Change in call option price}}{\text{Change in price of the shares}}$$

Delta measures the gradient of the option value line at any point in time or price point. As the share price falls towards zero, delta should also fall towards zero. The delta calculation can be used to determine the **amount** of the **underlying shares** or other instruments that the writer of the option position **should hold** in order to hedge the risk of the option position.

Theta

Theta represents a change in an option's **price** (specifically its time premium) over **time**. The time premium element of an option's price will diminish towards zero. At the money options have the greatest time premium and thus the greatest theta. Theta can be used to judge how the **option price** will **reduce** as **maturity approaches**.

Vega

Vega represents the sensitivity of an option's price to a change in its implied **volatility**. It is measured as the change in the value of an option from a 1% change in its volatility. The Black-Scholes model is very dependent upon the accurate estimation of an option price's volatility, and Vega is a measure of the **consequences of incorrect estimation**. Long-term options have larger vegas than short-term options; the longer the time period until expiration, the more uncertainty there is about the expiry price. Vega can be used to determine changes in value of both **put and call options**; these will **increase** as **volatility increases**, since there is an expectation of a potentially higher share price.

(b) **Find d_1**

(i) $$d_1 = \frac{\ln(P_s/X) + rT}{\sigma\sqrt{T}} + 0.5\sigma\sqrt{T}$$

$$= \frac{\ln\frac{2.00}{2\cdot20} + 0.06 \times 0.25}{0.5\sqrt{0.25}} + 0.5 \times 0.5\sqrt{0.25}$$

$$= -0.3212 + 0.125$$

$$= -0.1962$$

$$N(-0.1962) = 0.5 - 0.0753 - \frac{62}{100}[-0.0793 - (-0.0753)]$$

$$= 0.4222, \text{ the delta value}$$

You would need the following number of contracts to hedge the position

$$\text{Number of contracts} = \frac{\text{Number of shares}}{\text{Delta of option} \times \text{Size of contract}}$$

$$= \frac{100,000}{0.4222 \times 1,000}$$

$$= 236.9, \text{ rounding up 237 contracts}$$

(ii) The hedge is likely to need **constant adjustment** because of the volatility of the share price. Even a small change in the share price could produce a large change in the delta value. In practice therefore it may be difficult to maintain the hedge.

(c) The main **arguments for a firm to undertake hedging against risk** can be summarised as follows:

(i) Hedging reduces the risk imposed on the firm's managers, employees, suppliers and customers.

(ii) Hedging can control the conflict of interest between bondholders and shareholders, thus reducing the agency costs of debt.

(iii) Hedging can increase the value of a firm if capital market imperfections exist since it lowers the probability of the firm encountering financial distress which in turn lowers the expected costs of financial distress and the cost of capital. In addition, hedging encourages investment by the firm. According to the agency theory between shareholders and bondholders the issuance of bonds which have higher priority than equity creates incentives for the firm's equity holders to underinvest. Hedging reduces the incentive to underinvest since hedging reduces uncertainty and the risk of loss. Firms with more valuable growth opportunities and higher leverage are more likely to be affected by the underinvestment problem and so are more likely to hedge.

60 Folter

Text references. Chapter 15.

Top tips. Note that the comments in (a) are made with the benefit of hindsight and that the company has to weigh the higher premium cost against the potentially better deal that the 550 option offers.

(b) indicates the level of explanation you may need to give about delta hedges. The point that they are only valid for small movements in prices needs to be stressed. Note the explanation in (c) of why the intrinsic value of the option is zero.

Easy marks. (d) if you're not sure about delta hedging, but you wouldn't have chosen this question if you weren't.

(a)   **Share options**

Magterdoor's shares are currently trading (June 1) at 535 pence. To protect against a fall in share price Folter Inc can either purchase put options or sell call options.

Purchase of put options

If put options are purchased, they will be for the October contract and can be at strike prices of 500 or 550 pence. Clearly the 550 strike price has a higher premium cost as it enables Folter to sell the shares at above the current market price.

Share price 485c

Assuming the Magterdoor share price falls to 485c by the end of October and Folter must sell 2 million shares:

(i)   If **no options** are used, the shares would be **sold for 485c** each: total $9.7 million.

(ii)   If the **550 put option** is used, it would be **exercised**: sale price 550c less premium 51c = 499c: total $9.98 million.

(iii)   If the **500 put option** is used, it would be **exercised**: sale price 500p less premium 24.5c = 475.5c: total $9.51 million.

The **550 put option** gives the best hedge if the share price fell to 485c.

Share price 570c

If, on the other hand the share price had risen to 570c, the options would be abandoned (allowed to lapse). The best result would then be to have used **no option hedge**. The 500 hedge would be better than the 550 hedge simply because the premium is cheaper.

(b)   **Delta neutral hedge**

A delta neutral hedge consists of a **shareholding in combination** with the **sale of call options** on the shares. If the **share value falls**, the **call options also fall in value** and can be purchased cheaply to make a gain that compensates exactly for the fall in share price. Conversely if the **share price rises**, the **options rise in value** and a loss is made that offsets the share price gain.

Option delta value

The delta neutral hedge is therefore a **risk free portfolio**. To construct it the investor needs to know the option delta value for the shares in question. The option delta changes with the share price, which implies that the number of call options to be sold is **continually changing**. Consequently, **delta neutral hedges** are only **valid for small movements** in the share price.

Magterdoor

The option delta of Magterdoor is 0.47, which means that 1/0·47 call options need to be sold for every share held. For the holding of 2 million Magterdoor shares, 2m/0.47 call options need to be sold = 4.255m call options. The options are in 1,000 share contracts, so **4,255** contracts must be sold.

(c) **Intrinsic value of call option**

The intrinsic value of a call option is the **difference between the share price** and the **exercise price**, subject to a minimum of zero if the share price is below the exercise price. Thus the intrinsic value of the January 550 call option is zero, because 550 is higher than the current share price of 535.

Full value of share option

The full value of a share option is the **sum of its intrinsic value** and its **time value**. The time value arises because the option has time (in this case 7 months) before it expires, and in this time the share price is likely to rise above the exercise price. The **time value** depends on the **time to expiry**, the **volatility of the option** and the **level of interest rates**. The higher these variables, the higher the time value of the option. For the January 550 call option, the option premium of 34 pence is entirely time value.

(d) **Disclosure**

If Folter increases its holding in Magterdoor from 2% to 6%, it will have to declare this fact to Magterdoor. Under the City Code on Takeovers and Mergers, any holding over 3% must be disclosed to the target company.

Further acquisition

If Folter is considering a takeover of Magterdoor, then this disclosure may **make** the **acquisition of further parcels of shares** easier. On the other hand if the strategy is to be resisted by Magterdoor, Folter might do better if it aims for a larger holding than 6% when increasing its stake.

Effect on investment portfolio

The 6% will not give Folter any real power over Magterdoor and may excessively **increase the risk** of its overall investment portfolio.

(e) There are a number of defensive measures that can be taken where the management of the target takeover company perceives the bid as hostile. Takeover defences can be categorised into pre-offer and post-offer defences; tactics which are appropriate in the UK are:

(i) **Golden parachute**

Large compensation payments made to the top management of the target firm if their positions are eliminated due to a hostile takeover. This may include cash or bonus payments, stock options or a combination of these.

(ii) **Poison pill**

This is an attempt to make a company unattractive normally by giving the right to existing shareholders to buy shares at a very low price.

(iii) **White knights and white squires**

This would involve inviting a firm that would rescue the target from the unwanted bidder. The white knight would act as a friendly counter-bidder. A white squire is similar to a white knight but the former does not take control of the target firm.

(iv) **Crown jewels**

The firm's most valuable assets may be the main reason that the firm became a takeover target in the first place. By selling these or entering into arrangements such as sale and leaseback, the firm is making itself less attractive as a target.

(v) **Pacman defence**

This defence is carried out by mounting a counter bid for the attacker. The Pacman defence is an aggressive rather than defensive tactic and will only work where the original acquirer is a public company with diverse shareholdings. This tactic also appears to suggest that the company's management are in favour of the acquisition but they disagree about which company should be in control.

(vi) **Litigation or regulatory defence**

The target company can challenge the acquisition by inviting an investigation by the regulatory authorities or through the courts. The target may be able to sue for a temporary order to stop the predator from buying any more of its shares.

Mock Exams

ACCA Professional Level

Paper P4

Advanced Financial Management

Mock Examination 1
Pilot paper

Question Paper		
Time allowed		
Reading and Planning Writing		15 minutes 3 hours
Section A	BOTH questions are compulsory and MUST be attempted	
Section B	TWO questions ONLY to be attempted	
During reading and planning time only the question paper may be annotated		

DO NOT OPEN THIS PAPER UNTIL YOU ARE READY TO START UNDER EXAMINATION CONDITIONS

Section A: BOTH QUESTIONS are compulsory and MUST be attempted

Question 1

The senior managers of Daron, a company located in a European country, are reviewing the company's medium-term prospects. The company is heavily dependent on a single product. A general election will take place in the near future and the managers believe that the future level of inflation will depend upon the result of the election. Inflation is expected to remain at approximately 5% if political party A wins the election, or will quickly move to approximately 10% per year if party B wins the election. Opinion polls suggest that there is a 40% chance of party B winning.

Projected financial data for the next five years, including expected inflation where relevant, are shown below.

Political party A wins, inflation 5% per year

			$million		
	20X7	*20X8*	*20X9*	*20Y0*	*20Y1*
Operating cash flows:					
Sales	28	29	26	22	19
Variable costs	17	18	16	14	12
Fixed costs	3	3	3	3	3
Other financial data:					
Incremental working capital*	–	(1)	(2)	(3)	(3)
Tax allowable depreciation	4	3	3	2	1
Replacement investment (not tax allowable)	10	–	–	–	5

Political party B wins, inflation 10% per year

			$million		
	20X7	*20X8*	*20X9*	*20Y0*	*20Y1*
Operating cash flows:					
Sales	30	26	24	20	16
Variable costs	18	16	15	12	11
Fixed costs	3	3	4	4	4
Other financial data:					
Incremental working capital*	1	(2)	(2)	(3)	(3)
Tax allowable depreciation	4	3	3	2	1
Replacement investment (not tax allowable)	10	–	–	–	5

* A bracket signifies a decrease in working capital.

Tax allowable depreciation will be negligible after 20Y1 in both cases. Taxable cash flows after year 20Y1, excluding tax savings from tax allowable depreciation, are expected to be similar to year 20Y1 cash flows for a period of five years, after which substantial new fixed investment would be necessary in order to continue operations. However no replacement investment will be necessary between 20Y2 and 20Y6.

Working capital will remain approximately constant after the year 20Y1. Corporation taxation is at a rate of 30% per year, and is expected to continue at this rate. Tax may be assumed to be payable in the year that the income arises.

Daron's current ordinary share price is 46 centos. (100 centos = $1)

Summarised balance sheet of Daron as at 31 March 20X6

	$m
Tangible non-current assets	17
Net current assets	12
Total assets less current liabilities	29
Loans and other borrowings falling due after one year	7
Capital and reserves:	
Called up share capital (25 centos par value)	5
Reserves	17
	29

The company can currently borrow long-term from its bank at an interest rate of 10% per year. This is likely to quickly rise to 15.5% per year if the political party B wins the election. The real risk free rate (ie excluding inflation) is 4% and the real market return is 10%.

Daron's equity beta is estimated to be 1.25. This is not expected to significantly change if inflation increases.

Three alternatives are available to the managers of Daron.

(i) Recommend the sale of the company now. An informal, unpublicised, offer of $10 million for the company's shares has been received from a competitor.

(ii) Continue existing operations, with negligible capital investment for the foreseeable future.

(iii) If the political party A wins the election, diversify operations by buying a going concern in the hotel industry at a cost of $9 million. The purchase would be financed by the issue of 10% convertible loan stock. Issue costs are 2% of the gross sum raised. Daron has no previous experience of the hotel industry.

Financial projections for the hotel purchase

	\$million				
	20X7	20X8	20X9	20Y0	20Y1
Revenue	9	10	11	12	13
Variable costs	6	6	7	7	8
Fixed costs	2	2	2	2	2
Other financial data:					
Incremental working capital	1	–	–	1	–

Tax allowable depreciation is negligible for the hotel purchase. The after tax realisable value of the hotel at the end of year 20Y1 is expected to be $10 million, including working capital. The systematic risk of operating the hotels is believed to be similar to that of the company's existing operations.

Required

Using the above data, prepare a report advising the managers of Daron which, if any, of the three alternatives to adopt. Include in your report comment on any weaknesses/limitations of your data analysis. Relevant calculations, including:

(a) Estimates of the present values of future free cash flows from existing operations, and
(b) The estimated adjusted present value of diversifying into the hotel industry

should form appendices to your report.

The book value and market value of debt may be assumed to be the same. State clearly any other assumptions that you make.

(30 marks)

Question 2

(a)   Assume that you are the financial manager of a UK company which currently trades only with major European countries. Your managing director has strongly advocated that the UK should join the European Monetary Union (EMU) as sterling will then be replaced by the Euro, which will result in significant savings in transactions costs, and will eliminate all foreign exchange exposure for your company.

Discuss whether or not the managing director is correct in his comments.   **(5 marks)**

(b)   Retilon plc is a medium sized UK company that trades with companies in several European countries. Trade deals over the next three months are shown below. Assume that it is now 20 April.

	Two months time		Three months time	
	Receipts	*Payments*	*Receipts*	*Payments*
France	–	€393,265	€491,011	€60,505
Germany	–	–	€890,217	€1,997,651
Denmark	–	–	Kr 8.6m	–

Foreign exchange rates:

	Dkroner/£	Euro €/£
Spot	10.68 – 10.71	1.439 – 1.465
Two months forward	10.74 – 10.77	1.433 – 1.459
Three months forward	10.78 – 10.83	1.431 – 1.456

Annual interest rates (valid for 2 months or 3 months)

	Borrowing %	Investing %
United Kingdom	7.50	5.50
France	5.75	3.50
Germany	5.75	3.50
Denmark	8.00	6.00

Futures market rates

Three month Euro contracts (125,000 Euro contract size)

Contracts are for buying or selling Euros. Futures prices are in £ per Euro.

June	0.6964
September	0.6983
December	0.7013

Required

(i)   Using the forward market, money market and currency futures market as appropriate devise a foreign exchange hedging strategy that is expected to maximise the cash flows of Retilon plc at the end of the three month period.

Transactions costs and margin requirements may be ignored for this part of the question. Basis risk may be assumed to be zero at the time the contracts are closed out. Futures contracts may be assumed to mature at the month end.   **(15 marks)**

(ii)   Successive daily prices on the futures market for a June contract which you have sold are:

Selling price	0.6916
Day 1	0.6930
Day 2	0.6944
Day 3	0.6940

Initial margins are £1,000 per contract. Variation margin is 100% of the initial margin.

309

Spot exchange rates may be assumed not to change significantly during these three days.

Required

For each of the three days, show the effect on your cash flow of the price changes of the contract.

(4 marks)

(c)   Discuss the advantages and disadvantages of forward contracts and currency futures for hedging against foreign exchange risk.   **(6 marks)**

(Total = 30 marks)

Section B: TWO QUESTIONS ONLY to be attempted

Question 3

Cougar are developing a new product which they will be able to bring to the market in 24 months. Market research suggested that there is annual demand for 74,000 units at a selling price of $127 at today's prices but expect prices to rise by 3% on average each year with a price volatility of 18%. The shelf life of the product will be four years from launch.

The manufacturing cost of these units is $93 at current prices. This cost will grow steadily at 3% but will display no other volatility.

In order to be in production a factory will need to be re-tooled in 24 months at a cost of $150,000, however this cost will only be incurred if production proceeds. If selling prices fall then production may be shelved.

The development costs for the next two years are $1.2m and $1.4m respectively. Cougar has a 13% cost of capital and risk-free rates are 6%.

Requirements

(a)   Estimate the present value of this development opportunity and determine whether the company should proceed assuming all cost are incurred at the start of the year and revenues received at the end.

(12 marks)

(b)   Explain the significance of the existence of real options to the capital investment decisions and briefly discuss examples at real options that may arise.   **(8 marks)**

(Total = 20 marks)

Question 4

Discuss the main features of:

(a)   Corporate share repurchases (buy-backs)
(b)   Share (stock) splits
(c)   Rights issues

and why companies might use them. Include in your discussion comments on the possible effects on share price of share repurchases and share (stock) splits in comparison to the payment of dividends.   **(20 marks)**

Question 5

Servealot plc has issued the following statement as part of its annual report:

'This company aims at all times to serve its shareholders by paying a high level of dividends and adopting strategies that will increase the company's share price. Satisfying our shareholders will ensure our success. The company will reduce costs by manufacturing overseas wherever possible, and will attempt to minimise the company's global tax bill by using tax haven facilities.'

Required

(a)   Discuss the validity and implications of each of the comments and strategies in the above statement.

(15 marks)

(b)   Produce a short note outlining how the company should estimate its dividend capacity.   **(5 marks)**

(Total = 20 marks)

311

Answers

DO NOT TURN THIS PAGE UNTIL YOU HAVE
COMPLETED THE MOCK EXAM

Question 1

> **Top tips.** It is inappropriate to calculate expected values since the two scenarios are mutually exclusive. The only complex part of the present value analysis should be the calculation of the cost of capital. As we are told the financial data includes inflation but at varying rates, this means that the figures have to be discounted at the nominal cost of capital. Hence the real risk free rate and market return have to be adjusted for inflation.
>
> The starting point for the adjusted present value calculation is calculating the base case NPV by ungearing the company's equity beta, in order to obtain a beta that can used in the CAPM equation to find the ungeared cost of equity. The ungeared cost of equity is in turn used in the base case NPV calculation.
>
> Remember that Dt is only used to find the tax shield if interest is paid for an indefinite period (debt is irredeemable), Otherwise an NPV calculation has to be carried out.
>
> In your discussion it is important to identify the strategic implications as well as the technical limitations of the calculations.
>
> **Easy marks.** Best to do the calculations first in an appendix, but if you struggle for time, don't worry about finishing off the APV calculation.

REPORT

To: Managers of Daron
From: Company Accountant
Date: 14 December 20X6
Subject: **Long-term strategic options**

Strategic options

The purpose of this report is to evaluate the **strategic options** available to the company, namely an immediate sale of the company, continuation of existing operations, and diversification in the event of party A winning the forthcoming election.

Sale of the company

This option can be evaluated in terms of the value of the offer to the shareholders. The informal offer of $10m from the competitor compares with the current market value of the equity of $9.2m (20m × $0.46), a premium of 8.7%. However, it is perhaps more helpful to attempt a valuation of the company based on future cash flows, and figures illustrating this are included in Appendix 1 of this report. These suggest that if party A wins the election, the NPV of the future cash flows will amount to $18.8m, whereas if party B wins, the NPV will be $10.4m. Both of these are in excess of the competitor's offer, suggesting that if the shareholders do wish to sell they should seek a higher price for the company. However, these estimates are subject to a number of uncertainties which will be considered further in the next section of the report.

The shareholders will also need to consider some of the other implications of selling, such as the effect on the other stakeholders in the firm. For example, will many jobs be lost in redundancies? How will customers and the local community be affected by such a decision?

Continue existing operations

The figures contained in Appendix 1 represent a projection of performance for the ten year period up to 20Y6. However, when forecasting over such a long timescale the likelihood of inaccuracy increases, particular areas of potential error being as follows.

(a)   The assumption that the **cost of capital** will remain **constant** throughout the period
(b)   The assumptions made about the **inflation rate**
(c)   The **effect on economic conditions** of possible further elections beyond the one in the immediate future
(d)   The assumption that the **tax rate** will remain constant at 30%
(e)   Errors in the projections of sales revenues and costs

 315

A further major assumption built into the figures is that there will be no significant additional capital investment throughout this period. This raises a number of questions, including the following.

(a) Will **other opportunities** be **forgone** during this period if the company starts to lag behind its competitors in technology?

(b) Will significant major new investment be required beyond 20Y1 to allow the company to continue operations?

(c) What is the realisable value of the company in 20Y1?

This final factor could also have a significant impact on the calculations in Appendix 1, and could mean that the true value of the future cash flows for the period in question is even higher than the figures suggest.

In view of the uncertainties described, it is proposed that further work needs to be done, particularly in investigating the sensitivities of the NPVs to changes in assumptions concerning the key variables.

Diversification into hotel industry

The figures relating to the diversification are contained in Appendix 2. These suggest that the project should yield a NPV of $0.56m. However, a major element in this forecast is the **terminal value** of $10m **on disposal** in 20Y1, and any variation in the amount realised is likely to have a significant effect on the projections. Again it is suggested that sensitivity analysis be undertaken to establish the impact of changes in this variable.

In addition to making the financial evaluation, Daron needs to consider the **investment** in the light of its **strategic objectives**. If the investment is essentially opportunistic with the diversification being for the benefit of the shareholders in terms of reducing their level of risk, this may be a mistaken goal. The shareholders can achieve diversification of their portfolios by themselves in their choice of other investments, and are unlikely to look to Daron to achieve this for them.

The key question is what the **company strategy** is to be in the face of the declining market for its core business. It may well be appropriate to seek **diversification** as a means for survival and growth, but the markets into which Daron seeks to diversify should be carefully chosen and should ideally be related in some way, be it **technological basis** or customer spread, to those in which it currently operates. The greater the departure from its existing experience, the greater the risk that the diversification will be less successful than anticipated.

Conclusions

Daron needs to consider its **long-term strategic objectives** and the **desires** of its **shareholders** before making any choices between the options facing it. If sale is perceived to be the best option, then the directors should seek to present the company to the market in the best possible light so as to **maximise the disposal proceeds**, and not just take the offer from the competitor because it is there. If continuing the existing business is desired, careful attention should be given to **long-term market conditions** and to the effect of alternative investment policies. If diversification is to be pursued then products and markets should be properly evaluated to obtain the best fit with the existing business.

Appendix 1: Estimates of the present value of Daron

Scenario 1: Party A wins the election

	20X7 $m	20X8 $m	20X9 $m	20Y0 $m	20Y1 $m
Sales	28.0	29.0	26.0	22.0	19.0
Variable costs	(17.0)	(18.0)	(16.0)	(14.0)	(12.0)
Fixed costs	(3.0)	(3.0)	(3.0)	(3.0)	(3.0)
Taxable cash flows	8.0	8.0	7.0	5.0	4.0
Tax at 30%	(2.4)	(2.4)	(2.1)	(1.5)	(1.2)
Post tax cash flows	5.6	5.6	4.9	3.5	2.8
Tax credit on depreciation (30% × tax allowable depreciation)	1.2	0.9	0.9	0.6	0.3
Working capital movement		1.0	2.0	3.0	3.0
Replacement investment	(10.0)				(5.0)
Free cash flow	(3.2)	7.5	7.8	7.1	1.1
13% discount factors (see Note 1)	0.885	0.783	0.693	0.613	0.543
PV cash flow	(2.8)	5.9	5.4	4.4	0.6

Total PV = $13.5 million (20X7 – 20Y1)

To these figures must be added the PV cash flow for the period 20Y2-20Y6. This can be found by applying the 13% annuity value for periods 6 to 10 (5.426 –3.517=1.909) to the annual cash flows. These cash flows will be similar to those for 20Y1 excluding tax credit on depreciation, working capital movements and replacement investment.

	$m
Sales	19.0
Variable costs	(12.0)
Fixed costs	(3.0)
Taxable income	4.0
Tax at 30%	(1.2)
Annual cash flow	2.8
Annuity value	1.909
PV cash flow	5.3

The NPV of the free cash flows for the period 20X7 to 20Y6 is therefore $13.5m + $5.3m = $18.8m.

Note 1. The discount rate to be used is the cost of capital. This can be estimated by finding the cost of equity using the CAPM, and then weighting the relative costs of debt and equity on the basis of market values.

The current market value of equity is 20m × $0.46 = $9.2m. It is assumed that the balance sheet value of the debt approximates to its market value ie $7m. Its cost (Kd) is taken as the current bank rate of 10%. The risk free rate of return including inflation is $(1.05 \times 1.04) - 1 = 9.2\%$. The market rate of return including inflation is $(1.10 \times 1.05) - 1 = 15.5\%$.

Using the CAPM: $E(r_j) = r_f + [E(r_m) - r_f]\ \beta_j$
$$= 9.2\% + [15.5\% - 9.2\%] \times 1.25\% = 17.075\%$$

The WACC can now be estimated.

$$WACC = Ke\left(\frac{E}{E+D}\right) + Kd\ (1-t)\left(\frac{D}{E+D}\right)$$
$$= 17.075\% \times 9.2/(9.2 + 7) + 10\% \times (1 - 0.3) \times 7/(9.2 + 7)$$
$$= 12.72\% \text{ (approx 13\%)}$$

Scenario 2: Party B wins the election

	20X7	20X8	20X9	20Y0	20Y1
	$m	$m	$m	$m	$m
Sales	30.0	26.0	24.0	20.0	16.0
Variable costs	(18.0)	(16.0)	(15.0)	(12.0)	(11.0)
Fixed costs	(3.0)	(3.0)	(4.0)	(4.0)	(4.0)
Taxable cash flows	9.0	7.0	5.0	4.0	1.0
Tax at 30%	(2.7)	(2.1)	(1.5)	(1.2)	(0.3)
Post tax cash flows	6.3	4.9	3.5	2.8	0.7
Tax credit on depreciation	1.2	0.9	0.9	0.6	0.3
Working capital movement	(1.0)	2.0	2.0	3.0	3.0
Replacement capital expenditure	(10.0)				(5.0)
Net cash flow	(3.5)	7.8	6.4	6.4	(1.0)
18% discount factors (see Note 2)	0.847	0.718	0.609	0.516	0.437
PV cash flow	(3.0)	5.6	3.9	3.3	(0.4)

Total PV = $9.4 million (20X7-20Y1)

The PV cash flow for the period 20Y2-20Y6 can be found by applying the 18% annuity value for periods 6 to 10 (4.494 – 3.127=1.367) to the annual cash flows. These cash flows will be as for 20Y1 excluding depreciation, working capital movements and replacement capital expenditure.

	$m
Sales	16.0
Variable costs	(11.0)
Fixed costs	(4.0)
Taxable income	1.0
Tax at 30%	(0.3)
Annual cash flow	0.7
Annuity value	1.367
PV cash flow	1.0

The NPV of the free cash flows for the period 20X7 to 20Y6 is therefore $9.4m + $1.0m = $10.4m.

Note 2. The discount rate to be used is the cost of capital, which can be estimated by the same method as in Scenario 1.

The current market value of equity is again $9.2m. It is assumed that the balance sheet value of the debt approximates to its market value ie $7m, with its cost taken at the bank rate of 15.5%. The risk free rate of return including inflation is $(1.04 \times 1.1) - 1 = 14.4\%$. The market rate of return including inflation is $(1.10 \times 1.1) - 1 = 21.0\%$.

Using the CAPM: $Ke = r_f + [E(r_m) - r_f] \beta_j$

$$= 14.4\% + (21.0\% - 14.4\%) \times 1.25 = 22.65\%$$

The WACC can now be estimated.

$$WACC = Ke\left(\frac{E}{E+D}\right) + Kd(1-t)\left(\frac{D}{E+D}\right)$$

$$= 22.65\% \times 9.2/(9.2+7) + 15.5\% \times (1-0.3) \times 7/(9.2+7)$$

$$= 17.55\% \text{ (approx 18\%)}$$

Appendix 2: Cash flow evaluation of diversification project

To estimate the **APV**, it is first necessary to find the **base case NPV**. This is calculated using the ungeared cost of equity. This can be found using the expression:

	20X6	20X7	20X8	20X9	20Y0	20Y1
	$m	$m	$m	$m	$m	$m
Revenue		9.0	10.0	11.0	12.0	13.0
Variable costs		(6.0)	(6.0)	(7.0)	(7.0)	(8.0)
Fixed costs		(2.0)	(2.0)	(2.0)	(2.0)	(2.0)
Taxable income		1.0	2.0	2.0	3.0	3.0
Tax at 30%		(0.3)	(0.6)	(0.6)	(0.9)	(0.9)
Post tax income		0.7	1.4	1.4	2.1	2.1
Purchase cost	(9.0)					
Working capital movement		(1.0)			(1.0)	
Realisable value						10.0
Cash flow	(9.0)	(0.3)	1.4	1.4	1.1	12.1
14% discount factors (see Note 3)	1.000	0.877	0.769	0.675	0.592	0.519
PV cash flow	(9.0)	(0.3)	1.1	0.9	0.7	6.3

Total PV (base case NPV)= −$300,000

Note 3

$$\beta_a = \beta_e \frac{E}{E+D(1-t)}$$

where: β_a = ungeared beta

β_e = geared beta (1.25)

E = market value of equity ($9.2m)

D = market value of debt ($7.0m)

t = tax rate (30%)

β_a = $1.25 \times \dfrac{9.2}{9.2 + 7(1-0.3)} = 0.82$

The ungeared cost of equity can now be estimated using the CAPM:

$Ke_u = r_f + [E(r_m) - r_f]\beta$

= 9.2% + (15.5% − 9.2%) × 0.82 = 14.4% (say, approximately 14%)

This can be used to calculate the NPV of the project as if it were all equity financed.

Modigliani and Miller

The next stage is to use the **Modigliani and Miller formula** for the relationship between the value of geared and ungeared companies to establish the effect of gearing on the value of the project. The amount to be financed by debt will be the purchase cost of the hotel plus the issue costs: $9m/98% = $9.184m.

The present value of the tax shield on the debt interest can now be found.

Annual interest charge: $9.184m × 10%	$918,400
Tax saving: 30%	$275,520
Cost of debt (pre tax)	10%
PV of tax savings at 10% for 5 years: $275,520 × 3.791 (in round $'000)	$1,044,000

APV calculation

The APV is the base case NPV plus the financing side effects (including issue costs):

	$'000
Base case NPV	(300)
Issue costs	(184)
PV of tax savings	1,044
APV	560

This assumes firstly that all the funds required can be raised in the form of debt ie that Daron will have sufficient debt capacity, and secondly that the coupon rate of 10% is an accurate reflection of the risk of the convertible loan stock.

Question 2

Text references. Chapter 14.

Top tips. The elimination of foreign exchange risk with other members of the single currency is at the heart of the answer to (a).

It is not necessarily clear how best to tackle the futures part of (b) (i) given the absence of spot rates at the end of the contract. You need to come up with an answer that can be compared with the results on the forward and money markets. Our answer does this by saying that for the amount hedged, the results on the spot and futures market will balance out to give a net payment at the current futures price. This leaves in both instances a certain amount unhedged which can then be hedged on the forward market. We demonstrate this by using an example although this may not be necessary to gain full marks. Most marks would be available for the money and futures market parts of the answer.

The caveat about the lack of basis risk is important. (b) (ii) illustrates the importance of variation margin.

Easy marks. The list in (c) represents basic knowledge in this area. Your answer needs to focus on cost, flexibility and risk of loss.

(a)   **Foreign exchange exposure**

The managing director is certainly correct in saying that the **foreign exchange exposure** in dealing with other EMU countries will be eliminated. However foreign exchange exposure will still affect trade with countries that are not members of EMU.

Transaction costs

Similarly **transaction costs** involved in trade with other EMU members will disappear, and this could represent a considerable saving. However there will still be transaction costs when trading with other countries who are not EMU members.

Economic exposure

In addition the company would still face **economic exposure** even if it only traded with other countries within EMU. If the euro is over-valued with respect to non-members' currencies, companies from non-member countries may gain sales at the expense of the UK company because they can charge cheaper prices. The company may also face **indirect economic exposure** if it buys products from other EMU members who buy their raw materials from non-EMU members. Any adverse exchange movements meaning raw material prices increases would be passed on through the value chain.

BPP
LEARNING MEDIA

(b)   (i)   **Receipts**   **Payments**

Two months   €393,265

Three months Kr8.6m   491,011 + 890,217 − 60,505 − 1,997,651 = €676,928

Forward market hedge

Two months

Payment $\dfrac{€393,265}{1.433}$ = £274,435

Three months

Payment $\dfrac{€676,928}{1.431}$ = £473,045

Receipt $\dfrac{Kr8,600,000}{10.83}$ = £794,090

Money market hedge

(i)   **Two months payment**

We need to invest now to match the €393,265 we require.

Amount to be invested $= \dfrac{€393,265}{1+\dfrac{0.035}{6}}$

$= €390,984$

Converting at spot rate $\dfrac{390,984}{1.439}$ = £271,705

To obtain £271,705, we have to borrow for two months.

Amount to be paid to lender $= 271,705 \times \left(1+\dfrac{0.075}{6}\right)$

$= £275,101$

(ii) **Three months payment**

Again we need to invest

Amount to be invested $= \dfrac{€676,928}{1+\dfrac{0.035}{4}}$

$= €671,056$

Converting at spot rate $\dfrac{671,056}{1.439}$ = £466,335

Borrowing £466,335 for three months

Amount to be paid to lender $= 466,335 \times \left(1+\dfrac{0.075}{4}\right)$

$= £475,079$

(iii) **Three months receipt**

We need to borrow now to match the receipt we shall obtain.

Amount to be borrowed $= \dfrac{Kr8,600,000}{1 + \dfrac{0.08}{4}}$

$= Kr8,431,373$

Converting at spot rate $\dfrac{8,431,373}{10.71} = £787,243$

Amount to be received $= 787,243 \times \left(1 + \dfrac{0.055}{4}\right)$

$= £798,068$

Futures market

For the two months payment:

- We shall be buying June contracts as they mature just after payment date

- Buy € futures

- Number of contracts

$\dfrac{393,265}{125,000} = 3.15$, 3 contracts. This leaves €18,265 (393,265 − 375,000) not covered by futures contracts, and to be hedged on the forward market at 1.433.

- Tick size 125,000 × 0.0001 = £12.50.

The €375,000 will, assuming zero basis, be at the current futures price of 0.6964 to £261,150.

To demonstrate, let us assume spot market rate moves to 1.50.

On futures market:

Opening futures price	0.6964
Closing futures price	0.6667 (1/1.50)
Movement in ticks	297 ticks loss
Loss on futures market	297 × 12.50 × 3 = £11,138 loss

Net outcome

	£
Spot market payment (375,000 ÷ 1.50)	(250,000)
Loss on futures market	(11,138)
	261,138

allowing for rounding errors is the same as at the current futures price.

Therefore:

	£
Amount hedged on futures market	(261,150)
Forward market (18,265/1.433)	(12,746)
Total payment	273,896

We can use a similar argument for the three months payment. This time the number of contracts will be $\dfrac{676,928}{125,000} = 5.42$, say 5 contracts.

Amount hedged on the futures market will be €625,000, leaving €51,928 to be hedged on the forward market.

$$\text{Total payment} = (625{,}000 \times 0.6983) + \frac{51{,}928}{1.431}$$
$$= 436{,}438 + 36{,}288$$
$$= £472{,}726$$

Conclusion

For the three month Kr receipt, the money market will maximise cash flow. For the two Euro payments, the futures market should maximise cash flow assuming basis risk is negligible. If basis risk does have a significant impact, the forward market may be the best choice.

(ii) **Day 1** movement 0.6930 − 0.6916 = 14 ticks loss. Extra payment of £175 (14 × £12.50) is required. If the extra payment is not made, the contract will be closed out. Therefore:

Day 2 movement 0.6944 − 0.6930 = 14 ticks loss, extra payment of £175.

Day 3 movement 0.6940 − 0.6944 = 4 ticks profit. Profit = 4 × £12.50 = £50; this can be taken in cash.

(c) **Advantages of forward contracts**

(i) The contract can be tailored to the user's **exact requirements** with quantity to be delivered, date and price all flexible.

(ii) The trader will **know in advance** how much money will be received or paid.

(iii) **Payment** is **not required** until the contract is settled.

Disadvantages of forward contracts

(i) The user may not be able to negotiate **good terms**; the price may depend upon the **size** of the **deal** and how the user is rated.

(ii) Users have to **bear** the **spread** of the contract between the buying and selling price.

(iii) Deals can only be **reversed** by going back to the original party and offsetting the original trade.

(iv) The **creditworthiness** of the other party may be a problem.

Advantages of currency futures

(i) There is a **single specified price** determined by the market, and not the negotiating strength of the customer.

(ii) **Transactions costs** are generally **lower** than for forward contracts.

(iii) The exact date of **receipt** or **payment** of the currency does not have to be **known**, because the futures contract does not have to be closed out until the actual cash receipt or payment is made.

(iv) **Reversal** can easily take place in the market.

(v) Because of the process of **marking to market**, there is no default risk.

Disadvantages of currency futures

(i) The **fixing** of **quantity** and **delivery dates** that is necessary for the future to be traded means that the customer's risk may not be fully covered.

(ii) Futures contracts may not be **available** in the **currencies** that the customer requires.

(iii) **Volatile trading conditions** on the futures markets mean that the potential loss can be high.

Question 3

(a) Cougar must pay today (development cost) in order to have the opportunity/option to enter into production in 2 years' time. They will only choose to do this if the production option value exceeds the present value of the development costs.

Development costs

Time	Cash flow $'000	DF	AV $'000
0	1,200	1	1,200
1	1,400	$\dfrac{1}{1.13}$	1,239
PV at development cost			2,439

Production option

To evaluate this real call option we need to establish

S = PV at all volatile future cost flows if the project is undertaken.

X = PV **at the option expiry date** of any non-volatile cashflows arising if the project is undertaken

σ = Volatility of the returns from S.

r_f = Risk-free rate

t = Time of expiry

Consider the future volatile cashflows, based on the anticipated demand the annual revenue at today's prices would be $9,398,000 ($127 × 74,000). With inflation at 3% and a cost at capital at 13% this gives

Time	Cash flow $'000	DF	AV $'000
3	$9,398 \times 1.03^3 = 10,264$	$\dfrac{1}{1.13^3}$	7,117
4	$9,398 \times 1.03^4 = 10,578$	$\dfrac{1}{1.13^4}$	6,487
5	$9,398 \times 1.03^5 = 10,895$	$\dfrac{1}{1.13^5}$	5,913
6	$9,398 \times 1.03^6 = 11,222$	$\dfrac{1}{1.13^6}$	5,390
PV at development returns (S)			24,907

Now, the annual production cost in current prices is $6,882,000 ($93 × 74,000). Considering the non-volatile cash flows arising if the option is exercised, we have AS AT THE EXERCISE DATE in 24 months time

Time	Cash flow $'000	DF	AV $'000
2	150	$\dfrac{1}{1.13^2}$	118
2	$6882 \times 1.03^2 = 7,301$	$\dfrac{1}{1.13^2}$	5,718
3	$6882 \times 1.03^3 = 7,520$	$\dfrac{1}{1.13^3}$	5,212
4	$6882 \times 1.03^4 = 7,746$	$\dfrac{1}{1.13^4}$	4,751
5	$6882 \times 1.03^5 = 7,978$	$\dfrac{1}{1.13^5}$	4,330

	$'000
PV now	20,128
Compound factor for 2 years	$\times 1.13^2$
PV at exercise date (X)	25,701

So we have

S = $24,907 k

X = $25,701 k

σ = 18% pa

r_f = 6% pa

t = 2 years

$$d_1 = \frac{\ln\left[\dfrac{24,907}{25,701}\right] + (0.06 + 0.5 \times 0.18^2) \times 2}{0.18 \times \sqrt{2}} = 0.4754$$

$d_2 = d_1 - \sigma\sqrt{t} = 0.4752 - 0.18 \times \sqrt{2} = 0.2208$

$N(d_1) = N(0.48) = 0.5 + 0.1844 = 0.6844$

$N(d_2) = N(0.22) = 0.5 + 0.0871 = 0.5871$

$C = SN(d_1) - Xe^{-rt} N(d_2)$

$C = 24,907 \times 0.6844 - 25,701 \times e^{-0.06 \times 2} \times 0.5871 = \$3,664,000$

Conclusion	$'000
Value of development call option	3,664
PV of development costs	2,439
NPV of development opportunity	1,225

Hence the company should proceed with the development.

(b) An option is a choice which need to be exercised if it's to the investors advantage. A real option is a choice or opportunity arising from a capital investment. The choice may involve being able to change plans once the project is underway. The opportunity also may not have been envisaged when the original plans were made but may arise later on.

Real options include:

(i) **Option to delay** – where a business has the rights to a project or product but can choose to delay undertaking the project/producing the product until a later date. This may be useful if selling prices are currently low but are quite volatile. This is a call option, looking to obtain something at a later date.

(ii) **Option to abandon** – where a business has some current operations but has the opportunity to withdraw and recoup some invested capital. This is a put option on these operations.

(iii) **Option to expand** – where a business has the opportunity to make further future capital investments. This is a call option on these possible future operations.

(iv) **Option to redeploy** – where productive assets can be used for alternative purposes. This is a call option based on the benefits of the alternative production.

The significance of these options is that they add value to the project and should be taken into account as part of investment appraisal.

Question 4

Text references. Chapter 24.

Top tips. The main things that this question demonstrates are that questions on distributions may not be on dividends, and that the response of the market to the various measures will be conditioned by its degree of efficiency. This is a good demonstration of how the examiner brings in market efficiency. Note that both methods can affect the ownership of shares.

(a) **Share repurchases**

Purchase of own shares is a alternative means for companies to distribute shares to shareholders other than by a cash dividend. In certain regimes companies can purchase their own shares out of **distributable profits**, or the **proceeds of a new issue of shares**, provided certain conditions are fulfilled. In the UK private companies can **repurchase** their own shares out of capital.

Uses of share repurchase

(i) **No available buyer**

For a smaller private company, there may be **no immediate willing purchaser** at a time when a shareholder wishes to sell shares.

(ii) **Going private**

For a listed company, share repurchase can be a means of **withdrawing** from the stock market and going private.

(iii) **Surplus cash**

Share repurchase can be a **use for surplus cash**, particularly at a time when investment returns are low.

(iv) **Increase in share price**

Purchase of own shares can be a means of supporting share price during a **period of weakness**. A reduction of the number of shares in issue should lead to an **increase in earnings per share**, and hence an **increase in the market price of shares**.

(v) **Increase in gearing**

Companies whose gearing levels are low can **increase gearing** by purchasing their own shares. If debt finance is cheaper than equity finance this may **lower the company's weighted average cost of capital** and hence mean that **more potential investments** could be undertaken on the grounds that they have a positive NPV.

(vi) **Declining business**

If the company's business is in decline, purchase of equity can **lower its funding** to a more appropriate level for its level of business.

(vii) **Thwarting a takeover**

A share repurchase may be used to **buy out shareholders** who might be favourably disposed towards a takeover bid.

Response of market

(i) **Strong-form efficiency**

If the market is strong-form efficient, it may have understood the share repurchase as being the **best possible use of funds**, and the announcement of the purchase should not influence the share price.

(ii) **Signalling effect if markets are not strong-form efficient**

If the markets are not strong-form efficient, a repurchase of shares could be seen as an **admission** that the company **cannot make better use** of the funds than the shareholders, and its **share price may fall**. However the markets may take the contrary view, and see a share repurchase as a sign that the company has **more cash and more earnings potential** than previously believed.

The **price** at which shares are repurchased will influence the market response. If shares are repurchased by tender, it will often be at a price in excess of current market price.

(iii) **Investor preferences**

Investors may prefer share repurchase **to dividend payments** because of differences in the tax regime on capital gains and dividend income.

(b) **Stock splits**

A stock split occurs when each share is split into shares of smaller nominal values, for example each £1 share being split into 10 10p shares.

Uses of stock splits

(i) **Greater marketability**

Evidence suggests that shares of **smaller nominal value** are more marketable than shares of larger value. Companies whose shares are high valued often split their shares.

(ii) **Ownership**

Share splits may be a way of encouraging **wider ownership** of shares, by making it easier for shareholders to hold small holdings.

Market response

(i) **Strong-form efficiency**

If the market is strong-form efficient, the stock split should not make any **difference**, as it does not make any difference to the company's ability to undertake projects with a positive NPV.

(ii) **Signalling effect if markets are not strong-form efficient**

If the market is less than strongly efficient, it may interpret the stock split as **new information**, as a sign that the company is planning for earnings and dividend growth in the future. As a result, there may be short-term increases in the share price.

(c) **Rights issue**

A rights issue is an issue of new shares for cash to existing shareholders in proportion to their existing holding which is at a discount to the current market price. This is an attractive way of raising finance since

(i) There is no dilution of shareholders' interest.

(ii) The issue is at a discount to the current market price to make it attractive.

(iii) A shareholder who does not want to subscribe more cash and take up his rights can sell them, receiving cash as payment for the dilution of interest that he will suffer.

Such issues are generally underwritten to cater for those individuals who do not want to exercise their rights, thus the company can be sure of raising all the finance it requires.

Question 5

(a) (i) **Serving its shareholders by paying high dividends**

This assumes that shareholders **demand high dividends**, whereas some may not do so and may prefer appreciation of the value of their shares, particularly if **dividends are highly taxed**.

A policy of continuing to pay high dividends will mean that shareholders and the stock market may expect these levels to **continue indefinitely**; if dividends fall, these thwarted expectations may lead to the share price falling as well. However in the long-term high dividend levels may prove unsustainable, because insufficient monies are being retained for investment in projects that will yield the cash surpluses necessary for dividends.

(ii) **Adopting strategies that will increase the company's share price**

Maximising share price is not the same as **maximising shareholder wealth**. In addition Gordon's growth rate model suggests that the growth of dividends, and hence share price, is dependent on the **proportion of funds retained**; the higher the proportion retained, the more can be invested in projects that generate surpluses and hence higher long-term dividends.

(iii) **Satisfying our shareholders will ensure our success**

Other **stakeholders**, as well as shareholders, are affected by Servealot's activities and they will impact on Servealot's success to varying degrees. Loss of key employees because of poor working conditions may impact adversely, also suppliers stopping credit because Servealot has been a slow payer. Servealot will also have to fulfil **legal and regulatory requirements** imposed by the government and regulators; failure to do may lead to heavy costs and ultimately threaten its existence. Servealot may also be more attractive to consumers if it follows what is regarded as **ethical and environmental best practice**.

(iv) **Reducing costs by manufacturing overseas**

Manufacturing overseas may **reduce the costs of factors of production**. However Servealot will have to bear costs of investment, and also perhaps increased **selling and distribution costs**. There may also be increased costs arising from controlling the **quality of overseas output** and **managing the overseas operations**. Servealot's directors should also consider the risk implications; perhaps political instability might threaten the value of Servealot's investment. In addition there are threats to

Servealot's reputation due to **ethical concerns** over loss of home country employment and wealth generation.

(v) **Minimising global tax bill by using tax haven facilities**

Tax haven facilities may mean that Servealot has a **reduced burden of certain taxes**, including corporation taxes, capital gains taxes and taxes on remittances. Servealot may also benefit from **improved tax efficiencies**, if it has a number of subsidiaries and can channel transactions through the tax haven.

However there will be **some incorporation costs** and the benefits of the tax haven may decrease over the long-term as governments close tax loopholes and restrict the use of havens. Perhaps also the ethical climate is becoming less favourable to tax havens because of the **loss of tax** to governments and the **secrecy** surrounding the affairs of some companies who use tax havens, so Servealot might suffer some **loss of reputation** when using them.

(b) **Dividend capacity**

The **free cash flow** is the amount of money that is **available for distribution to the capital contributors**. If the project is financed by equity only, then these funds could be potentially distributed to the shareholders of the company.

However, if the company is financing the project by issuing **debt**, then the shareholders are entitled to the residual cash flow left over after meeting interest and principal payments. This **residual cash flow (free cash flow to equity)** represents **dividends that could potentially be paid to shareholders**. This is usually not the same as actual dividends in a given year because normally the management of a company **deliberately smoothes dividend** payments across time.

The **free cash flow to equity** is a measure of what is **available to the shareholders after providing for capital expenditures to maintain existing assets and to create new assets for future growth**. Thus, if a firm has substantial working capital and capital expenditure requirements then the free cash flow can be negative even if the earnings are positive.

Accurate financial forecasts covering timing and size of all cash flows are essential in order to determine the dividend capacity of a company.

ACCA Professional Level

Paper P4

Advanced Financial Management

Mock Examination 2

Question Paper	
Time allowed	
Reading and Planning Writing	**15 minutes** **3 hours**
Section A BOTH questions are compulsory and MUST be attempted **Section B** TWO questions ONLY to be attempted	
During reading and planning time only the question paper may be annotated	

DO NOT OPEN THIS PAPER UNTIL YOU ARE READY TO START UNDER EXAMINATION CONDITIONS

Section A: BOTH QUESTIONS are compulsory and MUST be attempted

Question 1

Novoroast plc manufactures microwave ovens which it exports to several countries, as well as supplying the home market. One of Novoroast's export markets is a South American country, which has recently imposed a 40% tariff on imports of microwaves in order to protect its local 'infant' microwave industry. The imposition of this tariff means that Novoroast's products are no longer competitive in the South American country's market but the government there is, however, willing to assist companies wishing to undertake direct investment locally. The government offers a 10% grant towards the purchase of plant and equipment, and a three-year tax holiday on earnings. Corporate tax after the three-year period would be paid at the rate of 25% in the year that the taxable cash flow arises.

Novoroast wishes to evaluate whether to invest in a manufacturing subsidiary in South America, or to pull out of the market altogether.

The total cost of an investment in South America is 155 million pesos (at current exchange rates), comprising:

- 50 million pesos for land and buildings
- 60 million pesos for plant and machinery (all of which would be required almost immediately)
- 45 million pesos for working capital

20 million pesos of the working capital will be required immediately and 25 million pesos at the end of the first year of operation. Working capital needs are expected to increase in line with local inflation.

The company's planning horizon is five years.

Plant and machinery is expected to be depreciated (tax allowable) on a straight-line basis over five years, and is expected to have negligible realisable value at the end of five years. Land and buildings are expected to appreciate in value in line with the level of inflation in the South American country.

Production and sales of microwaves are expected to be 8,000 units in the first year at an initial price of 1,450 pesos per unit, 60,000 units in the second year, and 120,000 units per year for the remainder of the planning horizon.

In order to control the level of inflation, legislation exists in the South American country to restrict retail price rises of manufactured goods to 10% per year.

Fixed costs and local variable costs, which for the first year of operation are 12 million pesos and 600 pesos per unit respectively, are expected to increase by the previous year's rate of inflation.

All components will be produced or purchased locally except for essential microchips which will be imported from the UK at a cost of £8 per unit, yielding a contribution to the profit of the parent company of £3 per unit. It is hoped to keep this sterling cost constant over the planning horizon.

Corporate tax in the UK is at the rate of 30% per year, payable in the year the liability arises. A bi-lateral tax treaty exists between the UK and the South American country, which permits the offset of overseas tax against any UK tax liability on overseas earnings. In periods of tax holiday assume that no UK tax would be payable on South American cash flows.

Summarised group data

	£m
Novoroast plc, summarised balance sheet:	
Fixed assets (net)	440
Current assets	370
Less current liabilities	(200)
	610

	£m
Financed by	
£1 ordinary shares	200
Reserves	230
	430
6% Eurodollar bonds, eight years until maturity	180
	610

Novoroast's current share price is 410 pence per share, and current bond price is $800 per bond ($1,000 par and redemption value).

Forecast inflation rates

	UK	South American country
Present	4%	20%
Year 1	3%	20%
Year 2	4%	15%
Year 3	4%	15%
Year 4	4%	15%
Year 5	4%	15%

Foreign exchange rates

	Peso/£
Spot	13.421
1 year forward	15.636

Novoroast plc believes that if the investment is undertaken the overall risk to investors in the company will remain unchanged.

The company's beta coefficients have been estimated as equity 1.25, debt 0.225.

The market return is 14% per annum and the risk free rate is 6% per annum.

Existing UK microwave production currently produces an after tax net cash flow of £30 million per annum. This is expected to be reduced by 10% if the South American investment goes ahead (after allowing for diversion of some production to other EU countries). Production is currently at full capacity in the UK.

Required

(a) Prepare a report advising whether or not Novoroast plc should invest in the South American country. Include in your report a discussion of the limitations of your analysis.

What other information would be useful to assist the decision process?

All relevant calculations must be shown in your report or as an appendix to it.

State clearly any assumptions that you make. **(25 marks)**

(b) If, once the investment had taken place, the government of the South American country imposed a block on the remittance of dividends to the UK, discuss how Novoroast might try to avoid such a block on remittances. **(5 marks)**

(Total = 30 marks)

Question 2

The CEO of Autocrat plc is reviewing the company's interest rate and currency risk strategies for the next few months. There has recently been considerable political instability with some countries showing signs of moving towards economic recession whilst others are still showing steady growth. Both interest rates and currency rates could become more volatile for many major trading countries.

Autocrat is expected to need to borrow £6,500,000 for a period of six months commencing in six months' time.

The company also needs to make a US$ payment of $4.3 million in 3 months' time.

Assume that it is now 1 December. Futures and options contracts may be assumed to expire at the end of the relevant month, and the company may be assumed to borrow at the 3 month LIBOR rate.

LIFFE futures prices, £500,000 contract size

March	95.56
June	95.29

LIFFE options on futures prices, £500,000 contract size. Premiums are annual %.

	Calls		Puts	
	March	*June*	*March*	*June*
95250	0.445	0.545	0.085	0.185
95500	0.280	0.390	0.170	0.280
95750	0.165	0.265	0.305	0.405

Three month LIBOR is currently 4.5%.

Foreign exchange rates

Spot	$1.4692 – 1.4735/£
3 month forward	$1.4632 – 1.4668/£

Currency option prices

Philadelphia Stock Exchange $/£ options, contract size £31,250, premiums are cents per £.

	Calls		Puts	
	March	*June*	*March*	*June*
1.450	3.12	–	1.56	–
1.460	2.55	2.95	1.99	2.51
1.470	2.14	–	2.51	–

Required

(a) Discuss the relevant considerations when deciding between futures and options to hedge the company's interest rate risk. **(6 marks)**

(b) Using the above information illustrate the possible results of

    (i)   Futures; and
    (ii)   Options

    hedges if interest rates in six months' time increase by 0.75%. Recommend which hedge should be selected and explain why there might be uncertainty as to the results of the hedges. **(11 marks)**

(c) Illustrate and discuss the possible outcomes of forward market and currency options hedges if possible currency rates in three months' time are either:

    (i) $1.4350 – $1.4386/£
    or   (ii) $1.4780 – $1.4820/£ **(8 marks)**

(d) Discuss and illustrate whether or not a currency straddle option with an exercise price of 1.460 might be an appropriate hedging strategy for Autocrat plc. Explain the circumstances in which straddle options could be a profitable strategy. **(5 marks)**

(Total = 30 marks)

Section B: TWO QUESTIONS ONLY to be attempted

Question 3

(a)   Briefly identify the key factors determining the value of options.   **(5 marks)**

(b)   The current share price of Cathlynn plc is £3.50. Using the Black-Scholes model, estimate the value of a European call option on the shares of the company that has an exercise price of £3.30 and 3 months to run before it expires. The risk free rate of interest is 8% and the variance of the rate of return on the share has been 12%.

Note. The Black-Scholes formula shows call price for a European option P_c where

$P_c = P_s N(d_1) - Xe^{-rT} N(d_2)$

Where   N(d)   =   cumulative distribution function

$$d_1 = \frac{\ln(P_s/X) + rT}{\sigma\sqrt{T}} + 0.5\sigma\sqrt{T}$$

$$d_2 = d_1 - \sigma\sqrt{T}$$

P_s =   share price

e   =   the exponential constant 2.7183

X   =   exercise price of option

r   =   annual (continuously compounded) risk free rate of return

T   =   time of expiry of option in years

σ =   share price volatility, the standard deviation of the rate of return on shares

$N(d_x)$ =   delta, the probability that a deviation of less than d_x will occur in a normal distribution with a mean of zero and a standard deviation of one

In   =   natural log   **(10 marks)**

(c)   Discuss the main limitations of the Black-Scholes model.   **(5 marks)**

(Total = 20 marks)

Question 4

Summarised financial data for TYR Inc is shown below.

Year	Post-tax earnings $m	Dividends $m	Issued shares million	Share price cents
20X0	86.2	34.5	180	360
20X1	92.4	36.2	180	410
20X2	99.3	37.6	180	345
20X3	134.1	51.6	240	459
20X4	148.6	53.3	240	448

Year	All-share index	Inflation rate
20X0	2895	6%
20X1	3300	5%
20X2	2845	4%
20X3	2610	3%
20X4	2305	3%

TYR's cost of equity is estimated to be 11%.

Required

(a) Explain, with supporting numerical evidence, the current dividend policy of TYR Inc, and briefly discuss whether or not this appears to be successful. **(6 marks)**

(b) Identify the additional information that might assist the managers of TYR in assessing whether the dividend policy has been successful. **(4 marks)**

(c) Evaluate whether or not the company's share price at the end of 20X4 was what might have been expected from the dividend growth model. Briefly discuss the validity of your findings. **(5 marks)**

(d) Explain what is meant by signalling and how this relates to the dividend policy of a firm. **(5 marks)**

(Total = 20 marks)

Question 5

Boster plc is a multinational that has investments in several developing countries. It is considering investing in three developing countries, Ammobia, Flassia and Hracland. Each country has a history of political instability, but Boster believes that the potential returns from the investments might justify the political risk.

A consultancy report has produced the following assessments of the countries.

	Expected investment return (%)	*Political Risk (%)*
Ammobia	21	33
Flassia	18	29
Hracland	28	42

Political risk was measured by investigating key variables in the relevant countries. These were: corruption, changes in government, social conditions, cultural issues, unfair trade and asset security.

Boster will invest in a maximum of two of the countries, with an equal amount invested in each country. The countries are in diverse parts of the world, and the returns from the investments in the three countries are believed to be independent.

Required

(a) Calculate the risk, return and coefficient of variation of the possible investment combinations. **(6 marks)**

(b) Discuss how useful the information calculated in (a) above might be to Boster in making its investment decisions. **(5 marks)**

(c) Briefly discuss other ways by which Boster might attempt to measure the potential political risk of the investments. **(4 marks)**

(d) Briefly describe the various strategies that Boster can adopt to limit the effects of political risk. **(5 marks)**

(Total = 20 marks)

Answers

DO NOT TURN THIS PAGE UNTIL YOU HAVE
COMPLETED THE MOCK EXAM

Question 1

(a) To: Board of Directors of Novoroast plc
     From: Strategic Financial Consultant
     Date:

Proposed Investment in South American Manufacturing Subsidiary

1   **Introduction**

     The proposed investment has been triggered by the imposition of a very **high import tariff** (40%) in the South American country. The effect of this tariff is that all sales from the UK to this country will be lost (10% of total UK sales). This loss of UK sales will occur whether or not the proposed investment is made, and has therefore been omitted from the financial evaluation which follows.

2   **Financial evaluation**

     A financial evaluation of the investment, based on discounting the sterling value of incremental cash flows at the company's weighted average cost of capital, shows a **negative net present value** of £610,000, indicating that the investment is not expected to show high enough returns over the five year time horizon to compensate for the risk involved. Calculations are followed by workings and assumptions.

Year	0	1	2	3	4	5
Profit and cash flow – peso million						
Total contribution (W1)		5.80	44.20	92.82	97.04	100.92
Fixed costs (per year inflation increases)		(12.00)	(14.40)	(16.56)	(19.04)	(21.90)
Tax allowable depreciation		(12.00)	(12.00)	(12.00)	(12.00)	(12.00)
Taxable profit		(18.20)	17.80	64.26	66.00	67.02
Tax: from year 4 only at 25%					(16.50)	(16.76)
Add back depreciation		12.00	12.00	12.00	12.00	12.00
Net after-tax cash flow from operations		(6.20)	29.80	76.26	61.50	62.26
Investment cash flows						
Land and buildings (W3)	(50)					104.94
Plant and machinery (less 10% govt. grant)	(54)					
Working capital (W4)	(20)	(29.00)	(7.35)	(8.45)	(9.72)	74.52
Cash remittable from/to UK	(124)	(35.20)	22.45	67.81	51.78	241.72
Exchange rate P/£	13.421	15.636	17.290	19.119	21.141	23.377
UK cash flows (£m)						
Cash remittable	(9.24)	(2.25)	1.30	3.55	2.45	10.34
Contribution from sale of chips (£3 per unit)		0.02	0.18	0.36	0.36	0.36
Tax on chips contribution at 30%		(0.01)	(0.05)	(0.11)	(0.11)	(0.11)
Additional UK tax at 5% on S.Am. profits					(0.16)	(0.14)
Net cash flow in £m	(9.24)	(2.24)	1.43	3.80	2.54	10.45
14% (W5) discount factors	1	0.877	0.769	0.675	0.592	0.519
Present value £m	(9.24)	(1.96)	1.10	2.57	1.50	5.42
Net present value	(£610,000)					

Workings

1

Year	0	1	2	3	4	5
Contribution per unit						
Sales price (10% increases – pesos)		1,450.0	1,595.0	1,754.5	1,930.0	2,123.0
Variable cost per unit in pesos (previous year inflation increases)		600.0	720.0	828.0	952.2	1,095.0
Chip cost per unit (£8 converted to pesos – W2)		125.1	138.3	153.0	169.1	187.0
Contribution per unit (pesos)		724.9	736.7	773.5	808.7	841.0
Sales volume ('000 units)		8	60	120	120	120

2 **Prediction of future exchange rates**

Future exchange rates have been predicted from expected inflation rates, on the principle of Purchasing Power Parity Theory, eg Year 1 exchange rate = 13.421 × 1.20/1.03 = 15.636, etc or

$$13.421 \times \left(\frac{(0.2 - 0.03)}{(1 + 0.03)} + 1 \right).$$

	Inflation			
	UK	SAm	Exchange rate	
Spot			13.421	
Year 1	3%	20%	15.636	
Year 2	4%	15%	17.290	
Year 3	4%	15%	19.119	
Year 4	4%	15%	21.141	
Year 5	4%	15%	23.377	

3 **Land and buildings**

Value after 5 years = P50m × 1.2 × 1.15^4 = P104.94m. It is assumed no tax is payable on the capital gain.

4   Working capital

Value of working capital increases in line with inflation each year. The relevant cash flow is the difference between the values from year to year. Working capital is assumed to be released at the end of year 5.

End of year	0	1	2	3	4	5
Local inflation		20%	15%	15%	15%	
Value of Year 0 investment	20	24	27.60	31.74	36.50	0.00
Year 1 investment		25	28.75	33.06	38.02	0.00
Cumulative investment	20	49	56.35	64.80	74.52	0.00
Incremental cash flow	(20)	(29)	(7.35)	(8.45)	(9.72)	74.52

5   Discount rate

The company's WACC has been used as a discount rate, on the grounds that overall risk to investors is not expected to change as a result of this investment.

From the CAPM, Ke = 6% + (14% − 6%)1.25 = 16%.

Kd = 6% + (14% − 6%)0.225 = 7.8% pre-tax. After-tax rate = 7.8%(1 − 0.3) = 5.46%.

Market values: Equity: 200m × £4.10 = £820m. Debt: £180m × 800/1,000 = £144m.

Total = £964m.

WACC = 16% × 820/964 + 5.46% × 144/964 = 14.42%.

The discount rate will be **rounded** to 14% for the calculation.

6   Limitations of the analysis

The calculations are based on many assumptions and estimates concerning future cash flows. For example:

(i)   **Purchasing power parity**, used to estimate exchange rates, is only a 'broad-brush' theory; many other factors are likely to affect exchange rates and could increase the risk of the project.

(ii) **Estimates** of inflation, used to estimate costs and exchange rates in the calculations, are subject to **high inaccuracies**.

(iii) **Assumptions** about future tax rates and the restrictions on price increases may be incorrect.

(iv) **Cash flows** beyond the five year time horizon may be crucial in determining the viability or otherwise of the project; economic values of the operational assets at year 5 may be a lot higher than the residual values included in the calculation.

The calculations show only the medium term financial implications of the project. Non-financial factors and potentially important strategic issues have not been addressed.

7   Other relevant information

In order to get a more realistic view of the overall impact of the project, a strategic analysis needs to be carried out assessing the long term plans for the company's products and markets. For example, the **long term potential growth** of the South American market may be of greater significance than the medium term problems of price controls and inflation. On the other hand, it may be of more importance to the company to **increase its product range** to existing customers in Europe. There may also be further opportunities in other countries or regions.

Before deciding whether to invest in the South American country, the company should commission an evaluation of the **economic, political and ethical environment**. **Political risks** include the likelihood of imposition of exchange controls, prohibition of remittances, or confiscation of assets.

The value of this project may be higher than is immediately obvious if it opens up longer term opportunities in South American markets. Option pricing theory can be used to value these opportunities.

As regards the existing financial estimates, the **uncertainties** surrounding the cash flows can be quantified and understood better by carrying out **sensitivity analysis**, which may be used to show how the final result varies with changes in the estimates used.

8 Conclusion

On the basis of the evaluation carried out so far, the project is not worthwhile. However other opportunities not yet quantified may influence the final decision.

(b) **Circumventing restrictions**

Restrictions on the transfer of dividends from one country to another can be circumvented by two main methods:

(i) **Adjusting transfer prices** for inter-company sales of goods or services between the subsidiary and other group companies; and/or

(ii) **'Dressing up'** equity finance as debt finance.

Transfer prices

Under the heading of transfer prices, the following techniques can be used:

(i) **Increasing prices** for the **subsidiary's purchases** from the parent or other group companies
(ii) **Reducing** (or abolishing) prices for sales by the subsidiary to other group companies
(iii) **Charging the subsidiary** for head office **overhead and management charges**
(iv) **Charging the subsidiary** for **royalties and patents** on processes used

The government of the South American country would probably attempt to prevent these arrangements from being effective.

Loan finance

If the company had foreseen the possibility of **dividend restriction**, it could have arranged for the subsidiary to be financed mainly by an inter-company loan, with equity investment nominally small. All expected returns could then be paid as inter-company loan interest.

Bank as intermediary

A less obvious way of achieving the same objective is for the parent to **lend the major part** of its **investment** to an independent international bank, which then lends to the South American subsidiary. Returns would be paid as interest to the bank, which would in turn pay interest to the parent company.

Parallel loans

If these financing arrangements have not already been made by the time dividend restrictions are imposed, the subsidiary may try to **lend its cash surpluses** to the **parent** (interest free) or, if this is prevented, to **lend** to the **subsidiary** of **another company** needing funds in the South American country, with an arrangement that the parent receives a corresponding loan from the parent of the other company. This device is known as a **parallel loan** and is, in effect, a currency swap.

Question 2

(a)   **Interest rate futures**

Hedging

A future is an agreement on the future price of a variable. Hedging with futures offers protection against **adverse movements in the underlying asset**; if these occur they will more or less be offset by a gain on the futures market. The person hedging may be worried about **basis risk**, the risk that the futures price may move by a different amount from the underlying asset being hedged.

Terms

The **terms, sums involved and periods** are **standardised** and hedge inefficiencies will be caused by either having too many contracts or too few, and having to consider what to do with the unhedged amount.

Deposit

Futures require the payment of a **small deposit**; this transaction cost is likely to be lower than the premium for a tailored forward rate agreement or any type of option.

Timescale

The majority of futures are taken out to **hedge borrowing** or **lending** for short periods.

Interest rate options

Guaranteed amounts

The main advantage of options is that the buyer cannot lose on the interest rate and can take advantage of any favourable rate movements. An interest rate option provides the **right to borrow a specified amount** at a **guaranteed rate of interest**. On the date of expiry of the option the buyer must decide **whether or not to exercise his right to borrow**. He will only exercise the option if actual interest rates have risen above the option rate.

Premium cost

However a premium must be paid regardless of whether or not the option is exercised, and the **premium cost** can be quite **high**, high enough not to make an option worthwhile if interest rate movements are expected to be marginal.

Types of option

Options can be **negotiated directly** with the bank (over the counter, OTC) or traded in a standardised form on the LIFFE. **OTC options** will be preferable if the buyers require an option **tailored to their needs** in terms of maturity date, contract size, currency or nature of interest. **OTC options** are also generally more appropriate if the buyer requires a **long time** to maturity or a large contract size. **Traded options** will be more appropriate if the buyers are **looking for options** that can be **exercised at any time**, is looking for a **quick, straightforward** deal, or might want to sell the options before the expiry date if they are not required.

(b) **Hedging the borrowing rate using futures**

Setup

(i)   June contracts as looking to borrow in six months time

(ii)   Sell June futures as borrowing

(iii)   Number of contracts

$$\frac{£6.5\,million}{£500,000} \times \frac{6}{3} = 26 \text{ contracts}$$

(iv)   Tick size

$$(0.01\% \times \frac{3}{12} \times 500,000) = £12.50$$

Estimate closing futures price

June contract expires in 7 months

LIBOR is currently 4.5% (95.50)

June contract basis risk 95.50 − 95.29 = 21 ticks, difference between current and futures price

1 June 1 month to expiry $21 \times \frac{1}{7} = 3$ ticks

$\Rightarrow$ If LIBOR rises to 5.25% (94.75) 94.75 − 0.03 = 94.72

Outcome

The results of the hedge under cases (i) and (ii) are shown below.

(i)   **Futures market**

1 Dec: Sell 26 @	95.29
1 Feb: Buy 26 @	94.72
Tick movement: $\frac{opening\,rate - closing\,rate}{0.01}$	57
Profit/(Loss) 26 contracts × £12.50 × tick movement	18,525

(ii)   **Net outcome**

		£
Payment in spot market 5.25% × £6.5m × 6/12		(170,625)
Profit/(Loss) in futures market		18,525
Net cost of loan		(152,100)

Effective interest cost is 152,100 × 2 /6,500,000 = **4.68%**

However this rate is dependent on the assumption that **basis declines linearly**; this may not be the case if **basis risk exists**.

Hedging the borrowing rate using options

Setup

(i)   June as above

(ii)   Buy put options

(iii)   Consider all three prices

(iv)   Number of contracts 26

(v)   Tick size £12.50

(vi)   Option premium

95250: 26 × 18.5 × 12.5 = £6,013
95500: 26 × 28 × 12.5 = £9,100
95750: 26 × 40.5 × 12.5 = £13,163

Closing price

94.72 as above

Outcome

(i)   **Option market outcome**

	95250	95500	95750
Put option strike price (right to sell)	95.25	95.50	95.75
June futures price	94.72	94.72	94.72
Exercise option? (prefer to sell at highest price)	Yes	Yes	Yes
Gain (ticks)	53	78	103
Option outcome (26 × 12.50 × tick gain)	17,225	25,350	33,475

(ii)   **Net position**

	95250	95500	95750
	£	£	£
Actual interest cost (as above)	(170,625)	(170,625)	(170,625)
Value of option gain	17,225	25,350	33,475
Premium	(6,013)	(9,100)	(13,163)
Net cost of loan	(159,413)	(154,375)	(150,313)
Effective interest cost (Cost × 2/6.5m)	4.91%	4.75%	4.63%

The 95750 option is the preferred hedging method, as it has a lower interest cost than the future. If interest rates fall, the option can lapse or be sold.

(c)   **Forward market**

4,300,000/1.4632 = £2,938,764

Currency options

Set up

(i)   March

(ii)   Type of contract put as wish to buy $/sell £ with option contract in £

(iii)   Consider all three exercise prices

(iv)   Number of contracts

Number of contracts = $4,300,000 ÷Exercise price/Contract price

1.450: $\dfrac{2,965,517}{31,250}$ = 94.8 say 95 contracts

1.460: $\dfrac{2,945,206}{31,250}$ = 94.2 say 94 contracts

1.470: $\dfrac{2,925,170}{31,250}$ = 93.6 say 94 contracts

(v)   Tick size = 0.0001 × £31,250

= $3.125

(vi)   Premium cost

1.450: 95 × $\dfrac{1.56}{100}$ × 31,250 =46,312/1.4692 = £31,522

1.460: 94 × $\dfrac{1.99}{100}$ × 31,250 = 58,456/1.4692 = £39,788

1.470: 94 × $\dfrac{2.51}{100}$ × 31,250 = 73,731/1.4692 = £50,184

Closing prices

$1.4350/$1.4780

Outcome

(i)   **Options**

If the strike price is 1.4780, none of the options will be exercised.

If the strike price is 1.4350, all of the options will be exercised.

Futures price	1.4500	1.4600	1.4700
Strike price	1.4350	1.4350	1.4350
Tick gain	150	250	350
Outcome of option position			
No of contracts × 3.125 × tick gain	$44,531	$73,438	$102,813

(ii) **Net outcome**

	1.4500		1.4600		1.4700	
	1.4350	1.4780	1.4350	1.4780	1.4350	1.4780
	£	£	£	£	£	£
Spot market	(2,996,516)	(2,909,337)	(2,996,516)	(2,909,337)	(2,996,516)	(2,909,337)
4,300,000 ÷ 1.4350/1.4780						
Option outcome ÷ 1.4350	31,032	–	51,176	–	71,647	–
Premium	(31,522)	(31,522)	(39,788)	(39,788)	(50,184)	(50,184)
Outcome	(2,997,006)	(2,940,859)	(2,985,128)	(2,949,125)	(2,975,053)	(2,959,521)

All of these outcomes are worst than the forward contract. The spot price would need to weaken further for options to be the best hedge.

Alternative method – options

If strike price is $1.4350 all options will be exercised.

	1.4500	1.4600	1.4700
	£	£	£
Costs of option contracts (£31,250 × no of contracts)	(2,968,750)	(2,937,500)	(2,937,500)
Amount hedged on forward market:			
(Cost of option contracts × exercise price) − 4,300,000 / Forward rate	(4,304,687 − 4,300,000) / 1.4668	(4,288,750 − 4,300,000) / 1.4632	(4,318,125 − 430,000) / 1.4668
	3,195	(7,689)	12,357
Premium	(31,522)	(39,788)	(50,184)
	(2,997,077)	(2,984,977)	(2,975,327)

If the strike price is 1.4780, none of the options will be exercised.

	1.4500	1.4600	1.4700
	£	£	£
Spot market 4,300,000/1.4780	(2,909,337)	(2,909,337)	(2,909,337)
Amount required to fulfil forward contract / Spot rate	(4,304,687 − 4,300,000) / 1.4780	(4,288,750 − 4,300,000) / 1.4820	(4,318,125 − 4,300,000) / 1.4780
	(3,171)	7,591	(12,263)
Premium	(31,522)	(39,788)	(50,184)
Outcome	(2,944,030)	(2,941,534)	(2,971,784)

The conclusion remains the same.

(d) **Straddle option**

A straddle is made by **buying a put and a call** at the same time at the **same exercise price**. This provides **protection in times of exchange rate volatility** against exchange rate movements in either direction.

Because **two options** are **purchased, two premiums** will be **payable** (unlike with a collar where one option is purchased, one sold, and the two premiums are netted against each other.) The straddle will be profitable if the exchange rate is outside $1.46: £1 +/− the sums of the two premiums. (4.54 cents per pound) where a put option would suffice to cover exposure.

Straddles are suitable for **two-way exposures,** but would not be suitable for the **one-way exposure** in dollars that Autocrat has, where a simple put option will supply sufficient cover.

Question 3

(a)   The value of an option is made up of the following.

    (i)   The **intrinsic value of the option** which depends on the

        (1)   Share price
        (2)   Exercise price

    (ii)   The **time value of the option** which is affected by:

        (1)   **Time period to expiry**

Value of all options will increase with the length of the expiry period, because in this period the price of the underlying security has time to move and create a gain for the option holder. If the underlying security falls in value, the option holder makes no loss other than the initial premium cost.

        (2)   **Volatility of the underlying security**

Options on volatile securities will be more valuable than options on securities whose prices do not change much. This is because volatile securities will either show large increases or large decreases in value. The holder of call options will gain a lot from a large increase in the value of the security but will lose nothing if it falls in value.

        (3)   **General level of interest rates**

The intrinsic value of an in-the-money call option is equal to the share price minus the exercise price. If the option has time to run before expiry, the exercise price will not have to be paid until the option is exercised.

The option's value will therefore depend on the current share price minus the present value of the exercise price.

If interest rates increase, this present value will decrease and the value of the call option will increase.

(b)   (i)   Find (d_1) and (d_2)

$$d_1 = \frac{\ln(3.50/3.30) + (0.08 \times 0.25)}{\sqrt{0.12}\sqrt{0.25}} + (0.5 \times (\sqrt{0.12} \times \sqrt{0.25}))$$

$$= 0.4552 + 0.0866$$
$$= 0.5418$$

$$d_2 = 0.5418 - (\sqrt{0.12}\sqrt{0.25})$$
$$= 0.5418 - 0.1732$$
$$= 0.3686$$

    (ii)   Find $N(d_1)$ and $N(d_2)$ using normal distribution tables

$N(0.5418) = 0.5 + 0.2060 = 0.7060$
$N(0.3686) = 0.5 + 0.1438 = 0.6438$

    (iii)   Using the Black-Scholes formula

$$C_0 = (3.50 \times 0.7060) - ((3.30e^{-0.08 \times 0.25}) \times 0.6438)$$
$$= 2.4710 - 2.0825$$
$$= 38.85c$$

(c)   The main limitations of the Black-Scholes model are:

(i)   The model is **only designed** for the valuation of **European call options**.

(ii)   The basic model is based on the assumption that **shares pay no dividends**.

(iii)   The model assumes that there will be **no transaction costs**.

(iv)   The model assumes knowledge of the **risk-free rate of interest**, and also assumes the risk-free rate will be constant throughout the option's life.

(v)   Likewise the model also assumes accurate knowledge of the **standard deviation of returns**, which is also assumed to be constant throughout the option's life.

Question 4

Text references. Chapter 24.

Top tips. The key things you are looking out for in (a) are (i) The relationship between earnings and dividend – no obvious link between the growth rates, and (ii) The relationship between dividends and inflation – the growth rates pretty much match indicating the company is paying constant real dividends. Don't forget though to take the dividend per share.

It would be acceptable in (a) to carry out a single calculation for the changes in levels between 20X1 and 20X5, but carrying out the calculation year-on-year gives a clearer impression of what has been happening and what the company is trying to achieve.

(b) emphasises the importance of being aware of the identity and viewpoints of shareholders. In (c) the fourth root method is better than a simple average.

Easy marks. The limitations of the divided valuation model will get you some easy marks.

(a)   **Dividend policy**

	Post tax EPS Cents	Growth %	Dividend per share Cents	Growth %	Inflation %	Payout ratio %
20X0	47.9	–	19.2	–	–	40.1
20X1	51.3	7.1	20.1	4.7	5	39.2
20X2	55.2	7.6	20.9	4.0	4	37.9
20X3	55.9	1.3	21.5	2.9	3	38.5
20X4	61.9	10.7	22.2	3.3	3	35.9

The data indicates that TYR is paying a **constant real dividend per share**, the nominal dividend per share being adjusted by the rate of inflation. As a result its **payout ratio** has declined.

Assessment of dividend policy

One way in which we can measure the success of the dividend policy is to compare the changes in the share price of TYR with the changes in the market index.

	FT all share index	Growth %	Share price Cents	Growth %
20X0	2895	–	360	–
20X1	3300	14.0	410	13.9
20X2	2845	(13.8)	345	(15.9)
20X3	2610	(8.3)	459	33.0
20X4	2305	(11.7)	448	(2.4)

TYR's shares have out-performed the market over the last two years, so by this measure their dividend policy has been a success, despite the decline in payout ratio.

Limitations of analysis

However TYR's share price may be affected by **factors other than its dividend policy**. Modigliani and Miller have suggested that shareholders will be indifferent between dividends and capital gains. Even if this view is not accepted, in a **reasonably efficient market** shareholders may be influenced by the present value of expected **future cash flows** rather than **present dividend policy**. The fact that TYR is retaining a higher proportion of its earnings may signal to shareholders that it has plans for significant investment in profitable opportunities. Other influences on share prices include rumours of a takeover bid.

(b)   **Additional information**

   (i)   Information about the **preferences of shareholders**. The managers need to determine whether shareholders are **happy with current levels** or whether they would prefer a different level, and hence a **different level of capital gains**.

   (ii)   Information on **who holds the shares**. This will help determine shareholder preferences, as individual shareholders may have different objectives from institutional shareholders.

   (iii)   Forecasts of **possible changes in levels of taxation on dividends**. These may affect shareholder preferences between dividends and capital gains.

   (iv)   **Forecast levels of investment**. As indicated above, these will influence **shareholder attitudes** in a **reasonably efficient market**.

   (v)   Indications of the **level of market efficiency**. If the market is not efficient, it might (wrongly perhaps) see the failure of dividend increases to match earnings increases as a sign of weakness.

   (vi)   Information about the **movement** in the **share prices of other companies** in the **same industry** rather than the index of the market as a whole may be a better point of comparison for TYR's shares.

(c)   Average growth rate = $\left(\sqrt[4]{\dfrac{22.2 - 19.2}{19.2} + 1} \right) - 1 = 3.7\%$

   $P_0 = \dfrac{22.2\,(1.037)}{0.11 - 0.037}$

   = 315.3 cents

The actual price (448c) is greater than the price predicted by the dividend growth model, suggesting that the shares are currently overvalued.

Problems with dividend valuation model

The problems with using the dividend valuation model are that:

   (i)   It assumes that the pattern of **past dividend growth rates** will continue. As argued above, the company's increased retention rate may indicate that new investments are planned, ultimately affecting earnings and dividends. It may be better to value the company on the basis on **earnings per share** rather than dividends.

   (ii)   However if directors' expectations are too optimistic, it is possible that there will be **insufficient future projects** to **maintain the dividend stream**.

   (iii)   Growth rates have been solely determined by the **rate of inflation**, and if the current policy is continued, growth rates will change if inflation rates change.

(d)   Signalling is the use of dividend policy to indicate the future prospects of an enterprise. The market would like to value shares on the basis of underlying cash flows on the company's projects. However, this information is not readily available to investors but is known to the directors. As a result, the dividend declared can be interpreted as a sign from directors to shareholders about the strength of underlying project cash flows.

Investors usually expect a consistent dividend policy from the company, either a fixed or increasing dividend in money or real terms, or less commonly, a constant or increasing proportion of its equity as dividends.

A large rise or fall in dividends in any year can have a marked effect on the company's share price. A cut in dividends may be treated by investors as signalling that the future prospects of the company are weak. Thus the dividend which is paid acts, possibly without justification, as a signal of the future prospects of the company.

The signalling effect of the company's dividend policy may also be used by the management of a company which faces a possible takeover. The dividend level might be increased as a defence against the takeover. Investors may take the increased dividend as a signal of improved future prospects, thus driving the share price higher and thereby making the company more expensive for a potential bidder to take over.

Question 5

> **Text references.** Chapter 9 covers the portfolio theory calculations, Chapter 20 the political risk issues.
>
> **Top tips.** The limited number of marks available for (a) – nine calculations for six marks – indicates you are expected to do these quickly. Factors to consider in (b) and (c) include the limitations of the information you've been given, the political risk factors that you haven't been given, and the other factors that will determine investment strategy. The micro-macro distinction is important and stressed in the marking scheme.
>
> **Easy marks.** If you remembered which formulae to use, the calculations. 6 out of 6 is very achievable. If this question was a last resort and you didn't know how to do the calculations, the best place to start for the discussion is taking apart what you're given, before widening your discussion to consider what's not there.

(a)   Return $\bar{r}_p = x\bar{r}_a + (1-x)\bar{r}_b$

Risk $\sigma_p = \sqrt{\sigma_a^2 x^2 + \sigma_b^2 (1-x)^2 + 2x(1-x)\rho_{ab} \sigma_a \sigma_b}$ where ρ_{ab} is zero

Coefficient of variation = Risk/Return

Ammonia/Flassia

Return = $(0.5 \times 21) + (0.5 \times 18) = 19.5\%$

Risk = $\sqrt{(33)^2(0.5)^2 + (29)^2(0.5)^2} = 22.0\%$

Coefficient of variation = 22/19.5 = 1.13

Ammonia/Hracland

Return = $(0.5 \times 21) + (0.5 \times 28) = 24.5\%$

Risk = $\sqrt{(33)^2(0.5)^2 + (42)^2(0.5)^2} = 26.7\%$

Coefficient of variation = 26.7/24.5 = 1.09

Flassia/Hracland

Return = $(0.5 \times 28) + (0.5 \times 18) = 23\%$

Risk = $\sqrt{(29)^2(0.5)^2 + (42)^2(0.5)^2} = 25.5\%$

Coefficient of variation = 25.5/23 = 1.11

The Ammonia/Hracland investment has the lowest coefficient of variation, and hence the lowest risk in relation to return. However there is a insignificant difference between the three investments.

(b)   The analysis is of little use to Boster for the following reasons:

(i)   There is **no information** about **what data was used** in making the assessment and **how reliable** it is.

(ii)   The return on investment may be **dependent upon the form the investment** takes, whether Boster sets up a full subsidiary, enters into a joint venture and so forth, also in **what sectors** the investment is made.

(iii)   There are other political risk factors which should be considered. These include **economic performance**, **debt default**, **credit ratings**, **remittance restrictions** and **access to capital**, also the impact of global risk factors such as terrorism.

(iv)   The analysis only takes into account political risk whereas other risks, including economic risks such as **foreign currency risk,** should also be considered when investing.

(v)   Presumably a system(s) of weightings was used to calculate political risk. Any such system might well have been arrived at **subjectively**, and if based on past experience, might **not be a reliable guide for the future.**

(vi)   Another difficulty is that the weighting system is not comparing like items; **underlying conditions** such as cultural trends and social issues are being compared with the impact of events such as changes of government.

(vii)   Bosler should seek information about **other countries in the region.**

In addition the risk analysis should only be a part of the decision-making process which should also take into account **strategic factors** and **financing.**

(c)   **Assessment of political risk** often has two aspects:

(i)   Seeking information about the **macro factors** affecting the country

(ii)   Seeking information about the **micro factors** that will affect the specific industry or company. Asset security for example may be higher in industries in which governments will welcome outside investment.

Methods of obtaining information

(i)   **Obtaining views from other sources** on **macro factors**. For example Boster could seek the **views of individuals** with direct experience of the countries in question, such as academics, diplomats and journalists.

(ii)   **Obtaining Information** about the **micro factors** that have most impact on the industry(ies) in which Boster intends to invest by consultancy reports focusing on the relevant industry/region, also again views of individuals.

(iii)   **Obtaining evidence itself** by for example the directors visiting the country rather than just relying on second-hand reports and views.

(d)   There are various strategies that Boster can adopt to limit potential risk. These are :

(i)   **Negotiations with host government**

The aim of these negotiations is to obtain a concession agreement covering matters such as transfer of capital, remittances and products, access to local finance, government intervention and taxation and transfer pricing. The problem with concession agreements can be that the initial terms of the agreement may not be satisfactory subsequently.

(ii)   **Insurance**

In the UK the Export Credits Guarantee Department provides protection against various threats including nationalisation, currency conversion problems, war and revolution.

(iii)   **Financial management**

Boster could obtain guarantees from the government for the investment that can be enforced by the company if the government takes any unfavourable action.

(iv)   **Management structure**

Possible methods include joint ventures or ceding control to local investors and obtaining profits by management contract. If governments do intervene, then Boster may have to make use of the advantage it holds or to threaten withdrawal. The threat of expropriation may be reduced by negotiation or legal threats.

ACCA Professional Level

Paper P4

Advanced Financial Management

Mock Examination 3
Pilot paper

Question Paper	
Time allowed	
Reading and Planning Writing	**15 minutes** **3 hours**
Section A BOTH questions are compulsory and MUST be attempted **Section B** TWO questions ONLY to be attempted	
During reading and planning time only the question paper may be annotated	

**DO NOT OPEN THIS PAPER UNTIL YOU ARE READY TO START UNDER
EXAMINATION CONDITIONS**

Section A: BOTH questions are compulsory and MUST be attempted

1   You are the chief financial officer of Fly4000 a large company in the airline and travel business whose principal market base is in Europe and the Middle East. Its principal hub is a major Northern European airport and Fly4000 has a small holiday business through its partnership with a number of independent tour operators. It has a good reputation as a business carrier within its European market, earned through very high standards of punctuality and service. Following the recent disinvestment of associated interests and a joint venture, it has cash reserves of $860 million.

FliHi is a smaller airline which also has its centre of operations at the same airport as Fly4000. It has, since it was founded in 1988, developed a strong transatlantic business as well as a substantial position in the long and medium haul holiday market. In the year to 31 December 2005 its reported turnover was in $1.7 billion and its profit after tax for the financial year was $50 million. The company's net assets are $120 million and it has $150 million of long term loans on its balance sheet. It has recently expanded its fleet of wide bodied jets suitable for its expanding holiday business and has orders placed for the new Airbus 380 super-Jumbo to supplement its long haul fleet. FliHi has route licenses to New York and six other major US cities.

FliHi's cash flow statement for the current and preceding year is as follows:

FliHi Consolidated Cash Flow Statement (extract)
For the year ended 31 December 2005

	31 December 2005		31 December 2004	
	$m	$m	$m	$m
Net cash inflow from operating activities		210.0		95.0
Return on investment and servicing of finance				
Interest received	12.0		6.0	
Interest paid	(4.0)		(3.0)	
Interest element on finance leases	(6.5)		(4.0)	
		1.5		(1.0)
Taxation		(4.1)		(0.2)
Capital Expenditure		(120.2)		(75.0)
Acquisitions and disposals				
Proceeds from the sale of interest in joint ventures		10.0		15.0
Cash inflow before management of Liquid resources and financing		97.2		33.8
Management of liquid resources				
Decrease/(increase) in short term deposits		35.5		(32.2)
Financing				
Repayment of secured loans		(31.0)		(25.0)
Increase/(decrease) in cash for the year		101.7		(23.4)

There is no other airline of comparable size and business mix to Fly4000 although analysts regard Rover Airways as a useful comparator. The statement below contains market data relating to Rover Airways:

Key Fundamentals

Forward P/E*	11.00	Dividend Yield	0.00
Price to Book value of equity	1.25	1Yr Total Return (%)**	25.07
Price To Cash Flow	3.00	Beta**	2.00
1Yr Sales Growth	-1.67	1Yr EPS Growth	80.50

** Equity Market Cap £3bn

You also note the following:

The current risk-free rate is 4.5 per cent and the equity risk premium is estimated at 3.5 percent. The prevailing share price for Rover Airways is 290¢ per share and its P/E ratio is 10. The corporation tax rate for both companies is 30 per cent.

The gearing ratio for Rover Airways, expressed as total debt to total capital (debt plus equity), is 60 per cent and as total debt to equity is 150 per cent.

You may assume that:

1   FliHi has undertaken a consistent programme of reinvestment
2   The debt in both companies is not expected to be sensitive to market risk.

There has been considerable consolidation in the airline industry and you are advising your board of directors of Fly4000 on the value of FliHi as a potential target for acquisition. It is anticipated that over the longer term the domestic airline industry will settle down to a rate of growth in line with GDP growth in the European economy which stands at 4 per cent per annum (nominal). However, the current rates of growth for this company are likely to be sustained for the next five years before reverting to the GDP growth rate from the sixth year forward.

Required:

(a) **Estimate the current cost of equity capital for FliHi using the Capital Asset Pricing Model, making notes on any assumptions that you have made.**   (9 marks)

(b) **Estimate the expected growth rate of Flihi using the current rate of retention of free cash flow and your estimate of the required rate of return on equity for each of the next six years. Make notes on any assumptions you have made.**   (6 marks)

(c) **Estimate the value of Flihi on the basis of its expected free cash flow to equity, explaining the limitations of the methods you have used.**   (7 marks)

(d) **Write a brief report outlining the considerations your colleagues on the board of Fly4000 might bear in mind when contemplating this acquisition.**   (8 marks)

                                                                                                   (30 marks)

2   You are the finance director of Sydonics Engineering and expect that a bid to build a new plant in Southern France may be accepted in three months time. If the contract is accepted, an immediate capital spend of €150million will be required in three months and the company will receive a €75million grant from the European Development Fund in nine months time. The current Euro/sterling exchange rate is EUR 0.6900 to the pound.

Three month and nine month Euro LIBOR is 2.76563 per cent and 3.05194 per cent respectively. The three and nine month sterling LIBOR is 4.62313 per cent and 4.73031 per cent respectively. You have decided to hedge the exchange rate risk by the purchase of EUR/STERLING at-the-money options which have a contract size of 100,000 Euros. The monthly volatility of the Euro against sterling is 6.35 per cent. At the current exchange rate, the project has a net present value of £25 million at the company's cost of capital of 8.5 per cent.

The board of directors are concerned about the use of derivatives in managing the firm's treasury operations. They argue that the diversity of the firm's interests in Europe, the UK and the United States means that such hedging transactions are unnecessary.

Required:

(a) Prepare a memorandum, to be considered at the next board meeting, which summarises the arguments for and against foreign currency risk hedging and recommends a general policy concerning the hedging of foreign exchange risk.
(10 marks)
(Including 2 professional marks)

(b) Prepare a short report justifying your use of derivatives to minimise the firm's exposure to foreign exchange risk. Your report should contain:

(i) The likely option price for an at-the-money option, stating the circumstances in which the option would be exercised. You should use the Grabbe variant of the Black-Scholes model for both transactions, adjusted on the basis that deposits generate a rate of return of LIBOR.
(10 marks)

(ii) A calculation of the number of contracts that would be required to eliminate the exchange rate risk and the cost of establishing a hedge to cover the likely foreign currency exposure.
(4 marks)

(iii) A summary of the issues the board should bear in mind when reviewing a hedging proposal such as this, taking into account the limitations of the modelling methods employed and the balance of risk to which the firm will still be exposed to when the position is hedged.
(6 marks)

(30 marks)

Section B: TWO questions ONLY to be attempted

3   The board of directors of Jonas Chemical Systems Limited has used payback for many years as an initial selection tool to identify projects for subsequent and more detailed analysis by its financial investment team. The firm's capital projects are characterised by relatively long investment periods and even longer recovery phases. Unfortunately, for a variety of reasons, the cash flows towards the end of each project tend to be very low or indeed sometimes negative. As the company's new chief financial officer (CFO), you are concerned about the use of payback in this context and would favour a more thorough pre-evaluation of each capital investment proposal before it is submitted for detailed planning and approval. You recognise that many board members like the provision of a payback figure as this, they argue, gives them a clear idea as to when the project can be expected to recover its initial capital investment.

All capital projects must be submitted to the board for initial approval before the financial investment team begins its detailed review. At the initial stage the board sees the project's summarised cash flows, a supporting business case and an assessment of the project payback and accounting rate of return.

A recent capital investment proposal, which has passed to the implementation stage after much discussion at board level, had summarised cash flows and other information as follows:

Distillation Plant at the Gulf Refining Centre

| | Investment Phase | | Recovery Phase | |
	Cash flow (tax adjusted, nominal) $m	Cumulative Cash Flow $m	Cash flow (tax adjusted, nominal) $m	Cumulative Cash Flow $m
01 January 2006	(9.50)	(9.50)		
31 December 2006	(5.75)	(15.25)		
31 December 2007	(3.00)	(18.25)		
31 December 2008			4.5	(13.75)
31 December 2009			6.40	(7.35)
31 December 2010			7.25	(0.10)
31 December 2011			6.50	6.40
31 December 2012			5.50	11.90
31 December 2013			4.00	15.90
31 December 2014			(2.00)	13.90
31 December 2015			(5.00)	8.90

Cost of Capital	8%
Expected net present value ($m)	1.964
Net present value volatility ($m)	1.02
Internal rate of return	11.0%
Payback (years)	5.015

The normal financial rules are that a project should only be considered if it has a payback period of less than five years. In this case the project was passed to detail review by the financial investment team who, on your instruction, have undertaken a financial simulation of the project's net present value to generate the expected value and volatility as shown above. The board minute of the discussion relating to the project's preliminary approval was as follows:

31 May 2005 Agenda Item 6
New capital projects – preliminary approvals

Outline consideration was given to the construction of a new distillation facility at the Gulf Refining Centre which is regarded as a key strategic component of the company's manufacturing capability. The cash flow projections had been prepared in accordance with existing guidelines and there was some uncertainty with respect to capital build and future profitability. Mrs Chua (chief financial officer) had given approval for the project to come to the board given its strategic importance and the closeness of the payback estimate to the company's barrier for long term capital investment of five years. Mr Lazar (non-executive director) suggested that they would need more information about the impact of risk upon the project's outcome before giving final approval. Mr Bright (operations director) agreed but asked why the board needed to consider capital proposals twice. The board was of the view that what was needed was clearer information about each proposal and the risks to which they were exposed. The chair requested the CFO to provide a review of the company's capital approval procedures to include better assessment of the firm's financial exposure. The revised guidelines should include procedures for both the preliminary and final approval stages. Approved (Action CFO to report)

Required:

(a) Prepare a paper for the next board meeting, recommending procedures for the assessment of capital investment projects. Your paper should make proposals about the involvement of the board at a preliminary stage and the information that should be provided to inform their decision. You should also provide an assessment of the alternative appraisal methods.

(8 marks)

(b) Using the appraisal methods you have recommended in (a), prepare a paper outlining the case for the acceptance of the project to build a distillation facility at the Gulf plant with an assessment of the company's likely value at risk. You are not required to undertake an assessment of the impact of the project upon the firm's financial accounts.

(12 marks)

(Including 2 professional marks)

(20 marks)

4 You are the chief financial officer of a multinational company in the Do-It-Yourself (DIY) retail business based in the United States. Your company is considering a major expansion into the rapidly developing China market where one of your competitors has already established a presence with three stores, one in Beijing and two in Shanghai. After conducting local market research and a personal review, you are convinced that, although your competitor has successfully opened a new market in those cities, the demand is considerably greater than its ability to supply. Your overseas operations group report that they can open the appropriate supply chains and that, unlike the competition, you will be able to get a greater variety of goods onto the shelves and maintain supply at competitive prices.

Your assessment is that the company will need to raise the equivalent of $380 million of new finance over 10 years for this venture, of which $80 million could come from the company's existing liquid reserves. You have completed your review of the financial merits of the case and the project offers a rate of return in excess of 80 per cent. The company's current credit rating is assessed at AA–. Its total market capitalisation is $3.5bn, which includes a ten year syndicated loan of $0.5 billion due for retirement in three years. The balance of the firm's capital is in the form of common stock (ordinary shares) trading on the New York and Hong Kong markets.

You wish to undertake a preliminary review of the options for financing this project. Your assessment is that borrowing the money is a possibility but that the increase in gearing would drop your credit rating to A+. You believe that the likelihood of that happening is 60 per cent, with a further 40 per cent chance that the company's rating could fall to A. The company's existing weighted average cost of capital (tax adjusted at the company's average corporation tax rate of 30 per cent) is 6.8 per cent. The current nominal yield curve and credit spreads for the retail sector are shown below:

Exhibit 1: 30 year yield curve

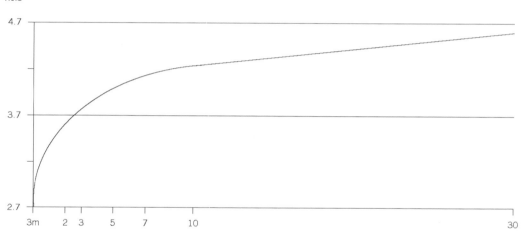

Exhibit 2: Yield spreads for retail sector (in basis points)

Rating	1yr	2yr	3yr	5yr	7yr	10yr	30yr
Aaa/AAA	4	8	12	18	20	30	50
Aa1/AA+	8	12	20	30	32	35	60
Aa2/AA	15	24	30	34	40	50	65
Aa3/AA–	24	35	40	45	54	56	78
A1/A+	28	37	44	55	60	70	82
A2/A	55	65	75	85	95	107	120

Required:

(a) Estimate the expected cost of capital for this project on the assumption that the additional finance is raised through a bond issue in the US market.

(10 marks)

(b) Draft a brief report for the board which outlines the alternative sources of finance that are potentially available for this project. Include, in your report, a brief discussion of the advantages and disadvantages and the likely impact of each alternative source upon the firm's cost of capital.

(10 marks)

(Including 2 professional marks)

(20 marks)

5   You have been appointed as the chief financial officer of a multimedia company which is financed by private equity. There is considerable public interest in the company and it continues a very rapid rate of growth under the leadership of its dynamic founder and chief executive officer, Martin Pickle. Martin Pickle owns over 30 per cent of the company's equity and has also loaned the business substantial sums to sustain its overseas development. The balance of the other investors consist of some small shareholdings held by current and past employees and the remainder is in the hands of a private equity company which is represented by two directors on the board.

You enjoy a substantial salary and package of other benefits. Your role description gives you overall responsibility to the board for the financial direction of the company, the management of its financial resources, direction and oversight of its internal control systems and responsibility for its risk management. After two months in the job you are called to a meeting with Martin Pickle and the company's non-executive chairman. In that time you have made significant progress in improving the financial controls of the business and the current year end, which is three weeks away, looks very promising. The company's underlying earnings growth promises to be in excess of 20 per cent and its cash generation is strong. The CEO tells you that he would like you to put together a plan to take the company to full listing as a first step to him undertaking a substantial reduction in his financial stake in the business. He tells you that this discussion must be confidential, as he expects that the market would react adversely to the news. However, he would like to see what could be done to make sure that the year end figures are as strong as possible. Given your performance, he also tell you that they would like to offer you a substantial incentive in the form of share options.

Required:

(a) **Prepare a board paper, describing the procedure for obtaining a listing on an international stock exchange such as the London or New York Stock Exchange.**
(6 marks)

(b) **Prepare a briefing note, itemising the advantages and disadvantages of such a step for a medium-sized company.**
(6 marks)
(Including 2 professional marks)

(c) **Discuss any ethical considerations or concerns you may have concerning this proposed course of action.**
(8 marks)

(20 marks)

Answers

DO NOT TURN THIS PAGE UNTIL YOU HAVE
COMPLETED THE MOCK EXAM

Question 1

Marks

30 marks distributed over four sections. Key numbers presented in the analysis must be contextualised and justified.

(a) **Estimate the current cost of equity capital for FliHi using the Capital Asset Pricing Model making notes on any assumptions that you have made**

Calculation of the asset beta for Rover Airways at 0.9756	2	
Regear for FliHi to 1.8294.	1	
Calculate FliHI's cost of equity at 10.90 per cent	2	
Notes on the assumptions relating to the CAPM	2	
Notes on the assumptions of more practical significance	2	
		9

(b) **Estimate the expected growth rate of this company using the current rate of retention of Free Cash Flow and your estimate of the required rate of return on equity for each of the next seven years. Make notes on any assumptions you have made.**

Calculation of the retention ratio as specified in the question as 0.58	2	
Estimate of the growth for the next six years (justifying the return on equity chosen)	2	
Assumptions embedded within the calculation of growth and Gordon's approximation	2	
		6

(c) **Value this company on the basis of its expected Free Cash Flow to Equity explaining the limitations of the methods you have used.**

Calculation and projection of the free cash flow to equity with explanations	2	
Discount these values at the rate of return on equity	2	
Calculate the present value of the perpetuity at 2011 with explanations	2	
Calculate the present value of the firm's equity	1	
		7

(d) **Write a brief report outlining the considerations your colleagues on the Board of Fly4000 might bear in mind when contemplating this acquisition.**

Discussion of synergies and their capture	2	
Examination of the risk exposure and the potential real options	3	
Review of the financing options	2	
Summary of valuation and recommendation of the next steps to the board of Fly4000	1	
		8
		30

(a) **FliHi cost of equity**

Since all three companies (Fly 4000, FliHi, Rover Airways) operate in the same sector it is reasonable to presume that they will all have the same asset beta.

Based on the information for Rover Airways we have

$\beta_e = 2.0$

D:E = 1.5:1.0 And so using

$$\beta_a = \beta_e \left(\frac{E}{E + D(1-T)} \right) + \beta_d \left(\frac{D(1-T)}{E + D(1-T)} \right)$$

and assuming zero systematic risk to the debt ($\beta_d = 0$), we have

$$\beta_a = 2.0 \left(\frac{1}{1 + 1.5(1 - 0.3)} \right) = 2 \times \frac{1}{2.05} = 0.9756$$

To obtain the equity beta (β_e) for FliHi we now need to re-gear based on the market values of FliHi's equity and debt. Since this information is not available we will use the book values as a proxy.

So using a rearrangement of the above formula to solve for β_e

$$\beta_e = \beta_a \left(\frac{E + D(1-T)}{E} \right) - \beta_d \left(\frac{D(1-T)}{E} \right)$$

and assuming again that $\beta_d = 0$, we have for FliHi

$$\beta_e = 0.9756 \times \left(\frac{120 + 150(1 - 0.3)}{120} \right) = 0.9756 \times \frac{225}{120} = 1.82925$$

Now, applying CAPM gives

$r_e = r_f + \beta(r_m - r_f) = 4.5 + 1.82925 \, (3.5) = 10.90\%$

Assumptions made in this calculation are:

- That we can use book values of equity and debt as proxy's for market values, this may be a reasonable assumption in a capital intensive business such as an airline, but certainly not in a service business where much of the value is in intangibles.

- All of the assumptions inherent in the theories of Modigliani and Miller whose gearing formulae we have applied, ie

  - Investors are rational and risk averse

  - Capital markets are perfect

  - Investors and companies can freely borrow at the same risk-free rate, hence individuals are indifferent between personal and corporate borrowings.

- All of the assumptions inherent in CAPM

  - Investors are rational and risk-averse

  - Investors are diversified

  - Capital markets are perfect, efficient and in equilibrium

  - All investors have the same expectations regarding the probability distribution of returns from each security

  - All investors can freely invest or borrow at the same risk-free rate

BPP
LEARNING MEDIA

- Specific assumption noted in the question that debt is not sensitive to market risk, ie $\beta_d = 0$.

  - That since all three companies operate in the same sector they will have the same asset beta, unless their operations are exactly the same this is unlikely to be true. Since it is a smaller company and will, therefore, be less internally diversified and at greater risk of default, perhaps a premium should be applied to its cost of capital through such variants of CAPM as the Fama and French 3 factor model.

(b) **FliHi growth rate**

We can estimate the growth rate (g) using

g = rb

Where

r = real return (after tax) on reinvested income/cash flows
b = proportion of profits/free cash retained and reinvested

Free cash flow to equity before reinvestment

	2005 $m	2004 $m
Operating cash flow	210.0	95.0
Net interest	1.5	(1.0)
Tax	(4.1)	(0.2)
FCFE (pre reinvestment)	207.4	93.8
Reinvestment	120.2	75.0
FCFE (part reinvestment)	87.2	18.8
b	0.58	0.80

These figures are clearly inconsistent and so we will use the most recent figures as indicative of the future, ie b = 0.58.

The rate of return on reinvested FCFE is harder to establish but, for a business in a competitive market where its shares are fairly valued, this should correspond to the return on equity (r_e) of 10.90%, giving

$g = r_b = 0.58 \times 10.9\% = 6.322\%$

Clearly this is substantially lower than the growth rate from 2004 to 2005 based on the FCFE calculated earlier, though this exceptional growth could be a function of higher reinvestments in earlier years that we are not assuming will continue into the future, and such growth appears unlikely to be sustainable in a highly competitive environment.

In conclusion, we expect future growth rates of:

Years	Growth	Comment
1-5	6.322%	Calculated above
6 onwards	4.000%	Assumption stated in question

The assumptions made here are as follows.

- Gordon's growth model can be validly applied based on the FCFE.
- That it is valid to use r_e as a proxy for r in a competitive business whose shares are fairly valued.
- That the shares of FliHi are fairly valued.
- That it is correct to use the reinvestment figure of 0.58 from 2005 as representative of the future.
- That the FCFE for 2005 are, indeed, typical, and likely to be repeated (subject to growth) in future years.
- That growth will be 4% from year 6.

(c)   **Value of FliHi**

Applying DVM ideas based on the 2005 FCFE post reinvestment of $87.2m, which represents a surrogate for the dividend that could be paid, we have

Time	Cash flow			DF	PV $
1	$d_1 = 87.2 \times 1.06322$	=	92.71	$\dfrac{1}{1.109}$	83.60
2	$d_2 = 87.2 \times 1.06322^2$	=	98.57	$\dfrac{1}{1.109^2}$	80.16
3	$d_3 = 87.2 \times 1.06322^3$	=	104.81	$\dfrac{1}{1.109^3}$	76.84
4	$d_4 = 87.2 \times 1.06322^4$	=	111.43	$\dfrac{1}{1.109^4}$	73.67
5	$d_5 = 87.2 \times 1.06322^5$	=	118.48	$\dfrac{1}{1.109^5}$	70.63
5	$E_5 =$	=	1,785.73	$\dfrac{1}{1.109^5}$	1,064.53
					1,449.43

Where E_5 is the share price at time 5 which can be calculated from the constant growth formulation of DCF as

$$E_5 = \frac{d_6}{r_e - g} = \frac{87.2 \times 1.06322^5 \times 1.04}{0.1090 - 0.04} = \frac{123.22}{0.0690} = 1,785.73$$

The assumptions made here are:

• The FCFE post reinvestment is a valued surrogate for the dividend payable.

• The growth pattern of dividends is correct and the FCFE is sustainable.

• The company is a going concern and will trade indefinitely into the future (the constant dividend growth model is a perpetuity).

• The required return of 10.9% will remain constant into perpetuity.

The limitations of our method hinge on the reality of the assumptions made. For example the 10.9% required was based (via CAPM) on a 4.5% risk-free rate and a 3.5% premium. It is most likely that these figures will vary as, say, the central bank charges interest rates in response to inflationary pressures. An interest rate of 4.5% is very low and may be expected to rise. Is a growth rate of 40% sustainable indefinitely into the future?

(d)   To: Whoever
        From: Chief financial officer
        Date: December 2005
        Subject: **Proposed acquisition of FliHi**

Having completed the divestment of various associated interests and joint ventures, we now have cash reserves of $860m. One of the alternative proposals for these funds is to partially finance the acquisition of FliHi, though the total cost of that acquisition may be of the order of $1,450m and hence require a further $590m finance. The factors I believe we should consider here, each of which I discuss below are:

• Strategic objectives
• Operating synergies
• Financial synergies
• Risk exposure
• Valuation

- Financing
- Other factors

Strategic objectives

A takeover should only be considered if it helps satisfy some strategic objectives of the business. Fly 4000's principal markets are in Europe and the Middle East from a Northern European hub. FliHi uses the same hub but has developed a strong transatlantic business as well as a substantial business in long-haul and medium-haul markets. As such, the business of FliHi is a good strategic fit with that of Fly 4000, allowing us to diversity into new markets.

In addition, FliHi is currently generating superior growth which helps to satisfy our strategic objective of achieving long-term growth in shareholder wealth.

Finally, from a strategic objective, the acquisition would provide defensive qualities since, as a larger more diversified operation, we would be able to compete more efficiently and effectively through offering a broader service range.

Operating synergies

Operating synergies that are likely to arise from a takeover would include:

- Revenue gains from being able to offer a broader range of flights, which is likely to enhance market share beyond that of the simple sum of the two entities.

- Cost savings and efficiency gains through the removal of any duplication (currently competition) between Fly 4000 and FliHi, resulting in planes operating with higher capacity loads.

- Revenue gains from the re-deployment of any planes released through this process.

- Cost savings from merging maintenance operations in our Northern European hub.

- Economies of scale with respect to fuel purchasing, in-flight catering, maintenance and ticketing operations.

Financial synergies

As a larger entity operating in a greater number of markets we are liable to be able to increase our borrowing capacity offering the opportunity for further expansion. In addition to this there may be tax benefits arising from how and when FliHi operates and the group structure it has.

Risk exposure

There is no reason why the market risk of our operations should be altered by this merger since both businesses operate in broadly the same sector.

We would need to recognise, however, that by increasing our geographical coverage we increase our exposure to overseas markets and exchange rates. There are obviously some diversification benefits to be gained from this, though we must also consider the associated risks, most particularly political risk, economic risk, exchange rate exposure (transaction risk, translation risk) as well as the increased risks of terrorism and the costs of anti-terrorist requirements especially on transatlantic markets.

Valuations

Our initial valuation of $1,450m for FliHi is a pessimistic figure based on our far from in-depth knowledge of the business based on FliHi's published accounts. This value has been established using discounted cash flow techniques.

Using a simple earnings based valuation gives a figure of $550m ($50m × 11.00) when applying the PE ratio of Power Airways to the earnings of FliHi. This is, however, very simplistic since the PE of 11.0 reflects the growth, management, prospects etc of Power, not FliHi which has achieved very strong recent growth.

As a result, a value in this range ($550m – $1,450m) would probably be achievable, but this is a very broad range and would be difficult to narrow without further information.

Financing

Clearly if we are at the lower end of this price range then we will need no additional finance to achieve this acquisition. If, however, we are at the higher end of this range then additional finance would be needed.

Consideration should be given to the practicability of raising new debt finance in the current economic circumstances for airlines, especially since many of our assets and many of those being acquired are subject to operating losses and cannot be offered as security for any debt.

On balance a combined cash plus shares offer would probably be advisable for this acquisition.

Other factors

- What is FliHi's reputation in its markets of operation?

- FliHi has recently expanded its fleet with the modern Airbus 380 super-Jumbo, which is ideal for its long-haul and transatlantic markets, with the result that little new investment is likely to be needed in aircraft.

- Are there any unique features to FliHi's offering such as limo's to and from the airport? We would need to assess the business case for any such items.

- Is FliHi dependent on a few key entrepreneurial individuals, and if so do we need to take any action to maintain their services?

- What is the age and experience of their flight crews and their industrial relations record?

Question 2

Marking scheme

	Marks
30 marks distributed over four sections.	

(a) **Prepare a memorandum, to be considered at the next board meeting, which summarises the arguments for and against forex risk hedging and recommends a general policy concerning the hedging of foreign exchange risk.**
Summary of the principle arguments for and against hedging with specific reference to the market perfection and reduction of cost of capital arguments. **4**
Clear policy recommendations focusing risk assessment, cost management, contracts and approvals, and monitoring. **4**
Quality of the memorandum assessed in terms of clarity, argumentation and persuasiveness. **2**

                                                                    10

(b) **Prepare a short report justifying your use of derivatives to minimise the firm's exposure to foreign exchange risk. Your report should contain:**

(i) **The likely option price for an at the money option stating the circumstances in which the option would be exercised (you should use the Grabbe variant of the Black-Scholes model for both transactions adjusted on the basis that deposits generate a rate of return of LIBOR).**

Correct calculation of d1 and d2 using the forward and spot rates as specified	5	
Calculation of N(x) from the tables given	1	
Correct calculation of the currency call	2	
Correct calculation of the currency put	2	
		10

(ii) **A calculation of the number of contracts that would be required to eliminate the exchange rate risk and the cost of establishing a hedge to cover the likely FOREX exposure.**

Calculation of the number of contracts for the 3 month hedge	2	
Calculation of the number of contracts for the 9 month hedge	2	
		4

(iii) **A summary of the issues the board should bear in mind when reviewing a hedging proposal such as this taking into account the limitations of the modelling methods employed and the balance of risk to which the firm will still be exposed when the position is hedged.**

Cost of the hedge and identification of alternatives	2	
Problems of establishing a perfect hedge (contract size)	2	
Understanding demonstrated of the nature of basis risk and how it is influenced by timing.	2	
		6
		30

(a) **Memorandum: Hedging Foreign Exchange Risk**

Foreign exchange risk exposure is driven by a mismatch of currency trade flows and the variability of the exchange rates. The volatility of the Euro against sterling is 22% (annualised). This indicates significant value at risk in any forward commitment to Euros and must be managed carefully.

For capital flows the ultimate target must be to match currency assets and liabilities. Hedging is costly. The expenses associated with establishing a treasury function and developing the in-house expertise can be considerable. Hedging through derivative contracts can be avoided can be avoided by the creation of internal hedging arrangements whereby finance is raised in the country of operations. This matches the borrowing costs with the revenue streams.

The firm's exposure to exchange rate volatility which is a market wide phenomenon can be controlled by hedging. The use of hedging would lead to a reduction in the form's beta and its cost of capital. Another benefit of hedging through the use of derivative contracts is that it allows us to manage uncertain risk exposure through the use of options contrast.

Hedging FOREX risk using derivatives can be expensive especially when exposure is uncertain. Where the exposure is certain, the use of futures or forward contracts can eliminate a large element of the risk at a much lower cost. The policy to hedge against FOREX will depend upon:

- The magnitude of the risk exposure (the high volatility and long-term exposure, as in this case, creates a high hedging cost). Value at risk may be an appropriate method for measuring the likely financial exposure.

- The materiality of the exposure in terms of the magnitude of the sums involved.

- The extent to which the risk can be mitigated by matching agreements.

- The extent to which the exposure has crystallised. If it is uncertain FOREX options allow the hedging of the downside risk but at a high cost.

A general policy concerning the hedging of foreign exchange risk should identify the principles which should be followed to cover:

- **Risk assessment**

  This involves the assessment of the likelihood and impact of any risk on the financial position of the firm. Derivative positions can be highly geared and this may expose the firm to high liabilities. It is recommended that derivatives should only be used for the management of specific risks and that no speculative or uncovered position should be taken.

- **Cost of hedging**

  This includes all direct costs as well as costs related to management time in establishing positions and operating the internal control procedures required when derivatives are used to hedge against risk. It is recommended that hedging costs are minimised to an agreed percentage of the value of risk through the unhedged position.

- **Contract and approval procedures**

  For both OTC and exchange traded products it is necessary to establish a clearly defined approval process with clear lines of responsibility and sign off on contracts (up to and including board level). It is recommend that the board appoint a risk management committee to review and monitor all hedging contracts where the value at risk is in excess of an agreed amount. The firm will also need to establish policies with respect to the legal aspects of the contracting process.

- **Hedging monitoring**

  It is necessary to establish a policy relating to the monitoring of all derivative positions and to stipulate the conditions under which any given position will be reversed. It is recommended that the risk management committee actively monitor all open positions.

(b)   To: Whoever
      From: Finance director
      Date: December 2006
      Subject: **Foreign Exchange Hedging with Derivatives**

In relation to hedging foreign exchange risk with derivatives I lay out the following:

- Likely option prices for at the money options.

- An assessment of the number of contracts needed for this hedge.

- A summary of the issues the board need to consider in reviewing the proposed hedge.

(i) **Option pricing**

The Grabble variant of the Black-Scholes model that can be used for pricing currency options is:

$C = [FN(d_1) - XN(d_2)]e^{-rt}$

$P = [XN(-d_2) - FN(-d_1)]e^{-rt}$

$$d_1 = \frac{\ln\left(\dfrac{F}{X}\right) + 0.5\sigma^2 t}{\sigma\sqrt{t}}$$

$d_2 = d_1 - \sigma\sqrt{t}$

Where

- F = currency forward price at the exercise date
- X = exercise price
- r = domestic interest rate (pa)
- t = time to exercise (years)
- σ = volatility of rates (pa)

There are two expiry dates we need to consider, 3 months where we wish to have a call option to allow us to buy €150m, and 9 months where we want to put option on €75m.

Relevant inputs are	3 months	9 months
Spot rate (X)	0.6900	0.6900
Sterling LIBOR	4.62313	4.73031
Euro LIBOR	2.76563	3.05194

3 month forward rate $= 0.69 \times \dfrac{(1 + 0.0462313 \times \frac{3}{12})}{(1 + 0.0276563 \times \frac{3}{12})} = 0.6932$

9 month forward rate $= 0.69 \times \dfrac{(1 + 0.0473031 \times \frac{9}{12})}{(1 + 0.0305194 \times \frac{9}{12})} = 0.6985$

Monthly volatility of exchange rates $= 6.35\%$, hence

Annual volatility $= 6.35\% \times \sqrt{12}$ $= 22.00\%$

Hence the inputs are:

	3 months	9 months
F	0.6932	0.6985
X (at the money)	0.6900	0.6900
r	4.62313%	4.73031%
t	0.25 yrs	0.75 yrs
σ	22.00%	22.00%

3 month call

$$d_1 = \frac{\ln\left(\dfrac{F}{X}\right) + 0.5\sigma^2 t}{\sigma\sqrt{t}} = \frac{\ln\left(\dfrac{0.6932}{0.6900}\right) + 0.5 \times 0.22^2 \times 0.25}{0.22 \times \sqrt{0.25}} = 0.0971$$

$d_2 = d_1 - \sigma\sqrt{t} = 0.0971 - 0.22 \times \sqrt{0.25} = -0.0129$

$N(d_1) = N(0.0971) \approx N(0.10) = 0.5000 + 0.0398 = 0.5398$

$N(d_2) = N(-0.0129) \approx N(-0.01) = 0.5000 - 0.0040 = 0.4960$

$C = [0.6932 \times 0.5398 - 0.6900 \times 0.4960] \times e^{-0.0462313 \times 0.25} = 0.03158$ or 3.158p

ie a three month call option will cost 3.158p per €1 or £3,158 per contract.

9 month put

$$d_1 = \frac{\ln\left(\dfrac{F}{X}\right) + 0.5\sigma^2 t}{\sigma\sqrt{t}} = \frac{\ln\left(\dfrac{0.6985}{0.6900}\right) + 0.5 \times 0.22^2 \times 0.25}{0.22 \times \sqrt{0.75}} = 0.1595$$

$$d_2 = d_1 - \sigma\sqrt{t} = 0.1595 - 0.22 \times \sqrt{0.75} = -0.0310$$

$$N(-d_1) = N(-0.1595) \approx N(-0.16) = 0.5000 - 0.0636 = 0.4364$$

$$N(-d_2) = N(+0.0310) \approx N(+0.03) = 0.5000 + 0.0120 = 0.5120$$

$$P = [0.6900 \times 0.5120 - 0.6985 \times 0.4364] \times e^{-0.0473031 \times 0.75} = 0.04677 \text{ or } 4.677p$$

ie a nine month put option will cost 4.677p per €1 or £4,677 per contract.

(ii) When using options to reduce or avoid risk there are two alternative strategies we can adopt, protection and hedging. Protection seeks to limit losses whilst retaining the opportunity to make a profit, and the number of options needed here would be.

$$\text{Number of contracts} \quad \frac{\text{Value of exposure}}{\text{Value of one contract}}$$

Hedging, on the other hand, seeks to eliminate loss potential but, as a consequence, must give up the profit potential and is achieved by taking account of the option delta (delta hedging) as follows.

$$\text{Number of contracts} = \frac{\text{Value of exposure}}{\text{Value of one contract}} \times \frac{1}{\text{option delta}}$$

The option delta being $N(d_1)/N(-d_1)$ for calls and puts respectively.

To eliminate exchange risk we need to delta hedge, hence

$$\text{No. of 3 month calls} = \frac{150m}{100,000} \times \frac{1}{0.5398} = 2,789$$

$$\text{No. of 9 month puts} = \frac{75m}{100,000} \times \frac{1}{0.4367} = 1,719$$

Cost of hedge

Contract	No.	Unit cost £	Total cost £
3 month calls	2,788	3,158	8,804,504
9 month puts	1,179	4,677	8,039,763
			16,844,267

(iii) Issues to bear in mind in respect of the hedging proposal are:

- Options can be used to protect against downside risk, leaving the upside available (unlike hedging with futures)

- Options can be used to hedge out all risk (delta hedging)

- The cost of any protection or hedging strategy can be very high, here we have a £16.8m cost to hedge a net payment of €75m

- Options are very useful if the exposure is uncertain, eg pre-contract since they give the right but not the obligation to buy or to sell.

- Given the fixed contract sizes (here €100,000) it may not always be possible to arrange the exact number of contracts needed, especially if delta hedging

- Since the options are European style and can only be exercised at expiry, we will be exposed to basis risk if the cash flows materialise earlier than is currently envisaged.

Question 3

Marks

(a) Prepare a paper for the next Board meeting recommending procedures for the assessment of capital investment projects. Your paper should make proposals about the involvement of the Board at a preliminary stage and the information that should be provided to inform their decision. You should also provide an assessment of the alternative appraisal methods.

Clear definition of a two stage process for Board involvement in capital expenditure decisions — 2

Recommendation for the stage 1 appraisal procedure and metrics focusing on the role of payback and viable alternatives — 3

Stage 2 appraisal focusing on the business plan, value and accounting impact and cash recovery. — 3

8

(b) **Using the appraisal methods you have recommended in (a) prepare a paper outlining the case for acceptance of the project to build a distillation facility at the Gulf plant with an assessment of the company's likely value at risk. You are not required to undertake an assessment of the impact of the project upon the firm's financial accounts.**

Calculation of the project VAR and assessment of its significance — 4

Estimation of the potential value impact using MIRR and the assumptions that underpin it. — 3

Estimation of the potential cash recovery using procedures recommended in (a) — 3

Quality and persuasiveness of the written report — 2

12
20

(a) **Board Paper Presenting Proposal Procedures for Large Capital Expenditure Projects.**

This paper proposes revised guidelines for the board approval of large capital investment projects. The current two stage process of preliminary and final approval serves an important role in ensuring that any initial concerns of the board in terms of strategic fit and risk are brought to the attention of the Financial Appraisal Team. The two stage process would consider:

Stage 1

- Business proposal including assessment of strategic requirement, business fit and identified risks.

- Outline financial appraisal to include capital requirement, mode of financing, expected net present value, modified internal rate of return and project duration.

- It is recommended that conventional payback is dropped because it ignores the cost of finance and the magnitude of post payback cash flows. Duration is recommended as this measures the time required to recover half of the project's weighted average present value.

Stage 2

- A proposed business plan must be presented giving the business case with an assessment of strategic benefits, risks, finalised capital spend and capital sources.

- A value impact assessment giving a NPV calculation supported by a calculation of the project value at risk. The net present value of the project represents our best estimate of the likely impact of the investment on the value of the firm.

  This is the key statistic from the capital market perspective in that, unless we are assured that the project NPV is positive, the investment will reduce and not enhance the value of the firm. This net present value calculation should be supported by a modified internal rate of return which measures the additional economic return of the project over the firm's cost of capital where intermediate cash flows are reinvested at that cost of capital. In a highly competitive business the reinvestment assumption implicit in the MIRR is more realistic than that assumed with IRR where intermediate cash flows are assumed to be reinvested at the IRR. This may be satisfactory for near-the-money projects but is far less satisfactory for projects which offer high levels of value addition to the firm.

- An accounting impact assessment including the differential rate of return on capital employed and a short term liquidity assessment. Although positive NPV projects are value enhancing, they may not do so in ways that are readily apparent in the financial reports. To manage investor expectations effectively the firm needs to be aware of the impact of the project on the firm's reported profitability and this is most accurately reflected by the differential rate of return measure. Accounting rate of return as normally calculated does not examine the impact of the project on the financial position of the firm but is restricted to the rate of return the investment offers on the average capital employed.

- An assessment of the project duration. This project, for example, reveals a duration of 4.461 years (Appendix 2) which is the mean time over which half of the project value is recovered. This is more useful than the other liquidity based measures especially when used as a relative as opposed to an absolute measure of the cash recovery. Cash recovery assumes that the future project cash flows are achieved at a constant rate over the life of the project.

(b) The proposed business case concludes that this is a key strategic investment for the firm to maintain operating capacity at the Gulf Plant. The financial assessment is detailed in the Appendix to this report (excluding an assessment of impact of the project on the financial reports of the firm).

(i) The net present value of this project calculated using a discount rate of 8% gives a value of $1.965 million (Appendix 3). The volatility attaching to the net present value of $1.02 million (given) indicates that there is (Z) standard deviations between the expected net present value and zero as follows:

$$Z = \frac{1.965 - 0}{1.02} = 1.9265$$

This suggests that this project has a 97.3 per cent probability that it will have a positive net present value or conversely a 2.7 per cent probability of a negative net present value.

The project value at risk relies upon an assessment of the number of years that the project cash flow is at risk (10 years), the annual volality ($1.02m) and the confidence level required by the firm. The formula for the project VaR is:

Project VaR = $\phi \sigma \sqrt{t}$

At the 98% level $\phi = 1.645$ giving

Project VaR = $1.645 \times \$1.02m \times 3.162 = \$5.3$ million

This assumes a 95% confidence level, at 99% the project VaR is $7.51 million. This value reflects the fact that the capital invested is at risk for ten years and assumes that the volality of the project is fairly represented by the volatility of its net present value.

(ii) **Project return**

The internal rate of return is given as 11.0%. The modified internal Rate of Return is calculated by

- Projecting forward the cash flows in the recovery stage of the project at 8% to future value of $41.7983 million. (Appendix 4)

- Discounting back the investment phase cash flows to give a present value of the investment of $17.3955 million. (Appendix 1)

The Modified Internal Rate of Return is therefore:

$$\text{MIRR} = \sqrt[10]{\frac{41.7983}{17.3955}} - 1 = 0.09162 \text{ or } 9.162\%$$

This rate suggests that the margin on the cost of capital is rather small with only a 1.162% premium for the strategic and competitive advantage implied by this project

(iii) **Project liquidity**

With a present value of the recovery phase of $19.3607 million and of the investment phase of $17.3955 million this suggests that the project will have recovery period of:

$$\text{Recovery} = 2 + \frac{17.3955}{19.3607} \times 8 = 9.1879 \text{ years}$$

In practice the actual recovery is shorter than this because the expected cash in flows occur earlier rather than later during the recovery phase of the project. The above calculation effectively assumes that the recovery cash flows arise evenly through the recovery period. The actual discounted payback period is just over 6 years. (Appendix 5)

The project duration of 4.461 years (Appendix 2) reveals that the project is more highly cash generative in the early years notwithstanding the two year investment phase.

In summery, the analysis confirms that this project is financially viable as it will be value adding to the firm. There is, however, substantial value at risk given the volatility of the net present value quoted. In terms of return, the premium over the firm's hurdle is small at 1.162% and any significant deterioration in the firms cost of capital would be damaging to the value of this project. The liquidity statistics reveal that the bulk of the project's cash returns are promised in the earlier part of the recovery phase and that value invested in the project should be recovered by year six. Taking this into account acceptance is recommended to the board.

Appendix

Note: All calculations have used the discount factor tables. If formulae are used unrounded on a calculator slightly different figures would arise.

1   **PV of investment/base**

Time	Cash flow $m	DF	PV $m
0	(9.50)	1.000	(9.5000)
1	(5.75)	0.926	(5.3245)
2	(3.00)	0.857	(2.5710)
			(17.3955)

2   **PV and duration of recovery phase**

The recovery phase duration is calculated by multiplying the present value of the cash recovered in each year by the relevant time from project commencement. The sum of the weighted years give the recovery phase duration.

Time	Cash flow	DF	PV @	tPV
t	$m		8%	
3	4.50	0.794	3.5730	10.7190
4	6.40	0.735	4.7040	18.8160
5	7.25	0.681	4.9372	24.6860
6	6.50	0.630	4.0950	24.5700
7	5.50	0.583	3.2065	22.4455
8	4.00	0.540	2.1600	17.2800
9	(2.00)	0.500	(1.0000)	(9.0000)
10	(5.00)	0.463	(2.3150)	(23.1500)
	27.15		19.3607	86.3725

$$\text{Project duration} = \frac{\text{Sum of time weighted present value of recovery phase}}{\text{Present value of recovery phase}}$$

$$\text{Project duration} = \frac{86.3725}{19.3607} = 4.461 \text{ years}$$

3   **PV of project**

	$m
PV investment phase	(17.3955)
PV recovery phase	19.3607
	1.9652

4   **TV if recovery phase cash flow**

$PV \times (1+r)^n$ = TV
19.3607×1.08^{10} = 41.7983

5   **Discounted payback period**

Time	PV	Cumulative PV
	$m	$m
0	(9.5000)	(9.5000)
1	(5.3245)	(14.8245)
2	(2.5710)	(17.3955)
3	3.5730	(13.8225)
4	4.7040	(9.1185)
5	4.9372	(4.1813)
6	4.0950	(0.0863)
7	3.2065	3.1202
8	2.1600	5.2802
9	(1.0000)	4.2802
10	(2.3150)	1.9652

Question 4

		Marks

(a) **Estimate the expected cost of capital for this project on the assumption that the additional finance is raised through a bond issue in the US market.**

	Marks	
Estimation of the current cost of debt capital at 4.324 per cent	3	
Calculation of the existing cost of equity capital at 7.48 per cent	2	
Ungearing and regearing the cost of equity capital using M&M proposition 2	3	
Calculation of the revised weighted average cost of capital and comment thereon	2	
		10

(b) **Draft a brief report for the board outlining the alternative sources of finance that are potentially available for this project including a brief discussion of their advantages and disadvantages and the likely impact upon the firm's cost of capital of each of the alternatives that you consider.**

	Marks	
Note of the theoretical issues in the selection of finance source (M&M, pecking order theory)	2	
Clear description of the potential sources of capital within the context of the Chinese economy, regulation and capital market	2	
Evaluation of the likely advantages and disadvantages of the principal sources of finance	2	
Discussion of the risk management strategies available	2	
Professional marks	2	
		10
		20

(a) **Current Financing**

Debt (3 year)

	%
Yield from yield curve	3.80
Spread of AA – debt	0.40
Cost of debt k_d	4.20

Finance structure	Current $bn	Now $bn
Equity	3.0	3.0
Debt – 3 year	0.5	0.5
– 10 year	–	0.3
	3.5	3.8

WACC and cost of equity

Current WACC = 6.8%

Now

$$\text{WACC} = \frac{E}{V} \times k_e + \frac{D}{V} \times k_d(1-T)$$

$$6.8 = \frac{3.0}{3.5} \times k_e + \frac{0.5}{3.5} \times 4.2 \times 0.7$$

$$6.8 = \frac{3.0}{3.5} \times k_e + 0.42$$

$$6.38 = \frac{3.0}{3.5} \times k_e$$

$$k_e = 6.38 \times \frac{3.5}{3.0} \times 7.443\%$$

Ungeared cost of equity

Since the proposed finance will alter the gearing level, the approach is to:

- Ungear from the current level to get the ungeared cost of equity.
- Re-gear to the new debt level.

Now using Modigliani and Miller we have:

$$k_e = k_u + (k_u - k_d) \times \frac{D}{E} \times (1-T)$$

$$k_e = k_u + k_u \times \frac{D}{E} \times (1-T) - k_d \times \frac{D}{E} \times (1-T)$$

$$k_e = k_d \times \frac{D}{E} \times (1-T) = k_u \left(1 + \frac{D}{E}(1-T)\right)$$

And so

$$7.443 + 4.20 \times \frac{0.5}{3.0} \times (1-0.30) = \left(k_u \left(1 + \frac{0.5}{3.0} \times (1-0.30)\right)\right)$$

$$7.933 = 1.1167\, k_u$$

$$k_u = \frac{7.933}{1.1167} = 7.104\%$$

New cost of debt

Following the new issue there is a 60% chance the credit rating will fall to At and a 40% chance it will fall to A. For the 3 and 10 year bands we have:

		3 year	10 year
Spread	– A+	0.440	0.700
	– A	0.750	1.070
	– 60:40	0.564	0.848
Yield from yield curve		3.800	4.200
Yield		4.364	5.048

Term	Value $m	Cost %	Weight	Weighted %
3 years	0.5	4.364	⅝	2.7275
10 years	0.3	5.048	⅜	1.8930
	0.8			4.6205

Re-gearing

$$k_e \;=\; k_u + (k_u - k_d) \times \frac{D}{E} \times (1 - T)$$

$$k_e \;=\; 7.104 + (7.104 - 4.6205) \times \frac{0.8}{3.0} \times 0.7 = 7.5676$$

New WACC

$$\text{WACC} \;=\; 7.5676 \times \frac{3.0}{3.8} + 4.6205 \times \frac{0.8}{3.8} \times 0.7 = 6.655\%$$

(b) **Briefing note on alternative sources of finance**

The choice of finance is party down to the cost and availability of various sources and partly down to the method the company chooses to hedge its FOREX exposure.

Ignoring foreign exchange considerations, the weighted average cost of capital suggest that the firm should increase its gearing to capture further tax shield effects which are not currently being offset by increased default risk. Thus debt finance should be preferred to equity finance. Raising $300 million of debt by bond issue is at the low end of the scale for a new debt issue of this type, although it may be possible to arrange a syndicated issue. The issue costs in terms of commission and underwriting fees are likely to be high. If finance is raised on the US market it will be necessary to consider entering into a swap arrangement to hedge against the currency risk for the ten year term. Finding a swap of this type would require the services of a financial institution specialising in such transactions.

Alternatively, it may be possible to raise finance directly in China. This has the benefit that this would eliminate the need to consider methods of hedging against currency risk. However, as with any emerging market, there are risks associated with inward investment and capital entry. These risks may be sufficient to raise the overall risk assessment and as a result the advantages of increased gearing mentioned above may not be realised in practice. In addition, given that Do-it-yourself is a US based company the cost of debt finance is likely to be higher than if it was raised in the US. The issue costs associated with a Chinese bond issue are likely to be as high as those for the US market.

A third source available would be to take out a loan in China to finance the project. Once again, this would avoid the need to consider entering into any hedging arrangements to reduce foreign exchange risks. However, given the lack of business history and performance in China the company is likely to be charged a premium for the debt finance. In addition, the lending institution may also insist upon a guarantee from the US company. The last two sources have the advantage of matching the borrowing and income flows and hence eliminating foreign currency exposure risk. Any appreciation in the Chinese currency, however, would increase the dollar value of the translated debt in the firm's balance sheet. If the borrowing is used to purchase matching assets in China then the translation risk is mitigated along with the transaction risk.

Final source of debt finance is on the sale and leaseback of assets. This could be either by the sale and leaseback of existing assets in the US or by the sale and leaseback of new assets purchased for the operation in China. If the assets are not owned but leased or rented then translation effects will impact upon the balance sheet and may be misread by the market. There are reporting implications for reporting under FASB 13 depending upon whether the leases are financing or operating leases.

Other sources of finance would be to raise equity capital by a rights or new issue. This would have the effect of increasing the weighted average cost of capital and would not provide any additional benefits of the tax shield. Finally, the finance can be raised by reducing the dividend payment policy and thereby using retained cash to finance part of the project. The change in the dividend policy is unlikely to be viewed favourably and could cause problems in the future.

Question 5

			Marks
(a)	**Prepare a board paper describing the procedure for obtaining a listing on an international stock exchange such as the London Stock Exchange.**		
	Outline of the three step procedure: registration, listing and admission to trading (2 marks for each step)	6	
			6
(b)	**Prepare a briefing note itemising the advantages and disadvantages of such a step for a medium sized company.**		
	Note of the advantages: capital market access, reputation effects	2	
	Note of the disadvantages: compliance costs, vulnerability to takeover, public scrutiny	2	
	Well written briefing note weighing the advantages and disadvantages and focusing on the judgements that the board would be required to make	2	
			6
(c)	**Discuss any ethical considerations or concerns you may have concerning this proposed course of action.**		
	Identification of the principal ethical issues involved	2	
	Note on the issue of transparency and the protection of minority rights	2	
	Discussion of alternative ways that the CFO could proceed and the ethical implications of each	2	
	Commentary on the ethical issues involved in earnings management	2	
			8
			20

(a) **Board Paper: Procedure for obtaining a listing on an International Stock Exchange**

Obtaining a listing on an international stock exchange such as the London or New York stock exchange consists of satisfying requirements in three broad areas; namely legal, regulatory and compliance.

A company must ensure that it is entitled to issue shares to the public as opposed to an issue by private treaty. In the UK a firm seeking a listing on the London Stock Exchange must register as a public limited company. This requires a change in the memorandum and articles of the company agreed by the existing shareholders at a special meeting convened for the express purpose of agreeing this change, and satisfying certain other requirements such as a minimum issued share capital of £50,000.

The company must meet the regulatory requirements of the Listing Authority which is part of Financial Services Authority in the UK. These regulatory requirements impose minimum size restrictions on a company and other conditions concerning length of time trading. Once these requirements are satisfied the company is placed on an official list and is allowed to make an initial public offering of its shares.

Once the company is on the official list it must then seek approval from the Stock Exchange to allow its shares to be traded. In principal, any company can seek a listing on any exchange where shares are traded. In practice, however, the exchanges such as the London Stock Exchange impose strict requirements which invariably mean that the applicant company will need the services of a sponsoring firm specialising in this area. This tends to be costly and therefore prohibitive for all but the larger companies. The restrictions (and costs) of obtaining a listing on a junior market (eg AIM in the UK) may be lower.

(b)   **Advantages and disadvantages of obtaining a public listing**

For a medium sized firm, the principal advantage of obtaining a public listing is the additional sources of finance available. A listed company would have access to equity capital from both institutional and private investors, and the sums that can be raised are usually much greater than through private equity sources. In addition, the presence of a firm as a limited company on a major exchange, such as the London Stock Exchange enhances the credibility of the firm both to potential investors and to the general public as it has opened itself to a much greater degree of public scrutiny than a privately financed firm.

The disadvantages are significant; the distributed shareholding places the firm in the market for investors seeking corporate control and also increases the likelihood that the firm will be subject to a takeover bid. The higher degree of public scrutiny imposes a significant regulatory burden on the firm as it must comply with a range of disclosure requirements and financial accounts must be prepared in accordance with relevant accounting standards. In the UK, this means in accordance with IFRS and the relevant GAAP as well as the Companies Acts. Under the rules of the London Stock Exchange companies must also comply with the governance requirements of the Combined Code and have an effective and ongoing business planning process in place. The requirement to comply or explain can impose a significant regulatory burden and can expose the company to critical comment.

(c)   Martin Pickle is a large shareholder, holding over 30% of the company's equity and thereby has certain duties towards other shareholders. He should not undertake any action which is prejudicial to them. It is unclear whether he has discussed his intentions with the other shareholders. Any move towards listed status would require their consent so he will need to provide them details of his future plans and intentions. It may well be that the private equity firm involved has its own exist strategy to mind and his proposed course of action is acceptable to them.

If the decision was made to go public then Martin Pickle's intention would be a material factor in the valuation of the firm and the offer price to subscribers. An immediate decision to disinvest would need to be disclosed.

At this stage, there would appear to be nothing wrong with asking the CFO to investigate the matter on a confidential basis although the request to enhance the earnings of the business should be resisted in so far as it represents an instruction to engage in earnings manipulation beyond that required to represent a true and fair view of the affairs of the business. Earnings management techniques whereby revenues and costs are accelerated/decelerated to achieve desired earnings are strictly limited by GAAP.

The proposal that the CFO would be offered share options places the CFO in a difficult position. The CFO must make it clear that he or she must act in the interests of all the shareholders and all the directors. An invitation to participate in a share option scheme appears to be a fairly crude attempt to win support for the proposed course of action and should be resisted.

ACCA
Examiner's answers

1 (a) The cost of equity capital is derived from the Capital Asset Pricing Model but given this is an unquoted company a proxy must be taken for the company's beta and regeared to reflect the different financial risk exposure of Fly4000.

Ideally, regearing beta requires an estimate of the market gearing for both companies. In the absence of that the book gearing can be used. However, the presence of corporation tax means that we need the values for both the debt and equity in Rover Airways.

$$BV(equity) = \frac{\$3bn}{1.25} = \$2.4bn$$

$$Gearing = \frac{BV(debt)}{BV(equity)}$$

$$BV(debt) = BV(equity) \times gearing$$

$$BV(debt) = \$2.4bn \times 1.5 = \$3.6bn$$

Using the formula for the asset beta where debt carries zero market risk:

$$\beta_A = \beta_e \times (1 - W_d)$$

where

$$W_d = \frac{BV_d \times (1-T)}{BV_e + BV_d \times (1-T)}$$

$$W_d = \frac{3.6 \times (0.7)}{2.4 + 3.6 \times (0.7)}$$

$$W_d = 0.5122$$

$$\beta_A = 2.0 \times (1 - 0.5122)$$

$$\beta_A = 0.9756$$

This is the asset beta for Rover Airways. We can now regear the beta to that for FliHi as follows:

Calculate the tax adjusted gearing ratio for FliHi.

$$W_d = \frac{BV_d \times (1-T)}{BV_e + BV_d \times (1-T)}$$

$$W_d = \frac{150 \times (0.7)}{120 + 150 \times (0.7)}$$

$$W_d = 0.4667$$

$$\beta_e = \frac{\beta_a}{(1 - W_d)}$$

$$\beta_e = \frac{0.9756}{(1 - 0.4667)}$$

$$\beta_e = 1.8294$$

This is the estimated equity beta for FliHi which, when applied to the CAPM, gives an expected rate of return as follows:

$$E(r_e) = R_F + \beta_e \times ERP$$
$$E(r_e) = 0.045 + 1.8294 \times 0.035$$
$$E(r_e) = 0.045 + 1.8294 \times 0.035$$
$$E(r_e) = 0.1090 (= 10.90\%)$$

The equity cost of capital for FliHi is therefore approximately 10.90 per cent.

The modelling of the equity cost of capital has embedded within it the assumptions implicit in the CAPM that:
- Investors are mean variance efficient
- Markets are frictionless
- Expectations are homogenous and,
- There is a risk free asset

However, of more practical significance we have also assumed that:
- The underlying exposure to market risk is the same for both companies (this is questionable given the differences in the markets in which they operate).
- That the book gearing ratio is a reasonable approximation to the market gearing ratio. The use of book values, can seriously distort the cost of capital that is calculated converting it into a measure of the average cost of capital in the firm's historical gearing ratio rather than in the ratio of the current capitalised values of the firm's equity and debt.
- That FliHi Ltd does not carry a size and default premium on its cost of capital. Default and size premia can be included through the use of such variants on the standard CAPM as the Fama and French 3 factor model which incorporates these elements of risk.

(b) Gordon's approximation requires a retention ratio which can be derived from the cash flow statement. The free cash flow to equity (before reinvestment) is defined as operating cash flow less interest and tax:

For 2005 the FCFE is as follows:

FCFE = operating cash flow – net interest paid – tax
FCFE ($m) = 210 + 1.5 – 4.1 = $207.4 million

In the current year $120.2m was reinvested. This implies a retention ratio (b) of:

$$b = \frac{reinvestment}{FCFE}$$

$$b = \frac{120.2}{207.4}$$

$$b = 0.58$$

Gordon's approximation was originally developed to measure the growth in earnings assuming a given retention ratio and rate of return. We can apply the same logic to the free cash flow model but here we are looking at the rate of cash generation by the business on new capital investment. The current rate of return is, in principle, the internal rate of return on the current business portfolio. If we assume that the business is highly competitive then the internal rate of return will be close to the company's equity cost of capital. Growth is therefore expected to be:

$g = bxr_e$
$g = 0.58x0.1090$
$g = 0.06322(=6.322\%)$

If we use the company's current rate of return on equity from the accounts we would have:

$$ROE = \frac{net\ profit}{equity\ employed\ (net\ assets)}$$

$$ROE = \frac{50}{120} = 42\%$$

This would suggest a rate of growth of 24.2 per cent which is unlikely in this industry.

On the basis of a growth rate of 6.322 per cent and given that the year six growth rate and forward will be 4 per cent, the pattern of growth we anticipate is therefore:

Year	1	2	3	4	5	6
Growth rate	6.322%	6.322%	6.322%	6.322%	6.322%	4.00%

The assumptions here are embedded within the method of measuring growth. Gordon's growth approximation will give the next year value for the FCFE for the business on the assumption that the cost of capital is achieved and no more. We have also assumed that the current figures for cash generation and reinvestment are typical and likely to be replicated over the near term. In this context we would note the significant increase in operating cash flow from 2004 and question whether this was sustainable.

(c) Using the free cash flow to equity net of reinvestment we have the free cash flow which is, in principle, distributable. We build a valuation model expanding this free cash flow through the next five years. From year six forward the rate of growth is a perpetuity and we use the free cash flow analogue of the dividend growth model to estimate the value at year six.

Step 1: take the growth rates as projected and estimate the future free cash flow to equity taking ($210m – $120.2m=$87.2m) as the starting point.
Step 2 discount these projected values at the cost of equity capital (10.9%) to give a present value of $384.89 million.
Step 3 using the formula:

$$V_e = \frac{FCFE_0(1+g)}{r_e-g}$$

Calculate the value of the growing perpetuity at the end of year 6 (note the timing of the year is important) using the expected FCFE in year 5. This gives a value at year 5 of $1,785.73.

Step 4: discount this at 10.9 per cent to give a present value of the residual term of $1,064.53

Step 5: add the two present values to give a valuation of the firm's equity at $1,449.42 million

Year	2006	2007	2008	2009	2010	2011
Growth	6.32%	6.32%	6.32%	6.32%	6.32%	4.00%
FCFE (2005)=$87.2m	92.71	98.57	104.81	111.43	118.48	
Discount at 10.9 per cent	83.60	80.15	76.84	73.67	70.63	
PV of year 1–6	$384.89					
PV of perpetuity at 2011						$1,785.73
PV of perpetuity at 2005	$1,064.53					
Present value of the firm's equity	$1,449.42					

The limitations of the method is that we assume:
- The current operating cash flows are sustainable
- The constant patterns of growth of operating cash flow will be achieved as specified.
- The rate of return required by investors is constant throughout the life of the business
- The business has an indefinite life beyond 2011.

These assumptions are unlikely to hold in practice and it should be noted that where the rate of growth (4%) is relatively low compared with the cost of equity that we would not expect the perpetuity to be a good approximation of residual value. It might be better to seek a likely break up value from the accounts as the residual value of the business. If we take the company's net asset figure and extrapolate forward at the rate of growth as shown above we obtain a figure of $169.55 million in 2011 which has a present value of $91.14 million. This would put a value on the business of $476.03 million. This incidentally gives a closer approximation to the market valuation if we apply the Rover Airlines P/E ratio to FliHi's net profit figure:

Value = benchmark P/E x FliHi Earnings
= 11.0 x $50million
= $550 million

(d) To whomsoever it may concern:

The proposed acquisition of FliHi represents a substantial capital investment for your airline. However, there are a number of issues which you might wish to consider before making a bid. These issues I have separated into synergies, risk exposure, future options, financing and valuation.

Synergies: From the perspective of your respective markets there would appear to be considerable advantage in integration. From the synergistic perspective these can be categorised as:

Revenue synergies: is there likely to be an enhancement in your ability to capture market share in a way that will add shareholder value. Simply acquiring the business as it stands will not be sufficient as investors can achieve the same at lower cost by diversification. Synergies only arise if a market opportunity presents itself which would not exist if both firms remain independent. One example would be where the domestic and European service can be used as a feeder system for an expanded long haul business from your principal airport and centre of operations.

Cost synergies: are there opportunities to save cost through more efficient operations? Economies of scale and scope are available in the airline business in the areas of in-flight catering, fuel supplies, maintenance and ticketing. The larger fleet size would also present operational opportunities.

Financial synergies: would the company have greater opportunities in the domestic and international capital market to acquire finance at more favourable rates and under better conditions.

Risk exposure: the larger operation would not necessarily improve the firm's exposure to market risk and indeed is likely to leave it unchanged as we would expect the underlying asset beta of both firms to be the same. There are a number of other risk areas that could be improved: operational risk may be mitigated by the firm's increased ability to hedge its operations (see the notes on the real options available below). Other risk effects include: economic, political, transactions and translation. Some of these are minimised (transactions) largely because your business is principally in the domestic market although this may change if you decide, for example, to develop your European network as a feeder system to your hub.

Future options: an acquisition of this type can create real options to expand, redeploy and exchange resources which add value to the proposition not easily captured with conventional valuation procedures. A real option is a claim upon some future course of action which can be exercised at your discretion. The availability of the new Airbus 380 offers potential both within the long haul business but also to medium haul holiday destinations at peak seasons. Access to your fleet of short to medium range aircraft offers the possibility of opening the European market to your long haul business. When and how you exercise these real options depends on circumstances at the time but paradoxically the more uncertain the underlying business the greater the value that attaches to this flexibility.

Financing: an acquisition of this type would require substantial extra financing. FIHi would appear to have a high level of off balance sheet value partly because of the scale of their operational leasing of aircraft but more significantly because of their business name and the quality of their operations. A substantial sum is likely to be paid for the goodwill of this business which suggests that this may not be a proposition that would be attractive to the debt market. Your own substantial cash reserves and the level of retained earnings suggest that this may be the route to financing this acquisition through a cash offer plus shares.

Valuation: we estimate the value of FliHi based upon its current cash flow generation to be of the order of $1.450 billion. Using market multiples a lower figure of $550million is obtained. The key point of this valuation process is to determine the lowest likely figure that the owners of FliHi would be prepared to accept. Our judgement is that the figure is likely to be closer to the upper end of this range. The free cash flow model relies upon our best forecast of future cash flow and reinvestment within the business. We believe that the owners of FliHi would have access to similar advice. The key question now to resolve is what would be the value of FliHi to your company. This has most of the characteristics of a type 2 acquisitions where the financial risk of the business is likely to be disturbed. For this reason we would need to value your current business using available market data and revalue it on the basis that the bid goes ahead using your preferred financing package. The potential increase in the value of your firm will reveal the potential control premium at any proposed offer price that may be decided upon.

2 (a) Sydonics Engineering
Memorandum

Our FOREX risk exposure is primarily driven by our European and US business and the variability of the Sterling/Euro and Sterling/Dollar exchange rates. The volatilities of both rates are of the order of 20 per cent (annualised) which indicates significant Value at Risk in any forward commitment to either currency. There are arguments for and against the use of derivative contracts to manage this transactions risk exposure.

In principal, nothing is added to the value of the firm if we attempt to do something which the investors can easily achieve, possibly, at lower cost. If the capital markets are perfect then investors should be indifferent to firm specific risk (which they can diversify away) and will only be concerned about the market driven risks as reflected in the firm's beta value. Arguably investors can diversify away the forex risk exposure within their portfolio much more efficiently and at lower cost than the company can through hedging. Hedging also brings costs: there are the direct costs of the treasury management function and the indirect costs of developing the in-house expertise required to assess hedging alternatives. There are also compliance costs in that any imperfect hedging agreement must be valued and shown in the accounts. Finally, hedging through derivative contracts can be avoided by the creation of internal hedging arrangements whereby finance is raised in the country of operations and hence borrowing costs are currency matched with the revenue streams.

On the other hand, the market perfection argument can be turned on its head. In as far as hedging is a means of reducing the firm's exposure to exchange rate volatility (a market wide phenomenon), then its impact will be to reduce the firm's beta and thus its cost of capital. This is a general argument for hedging but does not necessarily imply that we should use the derivative markets to manage our exposure to exchange rate risk. The empirical evidence on practice in industry is surprisingly sparse although Geczy, Minton and Schrand, (1997) found that 41 per cent of their sample of 370 US firms actively used derivative instruments to manage their forex risk. The benefits of hedging through the use of derivatives is that, with care, risk exposure can be tightly controlled although the use of exchange traded derivatives still leaves a residual 'basis risk' because of differences between the closeout rates and the underlying rates of exchange. Basis risk can be avoided through the use of OTC agreements wherever possible.

Hedging FOREX risk using derivatives can be expensive especially, as in this case, when the exposure is uncertain. Where the exposure is certain the use of futures or forward contracts can eliminate a large element of uncertainty at much lower cost. Any policy must therefore address the following issues:
- What is the magnitude of the risk exposure (in this case the very high volatility and long term exposure creates a very high hedging cost). Value at Risk (VaR) may be an appropriate method for measuring the likely financial exposure.
- The materiality of the exposure in terms of the magnitude of the sums involved.
- To what extent can the risk be mitigated by matching agreements (borrowing in the counter currency to mitigate CAPEX for example)?
- To what extent has the exposure crystallised? If it is uncertain FOREX options allow the hedging of the downside risk but at a high cost.

A policy would then lay down the principles that should be followed to cover the following:
- Risk assessment – an assessment of the likelihood and impact of any given risk upon the financial position of the firm. Derivative positions can be highly geared and the firm may be exposed to very high liabilities under certain exchange rate and/or interest rate conditions. It is recommended that derivatives should only be used for the management of specific risks and that no speculative or uncovered position should be taken.
- Cost of hedging – measured not only in terms of the direct costs involved but also in the use of scarce management time in establishing the positions and operating the internal control procedures appropriate where derivatives are used as a means of hedging risk. It is recommended that hedging costs should be minimised to an agreed percentage of the Value at Risk through the unhedged position.
- Contract and approval procedures – where OTC products are purchased and specific contracts are raised then the firm needs to establish policies with respect to the legal aspects of the contracting process. With both OTC and exchange traded products the firm should also establish an approval process with clear lines of responsibility and sign off on contracts up to and including board level. It is recommended that the board appoint a risk management committee to review and monitor all hedging contracts where the Value at Risk is in excess of an agreed amount.
- Hedge monitoring – policy needs to be established as to the monitoring of derivative positions and the conditions under which any given position will be reversed. It is recommended that the risk management committee actively monitor all open positions.

(b) This part of the question focuses on the use of options for foreign exchange hedging and deploys the Grabbe (1983) variant of the Black Scholes model.

The analytics for the question are shown in the tables below:

The price of the 'at the money' options are as follows:

	3 months	9 months
Sterling Euro Spot	0.6900	0.6900
Sterling Euro (indirect)	1.4493	1.4493
Euro Libor	2.7656	3.0519
Sterling Libor	4.6231	4.7303
Sterling Euro forward (indirect)	1.4426	1.4317
Sterling Euro forward (direct)	0.6932	0.6985
Annual volatility of £/Euro	0.2200	0.2200
D1	0.0968	0.1595
D2	-0.0132	-0.0310
N(d1)	0.5386	0.4367
N(d2)	0.4948	0.5124
3 month call and 9 month put price (pence per Euro)	3.1581	4.6853

(ie the price of a call or put to buy or sell one Euro at spot

Contract value (euro equivalent)	3158	4685

The values for d_1 and d_2 have been calculated as follows:

$$d_1 = \frac{\left(\ln\left(\frac{F}{S}\right) + \sigma^2 \frac{T}{2}\right)}{\sigma\sqrt{T}}$$

$$d_1 = \frac{\left(\ln\left(\frac{0.6932}{0.6900}\right) + 0.22^2 \frac{0.25}{2}\right)}{0.22\sqrt{0.25}}$$

$d_1 = 0.0968$
$d_2 = d_1 - \sigma\sqrt{T}$
$d_2 = 0.0968 - 0.22\sqrt{0.25}$
$d_2 = -0.0132$

Where F and S are the forward and spot rates respectively (note the forward must have the same maturity as the option), σ is the volatility, T is the time to maturity.

$N(d_1)$ and $N(d_2)$ are derived from the supplied tables for the normal density function for situations where $N(x) \geq 0$ and $N(x) \leq 0$.

The value of the currency call and the currency put are as follows:

$c = e^{-rT}[FN(d_1) - SN(d_2)]$

$c = e^{-0.046231 \times 0.25}[0.6932 \times 0.5386 - 0.6900 \times 0.4948]$

$c = 3.1581 pence$

and

$p = e^{-rT}[SN(-d_2) - FN(-d_1)]$

$p = e^{-0.047303 \times 0.75}[0.6900 \times 0.5124 - 0.6985 \times 0.4367]$

$p = 4.6853 pence$

The call should be exercised if the exchange rate rises above 0.6900 (thus making the sterling equivalent more expensive) and the nine month put should be exercised if the spot should be below 0.6900 at the exercise date.

The key points here are to note that the rates into the formula must all be direct, the volatility and interest rates are employed on an annual basis (they have been quoted as such in the question).

Candidates should also be aware of the money market conventions for quoting exchange rates that the base currency is shown first and the counter currency second. They should be sufficiently familiar with the relative values of the principal currencies to identify whether the quote is direct to indirect.

(iii) The hedge ratio (N(d1) and (N(-d1)) reveals the inverse of the number of option contracts we require to hedge a one euro exposure. Therefore the number of contracts we will require to hedge the exposures are as follows:

	3 months	9 months
Number of contracts	2,785	3,435
Cost of hedge	8,795,723	16,094,798
As percentage of value	0.058638	0.214597

(iv) The issues to be borne in mind are:
- Hedging with options eliminates downside risk (unlike futures) and are particularly useful when the exposure is uncertain.
- The cost of this type of hedge can be very high (especially for the long dated put) although the company may wish to reduce the cost by purchasing out of the money options. This will not eliminate the downside risk completely but will allow them to hedge to a known exposure.
- An alternative approach would be to hedge the three month exposure which is where the option is most valuable given the uncertainty over whether the bid will be accepted and then, if it is accepted, to enter into a future contract at that date to lock in the prevailing spot rate. Alternatively, purchasing the put option may be held back until the contract is won.
- Given the set contract sizes it is not possible to create a perfect hedge. The position would need continual monitoring and adjustment to offset gamma risk which is likely to be high for near-the-money options.
- There is timing risk given that currency options are quoted as Europeans. Early sale of the option if the requirement materialises early will create basis risk, if the requirement materialises late the residual time delay will be unhedged.

3 (a) Board Paper Presenting Proposed Procedures for Large CAPEX.

This paper proposes revised guidelines for the Board approval of large (in excess of $10,000) capital investment projects. The current two stage process of preliminary and final approval serves an important role in ensuring that any initial concerns of the Board in terms of strategic fit and risk are brought to the attention of the Financial Appraisal Team. The two stage process would consider:

Stage 1:
Business proposal including assessment of strategic requirement, business fit and identified risks.

Outline financial appraisal to include capital requirement, mode of financing, expected net present value, modified internal rate of return and project duration.

It is recommended that conventional payback is dropped because it ignores the cost of finance and the magnitude of post payback cash flows. Duration is recommended as this measures the time required to recover half of the project value.

Stage 2:
- A proposed business plan must be presented giving the business case with an assessment of strategic benefits, risks, finalised capital spend and capital source.
- A value impact assessment giving an NPV calculation supported by a calculation of the project value at risk. The net present value of the project represents our best estimate of the likely impact of the investment on the value of the firm. This is the key statistic from the capital market perspective in that, unless we are assured that the project NPV is positive, the investment will reduce and not enhance the value of the firm. This net present value calculation should be supported by a modified internal rate of return which measures the additional economic return of the project over the firm's cost of capital where intermediate cash flows are reinvested at that cost of capital. In a highly competitive business the reinvestment assumption implicit in the MIRR is more realistic that that assumed with IRR where intermediate cash flows are assumed to be reinvested at the IRR. This may be satisfactory for near-the-money projects but is far less satisfactory for projects which offer high levels of value addition to the firm.
- An accounting impact assessment including the differential rate of return on capital employed and a short term liquidity assessment. Although positive NPV projects are value enhancing they may not do so in ways that are readily apparent in the financial reports. To manage investor expectations effectively the firm needs to be aware of the impact of the project on the firm's reported profitability and this is most accurately reflected by the differential rate of return measure. Accounting rate of return as normally calculated does not examine the impact of the project on the financial position of the firm but is restricted to the rate of return the investment offers on the average capital employed.
- An assessment of the project duration. This project, for example, reveals a duration of 4.46 years which is the mean time over which half of the project value is recovered. This is more useful than the other liquidity based measures especially when used as a relative as opposed to an absolute measure of the cash recovery. Cash recovery assumes that the future project cash flows are achieved at a constant rate over the life of the project.

(b) The proposed business case concludes that this is a key strategic investment for the firm to maintain operating capacity at the Gulf Plant. The financial assessment is as detailed above (excluding an assessment of the impact of the project on the financial reports of the firm).

(i)   The net present value of this project is calculated using a discount rate of 8 per cent and gives a value of $1.964 million. The volatility attaching to the net present value of $1.02 million indicates that there is (z) standard deviations between the expected net present value and zero as follows:

$$z = \frac{1.964-0}{1.02} = 1.9255$$

This suggests that this project has a 97.3 per cent probability that it will have a positive net present value or conversely a 2.7 per cent probability of a negative net present value (these probabilities are taken from the normal density function tables supplied).

The project value at risk relies upon an assessment of the number of years that the project cash flow is at risk (10), the annual volatility and the confidence level required by the firm. The formula for project VaR is:

projectVaR = $N(0.95)s\sqrt{T}$

projectVaR = 1.645x1.02x3.162=$5.3million

This assumes a 95 per cent confidence level, at 99 per cent the project VaR is $7.51 million. This value reflects the fact that the capital invested is at risk for ten years and assumes that the volatility of the project is fairly represented by the volatility of its net present value.

(ii) Project Return

The internal rate of return is shown as 11.01 per cent. The Modified Internal Rate of Return is calculated by (i) projecting forward the cash flows in the recovery stage of the project at 8 per cent to future value of $41.798 million and (ii) discounting back the investment phase cash flows to give a present value of the investment of $17.396 million.

The Modified Internal Rate of Return is therefore:

$$MIRR = \sqrt[10]{\frac{41.798}{17.396}} -1$$

MIRR = 9.16%

This rate suggests that the margin on the cost of capital is rather small with only a 1.16 per cent premium for the strategic and competitive advantage implied by this project.

(iii) Project Liquidity

With a present value of the recovery phase of $19.6931 million and of the investment phase of $17.3961 million this suggests that the project will have a recovery period of:

$$recovery = 2 + \frac{17.396}{19.361} \text{ x } 8 = 9.188 \text{ years}$$

In practice the actual recovery is shorter than this because the expected cash in flows occur earlier rather than later during the recovery phase of the project.

The project duration is calculated by multiplying the proportion of cash recovered in each year (discounted recovery cash flow/present value of the recovery phase) by the relevant year number from project commencement. The sum of the weighted years gives the project duration.

Year		3	4	5	6	7	8	9	10
Discounted cash flow (recovery) ($m)		3.5722	4.7042	4.9342	4.0961	3.2092	2.1611	-1.0005	-2.316
Present value of recovery phase	19.3606								
duration of recovery phase proportion of CF recovered		0.1845	0.2430	0.2549	0.2116	0.1658	0.1116	-0.0517	-0.1196
weighted years		0.5535	0.9719	1.2743	1.2694	1.1603	0.8930	-0.4651	-1.1962
project duration (Years)	4.46								

The project duration reveals that the project is more highly cash generative in the early years notwithstanding the two year investment phase.

In summary, the analysis confirms that this project if financially viable, it will be value adding to the firm although there is substantial value at risk given the volatility of the net present value quoted. In terms of return the premium over the firm's hurdle rate is small at 1.16 per cent and any significant deterioration in the firms cost of capital would be very damaging to the value of this project. The liquidity statistics reveal that the bulk of the project's cash returns are promised in the early part of the recovery phase and that half the value invested in the project should be recovered by year five. Taking this into account acceptance is recommended to the board.

4 (a) Calculation of the expected WACC

A preliminary view suggests that the increased cost of debt is more than offset by the impact of the tax shield. The steps in the calculation are to estimate the cost of debt before and after the new issue. The existing cost of equity is calculated from the WACC and the ungeared equity cost calculated using M&M. The equity is then regeared to the new level assuming the higher level of gearing but not assuming any increase in the cost of debt through default or term structure. We then use the increased cost of debt to calculate the revised WACC. The analytics are as below:

Current WACC	**6.80%**			
	D/E	D/(D+E)		
Current gearing	0.1667	0.1429		
New gearing	0.2667	0.2105		
		risk free	spread	Total
Current yield on debt		0.03450	0.00400	0.03850
New yield on debt	3 years	0.03450	0.00440	0.03890
spread = 0.6x70 basis points (bp) + 0.4x107bp = 84.8bp	10 years	0.04200	0.00848	0.05048

Combined rate	MVd	Rd	
market value of 3 year debt	0.5	0.03890	0.02431
market value of new debt	0.3	0.05048	0.01893
Total market value of debt and combined rate	0.8		0.04324

Existing cost of equity	7.48%
Calculate ungeared cost of equity	7.11%
Calculate regeared cost of equity (keeping cost of debt constant)	7.72%
Calculate new weighted average cost of capital	6.73%

The existing cost of equity is calculated by rearranging the WACC as follows:

$$r_e = \frac{wacc - w_d r_d (1-T)}{(1-w_d)}$$

$$r_e = \frac{6.8\% - 0.1429 \times 3.85\% \times 0.7}{(1-0.1429)}$$

$$r_e = 7.48\%$$

The ungeared equity cost of capital (r_e^1) is discovered from Modigliani and Miller Proposition 2:

$$r_e = r_e^1 + (r_e^1 - r_d)\frac{D}{E}(1-T)$$

Rearranging and substituting:

$$r_e = r_e^1 + r_e^1 \frac{D}{E}(1-T) - r_d \frac{D}{E}(1-T)$$

$$r_e^1 = \frac{r_e + r_d \frac{D}{E}(1-T)}{1 + \frac{D}{E}(1-T)}$$

$$r_e^1 = \frac{7.48\% + 3.85\% \times 0.1667 \times 0.7}{1 + 0.1667 \times 0.7}$$

$$r_e^1 = 7.11\%$$

The regeared cost of equity capital assuming that the cost of debt remains unchanged is given by again using proposition 2:

$$r_e = r_e^1 + (r_e^1 - r_d)\frac{D}{E}(1-T)$$

$$r_e = 7.11\% + (7.11\% - 3.850\%) \times 0.2667 \times 0.7$$

$$r_e = 7.72\%$$

This assumes that the equity cost of capital is unaffected by the change in the level of default risk. This is a reasonable assumption at modest levels of gearing but would not be expected to hold at very high gearing levels.

Finally the new weighted average costs of capital is calculated using the revised equity cost and the revised debt cost as follows:

$wacc = (1-w_d)r_e + w_d r_d (1-T)$

$wacc = (1-0.2105) \times 7.72\% + 0.2105 \times 4.324\% \times 0.7$

$wacc = 6.73\%$

This demonstrates a less than 10 basis point fall in the weighted average cost of capital.

(b) Paper on the alternative sources of capital

For a company in this position the following sources of finance suggest themselves:

Sale and lease back of existing assets
US debt financed through a further bond issue
Debt raised on the Chinese market
Equity finance by rights or new issue

The choice of financing is partly down to the cost and availability of the various sources and partly down to the method the company chooses to hedge its FOREX exposure.

If we ignore foreign exchange considerations for a moment, pecking order theory suggests that debt should be preferred to equity and the weighted average cost of capital calculation suggests that the firm should increase its gearing to capture further tax shield effects which are not currently being offset by increased default risk (static trade off theory). However, issue costs may be expensive and the company may seek to raise finance by sale and lease back of existing assets. There are implications for reporting under FASB 13 depending upon whether the leases are financing or operating leases. Raising $300 million of debt by a bond issue is at the low end of the scale for new debt issues of this type although it may be possible that a syndicated issue where a number of companies of similar credit rating are joined by a lead bank could be arranged. It is to be expected that the costs of the issue will be high in terms of commissions and underwriting fees.

Raising finance directly in China has been eased considerably with recent changes in the rules of the Chinese Securities Regulatory Commission opening better access of foreign firms to the Chinese bond and equity markets. However, the entry of China into the WTO in 2002 is still feeding through the economy as tariff barriers and other constraints are removed. This process of liberalisation is likely to continue accelerating although, as with any emerging market, there are risks associated with inward investment and capital entry. These risks may be sufficient to raise the risk assessment against this company and as a result the benign implications of increased gearing outlined above may not be realised in practice.

The problem of hedging the foreign exchange exposure can be partly solved by borrowing directly in China and using the income flows from the new venture to finance the interest charges and capital repayments. Because the borrowing and the income flows are in the same currency transactions exposure is largely eliminated although any appreciation in the Chinese currency would increase the dollar value of the translated debt in the firm's balance sheet. If the borrowing is used to purchase matching assets in China then the translation risk is mitigated along with the transaction risk. However, if the assets are not owned but leased or rented then translation effects will impact upon the balance sheet and may be misread by the market. A second alternative would be to raise finance in the US and then engage in a currency swap for a ten year term. The effect of this would be to lock in the current exchange rate for the duration of the borrowing. However, finding a swap of this type would entail the services of a financial institution specialising in bringing appropriate counter-parties together. Such derivative arrangements have been mis-sold in the past with disastrous leveraging effects built into the contract.

5 **(a)** Normally, obtaining a listing consists of three steps: legal, regulatory and compliance. In the UK, as in many other jurisdictions a company must ensure that it is entitled to issue shares to the public as opposed to an issue by private treaty. In the UK a firm seeking listing must register as a public limited company. This entails a change in its memorandum and articles agreed by the existing members at a special meeting of the company.

The company must then meet the regulatory requirements of the Listing Agency which, in the UK, is part of the Financial Services Authority (FSA). These requirements impose a minimum size restriction on the company and other conditions concerning length of time trading. Once these requirements are satisfied the company is then placed on an official list and is allowed to make a public offering of its shares.

Once the company is on the official list it must then seek the approval of the Stock Exchange for its shares to be traded. In principal it is open to any company to seek a listing on any exchange where shares are traded. The London Exchange imposes strict requirements and invariably the applicant company will need the services of a sponsoring firm that specialises in this type of work.

(b) The advantages of seeking a public listing are that it opens the capital market to the firm. It offers the company access to equity capital from both institutional and private investors and the sums that can be raised are usually much greater than can be obtained through private equity sources. The presence of the firm as a listed company on a major exchange also enhances its credibility as investors and the general public are aware that by doing so it has opened itself to a much higher degree of public scrutiny than is the case for a firm that is privately financed. The disadvantages are significant. A distributed shareholding does place the firm in the market for corporate control increasing the likelihood that the firm will be subject to a takeover bid. There is also a much more public level of scrutiny with a range of disclosure requirements. Financial accounts must be prepared in accordance with IFRS or FASB and with the relevant GAAP as well as the Companies Acts. Under the rules of the London

Stock Exchange companies must also comply with the governance requirements of the Combined Code and also have in place an effective and ongoing business planning process. Much of this may be regarded as desirable within a privately owned company but the requirements to comply or explain imposed on a public company can impose a significant regulatory burden and exposure to critical comment.

(c) There is an ethical dimension to the request made by Martin Pickles. He is of course entitled to acquire or dispose of his equity claim as he sees fit but his position as a large shareholder does impose on him certain duties with respect to the other shareholders. He should not undertake any action which is prejudicial to them and in this case making any move towards listed status would require their consent. It may well be that the private equity firm involved has in mind its own exit strategy and that his proposed course of action would be acceptable to them. If the decision was made to go public his own intentions would be a material factor in the valuation of the firm and the offer price made to subscribers. An immediate intention to divest would need to be disclosed. There would appear to be nothing wrong at this stage with asking the CFO to investigate the matter on a confidential basis although the request that he or she should seek to enhance the earnings of the business should be resisted in as far as it represents an instruction to engage in earnings manipulation beyond that required to present a true and fair view of the affairs of the business.

Earnings management techniques whereby revenues and costs are accelerated/decelerated to achieve desired earnings figures are severely limited by GAAP and in the US for example could lead to arraignment under the Sarbanes Oxley Act. The proposal that the CFO would be offered share options adds a veneer of impropriatery to this discussion. He or she is in a difficult position but does need to make clear that he or she must act to preserve the interests of all the shareholders and all the directors. An invitation to participate in a share option scheme is a fairly crude attempt to win support for the proposed course of action (as the shares are not yet quoted) and should be resisted.

Marking Scheme

1   30 marks distributed over four sections. Key numbers presented in the analysis must be contextualised and justified.

   (a) Estimate the current cost of equity capital for FliHi using the Capital Asset Pricing Model making notes on any assumptions that you have made. **(9 marks)**

Calculation of the asset beta for Rover Airways at 0.9756	2
Regear for FliHi to 1.8294.	1
Calculate FliHI's cost of equity at 10.90 per cent	2
Notes on the assumptions relating to the CAPM	2
Notes on the assumptions of more practical significance	2

   (b) Estimate the expected growth rate of this company using the current rate of retention of Free Cash Flow and your estimate of the required rate of return on equity for each of the next seven years. Make notes on any assumptions you have made. **(6 marks)**

Calculation of the retention ratio as specified in the question as 0.58	2
Estimate of the growth for the next six years (justifying the return on equity chosen)	2
Assumptions embedded within the calculation of growth and Gordon's approximation	2

   (c) Value this company on the basis of its expected Free Cash Flow to Equity explaining the limitations of the methods you have used. **(7 marks)**

Calculation and projection of the free cash flow to equity with explanations	2
Discount these values at the rate of return on equity	2
Calculate the present value of the perpetuity at 2011 with explanations	2
Calculate the present value of the firm's equity	1

   (d) Write a brief report outlining the considerations your colleagues on the Board of Fly4000 might bear in mind when contemplating this acquisition. **(8 marks)**

Discussion of synergies and their capture	2
Examination of the risk exposure and the potential real options	3
Review of the financing options	2
Summary of valuation and recommendation of the next steps to the board of Fly4000	1

2   30 marks distributed over four sections.

   (a) Prepare a memorandum, to be considered at the next board meeting, which summarises the arguments for and against forex risk hedging and recommends a general policy concerning the hedging of foreign exchange risk. **(10 marks)**

Summary of the principle arguments for and against hedging with specific reference to the market perfection and reduction of cost of capital arguments.	4
Clear policy recommendations focusing risk assessment, cost management, contracts and approvals, and monitoring.	4
Quality of the memorandum assessed in terms of clarity, argumentation and persuasiveness.	2

   (b) Prepare a short report justifying your use of derivatives to minimise the firm's exposure to foreign exchange risk. Your report should contain:

   (iv) The likely option price for an at the money option stating the circumstances in which the option would be exercised (you should use the Grabbe variant of the Black-Scholes model for both transactions adjusted on the basis that deposits generate a rate of return of LIBOR). **(10 marks)**

Correct calculation of d1 and d2 using the forward and spot rates as specified	5
Calculation of N(x) from the tables given	1
Correct calculation of the currency call	2
Correct calculation of the currency put	2

   (v) A calculation of the number of contracts that would be required to eliminate the exchange rate risk and the cost of establishing a hedge to cover the likely FOREX exposure. **(4 marks)**

Calculation of the number of contracts for the 3 month hedge	2
Calculation of the number of contracts for the 9 month hedge	2

   (vi) A summary of the issues the board should bear in mind when reviewing a hedging proposal such as this taking into account the limitations of the modelling methods employed and the balance of risk to which the firm will still be exposed when the position is hedged. **(6 marks)**

Cost of the hedge and identification of alternatives	2
Problems of establishing a perfect hedge (contract size)	2
Understanding demonstrated of the nature of basis risk and how it is influenced by timing.	2

3 **(a)** Prepare a paper for the next Board meeting recommending procedures for the assessment of capital investment projects. Your paper should make proposals about the involvement of the Board at a preliminary stage and the information that should be provided to inform their decision. You should also provide an assessment of the alternative appraisal methods.

(8 marks)

Clear definition of a two stage process for Board involvement in capital expenditure decisions	2
Recommendation for the stage 1 appraisal procedure and metrics focusing on the role of payback and viable alternatives	3
Stage 2 appraisal focusing on the business plan, value and accounting impact and cash recovery.	3

(b) Using the appraisal methods you have recommended in (a) prepare a paper outlining the case for acceptance of the project to build a distillation facility at the Gulf plant with an assessment of the company's likely value at risk. You are not required to undertake an assessment of the impact of the project upon the firm's financial accounts. (12 marks)

Calculation of the project VAR and assessment of its significance	4
Estimation of the potential value impact using MIRR and the assumptions that underpin it.	3
Estimation of the potential cash recovery using procedures recommended in a)	3
Quality and persuasiveness of the written report	2

4 **(a)** Estimate the expected cost of capital for this project on the assumption that the additional finance is raised through a bond issue in the US market. (10 marks)

Estimation of the current cost of debt capital at 4.324 per cent	3
Calculation of the existing cost of equity capital at 7.48 per cent	2
Ungearing and regearing the cost of equity capital using M&M proposition 2	3
Calculation of the revised weighted average cost of capital and comment thereon	2

(b) Draft a brief report for the board outlining the alternative sources of finance that are potentially available for this project including a brief discussion of their advantages and disadvantages and the likely impact upon the firm's cost of capital of each of the alternatives that you consider. (10 marks)

Note of the theoretical issues in the selection of finance source (M&M, pecking order theory)	2
Clear description of the potential sources of capital within the context of the Chinese economy, regulation and capital market	2
Evaluation of the likely advantages and disadvantages of the principal sources of finance	2
Discussion of the risk management strategies available	2
Professional marks	2

5 **(a)** Prepare a board paper describing the procedure for obtaining a listing on an international stock exchange such as the London Stock Exchange. (6 marks)

Outline of the three step procedure: registration, listing and admission to trading (2 marks for each step)	6

(b) Prepare a briefing note itemising the advantages and disadvantages of such a step for a medium sized company.

(6 marks)

Note of the advantages: capital market access, reputation effects	2
Note of the disadvantages: compliance costs, vulnerability to takeover, public scrutiny	2
Well written briefing note weighing the advantages and disadvantages and focusing on the judgements that the board would be required to make	2

(c) Discuss any ethical considerations or concerns you may have concerning this proposed course of action. (8 marks)

Identification of the principal ethical issues involved	2
Note on the issue of transparency and the protection of minority rights	2
Discussion of alternative ways that the CFO could proceed and the ethical implications of each	2
Commentary on the ethical issues involved in earnings management	2

BPP
LEARNING MEDIA

Mathematical tables and exam formulae

Mathematical tables

Present value table

Present value of 1, ie $(1+r)^{-n}$

where r = discount rate

n = number of periods until payment

Periods	Discount rates (r)									
(n)	1%	2%	3%	4%	5%	6%	7%	8%	9%	10%
1	0.990	0.980	0.971	0.962	0.952	0.943	0.935	0.926	0.917	0.909
2	0.980	0.961	0.943	0.925	0.907	0.890	0.873	0.857	0.842	0.826
3	0.971	0.942	0.915	0.889	0.864	0.840	0.816	0.794	0.772	0.751
4	0.961	0.924	0.888	0.855	0.823	0.792	0.763	0.735	0.708	0.683
5	0.951	0.906	0.863	0.822	0.784	0.747	0.713	0.681	0.650	0.621
6	0.942	0.888	0.837	0.790	0.746	0.705	0.666	0.630	0.596	0.564
7	0.933	0.871	0.813	0.760	0.711	0.665	0.623	0.583	0.547	0.513
8	0.923	0.853	0.789	0.731	0.677	0.627	0.582	0.540	0.502	0.467
9	0.914	0.837	0.766	0.703	0.645	0.592	0.544	0.500	0.460	0.424
10	0.905	0.820	0.744	0.676	0.614	0.558	0.508	0.463	0.422	0.386
11	0.896	0.804	0.722	0.650	0.585	0.527	0.475	0.429	0.388	0.350
12	0.887	0.788	0.701	0.625	0.557	0.497	0.444	0.397	0.356	0.319
13	0.879	0.773	0.681	0.601	0.530	0.469	0.415	0.368	0.326	0.290
14	0.870	0.758	0.661	0.577	0.505	0.442	0.388	0.340	0.299	0.263
15	0.861	0.743	0.642	0.555	0.481	0.417	0.362	0.315	0.275	0.239

	11%	12%	13%	14%	15%	16%	17%	18%	19%	20%
1	0.901	0.893	0.885	0.877	0.870	0.862	0.855	0.847	0.840	0.833
2	0.812	0.797	0.783	0.769	0.756	0.743	0.731	0.718	0.706	0.694
3	0.731	0.712	0.693	0.675	0.658	0.641	0.624	0.609	0.593	0.579
4	0.659	0.636	0.613	0.592	0.572	0.552	0.534	0.516	0.499	0.482
5	0.593	0.567	0.543	0.519	0.497	0.476	0.456	0.437	0.419	0.402
6	0.535	0.507	0.480	0.456	0.432	0.410	0.390	0.370	0.352	0.335
7	0.482	0.452	0.425	0.400	0.376	0.354	0.333	0.314	0.296	0.279
8	0.434	0.404	0.376	0.351	0.327	0.305	0.285	0.266	0.249	0.233
9	0.391	0.361	0.333	0.308	0.284	0.263	0.243	0.225	0.209	0.194
10	0.352	0.322	0.295	0.270	0.247	0.227	0.208	0.191	0.176	0.162
11	0.317	0.287	0.261	0.237	0.215	0.195	0.178	0.162	0.148	0.135
12	0.286	0.257	0.231	0.208	0.187	0.168	0.152	0.137	0.124	0.112
13	0.258	0.229	0.204	0.182	0.163	0.145	0.130	0.116	0.104	0.093
14	0.232	0.205	0.181	0.160	0.141	0.125	0.111	0.099	0.088	0.078
15	0.209	0.183	0.160	0.140	0.123	0.108	0.095	0.084	0.074	0.065

Annuity table

Present value of an annuity of 1, ie $\dfrac{1-(1+r)^{-n}}{r}$

where r = discount rate

n = number of periods

Periods					Discount rates (r)					
(n)	1%	2%	3%	4%	5%	6%	7%	8%	9%	10%
1	0.990	0.980	0.971	0.962	0.952	0.943	0.935	0.926	0.917	0.909
2	1.970	1.942	1.913	1.886	1.859	1.833	1.808	1.783	1.759	1.736
3	2.941	2.884	2.829	2.775	2.723	2.673	2.624	2.577	2.531	2.487
4	3.902	3.808	3.717	3.630	3.546	3.465	3.387	3.312	3.240	3.170
5	4.853	4.713	4.580	4.452	4.329	4.212	4.100	3.993	3.890	3.791
6	5.795	5.601	5.417	5.242	5.076	4.917	4.767	4.623	4.486	4.355
7	6.728	6.472	6.230	6.002	5.786	5.582	5.389	5.206	5.033	4.868
8	7.652	7.325	7.020	6.733	6.463	6.210	5.971	5.747	5.535	5.335
9	8.566	8.162	7.786	7.435	7.108	6.802	6.515	6.247	5.995	5.759
10	9.471	8.983	8.530	8.111	7.722	7.360	7.024	6.710	6.418	6.145
11	10.37	9.787	9.253	8.760	8.306	7.887	7.499	7.139	6.805	6.495
12	11.26	10.58	9.954	9.385	8.863	8.384	7.943	7.536	7.161	6.814
13	12.13	11.35	10.63	9.986	9.394	8.853	8.358	7.904	7.487	7.103
14	13.00	12.11	11.30	10.56	9.899	9.295	8.745	8.244	7.786	7.367
15	13.87	12.85	11.94	11.12	10.38	9.712	9.108	8.559	8.061	7.606

	11%	12%	13%	14%	15%	16%	17%	18%	19%	20%
1	0.901	0.893	0.885	0.877	0.870	0.862	0.855	0.847	0.840	0.833
2	1.713	1.690	1.668	1.647	1.626	1.605	1.585	1.566	1.547	1.528
3	2.444	2.402	2.361	2.322	2.283	2.246	2.210	2.174	2.140	2.106
4	3.102	3.037	2.974	2.914	2.855	2.798	2.743	2.690	2.639	2.589
5	3.696	3.605	3.517	3.433	3.352	3.274	3.199	3.127	3.058	2.991
6	4.231	4.111	3.998	3.889	3.784	3.685	3.589	3.498	3.410	3.326
7	4.712	4.564	4.423	4.288	4.160	4.039	3.922	3.812	3.706	3.605
8	5.146	4.968	4.799	4.639	4.487	4.344	4.207	4.078	3.954	3.837
9	5.537	5.328	5.132	4.946	4.772	4.607	4.451	4.303	4.163	4.031
10	5.889	5.650	5.426	5.216	5.019	4.833	4.659	4.494	4.339	4.192
11	6.207	5.938	5.687	5.453	5.234	5.029	4.836	4.656	4.486	4.327
12	6.492	6.194	5.918	5.660	5.421	5.197	4.988	4.793	4.611	4.439
13	6.750	6.424	6.122	5.842	5.583	5.342	5.118	4.910	4.715	4.533
14	6.982	6.628	6.302	6.002	5.724	5.468	5.229	5.008	4.802	4.611
15	7.191	6.811	6.462	6.142	5.847	5.575	5.324	5.092	4.876	4.675

Standard normal distribution table

$Z = \dfrac{(x - \mu)}{\sigma}$	0.00	0.01	0.02	0.03	0.04	0.05	0.06	0.07	0.08	0.09
0.0	.0000	.0040	.0080	.0120	.0160	.0199	.0239	.0279	.0319	.0359
0.1	.0398	.0438	.0478	.0517	.0557	.0596	.0636	.0675	.0714	.0753
0.2	.0793	.0832	.0871	.0910	.0948	.0987	.1026	.1064	.1103	.1141
0.3	.1179	.1217	.1255	.1293	.1331	.1368	.1406	.1443	.1480	.1517
0.4	.1554	.1591	.1628	.1664	.1700	.1736	.1772	.1808	.1844	.1879
0.5	.1915	.1950	.1985	.2019	.2054	.2088	.2123	.2157	.2190	.2224
0.6	.2257	.2291	.2324	.2357	.2389	.2422	.2454	.2486	.2517	.2549
0.7	.2580	.2611	.2642	.2673	.2704	.2734	.2764	.2794	.2823	.2852
0.8	.2881	.2910	.2939	.2967	.2995	.3023	.3051	.3078	.3106	.3133
0.9	.3159	.3186	.3212	.3238	.3264	.3289	.3315	.3340	.3365	.3389
1.0	.3413	.3438	.3461	.3485	.3508	.3531	.3554	.3577	.3599	.3621
1.1	.3643	.3665	.3686	.3708	.3729	.3749	.3770	.3790	.3810	.3830
1.2	.3849	.3869	.3888	.3907	.3925	.3944	.3962	.3980	.3997	.4015
1.3	.4032	.4049	.4066	.4082	.4099	.4115	.4131	.4147	.4162	.4177
1.4	.4192	.4207	.4222	.4236	.4251	.4265	.4279	.4292	.4306	.4319
1.5	.4332	.4345	.4357	.4370	.4382	.4394	.4406	.4418	.4429	.4441
1.6	.4452	.4463	.4474	.4484	.4495	.4505	.4515	.4525	.4535	.4545
1.7	.4554	.4564	.4573	.4582	.4591	.4599	.4608	.4616	.4625	.4633
1.8	.4641	.4649	.4656	.4664	.4671	.4678	.4686	.4693	.4699	.4706
1.9	.4713	.4719	.4726	.4732	.4738	.4744	.4750	.4756	.4761	.4767
2.0	.4772	.4778	.4783	.4788	.4793	.4798	.4803	.4808	.4812	.4817
2.1	.4821	.4826	.4830	.4834	.4838	.4842	.4846	.4850	.4854	.4857
2.2	.4861	.4864	.4868	.4871	.4875	.4878	.4881	.4884	.4887	.4890
2.3	.4893	.4896	.4898	.4901	.4904	.4906	.4909	.4911	.4913	.4916
2.4	.4918	.4920	.4922	.4925	.4927	.4929	.4931	.4932	.4934	.4936
2.5	.4938	.4940	.4941	.4943	.4945	.4946	.4948	.4949	.4951	.4952
2.6	.4953	.4955	.4956	.4957	.4959	.4960	.4961	.4962	.4963	.4964
2.7	.4965	.4966	.4967	.4968	.4969	.4970	.4971	.4972	.4973	.4974
2.8	.4974	.4975	.4976	.4977	.4977	.4978	.4979	.4979	.4980	.4981
2.9	.4981	.4982	.4982	.4983	.4984	.4984	.4985	.4985	.4986	.4986
3.0	.4987	.4987	.4987	.4988	.4988	.4989	.4989	.4989	.4990	.4990

This table can be used to calculate $N(d_1)$, the cumulative normal distribution functions needed for the Black-Scholes model of option pricing. If $d_1 > 0$, add 0.5 to the relevant number above. If $d_1 < 0$, subtract the relevant number above from 0.5.

Formulae

Formulae provided to Paper P4 candidates are set out below.

Modigliani and Miller Proposition 2 (with tax)

$$k_e = k_e^i + (1-T)(k_e^i - k_d)\frac{V_d}{V_e}$$

Two asset portfolio

$$s_p = \sqrt{w_a^2 s_a^2 + w_b^2 s_b^2 + 2w_a w_b r_{ab} s_a s_b}$$

The capital asset pricing model

$$E(r_i) = R_f + \beta_i(E(r_m) - R_f)$$

The asset beta formula

$$\beta_a = \left[\frac{V_e}{(V_e + V_d(1-T))}\beta_e\right] + \left[\frac{V_d(1-T)}{(V_e + V_d(1-T))}\beta_d\right]$$

The growth model

$$P_0 = \frac{D_0(1+g)}{(r_e - g)}$$

Gordon's growth approximation

$$g = br_e$$

The weighted average cost of capital

$$WACC = \left[\frac{V_e}{V_e + V_d}\right]k_e + \left[\frac{V_e}{V_e + V_d}\right]k_d(1-T)$$

The Fisher formula

$$(1 + i) = (1 + r)(1 + h)$$

Purchasing power parity and interest rate parity

$$s_1 = s_0 \times \frac{(1+h_c)}{(1+h_b)}$$

$$f_0 = s_0 \times \frac{(1+i_c)}{(1+i_b)}$$

The Black Scholes option pricing model	The FOREX modified Black and Scholes option pricing model
$c = P_a N(d_1) - P_e N(d_2)e^{-rt}$	$c = e^{-rt} F_0 N(d_1) - XN(d_2)$
	Or
Where $\quad d_1 = \dfrac{\ln\left(\dfrac{P_a}{P_e}\right) + (r + 0.5s^2)t}{s\sqrt{t}}$	$p = e^{-rt} XN(-d_2) - F_0 N(-d_1)$
$\quad\quad d_2 = d_1 - s\sqrt{t}$	Where $\quad d_1 = \dfrac{\ln\left(\dfrac{F_0}{X}\right) + s^2\dfrac{T}{2}}{s\sqrt{T}}$
	and $\quad d_2 = d_1 - s\sqrt{T}$

The put call parity relationship

$$p = C - P_a + P_e e^{-rt}$$

Review Form & Free Prize Draw – Paper P4 Advanced Financial Management (5/07)

All original review forms from the entire BPP range, completed with genuine comments, will be entered into one of two draws on 31 July 2007 and 31 January 2008. The names on the first four forms picked out on each occasion will be sent a cheque for £50.

Name: _____   Address: _____

_____

_____

How have you used this Kit?
(Tick one box only)

☐ Home study (book only)

☐ On a course: college _____

☐ With 'correspondence' package

☐ Other _____

Why did you decide to purchase this Kit?
(Tick one box only)

☐ Have used the complementary Study text

☐ Have used other BPP products in the past

☐ Recommendation by friend/colleague

☐ Recommendation by a lecturer at college

☐ Saw advertising

☐ Other _____

During the past six months do you recall seeing/receiving any of the following?
(Tick as many boxes as are relevant)

☐ Our advertisement in *Student Accountant*

☐ Our advertisement in *Pass*

☐ Our advertisement in *PQ*

☐ Our brochure with a letter through the post

☐ Our website www.bpp.com

Which (if any) aspects of our advertising do you find useful?
(Tick as many boxes as are relevant)

☐ Prices and publication dates of new editions

☐ Information on product content

☐ Facility to order books off-the-page

☐ None of the above

Which BPP products have you used?

Text	☐	*Success CD*	☐	*Learn Online*	☐
Kit	☑	*i-Learn*	☐	*Home Study Package*	☐
Passcard	☐	*i-Pass*	☐	*Home Study PLUS*	☐

Your ratings, comments and suggestions would be appreciated on the following areas.

	Very useful	Useful	Not useful
Passing ACCA exams	☐	☐	☐
Passing 3.7	☐	☐	☐
Planning your question practice	☐	☐	☐
Questions	☐	☐	☐
Top Tips etc in answers	☐	☐	☐
Content and structure of answers	☐	☐	☐
Mock exam answers	☐	☐	☐

Overall opinion of this Kit   Excellent ☐   Good ☐   Adequate ☐   Poor ☐

Do you intend to continue using BPP products?   Yes ☐   No ☐

The BPP author of this edition can be e-mailed at: stelladinenis@bpp.com

Please return this form to: Nick Weller, ACCA Publishing Manager, BPP Learning Media Ltd, FREEPOST, London, W12 8BR

Review Form & Free Prize Draw (continued)

TELL US WHAT YOU THINK

Please note any further comments and suggestions/errors below.

Free Prize Draw Rules

1   Closing date for 31 July 2007 draw is 30 June 2007. Closing date for 31 January 2008 draw is 31 December 2007.

2   Restricted to entries with UK and Eire addresses only. BPP employees, their families and business associates are excluded.

3   No purchase necessary. Entry forms are available upon request from BPP Learning Media Ltd. No more than one entry per title, per person. Draw restricted to persons aged 16 and over.

4   Winners will be notified by post and receive their cheques not later than 6 weeks after the relevant draw date.

5   The decision of the promoter in all matters is final and binding. No correspondence will be entered into.